EDUCATION
REFLECTING OUR SOCIETY?

Barbara Klier

INFORMATION PLUS REFERENCE SERIES
Formerly published by Information Plus, Wylie, Texas

Detroit
New York
San Francisco
London
Boston
Woodbridge, CT

EDUCATION: REFLECTING OUR SOCIETY?

was produced for the Gale Group by Information Plus, Wylie, Texas

Information Plus Staff:

Barbara Klier, Author

Jacquelyn Quiram, Designer

Editorial: Abbey Begun, Cornelia Blair, Nancy R. Jacobs, Virginia Peterson, Mei Ling Rein, Mark A. Siegel

The Gale Group Staff:

Editorial: Rita Runchock, Managing Editor; John F. McCoy, Editor
Graphic Services: Randy Bassett, Image Database Supervisor; Robert Duncan, Senior Imaging Specialist
Product Design: Michelle DiMercurio, Senior Art Director; Michael Logusz, Graphic Artist
Production: NeKita McKee, Buyer; Dorothy Maki, Manufacturing Manager

EDUCATION — REFLECTING OUR SOCIETY?

CHAPTER I

AN OVERVIEW OF AMERICAN EDUCATION

American education is an embattled institution. During the 1980s, the nation became increasingly aware of critical issues, such as low academic performance, drug use and violence in the schools, and high dropout rates. Parents worry about the escalating cost of a college education. Political and community leaders question the ability of the nation's schools to produce high school graduates capable of competing in an increasingly technical and international environment. Voters and legislators debate whether parents who educate their children in private schools should receive federal or state subsidies.

Despite all the problems, the United States remains one of the most highly educated nations in the world. In fall 1998, approximately 75.4 million Americans were involved either directly or indirectly in providing or receiving formal education. About 67.3 million students were enrolled in schools and colleges, and 3.8 million instructors were teaching at the elementary, secondary, or college level. Another 4.2 million persons were professional, administrative, and support personnel at educational institutions. (See Table 1.1.)

A BETTER EDUCATED POPULATION

Over the past two generations, the median (half completed more; half completed less) number of school years completed among Americans age 25 and older rose from 8.6 years in 1940 to the current 13 years. In 1940, about 1 in 4 Americans (24.5 percent) 25 years old and older had completed four or more years of high school, and almost 1 in 7 (13.7 percent) had completed fewer than five years of elementary school. By 1997, 82.1 percent of Americans in the same age group had completed high school, while only 1.7 percent had fewer than five years of formal education. In 1940, less than

---

TABLE 1.1

Estimated number of participants in elementary and secondary education and in higher education: Fall 1998

[In millions]

Participants	All levels (elementary, secondary, and higher education)	Elementary and secondary schools			Institutions of higher education		
		Total	Public	Private	Total	Public	Private
1	2	3	4	5	6	7	8
Total	75.4	58.6	52.0	6.6	16.8	12.9	3.
Enrollment [1]	67.3	52.7	46.8	5.9	14.6	11.4	3.
Teachers and faculty	3.8	3.1	2.7	0.4	0.7	0.5	0.
Other professional, administrative, and support staff	4.2	2.8	2.5	0.2	1.5	1.0	0.

[1] Includes enrollments in local public school systems and in most private schools (religiously affiliated and nonsectarian). Excludes subcollegiate departments of institutions of higher education, residential schools for exceptional children, and federal schools. Elementary and secondary includes most kindergarten and some nursery school enrollment. Excludes preprimary enrollment in schools that do not offer first grade or above. Higher education comprises full-time and part-time students enrolled in degree-credit and non-degree-credit programs in universities, other 4-year colleges, and 2-year colleges.

NOTE.—The enrollment figures include all students in elementary and secondary schools and colleges and universities. However, the data for teachers and other staff public and private elementary and secondary schools and colleges and universities ar reported in terms of full-time equivalents. Because of rounding, details may not add t totals.

SOURCE: U.S. Department of Education, National Center for Education Statistic unpublished projections and estimates. (This table was prepared July 1998.)

Source: *Digest of Education Statistics 1998*, National Center for Education Statistics, Washington, DC, 1999

TABLE 1.2

Years of school completed by persons age 25 and over and 25 to 29, by race/ethnicity and sex: 1910 to 1997

Age, year, and sex	Percent, by years of school completed											
	All races			White, non-Hispanic [1]			Black, non-Hispanic [1]			Hispanic		
	Less than 5 years of elementary school	High school completion or higher [2]	4 or more years of college [3]	Less than 5 years of elementary school	High school completion or higher [2]	4 or more years of college [3]	Less than 5 years of elementary school	High school completion or higher [2]	4 or more years of college [3]	Less than 5 years of elementary school	High school completion or higher [2]	4 or more years of college [3]
1	2	3	4	5	6	7	8	9	10	11	12	13
Males and females												
25 and over												
1910 [4]	23.8	13.5	2.7	—	—	—	—	—	—	—	—	—
1920 [4]	22.0	16.4	3.3	—	—	—	—	—	—	—	—	—
1930 [4]	17.5	19.1	3.9	—	—	—	—	—	—	—	—	—
April 1940	13.7	24.5	4.6	10.9	26.1	4.9	41.8	7.7	1.3	—	—	—
April 1950	11.1	34.3	6.2	8.9	36.4	6.6	32.6	13.7	2.2	—	—	—
April 1960	8.3	41.1	7.7	6.7	43.2	8.1	23.5	21.7	3.5	—	—	—
March 1970	5.3	55.2	11.0	4.2	57.4	11.6	14.7	36.1	6.1	—	—	—
March 1980	3.4	68.6	17.0	1.9	71.9	18.4	9.1	51.4	7.9	15.8	44.5	7.6
March 1985	2.7	73.9	19.4	1.4	77.5	20.8	6.1	59.9	11.1	13.5	47.9	8.5
March 1986	2.7	74.7	19.4	1.4	78.2	20.1	5.3	62.5	10.9	12.9	48.5	8.4
March 1987	2.4	75.6	19.9	1.3	79.0	20.5	4.9	63.6	10.8	11.9	50.9	8.6
March 1988	2.5	76.2	20.3	1.2	79.8	21.8	4.8	63.5	11.2	12.2	51.0	10.0
March 1989	2.5	76.9	21.1	1.2	80.7	22.8	5.2	64.7	11.7	12.2	50.9	9.9
March 1990	2.5	77.6	21.3	1.1	81.4	23.1	5.1	66.2	11.3	12.3	50.8	9.2
March 1991	2.4	78.4	21.4	1.1	82.4	23.3	4.7	66.8	11.5	12.5	51.3	9.7
March 1992	2.1	79.4	21.4	0.9	83.4	23.2	3.9	67.7	11.9	11.8	52.6	9.3
March 1993	2.1	80.2	21.9	0.8	84.1	23.8	3.7	70.5	12.2	11.8	53.1	9.0
March 1994	1.9	80.9	22.2	0.8	84.9	24.3	2.7	73.0	12.9	10.8	53.3	9.1
March 1995	1.9	81.7	23.0	0.7	85.9	23.4	2.5	73.8	13.3	10.6	53.4	9.3
March 1996	1.8	81.7	23.6	0.6	86.0	25.9	2.2	74.6	13.8	10.4	53.1	9.3
March 1997	1.7	82.1	23.9	0.6	86.3	26.2	2.0	75.3	13.3	9.4	54.7	10.3
25 to 29												
1920 [4]	—	—	—	12.9	22.0	4.5	44.6	6.3	1.2	—	—	—
April 1940	5.9	38.1	5.9	3.4	41.2	6.4	27.0	12.3	1.6	—	—	—
April 1950	4.6	52.8	7.7	3.3	56.3	8.2	16.1	23.6	2.8	—	—	—
April 1960	2.8	60.7	11.0	2.2	63.7	11.8	7.2	38.6	5.4	—	—	—
March 1970	1.1	75.4	16.4	0.9	77.8	17.3	2.2	58.4	10.0	—	—	—
March 1980	0.8	85.4	22.5	0.3	89.2	25.0	0.7	76.7	11.6	6.7	58.0	7.7
March 1985	0.7	86.1	22.2	0.2	89.5	24.4	0.4	80.5	11.6	6.0	60.9	11.1
March 1986	0.9	86.1	22.4	0.4	89.6	25.2	0.5	83.5	11.8	5.6	59.1	9.0
March 1987	0.9	86.0	22.0	0.4	89.4	24.7	0.4	83.5	11.5	4.8	59.8	8.7
March 1988	1.0	85.9	22.7	0.3	89.7	25.1	0.3	80.9	12.0	6.0	62.3	11.3
March 1989	1.0	85.5	23.4	0.3	89.3	26.3	0.5	82.3	12.7	5.4	61.0	10.1
March 1990	1.2	85.7	23.2	0.3	90.1	26.4	1.0	81.7	13.4	7.3	58.2	8.2
March 1991	1.0	85.4	23.2	0.3	89.8	26.7	0.5	81.8	11.0	5.8	56.7	9.2
March 1992	0.9	86.3	23.6	0.3	90.7	27.2	0.8	80.9	11.1	5.2	60.9	9.5
March 1993	0.7	86.7	23.7	0.3	91.2	27.2	0.2	82.7	13.3	4.0	60.9	8.3
March 1994	0.8	86.1	23.3	0.3	91.1	27.1	0.6	84.1	13.6	3.6	60.3	8.0
March 1995	1.0	86.9	24.7	0.3	92.5	28.8	0.2	86.7	15.4	4.9	57.2	8.9
March 1996	0.8	87.3	27.1	0.2	92.6	31.6	0.4	86.0	14.6	4.3	61.1	10.0
March 1997	0.8	87.4	27.8	0.1	92.9	32.6	0.6	86.9	14.2	4.2	61.8	11.0
Males												
25 and over												
April 1940	15.1	22.7	5.5	12.0	24.2	5.9	46.2	6.9	1.4	—	—	—
April 1950	12.2	32.6	7.3	9.8	34.6	7.9	36.9	12.6	2.1	—	—	—
April 1960	9.4	39.5	9.7	7.4	41.6	10.3	27.7	20.0	3.5	—	—	—
March 1970	5.9	55.0	14.1	4.5	57.2	15.0	17.9	35.4	6.8	—	—	—
March 1980	3.6	69.2	20.9	2.0	72.4	22.8	11.3	51.2	7.7	16.5	44.9	9.2
March 1990	2.7	77.7	24.4	1.3	81.6	26.7	6.4	65.8	11.9	12.9	50.3	9.8
March 1994	2.1	81.1	25.1	0.8	85.1	27.8	3.9	71.8	12.7	11.4	53.4	9.6
March 1995	2.0	81.7	26.0	0.8	86.0	28.9	3.4	73.5	13.7	10.8	52.9	10.1
March 1996	1.9	81.9	26.0	0.7	86.1	28.8	2.9	74.6	12.5	10.2	53.0	10.3
March 1997	1.8	82.0	26.2	0.6	86.3	29.0	2.9	73.8	12.5	9.2	54.9	10.6
Females												
25 and over												
April 1940	12.4	26.3	3.8	9.8	28.1	4.0	37.5	8.4	1.2	—	—	—
April 1950	10.0	36.0	5.2	8.1	38.2	5.4	28.6	14.7	2.4	—	—	—
April 1960	7.4	42.5	5.8	6.0	44.7	6.0	19.7	23.1	3.6	—	—	—
March 1970	4.7	55.4	8.2	3.9	57.7	8.6	11.9	36.6	5.6	—	—	—
March 1980	3.2	68.1	13.6	1.8	71.5	14.4	7.4	51.5	8.1	15.3	44.2	6.2
March 1990	2.2	77.5	18.4	1.0	81.3	19.8	4.1	66.5	10.8	11.7	51.3	8.7
March 1994	1.7	80.8	19.6	0.7	84.7	21.1	1.8	73.9	13.1	10.3	53.2	8.6
March 1995	1.7	81.6	20.2	0.6	85.8	22.2	1.8	74.1	13.0	10.4	53.8	8.4
March 1996	1.7	81.6	21.4	0.5	85.9	23.2	1.6	74.6	14.8	10.6	53.3	8.3
March 1997	1.6	82.2	21.7	0.5	86.3	23.7	1.3	76.5	14.0	9.5	54.6	10.1

[1] Includes persons of Hispanic origin for years prior to 1980.
[2] Data for years prior to 1993 include all persons with at least 4 years of high school.
[3] Data for 1993 and later years are for persons with a bachelor's degree or higher.
[4] Estimates based on Bureau of the Census retrojection of 1940 Census data on education by age.
—Data not available.

NOTE.—Data for 1980 and subsequent years are for the noninstitutional population.

SOURCE: U.S. Department of Commerce, Bureau of the Census, *U.S. Census of Population, 1960*, Vol. 1, part 1; *Current Population Reports*, Series P-20 and unpublished data; and *1960 Census Monograph*, "Education of the American Population," by John K. Folger and Charles B. Nam. (This table was prepared July 1998.)

Source: *Digest of Education Statistics 1998*, National Center for Education Statistics, Washington, DC, 1999

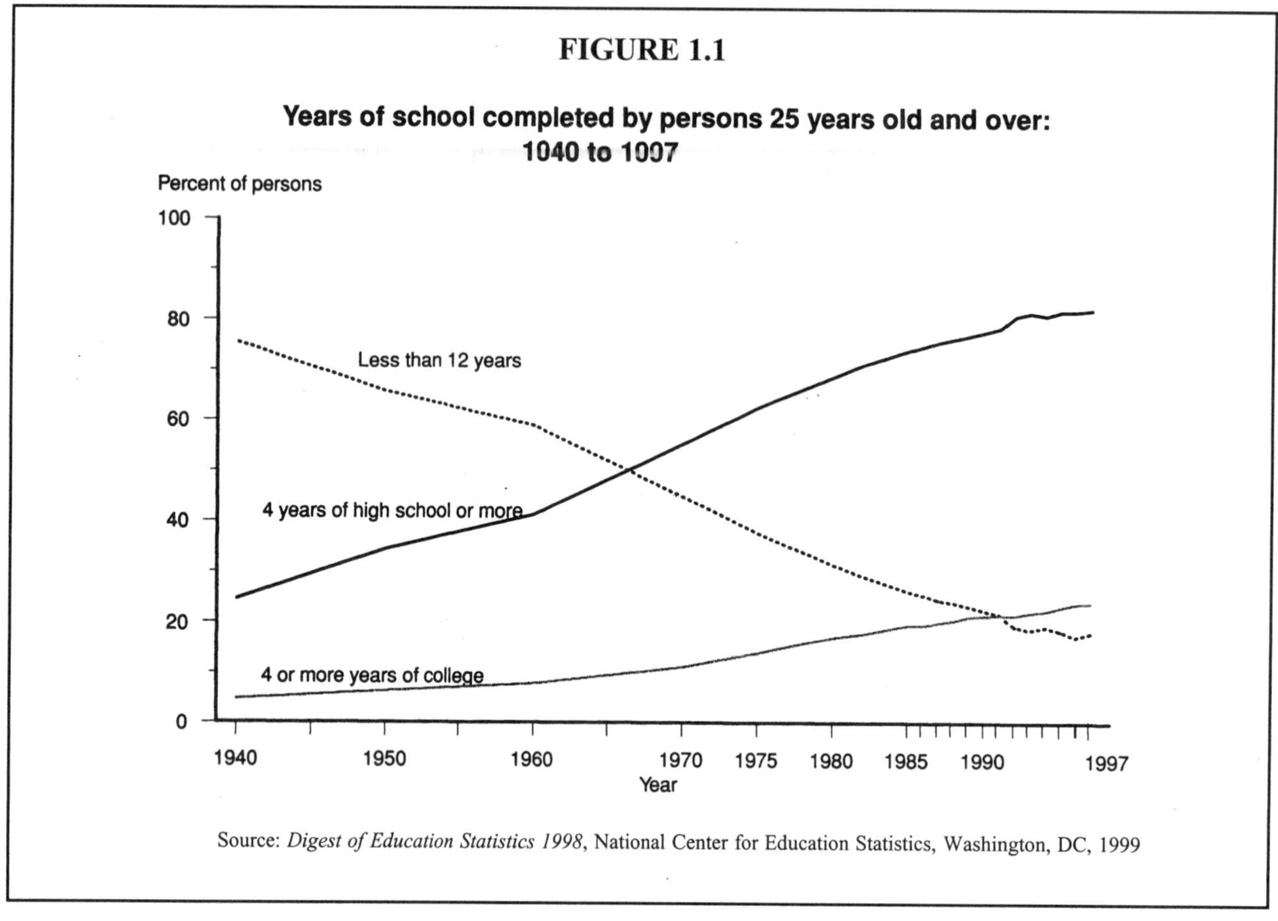

Source: *Digest of Education Statistics 1998*, National Center for Education Statistics, Washington, DC, 1999

5 percent of the population 25 years old and older had completed four or more years of college; by 1997, about 24 percent had done so. (See Table 1.2 and Figure 1.1.)

Among young people ages 25 to 29 years, 87.4 percent had completed four or more years of high school in 1997, while 27.8 percent had completed four or more years of college. White Americans were more likely than Black or Hispanic Americans to have completed both high school and college. (See Table 1.2.)

SCHOOL ENROLLMENT

Virtually all children 5 to 17 years old are enrolled in school. In 1997, more than 95 percent of all young people from 5 to 17 years old attended school. The enrollment of 3- and 4-year-olds has increased substantially over the past two decades, from 31.5 percent in 1975 to 52.6 percent in 1997. The proportion of children ages 5 and 6 enrolled in school changed little during this time period; in 1975, 94.7 percent of them were enrolled, and in 1997, 96.5 percent were enrolled. (See Table 1.3.)

The proportion of people enrolled in school drops sharply after age 18. By this age, young people either graduate from or leave high school and may not immediately go on to any form of higher education. However, the proportion of older teens attending school has increased during the past two decades. In 1997, the proportion of older teens enrolled in school reached 61.5 percent, up from 46.9 percent in 1975. (See Table 1.3.)

Enrollment Numbers Are Changing

The number of students enrolled in elementary and secondary schools and in colleges is directly proportional to the birth rates of the previous two decades. After World War II and the Korean conflict, the nation experienced a "baby boom" (1946-1964) as returning soldiers settled down to start families. Consequently, school enrollment grew rapidly during the 1950s and 1960s as these ba-

TABLE 1.3

Percent of the population 3 to 34 years old enrolled in school,[1] by race/ethnicity, sex, and age: October 1980 to October 1997

Year and age	Total				Male				Female			
	All races	White, non-Hispanic	Black, non-Hispanic	Hispanic origin	All races	White, non-Hispanic	Black, non-Hispanic	Hispanic origin	All races	White, non-Hispanic	Black, non-Hispanic	Hispanic origin
1	2	3	4	5	6	7	8	9	10	11	12	13
1975												
Total, 3 to 34 years	53.7	53.0	57.7	54.8	56.1	55.2	60.4	58.1	51.5	50.8	55.3	51.7
3 and 4 years	31.5	31.0	34.4	27.3	30.9	31.1	31.4	26.7	32.1	30.9	37.5	27.9
5 and 6 years	94.7	95.1	94.4	92.1	94.4	94.8	94.8	89.7	95.1	95.4	94.0	94.4
7 to 9 years	99.3	99.4	99.3	99.6	99.2	99.2	99.4	99.6	99.5	99.6	99.2	99.5
10 to 13 years	99.3	99.3	99.1	99.2	98.9	99.0	98.9	98.8	99.6	99.6	99.3	99.7
14 and 15 years	98.2	98.5	97.4	95.6	98.4	98.6	97.6	97.4	98.0	98.4	97.2	93.8
16 and 17 years	89.0	89.5	86.8	86.2	90.7	91.2	88.1	88.3	87.2	87.8	85.5	84.0
18 and 19 years	46.9	46.8	46.9	44.0	49.9	49.4	49.6	51.9	44.2	44.2	44.6	37.1
20 and 21 years	31.2	32.1	26.7	27.5	35.3	36.7	28.4	31.3	27.4	27.8	25.3	24.3
22 to 24 years	16.2	16.4	13.9	14.1	20.0	20.8	14.5	15.9	12.6	12.2	13.4	12.5
25 to 29 years	10.1	10.1	9.4	8.3	13.1	13.2	11.6	11.9	7.2	7.2	7.6	5.3
30 to 34 years	6.6	6.6	7.1	5.5	7.7	7.5	8.7	7.2	5.6	5.8	5.9	4.1
1980												
Total, 3 to 34 years	49.7	48.8	54.0	49.8	50.9	50.0	56.2	49.9	48.5	47.7	52.1	49.8
3 and 4 years	36.7	37.4	38.2	28.5	37.8	39.2	36.4	30.1	35.5	35.5	40.0	26.6
5 and 6 years	95.7	95.9	95.5	94.5	95.0	95.4	94.1	94.0	96.4	96.5	97.0	94.9
7 to 9 years	99.1	99.1	99.4	98.4	99.0	99.0	99.5	97.7	99.2	99.2	99.3	99.0
10 to 13 years	99.4	99.4	99.4	99.7	99.4	99.4	99.4	99.4	99.4	99.3	99.3	99.9
14 and 15 years	98.2	98.7	97.9	94.3	98.7	98.9	98.4	96.7	97.7	98.5	97.3	92.1
16 and 17 years	89.0	89.2	90.7	81.8	89.1	89.4	90.7	81.5	88.8	89.0	90.6	82.2
18 and 19 years	46.4	47.0	45.8	37.8	47.0	48.5	42.9	36.9	45.8	45.7	48.3	38.8
20 and 21 years	31.0	33.0	23.3	19.5	32.6	34.8	22.8	21.4	29.5	31.3	23.7	17.6
22 to 24 years	16.3	16.8	13.6	11.7	17.8	18.7	13.4	10.7	14.9	15.0	13.7	12.6
25 to 29 years	9.3	9.4	8.8	6.9	9.8	9.8	10.6	6.8	8.8	9.1	7.5	6.9
30 to 34 years	6.4	6.4	6.9	5.1	5.9	5.6	7.2	6.2	7.0	7.2	6.6	4.1
1985												
Total, 3 to 34 years	48.3	47.8	50.8	47.7	49.2	48.7	52.6	47.5	47.4	46.9	49.2	47.9
3 and 4 years	38.9	40.3	42.8	27.0	36.7	39.1	34.6	26.4	41.2	41.6	50.3	27.7
5 and 6 years	96.1	96.6	95.7	94.5	95.3	95.6	94.5	95.3	97.0	97.6	97.1	93.7
7 to 9 years	99.1	99.4	98.6	98.4	99.0	99.3	98.4	98.9	99.2	99.4	98.9	98.0
10 to 13 years	99.3	99.3	99.5	99.4	99.2	99.2	99.1	99.1	99.4	99.3	99.9	99.7
14 and 15 years	98.1	98.3	98.1	96.1	98.3	98.4	98.5	96.2	97.9	98.1	97.6	96.0
16 and 17 years	91.7	92.5	91.8	84.5	92.4	92.9	92.0	88.9	90.9	92.2	91.6	80.0
18 and 19 years	51.6	53.7	43.5	41.8	52.2	53.4	49.4	38.6	51.0	54.0	37.8	44.7
20 and 21 years	35.3	37.2	27.7	24.0	36.5	38.8	29.9	20.3	34.1	35.7	25.8	27.4
22 to 24 years	16.9	17.5	13.8	11.6	18.8	19.8	13.5	12.6	15.1	15.4	14.0	10.4
25 to 29 years	9.2	9.6	7.4	6.6	9.4	9.7	5.8	8.2	9.1	9.4	8.7	4.9
30 to 34 years	6.1	6.2	5.2	5.7	5.4	5.6	3.9	4.0	6.8	6.9	6.2	7.5
1990												
Total, 3 to 34 years	50.2	49.8	52.2	47.2	50.9	50.4	54.3	46.8	49.5	49.2	50.3	47.7
3 and 4 years	44.4	47.2	41.8	30.7	43.9	47.9	38.1	28.0	44.9	46.6	45.5	33.6
5 and 6 years	[illegible]	[illegible]	[illegible]	[illegible]	[illegible]	[illegible]	[illegible]	[illegible]	[illegible]	[illegible]	[illegible]	[illegible]
7 to 9 years	99.7	99.7	99.8	99.5	99.7	99.7	99.9	99.5	99.6	99.7	99.8	99.4
10 to 13 years	99.6	99.7	99.9	99.1	99.6	99.6	99.9	99.0	99.7	99.7	99.8	99.1
14 and 15 years	99.0	99.0	99.4	99.0	99.1	99.2	99.7	99.1	98.9	98.9	99.1	98.8
16 and 17 years	92.5	93.5	91.7	85.4	92.6	93.4	93.0	85.5	92.4	93.7	90.5	85.3
18 and 19 years	57.2	59.1	55.0	44.0	58.2	59.7	60.4	40.7	56.3	58.5	49.8	47.2
20 and 21 years	39.7	43.1	28.3	27.2	40.3	44.2	31.0	21.7	39.2	42.0	25.8	33.1
22 to 24 years	21.0	21.9	19.7	9.9	22.3	23.7	19.3	11.2	19.9	20.3	20.0	8.4
25 to 29 years	9.7	10.4	6.1	6.3	9.2	10.0	4.7	4.6	10.2	10.7	7.3	8.1
30 to 34 years	5.8	6.2	4.5	3.6	4.8	5.0	2.3	4.0	6.9	7.4	6.3	3.1
1997												
Total, 3 to 34 years	55.6	55.6	58.6	50.8	55.8	55.9	59.7	49.0	55.4	55.2	57.5	52.7
3 and 4 years[2]	52.6	54.9	60.0	36.6	51.9	54.9	57.4	35.5	53.2	55.0	62.9	37.7
5 and 6 years	96.5	96.9	95.7	96.6	96.7	97.3	94.0	97.7	96.4	96.4	97.1	95.7
7 to 9 years	98.8	98.9	99.2	98.6	98.6	98.8	98.7	97.7	99.1	99.0	99.8	99.6
10 to 13 years	99.3	99.2	99.4	99.6	99.4	99.3	99.1	99.8	99.3	99.1	99.7	99.5
14 and 15 years	98.9	98.9	99.2	98.4	99.1	99.0	99.5	99.5	98.7	98.8	98.9	97.3
16 and 17 years	94.3	95.1	93.5	91.1	94.2	94.5	93.8	92.5	94.4	95.7	93.2	89.6
18 and 19 years	61.5	64.0	57.8	49.4	60.5	63.3	56.2	45.4	62.4	64.9	59.4	53.9
20 and 21 years	45.9	49.9	36.0	28.9	44.4	48.5	35.1	27.6	47.4	51.3	36.7	30.4
22 to 24 years	26.4	27.8	25.7	16.4	25.4	27.5	21.8	14.0	27.4	28.1	28.9	19.2
25 to 29 years	11.8	12.2	10.6	7.3	11.7	12.0	10.1	5.9	11.9	12.4	10.9	8.8
30 to 34 years	5.7	5.6	6.5	3.7	4.7	4.6	5.8	2.7	6.6	6.6	7.2	4.9

[1] Includes enrollment in any type of graded public, parochial, or other private schools. Includes nursery schools, kindergartens, elementary schools, high schools, colleges, universities, and professional schools. Attendance may be on either a full-time or part-time basis and during the day or night. Enrollments in "special" schools, such as trade schools, business colleges, or correspondence schools, are not included.

[2] Preprimary enrollment collected using new procedures. May not be comparable to figures for earlier years.

NOTE.—Data are based upon sample surveys of the civilian noninstitutional population.

SOURCE: U.S. Department of Commerce, Bureau of the Census, Current Population Survey, unpublished data. (This table was prepared August 1998.)

Source: *Digest of Education Statistics 1998*, National Center for Education Statistics, Washington, DC, 1999

TABLE 1.4

Enrollment in educational institutions, by level and by control of institution: 1869–70 to fall 2008

[In thousands]

| Year | Total enrollment, all levels | Elementary and secondary, total | Public elementary and secondary schools | | | Private elementary and secondary schools [1] | | | Higher education [2] | | |
			Total	Pre-kindergarten through grade 8	Grades 9 through 12	Total	Kindergarten through grade 8	Grades 9 through 12	Total	Public	Private
1	2	3	4	5	6	7	8	9	10	11	12
1869–70	—	—	6,872	6,792	80	—	—	—	52	—	—
1879–80	—	—	9,868	9,757	110	—	—	—	116	—	—
1889–90	14,491	14,334	12,723	12,520	203	1,611	1,516	95	157	—	—
1899–1900	17,092	16,855	15,503	14,984	519	1,352	1,241	111	238	—	—
1909–10	19,728	19,372	17,814	16,899	915	1,558	1,441	117	355	—	—
1919–20	23,876	23,278	21,578	19,378	2,200	1,699	1,486	214	598	—	—
1929–30	29,430	28,329	25,678	21,279	4,399	2,651	2,310	341	1,101	—	—
1939–40	29,539	28,045	25,434	18,832	6,601	2,611	2,153	458	1,494	797	698
1949–50	31,151	28,492	25,111	19,387	5,725	3,380	2,708	672	2,659	1,355	1,304
Fall 1959	44,497	40,857	35,182	26,911	8,271	5,675	4,640	1,035	3,640	2,181	1,459
Fall 1964	52,996	47,716	41,416	30,025	11,391	[3] 6,300	[3] 5,000	1,300	5,280	3,468	1,812
Fall 1965	54,394	48,473	42,173	30,563	11,610	6,300	4,900	1,400	5,921	3,970	1,951
Fall 1966	55,629	49,239	43,039	31,145	11,894	[3] 6,200	[3] 4,800	[3] 1,400	6,390	4,349	2,041
Fall 1967	56,803	49,891	43,891	31,641	12,250	[3] 6,000	[3] 4,600	[3] 1,400	6,912	4,816	2,096
Fall 1968	58,257	50,744	44,944	32,226	12,718	5,800	4,400	1,400	7,513	5,431	2,082
Fall 1969	59,055	51,050	45,550	32,513	13,037	[3] 5,500	[3] 4,200	[3] 1,300	8,005	5,897	2,108
Fall 1970	59,838	51,257	45,894	32,558	13,336	5,363	4,052	1,311	8,581	6,428	2,153
Fall 1971	60,220	51,271	46,071	32,318	13,753	[3] 5,200	[3] 3,900	[3] 1,300	8,949	6,804	2,144
Fall 1972	59,941	50,726	45,726	31,879	13,848	[3] 5,000	[3] 3,700	[3] 1,300	9,215	7,071	2,144
Fall 1973	60,047	50,445	45,445	31,401	14,044	[3] 5,000	[3] 3,700	[3] 1,300	9,602	7,420	2,183
Fall 1974	60,297	50,073	45,073	30,971	14,103	[3] 5,000	[3] 3,700	[3] 1,300	10,224	7,989	2,235
Fall 1975	61,004	49,819	44,819	30,515	14,304	[3] 5,000	[3] 3,700	[3] 1,300	11,185	8,835	2,350
Fall 1976	60,490	49,478	44,311	29,997	14,314	5,167	3,825	1,342	11,012	8,653	2,359
Fall 1977	60,003	48,717	43,577	29,375	14,203	5,140	3,797	1,343	11,286	8,847	2,439
Fall 1978	58,897	47,637	42,551	28,463	14,088	5,086	3,732	1,353	11,260	8,786	2,474
Fall 1979	58,221	46,651	41,651	28,034	13,616	[3] 5,000	[3] 3,700	[3] 1,300	11,570	9,037	2,533
Fall 1980	58,305	46,208	40,877	27,647	13,231	5,331	3,992	1,339	12,097	9,457	2,640
Fall 1981	57,916	45,544	40,044	27,280	12,764	[3] 5,500	[3] 4,100	[3] 1,400	12,372	9,647	2,725
Fall 1982	57,591	45,166	39,566	27,161	12,405	[3] 5,600	[3] 4,200	[3] 1,400	12,426	9,696	2,730
Fall 1983	57,432	44,967	39,252	26,981	12,271	5,715	4,315	1,400	12,465	9,683	2,782
Fall 1984	57,150	44,908	39,208	26,905	12,304	[3] 5,700	[3] 4,300	[3] 1,400	12,242	9,477	2,765
Fall 1985	57,226	44,979	39,422	27,034	12,388	5,557	4,195	1,362	12,247	9,479	2,768
Fall 1986	57,709	45,205	39,753	27,420	12,333	[3] 5,452	[3] 4,116	[3] 1,336	12,504	9,714	2,790
Fall 1987	58,254	45,488	40,008	27,933	12,076	5,479	4,232	1,247	12,767	9,973	2,793
Fall 1988	58,485	45,430	40,189	28,501	11,687	[3] 5,241	[3] 4,036	[3] 1,206	13,055	10,161	2,894
Fall 1989	59,436	45,898	40,543	29,152	11,390	[3] 5,355	[3] 4,162	[3] 1,193	13,539	10,578	2,961
Fall 1990	60,267	46,448	41,217	29,878	11,338	5,232	4,095	1,137	13,819	10,845	2,974
Fall 1991	61,605	47,246	42,047	30,506	11,541	[3] 5,199	[3] 4,074	[3] 1,125	14,359	11,310	3,049
Fall 1992	62,686	48,198	42,823	31,088	11,735	[3] 5,375	[3] 4,212	[3] 1,163	14,487	11,385	3,103
Fall 1993	63,241	48,936	43,465	31,504	11,961	[3] 5,471	[3] 4,280	[3] 1,191	14,305	11,189	3,116
Fall 1994	63,986	49,707	44,111	31,898	12,213	[3] 5,596	[3] 4,360	[3] 1,236	14,279	11,134	3,145
Fall 1995	64,803	50,540	44,840	32,341	12,500	[3] 5,700	[3] 4,431	[3] 1,269	14,262	11,092	3,169
Fall 1996 [4]	65,674	51,375	45,592	32,759	12,834	[3] 5,783	[3] 4,486	[3] 1,297	14,300	11,090	3,210
Fall 1997 [5]	66,170	51,821	45,953	32,951	13,003	5,867	4,545	1,322	14,350	11,208	3,143
Fall 1998 [5]	67,309	52,718	46,792	33,522	13,270	5,927	4,588	1,339	14,590	11,395	3,194
Fall 1999 [5]	67,871	53,112	47,143	33,722	13,420	5,970	4,616	1,354	14,758	11,525	3,233
Fall 2000 [5]	68,334	53,445	47,439	33,903	13,537	6,006	4,640	1,366	14,889	11,626	3,263
Fall 2001 [5]	68,728	53,736	47,698	34,055	13,643	6,038	4,661	1,376	14,992	11,705	3,287
Fall 2002 [5]	69,040	53,987	47,924	34,124	13,800	6,063	4,671	1,392	15,053	11,751	3,303
Fall 2003 [5]	69,338	54,153	48,075	34,124	13,951	6,078	4,671	1,407	15,185	11,849	3,335
Fall 2004 [5]	69,657	54,308	48,221	33,958	14,263	6,087	4,648	1,439	15,349	11,975	3,374
Fall 2005 [5]	69,942	54,426	48,335	33,756	14,579	6,091	4,620	1,471	15,516	12,101	3,415
Fall 2006 [5]	70,160	54,457	48,368	33,584	14,785	6,088	4,597	1,491	15,703	12,242	3,461
Fall 2007 [5]	70,305	54,425	48,342	33,489	14,854	6,082	4,584	1,498	15,880	12,378	3,502
Fall 2008 [5]	70,351	54,268	48,201	33,455	14,746	6,067	4,579	1,488	16,083	12,534	3,549

[1] Beginning in fall 1980, data include estimates for an expanded universe of private schools. Therefore, these totals may differ from figures shown in other tables, and direct comparisons with earlier years should be avoided.

[2] Data for 1869–70 through 1949–50 include resident degree-credit students enrolled at any time during the academic year. Beginning in 1959, data include all resident and extension students enrolled at the beginning of the fall term.

[3] Estimated.

[4] Preliminary data.

[5] Projected.

—Data not available.

NOTE.—Elementary and secondary enrollment includes pupils in public school systems and in most private schools (religiously affiliated and nonsectarian), but generally excludes pupils in subcollegiate departments of colleges, residential schools for exceptional children, federal schools, and home-schooled children. Based on Department estimates, the home-schooled children numbered approximately 800,000 to 1,000,000 in 1997–98. Public elementary enrollment includes most preprimary school pupils. Private elementary enrollment includes some preprimary students. Higher education includes colleges, universities, professional schools, and 2-year colleges. Higher education enrollment projections are based on the middle alternative projections published by the National Center for Education Statistics. Some data have been revised from previously published figures. Because of rounding, details may not add to totals.

SOURCE: U.S. Department of Education, National Center for Education Statistics, *Statistics of State School Systems; Statistics of Public Elementary and Secondary School Systems; Statistics of Nonpublic Elementary and Secondary Schools; Projections of Education Statistics to 2008; Common Core of Data; Higher Education General Information Survey* (HEGIS), "Fall Enrollment in Institutions of Higher Education" surveys; and Integrated Postsecondary Education Data System (IPEDS), "Fall Enrollment" surveys. (This table was prepared July 1998.)

Source: *Digest of Education Statistics 1998*, National Center for Education Statistics, Washington, DC, 1999

bies matured to school age. Total enrollment peaked at 61 million in 1975, a number not attained again until 1991. Elementary enrollment (36.7 million) reached a record high in 1969, and high school enrollment (15.7 million) peaked in 1976. (See Table 1.4.)

Following the baby boom, birth rates declined, and so did school enrollments in the 1970s. An "echo effect" occurred in the 1980s, when those born during the baby boom started their own families. This increase in birth rates triggered an increase in school enrollment in the early 1990s. In 1991, 61.6 million students were enrolled in schools at all levels. In the years following 1991, school enrollment grew at about 1 to 2 percent annually, a trend expected to continue into the 2000s. (See Table 1.4.)

For the past two decades, elementary enrollment in public and private schools has gradually declined from a high of 36.7 million in 1969. Af-

TABLE 1.5

Total expenditures of educational institutions related to the gross domestic product, by level of institution: 1959–60 to 1997–98

Year	Gross domestic product (in billions)	School year	Total expenditures for education (amounts in millions of current dollars)					
			All educational institutions		All elementary and secondary schools		All colleges and universities	
			Amount	As a percent of gross domestic product	Amount	As a percent of gross domestic product	Amount	As a percent of gross domestic product
1	2	3	4	5	6	7	8	9
1959	$507.2	1959–60	$23,860	4.7	$16,713	3.3	$7,147	1.4
1961	544.8	1961–62	28,503	5.2	19,673	3.6	8,830	1.6
1963	617.4	1963–64	34,440	5.6	22,825	3.7	11,615	1.9
1965	719.1	1965–66	43,682	6.1	28,048	3.9	15,634	2.2
1967	833.6	1967–68	55,652	6.7	35,077	4.2	20,575	2.5
1969	982.2	1969–70	68,459	7.0	43,183	4.4	25,276	2.6
1970	1,035.6	1970–71	75,741	7.3	48,200	4.7	27,541	2.7
1971	1,125.4	1971–72	80,672	7.2	50,950	4.5	29,722	2.6
1972	1,237.3	1972–73	86,875	7.0	54,952	4.4	31,923	2.6
1973	1,382.6	1973–74	95,396	6.9	60,370	4.4	35,026	2.5
1974	1,496.9	1974–75	108,664	7.3	68,846	4.6	39,818	2.7
1975	1,630.6	1975–76	118,706	7.3	75,101	4.6	43,605	2.7
1976	1,819.0	1976–77	126,417	6.9	79,194	4.4	47,223	2.6
1977	2,026.9	1977–78	137,042	6.8	86,544	4.3	50,498	2.5
1978	2,291.4	1978–79	148,308	6.5	93,012	4.1	55,296	2.4
1979	2,557.5	1979–80	165,627	6.5	103,162	4.0	62,465	2.4
1980	2,784.2	1980–81	182,849	6.6	112,325	4.0	70,524	2.5
1981	3,115.9	1981–82	197,801	6.3	120,486	3.9	77,315	2.5
1982	3,242.1	1982–83	212,081	6.5	128,725	4.0	83,356	2.6
1983	3,514.5	1983–84	228,597	6.5	139,000	4.0	83,597	2.5
1984	3,902.4	1984–85	247,657	6.3	149,400	3.8	98,257	2.5
1985	4,180.7	1985–86	269,485	6.4	161,800	3.9	107,685	2.6
1986	4,422.2	1986–87	291,974	6.6	175,200	4.0	116,774	2.6
1987	4,692.3	1987–88	313,375	6.7	187,999	4.0	125,376	2.7
1988	5,049.6	1988–89	346,883	6.9	209,377	4.1	137,506	2.7
1989	5,438.7	1989–90	381,525	7.0	230,970	4.2	150,555	2.8
1990	5,743.8	1990–91	412,652	7.2	248,930	4.3	163,722	2.9
1991	5,916.7	1991–92	432,987	7.3	261,255	4.4	171,732	2.9
1992	6,244.4	1992–93	456,070	7.3	274,335	4.4	181,735	2.9
1993	6,558.1	1993–94	477,237	7.3	287,507	4.4	189,730	2.9
1994	6,947.0	1994–95	503,925	7.3	302,400	4.4	201,525	2.9
1995	7,269.6	[1] 1995–96	529,561	7.3	318,211	4.4	211,350	2.9
1996	7,661.6	[2] 1996–97	559,500	7.3	336,000	4.4	223,500	2.9
1997	8,110.9	[2] 1997–98	583,800	7.2	351,300	4.3	232,500	2.9

[1] Preliminary.
[2] Estimated.

NOTE.—Total expenditures for public elementary and secondary schools include current expenditures, interest on school debt, and capital outlay. Data for private elementary and secondary schools are estimated. Total expenditures for colleges and universities include current-fund expenditures and additions to plant value. Excludes expenditures of noncollegiate postsecondary institutions. Data for 1995–96 through 1997–98 are for 4-year and 2-year degree-granting institutions that were eligible to participate in Title IV federal financial aid programs. Some data revised from previously published figures. Because of rounding, details may not add to totals.

SOURCE: U.S. Department of Education, National Center for Education Statistics, *Statistics of State School Systems; Revenues and Expenditures for Public Elementary and Secondary Education; Financial Statistics of Institutions of Higher Education;* Common Core of Data survey; Higher Education General Information Survey (HEGIS), "Financial Statistics of Institutions of Higher Education" survey, Integrated Postsecondary Education Data System (IPEDS) "Finance" survey, and unpublished data; Council of Economic Advisers, *Economic Indicators;* and National Education Association, *Estimates of School Statistics,* various years. (This table was prepared November 1998.)

Source: *Digest of Education Statistics 1998*, National Center for Education Statistics, Washington, DC, 1999

ter leveling off in the late 1980s at around 33 million, elementary enrollment has risen through the 1990s and is expected to stay fairly stable into the twenty-first century. (See Table 1.1.)

High school enrollment, which began to decline in the late 1970s, started to increase again in the mid-1990s and is expected to continue this trend beyond the year 2000. College enrollments, unlike elementary and secondary enrollments, have risen consistently and are expected to reach 16.1 million by 2008. (See Table 1.4.)

EDUCATIONAL DIFFERENCES

Race

The marked difference in educational attainment that once existed between Whites and minorities has narrowed. About 86 percent of White adults age 25 years and older were high school graduates in 1997, while 75.3 percent of Blacks and 54.7 percent of Hispanics were graduates. The most significant advances can be seen among young adults ages 25 to 29. In 1997, 92.9 percent of Whites, 86.9 percent of Blacks, and 61.8 percent of Hispanics ages 25 to 29 years old were high school graduates, compared to 41.2 percent of Whites and 12.3 percent of Blacks and other races in 1940. (See Table 1.2.)

In 1940, White adults age 25 and older were far more likely than Blacks and other minorities to have completed four years of college (4.9 percent versus 1.3 percent). By 1997, however, the gap had narrowed. Twenty-six percent of Whites, 13.3 percent of Blacks, and 10.3 percent of Hispanics had completed four or more years of college. About one-third of White young adults (32.6 percent) ages 25 to 29 were college graduates, compared to 14.2 percent of Blacks and 11 percent of Hispanics in the same age group (Table 1.2). The differences remain significant.

Gender

Traditionally, women were slightly more likely than men to complete high school but less likely to go on to college. In recent years, the differences in high school graduation have disappeared. In 1997, 82 percent of both young women and young men age 25 and older had completed four or more years of high school. The proportion of women 25 years old and older graduating from college has increased steadily, from 3.8 percent in 1940 to 21.7 percent in 1997. Nevertheless, the proportion of male students (26.2 percent in 1997) who completed four or more years of college was still significantly higher. (See Table 1.2.)

PROJECTIONS TO 2008

The National Center for Education Statistics (NCES) estimates that the total public and private elementary and secondary enrollment will increase about 5 percent between 1997 and 2008, from 51.8 million to 54.3 million. Enrollment in kindergarten through eighth grade is projected to increase only about 1 percent through 2008, while enrollment in grades nine through 12 is expected to rise 13 percent. The number of persons attending institutions of higher learning is projected to increase from 14.4 million in 1997 to 16.1 million by 2008. (See Table 1.4.) The majority of college students through 2008 will likely be women.

EDUCATION SPENDING

Expenditures for public and private education from preprimary through graduate school rose to an estimated high of $583.8 billion for the 1997-98 school year. Expenditures for elementary and secondary schools reached $351.3 billion (60 percent of total education spending), and outlays for institutions of higher learning were estimated at $232.5 billion (40 percent). In 1997-98, the United States spent over 7 percent of its gross domestic product (GDP— the total value of goods and services produced within the United States) on education. (See Table 1.5.) About 70 percent of state and local funds for education was spent on elementary and secondary schools, 26 percent on colleges and universities, and 4 percent on other educational programs.

CHAPTER II

PREPRIMARY, ELEMENTARY, AND SECONDARY SCHOOLS

SCHOOL ENROLLMENTS

Preprimary, elementary, and secondary school enrollments reflect the number of births over a specific period. Because of the baby boom (see Chapter I), school enrollment grew rapidly during the 1950s and 1960s and then declined steadily during the 1970s and 1980s. In fall 1985, public elementary and secondary school enrollment increased for the first time since 1971. Enrollment has grown slowly but steadily since, reaching an estimated 46.8 million in public schools and 5.9 million in private schools in fall 1998. Slow but steady growth is projected to continue into the twenty-first century. (See Table 2.1 and Figure 2.1.)

Preprimary Growth

In contrast to the declining elementary and secondary school enrollment during the 1970s and early 1980s, preprimary enrollment showed substantial growth. Between 1970 and 1980, preprimary enrollment rose by 19 percent, from 4.1 million to 4.9 million. While the population of 3- to 5-year-olds grew 31 percent from 1980 to 1997, enrollment in preprimary programs rose 61 percent to 7.9 million. This increase reflects not only the growth in the number of children ages 3 to 5, but also the greater availability of and interest in preschool education. In 1965, of the 12.5 million children in this age group, only 27.1 percent were enrolled in nursery school or kindergar-

---

TABLE 2.1

Elementary and secondary school enrollment (in thousands), by control and grade level of school, with projections: Fall 1970–2008

Year/period	Public schools			Private schools[1]		
	Grades PreK–12	Grades PreK–8	Grades 9–12	Grades PreK–12	Grades PreK–8	Grades 9–12
1970	45,894	32,558	13,336	5,363	4,052	1,311
1988	40,189	28,501	11,687	5,241	4,036	1,206
1998	46,792	33,522	13,270	5,927	4,588	1,339
	Projected[2]			Projected[2]		
2008	48,201	33,455	14,746	6,067	4,579	1,488
	Percentage change			Percentage change		
1970–88	-12.4	-12.5	-12.4	-2.3	-0.4	-8.0
	Projected percentage change			Projected percentage change		
1988–98	16.4	17.6	13.5	13.1	13.7	11.0
1998–2008	3.0	-0.2	11.1	2.4	-0.2	11.1

[1] Beginning in fall 1980, data include estimates for the expanded universe of private schools.

[2] Enrollment includes students in kindergarten through grade 12 and some nursery school students.

NOTE: Details may not add to totals due to rounding.

SOURCE: U.S. Department of Education, National Center for Education Statistics, *Digest of Education Statistics 1998* (based on Common Core of Data) and *Projections of Education Statistics to 2008*, 1998.

Source: *The Condition of Education 1999*, National Center for Education Statistics, Washington, DC 1999

FIGURE 2.1

Elementary and secondary school enrollment

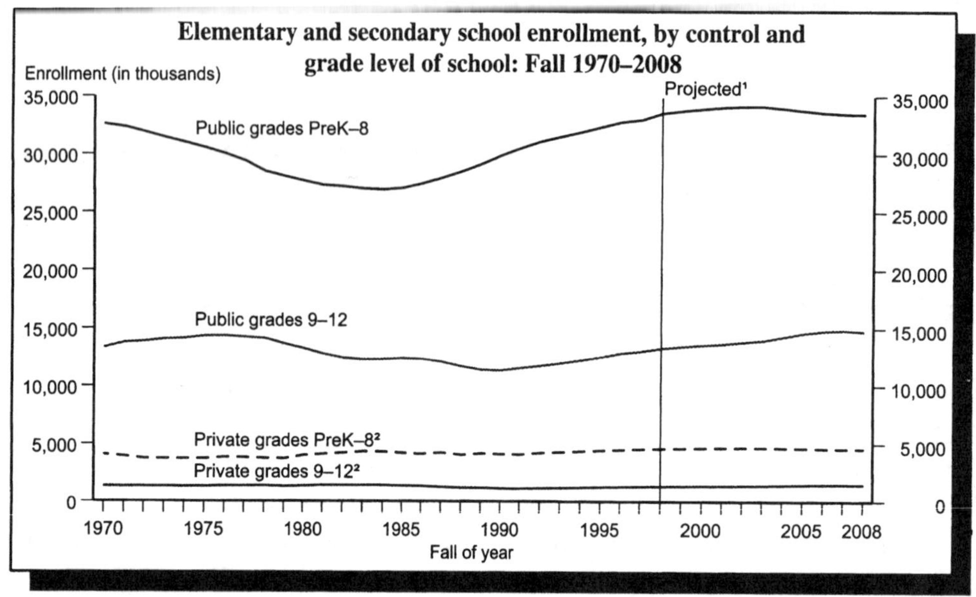

¹ Enrollment includes students in kindergarten through grade 12 and some nursery school students.

² Beginning in fall 1980, data include estimates for the expanded universe of private schools.

SOURCE: U.S. Department of Education, National Center for Education Statistics, *Digest of Education Statistics 1998* (based on Common Core of Data) and *Projections of Education Statistics to 2008*, 1998.

Source: *The Condition of Education 1999*, National Center for Education Statistics, Washington, DC, 1999

TABLE 2.2

Enrollment of 3-, 4-, and 5-year-old children in preprimary programs, by level and control of program and by attendance status: October 1965 to October 1997

[In thousands]

Year and age	Total population, 3 to 5 years old	Enrollment by level and control						Enrollment by attendance		
		Total	Percent enrolled	Nursery school		Kindergarten		Full-day	Part-day	Percent full-day
				Public	Private	Public	Private			
1	2	3	4	5	6	7	8	9	10	11
Total, 3 to 5 years old										
1965	12,549	3,407	27.1	127	393	2,291	596	—	—	—
1970	10,949	4,104	37.5	332	762	2,498	511	698	3,405	17.0
1975	10,185	4,955	48.7	570	1,174	2,682	528	1,295	3,659	26.1
1980	9,284	4,878	52.5	628	1,353	2,438	459	1,551	3,327	31.8
1985	10,733	5,865	54.6	846	1,631	2,847	541	2,144	3,722	36.6
1986	10,866	5,971	55.0	829	1,715	2,859	567	2,241	3,730	37.5
1987	10,872	5,931	54.6	819	1,736	2,842	534	2,090	3,841	35.2
1988	10,993	5,978	54.4	851	1,770	2,875	481	2,044	3,935	34.2
1989	11,039	6,026	54.6	930	1,894	2,704	497	2,238	3,789	37.1
1990	11,207	6,659	59.4	1,199	2,180	2,772	509	2,577	4,082	38.7
1991	11,370	6,334	55.7	996	1,828	2,967	543	2,408	3,926	38.0
1992	11,545	6,402	55.5	1,073	1,783	2,995	550	2,410	3,992	37.6
1993	11,954	6,581	55.1	1,205	1,779	3,020	577	2,642	3,939	40.1
1994 ¹	12,328	7,514	61.0	1,848	2,314	2,819	534	3,468	4,046	46.2
1995 ¹	12,518	7,739	61.8	1,950	2,381	2,800	608	3,689	4,051	47.7
1996 ¹	12,378	7,580	61.2	1,830	2,317	2,853	580	3,562	4,019	47.0
1997 ¹	12,121	7,860	64.9	2,207	2,231	2,847	575	3,922	3,939	49.9

¹ Data collected using new procedures. May not be comparable with figures prior to 1994.

—Data not available.

NOTE.—Data are based on sample surveys of the civilian noninstitutional population. Although cells with fewer than 75,000 children are subject to wide sampling variation, they are included in the table to permit various types of aggregations. Enrollment data for 5-year-olds include only those students in preprimary programs. Because of rounding, details may not add to totals.

SOURCE: U.S. Department of Education, National Center for Education Statistics, *Preprimary Enrollment*, various years; and U.S. Department of Commerce, Bureau of the Census, Current Population Survey, unpublished data. (This table was prepared September 1998.)

Source: *Digest of Education Statistics 1998*, National Center for Education Statistics, Washington, DC, 1999

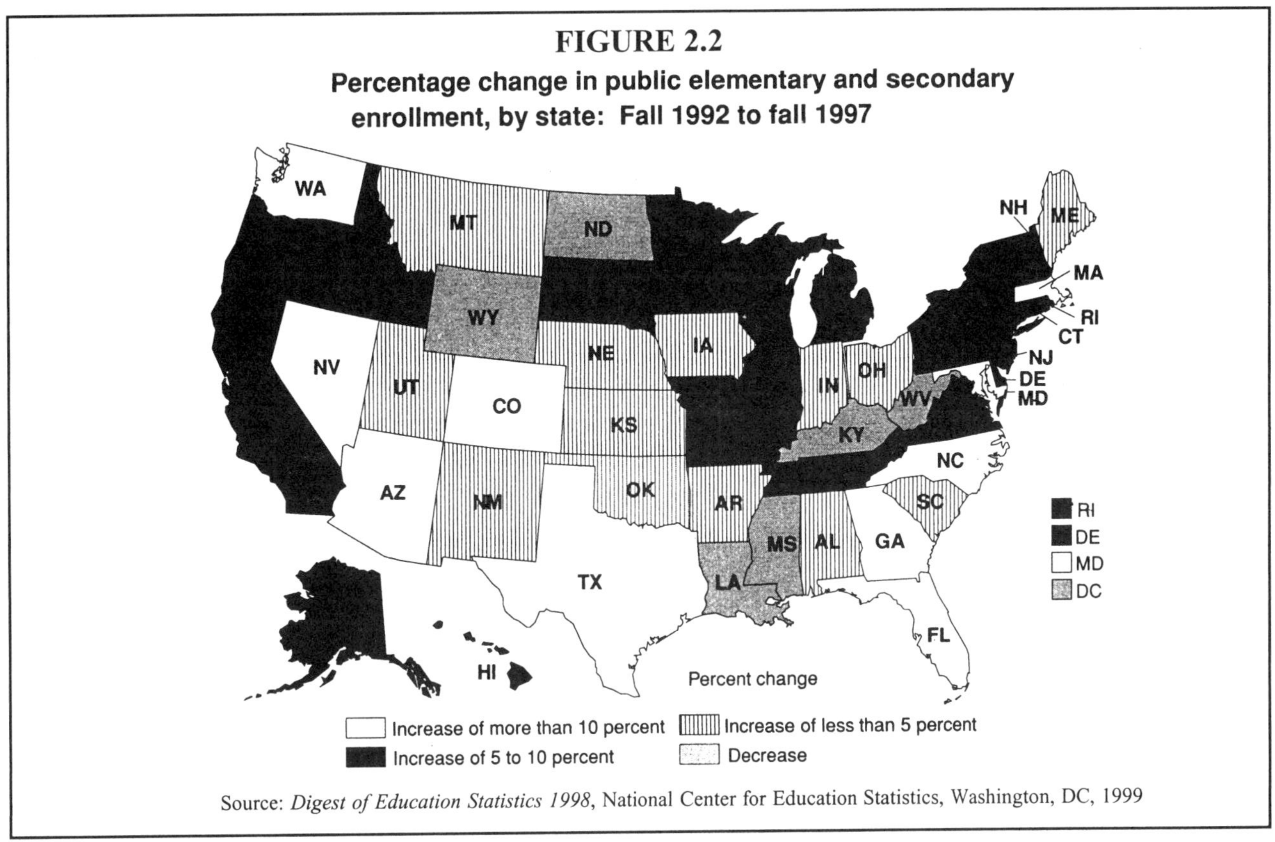

Source: *Digest of Education Statistics 1998*, National Center for Education Statistics, Washington, DC, 1999

ten. By October 1997, 64.9 percent of the 12.1 million preschool-age children in this country were enrolled in preprimary programs. (See Table 2.2.)

As the proportion of working mothers has grown, the proportion of young children in full-day preprimary programs has also increased. In 1997, one-half (49.9 percent) of children in preprimary programs attended school all day, compared to 31.8 percent in 1980 and 17 percent in 1970 (Table 2.2).

Geographic Shifts

The general shift in population away from the Northeast and North Central regions toward the South and West has led to significant changes in regional school enrollment. Between 1970 and

TABLE 2.3

Enrollment in public elementary and secondary schools, by race or ethnicity and state:
Fall 1986 and fall 1996

State or other area	Percent distribution, fall 1986						Percent distribution, fall 1996					
	Total	White [1]	Black [1]	Hispanic	Asian or Pacific Islander	American Indian/ Alaskan Native	Total	White [1]	Black [1]	Hispanic	Asian or Pacific Islander	American Indian/ Alaskan Native
1	2	3	4	5	6	7	8	9	10	11	12	13
United States [2]	100.0	70.4	16.1	9.9	2.8	0.9	100.0	64.2	16.9	14.0	3.8	1.1

[1] Excludes persons of Hispanic origin.
[2] U.S. totals for 1996 include estimate for New Jersey.

NOTE.—The 1986–87 data were derived from the 1986 Elementary and Secondary School Civil Rights sample survey of public school districts. Because of rounding, details may not add to totals.

SOURCE: U.S. Department of Education, Office for Civil Rights, *1986 State Summaries of Elementary and Secondary School Civil Rights Survey;* and National Center for Education Statistics, Common Core of Data survey. (This table was prepared May 1998.)

Source: *Digest of Education Statistics 1998*, National Center for Education Statistics, Washington, DC, 1999

TABLE 2.4

People and Families in Poverty by Selected Characteristics: 1989, 1997, and 1998

Numbers in thousands.

Characteristic	Below poverty, 1998				Below poverty, 1997				Below poverty, 1989[r]			
	Number	90-pct. C.I. (±)	Percent	90-pct. C.I. (±)	Number	90-pct. C.I. (±)	Percent	90-pct. C.I. (±)	Number	90-pct. C.I. (±)	Percent	90-pct. C.I. (±)
PEOPLE												
Total	**34,476**	**920**	**12.7**	**0.3**	**35,574**	**931**	**13.3**	**0.3**	**32,415**	**859**	**13.1**	**0.3**
Family Status												
In families...................	25,370	804	11.2	0.4	26,217	814	11.6	0.4	24,882	765	11.8	0.4
Householder	7,186	248	10.0	0.4	7,324	252	10.3	0.4	6,895	232	10.4	0.4
Related children under 18......	12,845	479	18.3	0.7	13,422	485	19.2	0.7	12,541	454	19.4	0.7
Related children under 6.....	4,775	309	20.6	1.4	5,049	316	21.6	1.4	5,116	306	22.5	1.4
In unrelated subfamilies	628	66	48.8	6.0	670	67	46.5	5.5	727	67	54.6	6.1
Reference person	247	41	47.4	9.2	259	41	45.0	8.5	284	41	51.8	9.1
Children under 18	361	89	50.5	14.2	403	94	48.9	13.0	430	92	60.5	15.3
Unrelated individual	8,478	275	19.9	0.7	8,687	280	20.8	0.7	6,807	230	19.3	0.7
Male	3,465	161	17.0	0.8	3,447	161	17.4	0.9	2,577	132	15.8	0.8
Female	5,013	201	22.6	1.0	5,240	206	24.0	1.0	4,230	174	22.3	1.0
Race and Hispanic Origin												
White, total..................	23,454	776	10.5	0.3	24,396	790	11.0	0.4	21,294	712	10.2	0.3
White, not Hispanic...........	15,799	646	8.2	0.3	16,491	660	8.6	0.3	15,499	615	8.3	0.3
Black, total	9,091	434	26.1	1.2	9,116	434	26.5	1.3	9,525	423	30.8	1.4
Asian and Pacific Islander, total ...	1,360	181	12.5	1.7	1,468	186	14.0	1.8	1,032	155	14.2	2.1
Hispanic origin, all races........	8,070	411	25.6	1.3	8,308	413	27.1	1.3	6,086	357	26.3	1.5
Age												
Under 18 years................	13,467	487	18.9	0.7	14,113	495	19.9	0.7	13,154	462	20.1	0.7
18 to 64 years	17,623	674	10.5	0.4	18,085	681	10.9	0.4	15,950	617	10.4	0.4
18 to 24 years...............	4,312	201	16.6	0.8	4,416	204	17.5	0.8	4,132	189	15.4	0.7
25 to 34 years...............	4,582	214	11.9	0.6	4,759	219	12.1	0.6	4,873	212	11.2	0.5
35 to 44 years...............	4,082	202	9.1	0.5	4,251	207	9.6	0.5	3,115	171	8.3	0.5
45 to 54 years...............	2,444	158	6.9	0.4	2,439	158	7.2	0.5	1,873	133	7.5	0.5
55 to 59 years...............	1,165	110	9.2	0.9	1,092	107	9.0	0.9	971	97	9.5	0.9
60 to 64 years...............	1,039	104	10.1	1.0	1,127	109	11.2	1.1	986	97	9.4	0.9
65 years and over	3,386	179	10.5	0.6	3,376	179	10.5	0.6	3,312	171	11.4	0.6
Nativity												
Native.....................	29,707	860	12.1	0.4	30,336	869	12.5	0.4	NA	NA	NA	NA
Foreign-born.................	4,769	413	18.0	1.6	5,238	433	19.9	1.6	NA	NA	NA	NA
Naturalized citizen............	1,087	199	11.0	2.0	1,111	201	11.4	2.1	NA	NA	NA	NA
Not a citizen	3,682	364	22.2	2.2	4,127	385	25.0	2.3	NA	NA	NA	NA
Region												
Northeast	6,357	385	12.3	0.8	6,474	388	12.6	0.8	5,213	336	10.2	0.7
Midwest	6,501	428	10.3	0.7	6,493	428	10.4	0.7	7,088	429	12.0	0.7
South	12,992	612	13.7	0.7	13,748	628	14.6	0.7	13,277	594	15.6	0.7
West.......................	8,625	505	14.0	0.8	8,858	512	14.6	0.9	6,838	433	12.8	0.8
Residence												
Inside metropolitan areas	26,997	827	12.3	0.4	27,273	829	12.6	0.4	23,726	748	12.3	0.4
Inside central cities	14,921	630	18.5	0.8	15,018	632	18.8	0.8	14,151	589	18.5	0.8
Outside central cities.........	12,076	569	8.7	0.4	12,255	572	9.0	0.4	9,574	489	8.2	0.4
Outside metropolitan areas.......	7,479	554	14.4	1.1	8,301	582	15.9	1.1	8,690	571	15.9	1.1
FAMILIES												
Total	**7,186**	**248**	**10.0**	**0.4**	**7,324**	**252**	**10.3**	**0.4**	**6,895**	**232**	**10.4**	**0.4**
White, total....................	4,829	196	8.0	0.3	4,990	199	8.4	0.3	4,457	179	7.9	0.3
White, not Hispanic...........	3,264	156	6.1	0.3	3,357	160	6.3	0.3	3,287	151	6.4	0.3
Black, total	1,981	118	23.4	1.5	1,985	118	23.6	1.5	2,108	118	27.9	1.7
Asian and Pacific Islander, total ...	270	43	11.0	1.8	244	41	10.2	1.8	201	35	12.2	2.2
Hispanic origin, all races........	1,648	109	22.7	1.5	1,721	110	24.7	1.6	1,227	89	23.7	1.8
Type of Family												
Married-couple	2,879	146	5.3	0.3	2,821	145	5.2	0.3	2,965	143	5.7	0.3
White........................	2,400	132	5.0	0.3	2,312	130	4.8	0.3	2,347	125	5.0	0.3
White, not Hispanic	1,639	107	3.8	0.2	1,501	102	3.5	0.2	1,776	107	4.1	0.3
Black........................	290	44	7.3	1.1	312	46	8.0	1.2	444	53	11.7	1.4
Hispanic origin, all races	775	72	15.7	1.5	836	76	17.4	1.6	592	61	16.4	1.8
Female householder, no husband present	3,831	171	29.9	1.5	3,995	176	31.6	1.5	3,575	158	32.6	1.6
White........................	2,123	123	24.9	1.6	2,305	130	27.7	1.7	1,886	112	25.8	1.7
White, not Hispanic	1,428	100	20.7	1.6	1,598	107	23.4	1.7	1,341	92	21.7	1.6
Black........................	1,557	105	40.8	3.1	1,563	105	39.8	3.0	1,553	100	46.7	3.4
Hispanic origin, all races	756	72	43.7	4.7	767	72	47.6	5.1	576	59	48.0	5.7

Source: *Poverty in the United States — 1998*, Bureau of the Census, Washington, DC, 1999

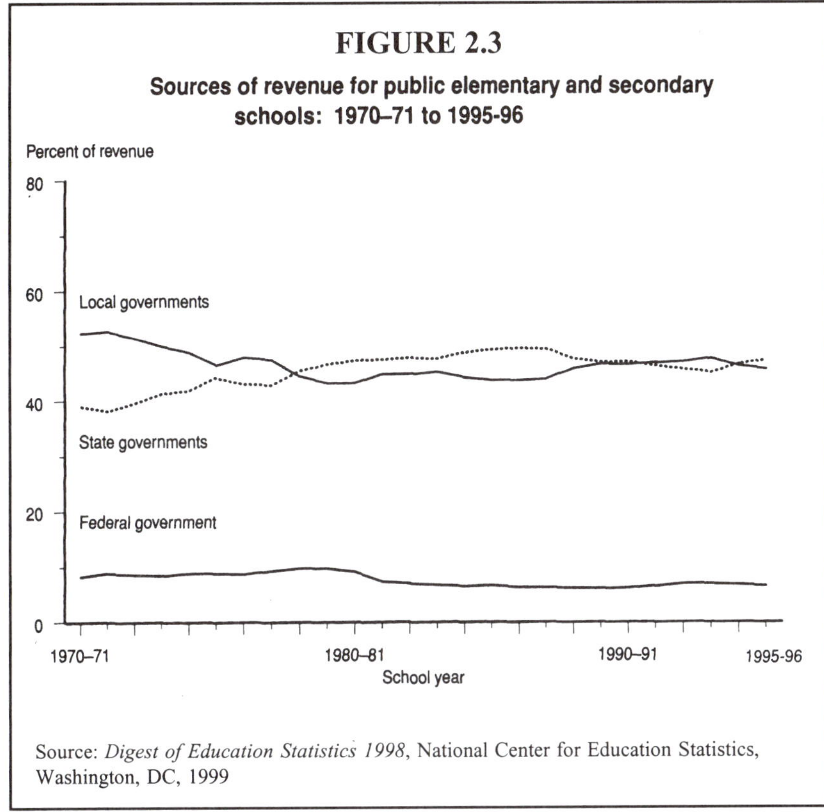

FIGURE 2.3

Sources of revenue for public elementary and secondary schools: 1970–71 to 1995-96

Source: *Digest of Education Statistics 1998*, National Center for Education Statistics, Washington, DC, 1999

1980, school enrollment in 41 states and the District of Columbia dropped, with most of the decline occurring at the elementary level. Between fall 1992 and fall 1997, 31 states increased enrollment by 5 percent or more, while 13 other states reported increases of less than 5 percent. Only West Virginia, Wyoming, North Dakota, Louisiana, Mississippi, Kentucky, and the District of Columbia reported decreases in school enrollment. (See Figure 2.2.)

Racial and Ethnic Diversity

Public-school enrollment has become more racially and ethnically diverse, reflecting the nation's changing demographics. Between 1986 and 1996, the proportion of non-Hispanic White students declined from 70.4 percent to 64.2 percent, while the proportion of non-Hispanic Black students increased only slightly. The proportion of Hispanic students rose from 9.9 percent to 14 percent; Asian/Pacific Islander students, from 2.8 percent to 3.8 percent; and American Indian/Alaskan Native students, from less than 1 percent to slightly over 1 percent. (See Table 2.3.) The increases in diversity among the school-age population are pro-

jected to continue well into the twenty-first century.

Changes in the demographics of the school-age population have increased the challenges facing many schools and school districts. These challenges, caused by a greater degree of language and cultural diversity, mean that schools must work harder to help these students take full advantage of educational opportunities. The bulk of this assistance often comes from the federal government, so the proportion of children who need help directly affects the distribution of federal funds.

THE SCHOOL-AGE POPULATION

The 1990 Census counted approximately 45.3 million elementary- and secondary-age children (ages 5 to 17). In 1998, the U.S. Bureau of the Census estimated that there were 52.1 million school-age children, an increase of 15 percent. Overall, 20 percent of the total U.S. population were school-age children.

Poor School-Age Children

Although poverty rates have declined significantly since 1960, poverty remains a persistent problem for the nation and its schools. In 1998, 12.7 percent of all Americans lived in poverty. For children, however, the proportion was even higher; 18.9 percent of all children under age 18 lived in poverty. (See Table 2.4.) Children who are poor are more likely to be poorly nourished, subject to frequent illnesses, and generally much less ready for learning.

Poverty rates vary widely by race and ethnicity, as well as by the type of household in which a child lives. In 1998, 15 percent of White children below age 18 were poor, compared to 36.7 percent of

TABLE 2.5

Total Funding Gaps Between Poor and Wealthy Districts

State	Total funding per weighted pupil[a]			Wealthy group funding compared with poor group funding[b]
	State average	For the poor group	For the wealthy group	
Alabama	$3,277	$3,213	$3,795	1.18
Alaska	8,030	8,912	8,877	1.00
Arizona	4,507	4,146	5,473	1.32
Arkansas	3,784	3,747	4,282	1.14
California	4,543	4,407	4,965	1.13
Colorado	5,047	5,109	5,501	1.08
Connecticut	8,221	7,426	9,985	1.34
Delaware	5,576	5,316	5,817	1.09
Florida	5,555	5,286	6,264	1.18
Georgia	4,324	3,867	5,029	1.30
Idaho	3,504	3,246	4,075	1.26
Illinois	4,970	4,330	7,249	1.67
Indiana	4,993	4,804	5,299	1.10
Iowa	4,849	5,051	4,855	.96
Kansas	4,973	4,648	5,089	1.09
Kentucky	3,728	3,601	4,143	1.15
Louisiana	3,912	3,507	4,238	1.21
Maine	5,681	5,469	6,399	1.17
Maryland	6,039	4,686	7,728	1.65
Massachusetts	6,264	5,227	8,037	1.54
Michigan	5,851	5,275	7,198	1.36
Minnesota	5,646	5,613	6,212	1.11
Mississippi	2,831	3,034	2,974	.98
Missouri	3,972	2,912	4,937	1.70
Montana	4,835	4,006	6,942	1.73
Nebraska	5,148	5,367	5,614	1.05
Nevada	3,597	4,518	3,117	.69
New Hampshire	5,850	5,592	7,284	1.30
New Jersey	9,239	8,434	11,087	1.31
New Mexico	3,830	3,891	4,094	1.05
New York	7,787	8,309	10,950	1.32
North Carolina	4,424	4,183	4,919	1.18
North Dakota	4,079	4,006	4,709	1.18
Ohio	4,709	4,305	5,688	1.32
Oklahoma	3,623	3,735	3,528	.94

(continued)

Black children and 34.4 percent of Hispanic children. White (40 percent) and Black (54.7 percent) living in households headed by a female with no spouse present were very likely to be poor. Most Hispanic children (59.6 percent) living in female-headed households were poor.

Poverty is generally a worse problem in central cities and rural areas. In 1998, 18.5 percent of the residents of central cities and 14.4 percent of those in rural areas were poor. (See Table 2.4.)

14

TABLE 2.5 (Continued)

Total Funding Gaps Between Poor and Wealthy Districts (Continued)

State	Total funding per weighted pupil[a]			Wealthy group funding compared with poor group funding[b]
	State average	For the poor group	For the wealthy group	
Oregon	5,087	4,860	5,910	1.22
Pennsylvania	6,406	5,812	7,674	1.32
Rhode Island	5,939	5,507	6,553	1.19
South Carolina	4,112	3,840	4,151	1.08
South Dakota	3,756	3,297	4,228	1.28
Tennessee	3,329	3,038	3,671	1.21
Texas	4,603	4,689	4,691	1.00
Utah	3,177	3,333	3,301	.99
Vermont	7,722	6,478	8,454	1.31
Virginia	4,713	4,138	5,702	1.38
Washington	5,302	5,252	5,481	1.04
West Virginia	4,927	4,859	5,044	1.04
Wisconsin	5,865	5,974	6,455	1.08
Wyoming	5,920	6,573	5,514	.84

[a]All funding figures have been adjusted for statewide differences in cost and need. We assigned weights of 1.2 to poor students and 2.3 to disabled students.

[b]We calculated this ratio by dividing the wealthy districts' funding by the poor districts' funding, for example, $3,795/$3,213 in Alabama.

Source: *School Finance: State Efforts to Reduce Funding Gaps Between Poor and Wealthy Districts*, U.S. General Accounting Office, Washington, DC, 1997

FINANCING THE SCHOOLS

Sources of Funding

Public schools obtain funds from three sources: local, state, and federal governments. Typically, local governments rely on property taxes to finance education, while state governments use revenues from sales taxes and, in some instances, income taxes. Local and state governments have traditionally been the primary sources of revenues for elementary and secondary schools, with the federal government contributing a relatively small proportion. (See Figure 2.3.)

During the late 1970s, the federal government supplied almost 10 percent of the revenues for public schools, while state and local authorities divided the remainder. Since 1980, the federal proportion has dropped, reaching about 6 percent in 1990, although it increased slightly to 6.6. percent in 1995-96 (Figure 2.3). The growing dependence on state and local revenues has significant meaning for school funding.

State revenues, which rely on sales and income taxes, are tied to business cycles. Local school funding is usually tied to property taxes. When a recession occurs or businesses close or move away so that property values decline, school funding is directly affected. Also, per capita income and property values are typically lower in rural areas, and local taxes may not be enough to fund the district's schools. In these cases, states must find ways to fill the gap.

To try to resolve these problems, many states now use complex formulas for distributing state education funds to equalize the per pupil expenditure statewide — that is, they give proportionately more state funds per student to poor districts than to wealthy districts. Table 2.5 shows the total fund-

TABLE 2.6

Revenues for public elementary and secondary schools, by source and state: 1995–96

[Amounts in thousands of dollars]

State or other area	Total	Federal		State		Local and intermediate		Private [1]	
		Amount	Percent of total	Amount	Percent of total	Amount	Percent of total	Amount	Percent of total
1	2	3	4	5	6	7	8	9	10
United States	**$287,702,844**	**$19,104,019**	**6.6**	**$136,670,754**	**47.5**	**$124,308,202**	**43.2**	**$7,619,869**	**2.6**
Alabama	3,771,940	348,717	9.2	2,310,952	61.3	790,919	21.0	321,353	8.5
Alaska	1,183,127	130,903	11.1	782,559	66.1	239,553	20.2	30,112	2.5
Arizona	4,151,421	375,299	9.0	1,829,488	44.1	1,850,818	44.6	95,817	2.3
Arkansas	2,204,845	188,064	8.5	1,322,273	60.0	580,387	26.3	114,121	5.2
California	30,858,564	2,742,893	8.9	17,207,011	55.8	10,546,059	34.2	362,602	1.2
Colorado	3,804,992	200,537	5.3	1,665,138	43.8	1,811,053	47.6	128,263	3.4
Connecticut	4,786,247	177,394	3.7	1,819,099	38.0	2,656,280	55.5	133,474	2.8
Delaware	822,226	54,837	6.7	547,837	66.6	207,183	25.2	12,369	1.5
District of Columbia	675,409	54,405	8.1	—	—	617,760	91.5	3,244	0.5
Florida	13,214,948	972,473	7.4	6,422,329	48.6	5,317,562	40.2	502,583	3.8
Georgia	7,627,823	520,690	6.8	3,956,281	51.9	3,005,940	39.4	144,911	1.9
Hawaii	1,201,888	94,261	7.8	1,079,096	89.8	5,294	0.4	23,238	1.9
Idaho	1,179,927	83,787	7.1	758,538	64.3	316,851	26.9	20,750	1.8
Illinois	12,290,140	745,113	6.1	3,359,525	27.3	7,898,466	64.3	287,036	2.3
Indiana	6,191,534	319,237	5.2	3,362,035	54.3	2,312,251	37.3	198,012	3.2
Iowa	3,033,687	154,638	5.1	1,486,472	49.0	1,231,268	40.6	161,308	5.3
Kansas	2,948,036	160,308	5.4	1,690,101	57.3	1,022,587	34.7	75,040	2.5
Kentucky	3,492,890	290,625	8.3	2,280,140	65.3	895,219	25.6	26,906	0.8
Louisiana	3,934,998	477,761	12.1	1,978,050	50.3	1,374,937	34.9	104,250	2.6
Maine	1,451,987	80,876	5.6	681,853	47.0	673,602	46.4	15,656	1.1
Maryland	5,695,850	281,709	4.9	2,175,948	38.2	3,058,142	53.7	180,051	3.2
Massachusetts	6,772,855	318,591	4.7	2,593,935	38.3	3,749,747	55.4	110,582	1.6
Michigan	12,698,697	777,325	6.1	8,483,312	66.8	3,184,072	25.1	253,987	2.0
Minnesota	5,939,765	253,845	4.3	3,458,503	58.2	2,000,762	33.7	226,655	3.8
Mississippi	2,225,798	304,024	13.7	1,285,426	57.8	560,821	25.2	75,527	3.4
Missouri	5,263,003	317,991	6.0	2,113,958	40.2	2,618,966	49.8	212,088	4.0
Montana	941,538	92,802	9.9	457,958	48.6	350,452	37.2	40,326	4.3
Nebraska	1,876,494	104,388	5.6	593,662	31.6	1,067,218	56.9	111,226	5.9
Nevada	1,554,888	69,857	4.5	497,744	32.0	930,476	59.8	56,810	3.7
New Hampshire	1,217,104	40,623	3.3	84,764	7.0	1,060,083	87.1	31,633	2.6
New Jersey	11,882,657	402,135	3.4	4,582,794	38.6	6,615,530	55.7	282,198	2.4
New Mexico	1,783,804	216,810	12.2	1,318,739	73.9	209,699	11.8	38,556	2.2
New York	25,849,431	1,507,150	5.8	10,261,383	39.7	13,840,857	53.5	240,040	0.9
North Carolina	6,154,971	443,121	7.2	3,971,825	64.5	1,565,289	25.4	174,735	2.8
North Dakota	618,322	71,300	11.5	260,260	42.1	253,276	41.0	33,486	5.4
Ohio	11,794,089	738,880	6.3	4,797,764	40.7	5,775,786	49.0	481,659	4.1
Oklahoma	2,856,688	266,970	9.3	1,694,433	59.3	738,270	25.8	157,016	5.5
Oregon	3,366,831	218,785	6.5	1,821,888	54.1	1,203,913	35.8	122,245	3.6
Pennsylvania	14,047,905	776,499	5.5	5,589,707	39.8	7,425,427	52.9	256,273	1.8
Rhode Island	1,138,171	57,906	5.1	472,134	41.5	593,824	52.2	14,308	1.3
South Carolina	3,697,232	308,082	8.3	1,955,378	52.9	1,271,210	34.4	162,561	4.4
South Dakota	717,005	70,519	9.8	213,290	29.7	410,705	57.3	22,491	3.1
Tennessee	4,142,148	358,035	8.6	1,985,414	47.9	1,530,085	36.9	268,614	6.5
Texas	21,689,792	1,557,597	7.2	9,312,159	42.9	10,246,162	47.2	573,876	2.6
Utah	2,066,218	137,707	6.7	1,209,925	58.6	612,311	29.6	106,275	5.1
Vermont	773,448	36,481	4.7	215,275	27.8	501,925	64.9	19,767	2.6
Virginia	6,826,448	361,752	5.3	2,123,203	31.1	4,106,568	60.2	234,925	3.4
Washington	6,327,993	365,988	5.8	4,302,300	68.0	1,464,556	23.1	195,150	3.1
West Virginia	1,990,094	160,084	8.0	1,253,995	63.0	544,803	27.4	31,213	1.6
Wisconsin	6,304,318	273,225	4.3	2,705,278	42.9	3,192,597	50.6	133,219	2.1
Wyoming	662,660	41,022	6.2	339,624	51.3	270,684	40.8	11,331	1.7
Outlying areas									
American Samoa	45,087	34,218	75.9	10,801	24.0	0	—	68	0.2
Guam	171,464	19,524	11.4	0	—	150,544	87.8	1,397	0.8
Northern Marianas	44,418	11,785	26.5	32,504	73.2	70	0.2	58	0.1
Puerto Rico	1,821,858	536,899	29.5	1,284,218	70.5	256	(2)	484	(2)
Virgin Islands	142,016	24,495	17.2	0	—	117,434	82.7	87	0.1

[1] Includes revenues from gifts, and tuition and fees from patrons.
[2] Less than .05 percent.
—Data not available or not applicable.

NOTE.—Excludes revenues for state education agencies. Because of rounding, details may not add to totals.

SOURCE: U.S. Department of Education, National Center for Education Statistics, Common Core of Data survey. (This table was prepared February 1998.)

Source: *Digest of Education Statistics 1998*, National Center for Education Statistics, Washington, DC, 1999

16

In *School Finance: State Efforts to Equalize Funding Between Poor and Wealthy School Districts* (Washington, DC, 1997), the General Accounting Office (GAO), the investigatory arm of the Congress, analyzed state efforts to equalize funding. A phone survey showed that half the states reported little or no changes in their finance systems. Between November 1996 and May 1998, the GAO further researched four states — Oregon, Kansas, Rhode Island, and Louisiana — which represented a wide variety of school finance strategies. Two key factors were found to have reduced the size of the funding gap between poor and wealthy districts: 1) a greater tax effort by poor districts and 2) the state's effort to compensate for differences in district funding with specific equalization policies.

Increased equalization in the four states showed mixed results. Oregon and Kansas reduced their funding gaps between poor and wealthy districts. Oregon's success was largely the result of a 75 percent increase in its share of education funding. Louisiana's equalization efforts increased its fund-

ing gaps between poor and wealthy groups in each state. (A ratio close to 1.00 means that the state has equalized its per student expenditures in wealthy and poor areas.)

TABLE 2.7

Current expenditure per pupil in average daily attendance: 1980–81 to 1997–98

School year	Unadjusted dollars	Constant dollars (1997–98)
1980–81	$2,502	$4,671
1981–82	2,726	4,685
1982–83	2,955	4,870
1983–84	3,173	5,043
1984–85	3,470	5,307
1985–86	3,756	5,582
1986–87	3,970	5,773
1987–88	4,240	5,920
1988–89	4,645	6,199
1989–90	4,980	6,343
1990–91	5,258	6,350
1991–92	5,421	6,344
1992–93	5,584	6,337
1993–94	5,767	6,380
1994–95	5,989	6,440
1995–96	6,146	6,434
1996–97 *	6,387	6,501
1997–98 *	6,624	6,624

* Estimated.

Source: *Mini-Digest of Education Statistics — 1998*, National Center for Education Statistics, Washington, DC, 1999

TABLE 2.8

Public and private expenditures on educational institutions[1] in G-7 countries as a percentage of GDP, by level of education, funding source, and country: 1995

G-7 country	As a percent of GDP				All levels and sources combined[6]	Per student[2] Constant 1995 U.S dollars[3]		
	Elementary–secondary		Higher education			Elementary	Secondary	Higher education
	Public sources[4]	Private sources[5]	Public sources[4]	Private sources[5]				
Canada	4.0	0.3	2.0	0.5	7.0	—	—	$11,471
France	4.1	0.3	1.0	0.2	6.3	$3,379	$6,182	6,569
Germany	2.9	0.9	1.0	0.1	5.8	3,361	6,254	8,897
Italy	3.2	(7)	0.8	0.1	4.7	4,673	5,348	5,013
Japan	2.8	0.3	0.4	0.6	4.7	4,065	4,465	8,768
United Kingdom	3.8	—	0.9	0.1	—	3,328	4,246	7,225
United States	3.5	0.4	1.1	1.2	6.7	5,371	6,812	16,262

— Not available.

[1] Includes all institutions, public and private, with the exception of Germany and Italy, which include only public institutions, and the United Kingdom, which includes public and government-dependent private institutions.

[2] Per student expenditures are calculated based on public and private Full-Time-Equivalent (FTE) enrollment figures and expenditures from both public and private sources, where data are available.

[3] Purchasing Power Parity (PPP) indices were used to convert other currencies to U.S. dollars. Because the fiscal year has a different starting date in different countries, within-country Consumer Price Indices (CPIs) were used to adjust the PPP indices to account for inflation. See the supplemental note to this indicator for further explanation.

[4] Public expenditures are defined as direct public expenditures on education institutions plus public subsidies to households and other private entities for education (e.g., tuition and fees), excluding other education-related public aid to students and households (e.g., subsidies for student living costs).

[5] Private expenditures are defined as private payments from households and other private entities to education institutions, minus any portion derived from public subsidies.

[6] "All levels combined" includes expenditures on preprimary education and funds classified as "undistributed," a classification reserved for enrollments, expenditures, or programs that cannot be classified by level (e.g., nongraded special education).

[7] Percentage is less than 0.05.

SOURCE: Organisation for Economic Co-operation and Development, Center for Educational Research and Innovation, *Education at a Glance: OECD Indicators*, 1998.

Source: *The Condition of Education 1999*, National Center for Education Statistics, Washington, DC, 1999

ing gap, and Rhode Island's gap stayed about the same.

The GAO found that equalization efforts are undermined in states without some kind of ceiling on wealthy districts' spending. Even when states fund poor districts at a higher rate than wealthy districts, wealthy districts are able to raise more funds locally. In some states, wealthy districts may have to contribute locally raised revenue to the state for redistribution to poor districts.

A newer issue than financial equity is the issue of the adequacy of the education the state offers children. Education experts are developing standards — what it takes in terms of teachers, curriculum, and expenditures — to define an adequate education. The next step will be to determine how much money each school needs to meet those standards.

Revenues

In 1995-96, revenues for public elementary and secondary schools totaled $287.7 billion. States (47.5 percent) and local authorities (43.2 percent) provided most of the revenues, with less than 7 percent coming from the federal government and

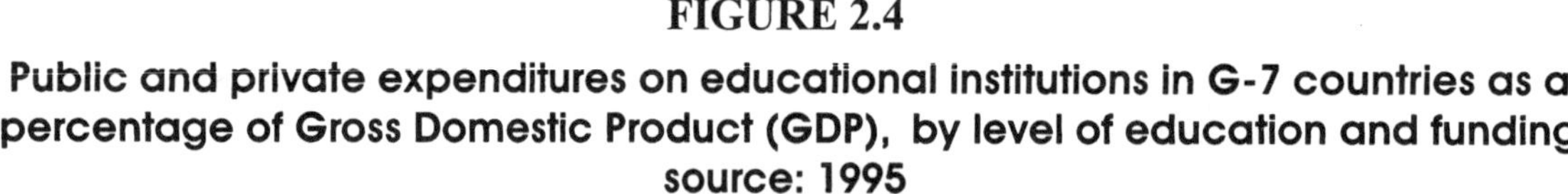

FIGURE 2.4

Public and private expenditures on educational institutions in G-7 countries as a percentage of Gross Domestic Product (GDP), by level of education and funding source: 1995

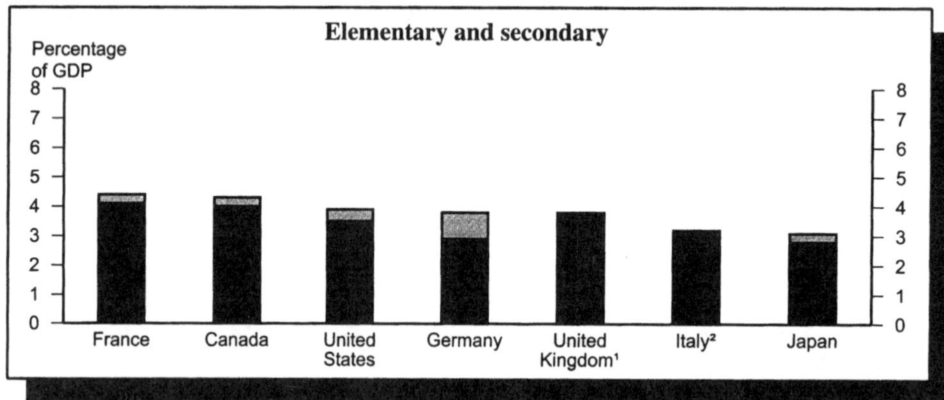

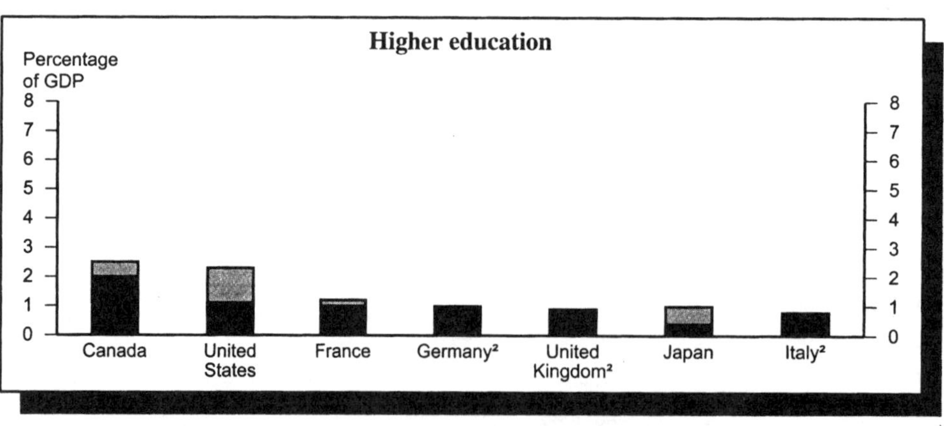

¹ Sources of funds for the United Kingdom were not available.

² Private sources of funds for some countries are less than 1 percent; therefore, percentages may not be discernable in the graphs.

reserved for enrollments, expenditures, or programs that cannot be classified by level (e.g., nongraded special education).

SOURCE: Organisation for Economic Co-operation and Development, Center for Educational Research and Innovation, *Education at a Glance: OECD Indicators*, 1998.

Source: *The Condition of Education 1999*, National Center for Education Statistics, Washington, DC, 1999

less than 3 percent from private sources. The proportions of federal, state, and local funding varied by state. In Hawaii, the state provided nearly 90 percent of revenue, while in New Hampshire, the state provided only 7 percent. The federal government supplied 13.7 percent of the school revenue for Mississippi and 3.3 percent for New Hampshire. (See Table 2.6.)

Expenditures

According to the National Center for Education Statistics (NCES), the nation spent $259.4 billion (in current expenditures) for public elementary and secondary education in 1996 — an 89 percent increase since 1986. By 2002, the current expenditures are projected to reach $308.4 billion, and by 2008, the total is projected to be $341.5 billion (in constant 1995-96 dollars, adjusted for inflation).

In 1997-98, the average per pupil expenditure was estimated to be $6,624. Allowing for inflation (constant 1997-98 dollars), the expenditure per student has risen significantly (42 percent) since 1980-81. (See Table 2.7.) The NCES projects that expenditures per student will reach $7,622 by 2008.

TABLE 2.9

Number and percent of private schools, students, by selected characteristics: United States, 1995–96

Characteristics	Schools		Students	
	Number	Percent	Number	Percent
Total	**27,686**	**100.0 %**	**5,032,200**	**100.0 %**
Private school type				
Catholic	8,248	29.8 %	2,519,205	50.1 %
Parochial	4,879	17.6	1,369,997	27.2
Diocesan	2,516	9.1	813,641	16.2
Private	853	3.1	335,567	6.7
Other religious	13,081	47.3 %	1,743,791	34.7 %
Conservative Christian	5,109	18.5	705,547	14.0
Affiliated	3,677	13.3	590,299	11.7
Unaffiliated	4,295	15.5	447,945	8.9
Non-sectarian	6,357	23.0 %	769,204	15.3 %
Regular	2,646	9.6	512,256	10.2
Special emphasis	2,425	8.8	174,673	3.5
Special education	1,286	4.6	82,276	1.6
School level				
Elementary	16,744	60.5 %	2,835,247	56.3 %
Secondary	2,533	9.2	811,422	16.1
Combined	8,409	30.4	1,385,531	27.5
Program emphasis				
Regular elementary, secondary	22,108	79.9 %	4,621,731	91.8 %
Montessori	1,260	4.6	73,468	1.5
Special program emphasis	639	2.3	113,702	2.3
Special education	1,451	5.2	92,268	1.8
Vocational/technical	—	—	—	—
Early childhood	119	0.4	4,813	0.1
Alternative	2,096	7.6	124,784	2.5
Size				
Less than 150	15,843	57.2 %	925,845	18.4 %
150 to 299	6,667	24.1	1,443,244	28.7
300 to 499	3,187	11.5	1,211,421	24.1
500 to 749	1,333	4.8	790,747	15.7
750 or more	657	2.4	660,942	13.1
Region				
Northeast	6,370	23.0 %	1,289,355	25.6 %
Midwest	7,508	27.1	1,348,736	26.8
South	8,038	29.0	1,444,685	28.7
West	5,770	20.8	949,424	18.9
Community type				
Central city	11,357	41.0 %	2,492,539	49.5 %
Urban fringe/large town	10,325	37.3	1,968,029	39.1
Rural/small town	6,003	21.7	571,632	11.4

—Too few sample cases for a reliable estimate.

NOTE: Details may not add to totals due to rounding or missing values in cells with too few sample cases.

Source: *Private School Universe Survey, 1995-96*, National Center for Education Statistics, Washington, DC, 1998

International Comparisons of Expenditures Per Student

One method of measuring a country's commitment to education is to examine what portion of its GDP (gross domestic product, the total value of goods and services produced in the nation) goes to educating its young people. In 1995, the United States spent 6.7 percent of its GDP for education, 3.5 percent (from public sources) for primary and secondary education and another 1.1 percent (from public sources) for higher education. Comparing expenditures from public (federal, state, and local) sources, only France (4.1 percent), Canada (4 percent) and the United Kingdom (3.8 percent) spent a higher proportion of GDP on primary and secondary education. For higher education, only Canada spent a larger fraction of its GDP than the United States (2.0 and 1.1 percent, respectively). (See Table 2.8 and Figure 2.4.)

In 1995, public expenditures per student in elementary and secondary schools ranged from $5,371 and $6,812, respectively, in the United

TABLE 2.10

Private elementary and secondary enrollment and schools, by amount of tuition, level, and orientation of school: 1993–94

Orientation and tuition	Kindergarten through 12th grade enrollment [1]				Schools				Average tuition paid by students [2]			
	Total	Elementary	Secondary	Combined	Total	Elementary	Secondary	Combined	Total	Elementary	Secondary	Combined
1	2	3	4	5	6	7	8	9	10	11	12	13
Total	4,970,646	2,803,359	811,087	1,356,199	26,093	15,538	2,551	8,004	$3,116	$2,138	$4,578	$4,266
Catholic	2,516,130	1,848,257	592,011	75,862	8,351	6,924	1,161	266	2,178	1,628	3,643	4,153
Less then $1,000	393,901	378,724	(3)	(3)	1,786	1,706	(3)	(3)	—	—	—	—
$1,000 to $2,499	1,368,046	1,274,601	81,955	(3)	4,834	4,542	235	(3)	—	—	—	—
$2,500 to $4,999	675,708	188,123	452,901	(3)	1,533	642	782	(3)	—	—	—	—
$5,000 or more	71,929	(3)	(3)	(3)	(3)	(3)	(3)	(3)	—	—	—	—
Other religious	1,686,064	718,170	124,447	843,448	12,180	6,328	612	5,240	2,915	2,606	5,261	2,831
Less then $1,000	113,382	66,259	(3)	45,878	2,435	1,386	(3)	1,044	—	—	—	—
$1,000 to $2,499	839,447	387,917	(3)	435,788	6,759	3,645	(3)	3,012	—	—	—	—
$2,500 to $4,999	513,773	187,164	62,993	263,615	2,198	970	316	913	—	—	—	—
$5,000 or more	203,014	68,255	38,655	96,104	738	303	172	263	—	—	—	—
Non-sectarian	768,451	236,932	94,629	436,890	5,563	2,287	778	2,498	6,631	4,693	9,525	7,056
Less then $1,000	49,128	(3)	(3)	(3)	912	(3)	(3)	(3)	—	—	—	—
$1,000 to $2,499	121,869	(3)	(3)	(3)	666	(3)	(3)	(3)	—	—	—	—
$2,500 to $4,999	200,857	119,326	(3)	74,395	1,810	1,301	(3)	465	—	—	—	—
$5,000 or more	396,244	82,596	74,283	239,364	2,166	456	408	1,302	—	—	—	—

[1] Only includes kindergarten students who attend schools that offer first grade or above.
[2] Tuition weighted by the number of students enrolled in schools.
[3] Too few sample cases (fewer than 30 schools) for reliable estimates.
—Data not applicable.

NOTE.—Data are based upon a sample survey and may not be strictly comparable with data reported elsewhere. Elementary schools have grade 6 or lower and no grade higher than 8. Secondary schools have no grade lower than 7. Combined schools have grades lower than 7 and higher than 8. Excludes prekindergarten students. Because of rounding and missing values in cells with too few sample cases, details may not add to totals.

SOURCE: U.S. Department of Education, National Center for Education Statistics, "Schools and Staffing Survey, 1993–94." (This table was prepared August 1995.)

Source: *Digest of Education Statistics 1998*, National Center for Education Statistics, Washington, DC, 1999

States to $3,328 and $4,246 in the United Kingdom. (Per student data for Canada were not available.) For higher education, spending ranged from $16,262 per student in the United States to $5,013 in Italy. (See Table 2.8.)

PRIVATE SCHOOLS

In the fall of 1995, about 5 million students attended 27,686 private elementary and secondary schools throughout the country. (See Table 2.9.) Private schools served approximately 10 percent

TABLE 2.11

Public elementary and secondary students, schools, pupil/teacher ratios, and finances, by type of locale: 1995 and 1996

Characteristic	Total	Large central city [1]	Mid-size central city [2]	Urban fringe of large city [3]	Urban fringe of mid-size city [4]	Large town [5]	Small town [6]	Rural [7]
1	2	3	4	5	6	7	8	9
Schools, enrollment, and teachers, 1996–97								
Enrollment, in thousands	45,705	8,300	7,597	13,588	4,330	803	5,279	5,808
Schools	88,223	12,109	13,019	21,523	7,828	1,616	12,516	19,609
Average school size [8]	527	729	590	635	560	506	430	299
Pupil/teacher ratio [9]	17.3	18.5	17.1	17.9	17.4	17.2	16.5	15.6
Enrollment (percent distribution)	100.0	18.2	16.6	29.7	9.5	1.8	11.6	12.7
Schools (percent distribution)	100.0	13.7	14.8	24.4	8.9	1.8	14.2	22.2

[1] Central city of metropolitan statistical area (MSA) with population of 400,000 or more or a population density of 6,000 or more persons per square mile.
[2] Central city of an MSA but not designated as a large central city.
[3] Place within the MSA of a large central city.
[4] Place within the MSA of a mid-size central city.
[5] Place not within an MSA but with population of 25,000 or more and defined as urban.
[6] Place not within an MSA with a population of at least 2,500 but less than 25,000.
[7] Place with a population of less than 2,500.
[8] Average for schools reporting enrollment.
[9] Ratio for schools reporting both FTE teachers and fall enrollment data.

NOTE.—Locale classification procedures not comparable with previous years. Enrollments by locale were used to distribute school district revenue and expenditure amounts by locale classification.

SOURCE: U.S. Department of Education, National Center for Education Statistics, Common Core of Data survey; and U.S. Department of Commerce, Bureau of the Census, *Survey of Local Government Finances*, unpublished data. (This table was prepared February 1999.)

Source: *Digest of Education Statistics 1998*, National Center for Education Statistics, Washington, DC, 1999

of all students. By 2008, enrollment is projected to be 6.1 million.

Characteristics

Most (60.5 percent) private schools in 1995-96 were at the elementary level, while 9.2 percent were high schools. About 30 percent were combined elementary and secondary schools. Twenty-three percent were nonsectarian schools — those with no religious affiliation. (See Table 2.9.)

Catholic schools constituted 29.8 percent of all private schools in 1995-96. Economic and social changes have caused a decline in Catholic school enrollment and in the number of Catholic schools. In fall 1960, there were 5.3 million students attending 12,893 Catholic elementary and second-ary schools. By 1995-96, the number of students had dropped to 2.5 million, and the number of schools had fallen to 8,248. Many closures took place in inner cities, where the racial makeup of the schools has changed in recent years and financial difficulties made closure necessary. Despite the declines, Catholic schools still accounted for half (50.1 percent) of all students attending private schools. (See Table 2.9.)

Religiously affiliated schools charged much lower tuition than nonsectarian schools. In 1993-94, only about 18 percent of Catholic schools and 24 percent of schools with other religious affiliations charged $2,500 or more per year for tuition, compared to 71 percent of the nonsectarian private schools. (See Table 2.10.) The average tuition paid by students at Catholic elementary

TABLE 2.12

Public and private elementary and secondary teachers and pupil/teacher ratios, by level: Fall 1955 to fall 1998

Year	Public and private elementary and secondary			Public elementary and secondary			Private elementary and secondary		
	Kindergarten to grade 12	Elementary	Secondary	Kindergarten to grade 12	Elementary	Secondary	Kindergarten to grade 12	Elementary	Secondary
1	2	3	4	5	6	7	8	9	10
Pupil/teacher ratios									
1955	27.4	31.4	20.3	26.9	30.2	20.9	[1]31.7	[1]40.4	[1]15.7
1960	26.4	29.4	21.4	25.8	28.4	21.7	[1]30.7	[1]36.1	[1]18.6
1965	25.1	28.4	20.6	24.7	27.6	20.8	28.3	33.3	18.4
1968	23.5	26.0	20.2	23.2	25.4	20.4	25.8	29.9	17.9
1969	22.7	25.1	19.7	22.6	24.7	20.0	[1]24.0	[1]27.8	[1]16.7
1970	22.4	24.6	19.5	22.3	24.3	19.8	23.0	26.5	16.4
1971	22.4	25.0	19.1	22.3	24.9	19.3	[1]22.6	[1]25.7	[1]16.7
1972	21.7	24.0	18.9	21.7	23.9	19.1	[1]21.6	[1]24.0	[1]16.9
1973	21.3	23.0	19.1	21.3	23.0	19.3	[1]21.2	[1]23.0	[1]16.5
1974	20.8	22.6	18.5	20.8	22.6	18.7	[1]20.4	[1]22.6	[1]16.0
1975	20.3	21.7	18.6	20.4	21.7	18.8	[1]19.6	[1]21.5	[1]15.7
1976	20.1	21.7	18.3	20.2	21.8	18.5	19.3	20.9	15.8
1977	19.6	20.9	17.9	19.7	21.1	18.2	18.4	20.0	15.1
1978	19.2	20.9	17.1	19.3	21.0	17.3	18.7	20.2	15.6
1979	19.0	20.5	17.0	19.1	20.6	17.2	[1]18.1	[1]19.7	[1]14.8
1980	18.6	20.1	16.6	18.7	20.4	16.8	17.7	18.8	15.0
1981	18.7	20.0	16.8	18.8	20.3	16.9	[1]17.6	[1]18.6	[1]15.2
1982	18.4	19.8	16.4	18.6	20.2	16.6	[1]17.2	[1]18.2	[1]14.9
1983	18.2	19.6	16.2	18.4	19.9	16.4	17.0	18.0	14.4
1984	17.9	19.3	16.0	18.1	19.7	16.1	[1]16.8	[1]17.7	[1]14.4
1985	17.6	19.1	15.6	17.9	19.5	15.8	16.2	17.1	14.0
1986	17.4	18.8	15.5	17.7	19.3	15.7	[1]15.7	[1]16.5	[1]13.6
1987	17.3	18.8	15.0	17.6	19.3	15.2	[1]15.5	[1]16.5	[1]13.1
1988	17.0	18.6	14.7	17.3	19.0	14.9	[1]15.2	[1]16.1	[1]12.8
1989	16.8	18.4	14.3	17.2	19.0	14.6	[1]14.2	[1]15.1	[1]11.7
1990	16.9	18.5	14.3	17.2	18.9	14.6	[1]14.7	[1]16.1	[1]11.3
1991	17.0	18.4	14.6	17.3	18.8	15.0	[1]14.6	[1]16.0	[1]11.1
1992	17.1	18.4	14.8	17.4	18.8	15.2	[1]14.8	[1]16.2	[1]11.3
1993	17.1	18.5	14.7	17.4	18.9	15.1	[1]14.9	[1]16.3	[1]11.5
1994	17.0	18.6	14.4	17.3	19.0	14.8	[1]15.0	[1]16.4	[1]11.4
1995	17.0	18.9	14.1	17.3	19.3	14.4	[1]15.0	[1]16.5	[1]11.4
1996	16.8	18.4	14.3	17.1	18.8	14.6	[1]14.9	[1]16.4	[1]11.5
1997[2]	16.7	18.3	14.2	17.0	18.6	14.5	[1]14.9	[1]16.3	[1]11.4
1998[3]	16.9	18.5	14.4	17.2	18.9	14.7	14.9	16.3	11.4

[1] Estimated.
[2] Preliminary data.
[3] Projected.

NOTE.—Data for teachers are expressed in full-time equivalents. Distribution of unclassified teachers by level is estimated. Distribution of elementary and secondary school teachers by level is determined by reporting units. Kindergarten includes a relatively small number of nursery school teachers and students. Some data have been revised from previously published figures. Because of rounding, details may not add to totals.

SOURCE: U.S. Department of Education, National Center for Education Statistics, *Statistics of Public Elementary and Secondary Day Schools;* Common Core of Data surveys; and *Projections of Education Statistics to 2008.* (This table was prepared July 1998.)

Source: *Digest of Education Statistics 1998*, National Center for Education Statistics, Washington, DC, 1999

schools was $1,628, compared to $2,606 at other religiously affiliated schools and $4,693 at nonsectarian schools. Average tuition paid by secondary school students was much higher: $3,643 at Catholic schools, $5,261 at other religiously oriented schools, and $9,525 at nonsectarian schools.

COMPARISONS OF PUBLIC AND PRIVATE SCHOOLS

Location, Teachers, and Size

In 1996, 36 percent of the 88,223 public schools in the United States were located in rural communities or small towns. Another 30,967 (35 percent) were located in urban fringe areas or large towns, and 25,128 (28 percent) were in large central or mid-sized central cities. (See Table 2.11.) In 1995, private school distribution was somewhat different. Over 11,000 private schools (41 percent) were in central cities, 10,325 (37.3 percent) were in urban fringe/large town areas, and 6,003 (21.7 percent) were in rural/small town communities. (See Table 2.9.)

In fall 1998, there were 2.7 million teachers and other faculty in public elementary and secondary schools and 399,000 in private schools. The average ratio of students to teachers was about 17 pupils to every teacher. In general, the pupil-teacher ratio was higher in elementary schools (18.5) than in secondary schools (14.4). Public schools, on average, had higher pupil/teacher ratios (17.2) than private schools (14.9). These ratios were considerably lower in the 1990s than they were from the 1950s to the early 1980s. (See Table 2.12.) (For more information about pupil/teacher ratios, see Chapter VIII.)

In 1996-97, about 38 percent of public elementary and secondary schools had enrollments of 300 to 599 students. The average enrollment was 527 students per school — 478 in elementary schools and 703 in secondary schools. (See Table 2.13.) Private schools, in 1995-96, tended to have lower enrollments. Eighty-one percent of private elementary and secondary schools had enrollments below 300 students. (See Table 2.9.) The average enrollment for private schools was about 190 students per school.

In the 1995-96 school year, 68 percent of all schools were elementary schools, while 20 percent were secondary. Another 12 percent were combined elementary and secondary schools and special-purpose schools. Combined schools were more common in the private sector (30 percent) than in the public sector (3 percent).

Supportive Programs and Services

The type of supportive programs and services available to schools and school districts is one indicator of the access students have to educational opportunities. Although individual schools can apply directly for these programs and services, the school district (especially in public schools) usually decides whether the programs and services will be provided in its schools.

In 1993-94, schools offered a variety of student services, such as

- Free or reduced-price lunches financed by public funds — public schools, 94.3 percent; private schools, 22.4 percent.

- Services for disabled students — public, 89.2 percent; private, 24.8 percent.

- Remedial programs — public, 83.2 percent; private, 54.5 percent.

- Programs for gifted and talented students — public, 70.7 percent; private, 24.9 percent.

TABLE 2.14		
Percentage of schools in which various services were available to students: 1993–94		
Service	Public	Private
Academic support		
Remedial	83.2	54.5
Gifted and talented	70.7	24.9
Bilingual	17.8	4.2
ESL	42.7	11.3
Chapter I	61.6	22.7
Disability	89.2	24.8
Diagnostic services	82.6	43.5
Library	95.6	80.3
Health-related		
Medical services	58.7	31.0
Drug and alcohol prevention	93.6	70.6
Substance abuse counseling	36.2	14.4
Free or reduced-price lunches	94.3	22.4

U.S. Department of Education, National Center for Education Statistics, *Schools and Staffing in the United States: A Statistical Profile, 1993–94,* pp. 26–29.

FIGURE 2.5

Percentage of elementary and combined schools that offered extended-day programs, by control of school: 1987–88, 1990–91, and 1993–94

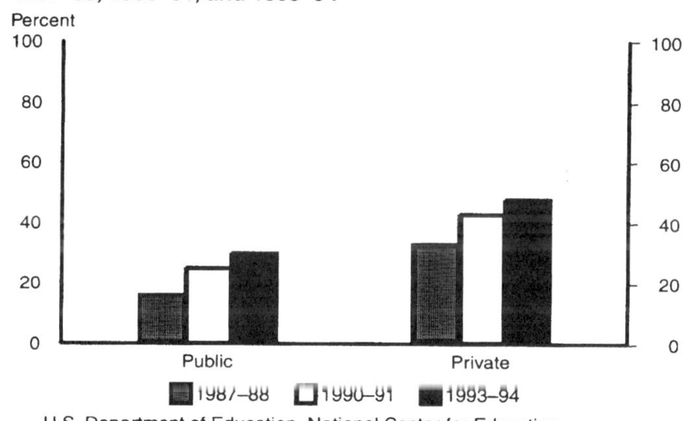

U.S. Department of Education, National Center for Education Statistics, *Extended-Day Programs in Elementary and Combined Schools* Issue Brief, 1996 and *Schools and Staffing in the United States: A Statistical Profile,1993–94,* pp. 30–31.

Source of table and figure: Thomas M. Smith et al., *The Condition of Education 1997*, National Center for Education Statistics, Washington, DC, 1997

- Programs under Chapter I (federal funds designated for special educational programs for disadvantaged children) of the Elementary and Secondary Education Act (PL 89-10) — public, 61.6 percent; private, 22.7 percent.

- Drug and alcohol prevention programs — public, 93.6 percent; private, 70.6 percent.

- English as a second language (ESL) programs — public, 42.7 percent; private, 11.3 percent.

TABLE 2.15

Characteristics of educational systems participating in the International Assessment of Educational Progress: 1991

Country	Ethnic homogeneity [1]	Age for starting school	Average days in school year [2]	Average minutes of instruction in school day [2]	National curriculum	Percent of schools with one or more problems [2,3]
1	2	3	4	5	6	7
Populations (comprehensive)						
Canada [4]	No	6	188 (0.2)	304 (0.8)	No	13 (1.3)
France	Yes	6	174 (1.7)	370 (3.4)	Yes	29 (4.9)
Hungary	Yes	6	177 (1.5)	223 (1.3)	Yes	32 (4.2)
Ireland	Yes	6	173 (0.9)	323 (4.4)	Yes	39 (5.8)
Israel [5]	No	6	215 (2.2)	278 (6.5)	Yes	46 (6.7)
Jordan	Yes	6	191 (0.9)	260 (2.9)	Yes	63 (5.3)
Korea	Yes	6	222 (2.5)	264 (2.4)	Yes	24 (4.9)
Scotland	Yes	5	191 (0.9)	324 (2.3)	Yes	23 (4.0)
Slovenia	Yes	7	190 (1.5)	248 (2.5)	Yes	50 (5.3)
Spain [6]	No	6	188 (2.3)	285 (3.2)	Yes	33 (5.0)
(Former) Soviet Union [7]	No	6 or 7	198 (2.1)	243 (2.6)	Yes	72 (5.1)
Switzerland [8]	No	6 or 7	207 (3.2)	305 (7.4)	No	11 (3.5)
Taiwan	No	6	222 (2.5)	318 (6.9)	Yes	10 (2.8)
United States	No	6	178 (0.4)	338 (5.0)	No	5 (2.2)
Populations (with exclusions or low participation)						
Brazil, Fortaleza	No	7	183 (1.1)	223 (9.8)	No	62 (5.3)
Brazil, Sao Paulo	No	7	181 (0.2)	271 (9.3)	No	60 (4.6)
China	Yes	6.5 or 7	251 (2.1)	305 (7.1)	Yes	43 (6.3)
England	Yes	5	192 (1.8)	300 (4.4)	Yes	24 (8.3)
Italy [9]	Yes	6	204 (0.5)	289 (5.0)	Yes	18 (5.1)
Mozambique, Maputo, and Beira	No	7	193 (0.0)	272 (0.0)	Yes	92 (0.0)
Portugal	Yes	6	172 (1.1)	334 (6.5)	Yes	56 (7.9)

[1] 90 percent of entire population from one ethnic group.
[2] For 13–year-olds.
[3] Problems included: overcrowded classrooms, inadequate facilities and maintenance, shortages of textbooks and other educational materials, student absenteeism, lack of discipline, and vandalism of school property.
[4] Four provinces assessed 9-year-olds. Nine provinces assessed 13-year-olds.
[5] Schools where instruction is in Hebrew.
[6] Schools where instruction is in Spanish, in all regions except Cataluna.
[7] Schools in 14 republics, where instruction is in Russian.
[8] Fifteen Cantons.
[9] Emilia-Romagna province only.

NOTE.—Standard errors appear in parentheses.

U.S. Department of Education, National Center for Education Statistics, International Assessment of Educational Progress, *Learning Science* and *Learning Mathematics*, by Educational Testing Service. (This table was prepared February 1992.)

Source: *Digest of Education Statistics 1996*, National Center for Education Statistics, Washington, DC, 1996

- Bilingual programs — public, 17.8 percent; private, 4.2 percent. (See Table 2.14.)

Prekindergarten and Kindergarten

Most public and private schools provide prekindergarten and kindergarten programs. Seventy-seven percent of public and 79 percent of private elementary and combined schools offer kindergarten programs. Among public schools, 83 percent of those in central cities, 81 percent in urban fringe/large town communities, and 75 percent in rural/small town communities offer early childhood programs. The corresponding percentages for private schools were 86 percent, 89 percent, and 70 percent, respectively.

In 1993-94, private schools were more likely to offer extended-day programs: 48 percent of private elementary and combined schools reported full-day care, compared to 30 percent of all public elementary and combined schools. (See Figure 2.5.)

SCHOOL ATTENDANCE

Days in Attendance

In 1991, American 13-year-old students spent an average of 178 days a year in school, with 5.6 hours of instruction per day. Among other Western nations, only students in France, Hungary, Ireland, and Portugal have fewer school days. (See Table 2.15.) In Japan, eighth-graders attend 243 days of school per year, and high school seniors attend 216 days.

Compulsory Attendance

Most industrialized Western nations require children to attend school for about 10 years. In 1997, all U.S. states required students to attend school at least through age 16 (Table 2.16). In 1992-93, Indiana enacted legislation requiring a student between the ages of 16 and 18 to submit to an exit interview and have written parental approval

TABLE 2.16

Ages for compulsory school attendance, special education services for students, policies for kindergarten programs, and year-round schools, by state: 1997 and 1995

State	Compulsory attendance, 1997	Compulsory special education services, 1997 [1]	Year-round schools, 1995		Provision of kindergarten education, 1995			
			Has policy on year-round schools	Has districts with year-round schools	School districts required to offer		Attendance required	
					Half day	Full day	Half day	Full day
	2	3	4	5	6	7	8	9
Alabama	7 to 16	3 to 21		X		X		
Alaska	[2] 7 to 16	3 to 21		X				
Arizona	[3] 6 to 16	3 to 21	X	X	X		X	
Arkansas	5 to 17	3 to 21	X	X		X		X
California	6 to 18	3 to 21	X	X	X			
Colorado	7 to 16	[4] 3 to 20		X				
Connecticut	7 to 16	3 to 20			X			
Delaware	5 to 16	3 to 20			X			
District of Columbia	5 to 18	[5] 3 to 21				X		X
Florida	6 to 16	3 to 20	X	X		X		X
Georgia	7 to 16	3 to 21		X		X		
Hawaii	[6] 6 to 18	3 to 20		X				
Idaho	7 to 16	3 to 20	X	X				
Illinois	7 to 16	3 to 20	X	X	X			
Indiana	[7] 7 to 18	3 to 21		X	X			
Iowa	6 to 16	Birth to 20						
Kansas	7 to 16	3 to 20						
Kentucky	[8] 6 to 16	3 to 20		X	X			
Louisiana	7 to 17	3 to 21	—	—	—	—	—	—
Maine	7 to 17	3 to 19						
Maryland	5 to 16	Birth to 20			X			
Massachusetts	6 to 16	3 to 21			X			
Michigan	6 to 16	Birth to 25						
Minnesota	[9] 7 to 16	Birth to 20	X	X	X			
Mississippi	6 to 17	3 to 20		X		X		
Missouri	7 to 16	3 to 20		X	X		X	
Montana	[10] 7 to 16	3 to 18			X			
Nebraska	7 to 16	Birth to 20	X					
Nevada	7 to 17	3 to 21		X	X			
New Hampshire	6 to 16	3 to 20						
New Jersey	6 to 16	3 to 21						
New Mexico	5 to 18	3 to 21		X	X		X	
New York	[11] 6 to 16	3 to 21	X	X				
North Carolina	7 to 16	3 to 20	X	X				
North Dakota	7 to 16	3 to 20			X	X	X	X
Ohio	6 to 18	3 to 21		X	X		X	
Oklahoma	5 to 18	3 to 21	X	X	X			
Oregon	7 to 18	3 to 21		X	X			
Pennsylvania	8 to 17	3 to 20			X			
Rhode Island	6 to 16	3 to 20			X		X	
South Carolina	[12] 5 to 17	[4] 3 to 21		X	X		X	
South Dakota	[10] 6 to 16	3 to 21	X		X		X	
Tennessee	7 to 17	3 to 21		X	X		X	
Texas	6 to 17	3 to 21	X	X	X		X	
Utah	6 to 18	3 to 21	X	X	X		X	
Vermont	7 to 16	3 to 21						
Virginia	5 to 18	2 to 21		X	X	X	X	X
Washington	[13] 8 to 18	3 to 20		X				
West Virginia	6 to 16	3 to 20	X		X			
Wisconsin	[14] 6 to 18	[4] 3 to 20			X			
Wyoming	7 to 16	[4] 3 to 20			X			

[1] Most states have an upper age limit whereby education is provided up to a certain age or completion of secondary school, whichever comes first.
[2] Ages 7 to 16 or high school graduation.
[3] Ages 6 to 16 or tenth grade completion.
[4] Upper age limit for eligibility has been updated for 1997.
[5] State has established two points in the program year by which children must be 3 years of age to be eligible for services.
[6] Students over the age of 16 may withdraw with the approval of a principal and student's guardians, and if an alternative education program exists.
[7] From age 7 until student (1) graduates; (2) between age 16 to 18 and meets requirements for exit interview before graduation; or (3) reaches 18. Withdrawal before 18 requires parent/guardian and principal written permission.
[8] Must have parental signature for leaving school between ages 16 to 18.
[9] Age 18 takes effect in 2000.
[10] Age 16 or completion of eighth grade.
[11] Ages 6 to 17 for New York City and Buffalo.
[12] Permits parental waiver of kindergarten at age 5.
[13] Or can exit if age 16 or older, has a useful occupation, has met graduation requirements or has a certificate of education competency.
[14] Ages 6 to 18 or high school graduation.

—Data not available.

NOTE.—The Education of the Handicapped Act (EHA) Amendments of 1986 make it mandatory for all states receiving EHA funds to serve all 3- to 18-year-old disabled children.

SOURCE: U.S. Department of Education, Office of Special Education and Rehabilitative Services, *The Eighteenth Annual Report to Congress on the Implementation of The Individuals with Disabilities Education Act, 1996*; National Association of State Directors of Special Education, Inc., unpublished data; Education Commission of the States, "Clearinghouse Notes," March 1997; and Council of Chief State School Officers, *State Education Policies on Student Attendance and Use of Time: 1995*. (This table was prepared May 1997.)

Source: *Digest of Education Statistics 1998*, National Center for Education Statistics, Washington, DC, 1999

TABLE 2.17

High school graduates compared with population 17 years of age, by sex and control of school: 1869–70 to 1997–98

[Numbers in thousands]

School year	Population 17 years old [1]	High school graduates					Graduates as a percent of 17-year-old population
		Total [2]	Sex		Control		
			Male	Female	Public [3]	Private [4]	
1	2	3	4	5	6	7	8
1869–70	815	16	7	9	—	—	2.0
1879–80	946	24	11	13	—	—	2.5
1889–90	1,259	44	19	25	22	22	3.5
1899–1900	1,489	95	38	57	62	33	6.4
1909–10	1,786	156	64	93	111	45	8.8
1919–20	1,855	311	124	188	231	80	16.8
1929–30	2,296	667	300	367	592	75	29.0
1939–40	2,403	1,221	579	643	1,143	78	50.8
1947–48	2,261	1,190	563	627	1,073	117	52.6
1949–50	2,034	1,200	571	629	1,063	136	59.0
1951–52	2,086	1,197	569	627	1,056	141	57.4
1953–54	2,135	1,276	613	664	1,129	147	59.8
1955–56	2,242	1,415	680	735	1,252	163	63.1
1956–57	2,272	1,434	690	744	1,270	164	63.1
1957–58	2,325	1,506	725	781	1,332	174	64.8
1958–59	2,458	1,627	784	843	1,435	192	66.2
1959–60	2,672	1,858	895	963	1,627	231	69.5
1960–61	2,892	1,964	955	1,009	1,725	239	67.9
1961–62	2,768	1,918	938	980	1,678	240	69.3
1962–63	2,740	1,943	956	987	1,710	233	70.9
1963–64	2,978	2,283	1,120	1,163	2,008	275	76.7
1964–65	3,684	2,658	1,311	1,347	2,360	298	72.1
1965–66	3,489	2,665	1,323	1,342	2,367	298	76.4
1966–67	3,500	2,672	1,328	1,344	2,374	298	76.3
1967–68	3,532	2,695	1,338	1,357	2,395	300	76.3
1968–69	3,659	2,822	1,399	1,423	2,522	300	77.1
1969–70	3,757	2,889	1,430	1,459	2,589	300	76.9
1970–71	3,872	2,938	1,454	1,484	2,638	300	75.9
1971–72	3,973	3,002	1,487	1,515	2,700	302	75.6
1972–73	4,049	3,035	1,500	1,535	2,729	306	75.0
1973–74	4,132	3,073	1,512	1,561	2,763	310	74.4
1974–75	4,256	3,133	1,542	1,591	2,823	310	73.6
1975–76	4,272	3,148	1,552	1,596	2,837	311	73.7
1976–77	4,272	3,152	1,548	1,604	2,837	315	73.8
1977–78	4,286	3,127	1,531	1,596	2,825	302	73.0
1978–79	4,327	3,101	1,517	1,584	2,801	300	71.7
1979–80	4,262	3,043	1,491	1,552	2,748	295	71.4
1980–81	4,212	3,020	1,483	1,537	2,725	295	71.7
1981–82	4,134	2,995	1,471	1,524	2,705	290	72.4
1982–83	3,962	2,888	1,437	1,451	2,598	290	72.9
1983–84	3,784	2,767	—	—	2,495	272	73.1
1984–85	3,699	2,677	—	—	2,414	263	72.4
1985–86	3,670	2,643	—	—	2,383	260	72.0
1986–87	3,754	2,694	—	—	2,429	265	71.8
1987–88	3,849	2,773	—	—	2,500	273	72.1
1988–89	3,842	2,727	—	—	2,459	268	71.0
1989–90	3,505	2,586	—	—	2,320	266	73.8
1990–91	3,421	2,503	—	—	2,235	268	73.2
1991–92	3,391	2,482	—	—	2,226	256	73.2
1992–93	3,447	2,490	—	—	2,233	257	72.2
1993–94	3,459	2,479	—	—	2,221	258	71.7
1994–95	3,588	2,538	—	—	2,274	264	70.7
1995–96	3,641	2,548	—	—	2,281	267	70.0
1996–97 [5]	3,773	2,623	—	—	2,360	267	69.6
1997–98 [5]	3,923	2,708	—	—	2,433	275	69.0

[1] Derived from *Current Population Reports*, Series P-25. 17-year-old population adjusted to reflect October 17-year-old population.

[2] Includes graduates of public and private schools.

[3] Data for 1929–30 and preceding years are from *Statistics of Public High Schools* and exclude graduates of high schools which failed to report to the Office of Education.

[4] For most years, private school data have been estimated based on periodic private school surveys. For years through 1957–58, private includes data for subcollegiate departments of institutions of higher education and residential schools for exceptional children.

[5] Public high school graduates based on state estimates.

—Data not available.

NOTE.—Includes graduates of regular day school programs. Excludes graduates of other programs, when separately reported, and recipients of high school equivalency certificates. Some data have been revised from previously published figures. Because of rounding, details may not add to totals.

SOURCE: U.S. Department of Education, National Center for Education Statistics, *Statistics of Public High Schools; Biennial Survey of Education in the United States; Statistics of State School Systems; Statistics of Nonpublic Elementary and Secondary Schools; Projections of Education Statistics;* Common Core of Data surveys; and U.S. Department of Commerce, Bureau of the Census, *Current Population Reports,* Series P-25. (This table was prepared June 1998.)

Source: *Digest of Education Statistics 1998*, National Center for Education Statistics, Washington, DC, 1999

before leaving high school. Montana and South Dakota permit students age 16 and over to leave school after completion of the eighth grade, if they wish. In 2000, Minnesota will extend the age of compulsory school attendance to age 18.

GRADUATING FROM HIGH SCHOOL

In 1899-1900, only 6.4 percent of 17-year-olds had graduated from high school. By 1929-30, this proportion had risen to 29 percent, and by 1949-50,

TABLE 2.18

General Educational Development (GED) credentials issued, and number and age of test takers: United States and outlying areas, 1971 to 1996

Year	Number of credentials issued, in thousands [1]	Number completing test battery, in thousands [2]	Number of test takers, in thousands [3]	Percentage distribution of test takers, by age				
				19 years old or less	20- to 24-year-olds	25- to 29-year-olds	30- to 34-year-olds	35 years old or over
1	2	3	4	5	6	7	8	9
1971	227	—	377	—	—	—	—	—
1972	245	—	419	—	—	—	—	—
1973	249	—	423	—	—	—	—	—
1974	295	412	540	35	27	13	9	17
1975	342	507	652	33	26	14	9	18
1976	337	507	656	31	28	14	10	17
1977	331	488	680	40	24	13	9	14
1978	381	467	641	31	27	13	10	19
1979	435	583	744	35	27	13	8	16
1980	488	708	779	37	27	13	8	15
1981	500	701	770	37	27	13	8	15
1982	494	692	756	37	28	13	8	15
1983	477	678	740	34	29	14	9	15
1984	437	613	676	32	28	15	9	16
1985	427	622	685	33	26	15	10	16
1986	439	648	713	33	26	15	10	16
1987	458	662	729	33	24	15	10	18
1988	421	617	701	36	23	14	10	17
1989	364	554	645	36	24	13	10	16
1990	419	628	727	35	25	14	10	17
1991	471	672	770	33	27	14	10	17
1992	465	653	754	32	28	13	11	16
1993	476	652	757	33	27	14	11	16
1994	499	684	793	34	26	13	10	16
1995	513	698	803	37	25	13	10	15
1996	514	733	842	40	25	13	9	15

[1] Number of people receiving high school equivalency credentials based on the GED tests.

[2] Number of people completing the entire GED battery of five tests.

[3] Number of people taking the GED tests (one or more subtests).

—Data not available.

NOTE.—Because of rounding, percentages may not add to 100. Some data have been revised from previously published figures.

SOURCE: American Council on Education, General Educational Development Testing Service. (This table was prepared August 1998.)

Source: *Digest of Education Statistics 1998*, National Center for Education Statistics, Washington, DC, 1999

it had grown to 59 percent. The proportion peaked at about 77 percent in 1968-69 and then dropped to around 72 percent from 1978-79 through 1980-81. The proportion remained about 71 to 73 percent throughout much of the 1980s and the early 1990s. (See Chapter VI for a discussion of dropouts.) At the end of the 1997-98 school year, 2.7 million students graduated from high school, representing about 69 percent of all 17-year-olds. (See Table 2.17.) This is not a completion percentage since many students complete their high school education through alternative programs, such as the General Educational Development (GED) program.

General Educational Development (GED) Diplomas

The General Educational Development (GED) diploma is an alternative way for young people who have left school to get equivalency credit for high school graduation. The number of those getting GED diplomas rose sharply from 295,000 in 1974 to 514,000 in 1981. The number gaining a GED diploma generally dropped during the 1980s, falling to 364,000 in 1989, but increased to 514,000 in 1996. (See Table 2.18.) The GED Testing Service estimates that 1 in every 7 high school graduates holds a GED high school credential.

CHAPTER III

EDUCATION FOR SPECIAL SCHOOL POPULATIONS

The right to public education is guaranteed to all children in the United States. For many children, however, acquiring an education that fits their special needs is not always easy. For the mentally or physically disabled, gifted or talented, or significantly disadvantaged, preparation for adulthood requires extra effort on the part of both the children and the education system. In addition, many students need vocational education to prepare them to go straight from high school to work or to further occupational training.

DISABLED CHILDREN

In 1975, Congress passed the Education for All Handicapped Children Act (PL 94-142, amended in 1983 by PL 98-199), which required schools to develop programs for disabled children. In 1992, the act was renamed the Individuals with Disabilities Education Act (IDEA). The act defines disabled children as those who are

... mentally retarded, hard of hearing, deaf, orthopedically impaired, other health impaired, speech and language impaired, visually impaired, seriously emotionally disturbed, children with specific learning disabilities who, by reason thereof, require special education and related services (20 U.S.C. 1401 [a][1]).

In its 1993 report, *To Assure the Free Appropriate Public Education of All Children with Disabilities*, the U.S. Department of Education Office

---

TABLE 3.1

Children 0 to 21 years old served in federally supported programs for the disabled, by type of disability: 1976–77 to 1996–97

Type of disability	1976–77	1980–81	1984–85	1985–86	1986–87	1987–88	1988–89	1989–90	1990–91	1991–92	1992–93	1993–94	1994–95	1995–96	1996–97
1	2	3	4	5	6	7	8	9	10	11	12	13	14	15	16
	Number served,[1] in thousands														
All disabilities	3,692	4,142	4,315	4,317	4,374	4,446	4,527	4,641	4,762	4,949	5,176	5,365	5,539	5,745	5,920
Specific learning disabilities	796	1,462	1,832	1,862	1,914	1,928	1,970	2,050	2,130	2,234	2,351	2,408	2,489	2,579	2,651
Speech or language impairments	1,302	1,168	1,126	1,125	1,136	953	967	973	985	997	994	1,014	1,015	1,022	1,045
Mental retardation	959	829	694	660	643	582	564	548	534	538	518	536	555	570	579
Serious emotional disturbance	283	346	372	375	383	373	376	381	390	399	400	414	427	438	446
Hearing impairments	87	79	69	66	65	56	56	57	58	60	60	64	64	67	68
Orthopedic impairments	87	58	56	57	57	47	47	48	49	51	52	56	60	63	66
Other health impairments	141	98	68	57	52	45	43	52	55	58	65	82	106	133	160
Visual impairments	38	31	28	27	26	22	23	22	23	24	23	24	24	25	25
Multiple disabilities	—	68	69	86	97	77	85	86	96	97	102	108	88	93	98
Deaf-blindness	—	3	2	2	2	1	2	2	1	1	1	1	1	1	1
Autism and other	—	—	—	—	—	—	—	—	—	5	19	24	30	38	45
Preschool disabled[2]	(3)	(3)	(3)	(3)	(3)	363	394	422	441	484	590	634	680	717	737

[1] Includes students served under Chapter I and Individuals with Disabilities Education Act (IDEA), formerly the Education of the Handicapped Act.

[2] Includes preschool children 3–5 years and 0–5 years served under Chapter I and IDEA, respectively.

[3] Prior to 1987–88, these students were included in the counts by handicapping condition. Beginning in 1987–88, states were no longer required to report preschool handicapped students (0–5 years) by handicapping condition.

NOTE.—Counts are based on reports from the 50 states and District of Columbia only (i.e., figures from U.S. territories are not included). Increases since 1987–88 are due in part to new legislation enacted fall 1986, which mandates public school special education services for all handicapped children ages 3 through 5. Some data have been revised from previously published figures. Because of rounding, details may not add to totals.

SOURCE: U.S. Department of Education, Office of Special Education and Rehabilitative Services, *Annual Report to Congress on the Implementation of The Individuals with Disabilities Education Act*, various years, and unpublished tabulations; and National Center for Education Statistics, Common Core of Data survey. (This table was prepared May 1998.)

Source: *Digest of Education Statistics 1998*, National Center for Education Statistics, Washington, DC, 1999

---

of Special Education Programs stated the purposes of IDEA.

- To help states develop early intervention services for infants and toddlers with disabilities and their families.

- To assure a free appropriate public education to all children and youth with disabilities.

- To protect the rights of disabled children and youth from birth to age 21 and their families.

- To help provide early intervention services and the education of all children with disabilities.

- To assess and assure the effectiveness of efforts to provide early intervention services and education of children with disabilities.

Increase in the Number Served

As a result of the Individuals with Disabilities Education Act, an increasing number and percentage of students have been served in programs for the disabled. During 1996-97, an estimated 5.9 million disabled children and youth from birth through age 21 were served. From 1976-77 to 1997, the number of children served under the programs rose by more than 2.2 million, a 60 percent increase. (See Table 3.1.) The U.S. Department of Education reported that the proportion of children and youth with disabilities, as a percent of public school enrollment, has risen steadily from 8.3 percent in 1976-77 to 13 percent in 1996-97. Much of this increase probably reflects more effective identification of persons with disabilities.

The majority (80 percent) of students with disabilities served in 1996-97 were those identified as having specific learning disabilities (44.8 percent), speech or language impairments (17.6 percent), mental

retardation (9.8 percent), or serious emotional disturbance (7.5 percent). Students with multiple disabilities, hearing impairments, orthopedic impairments, other health impairments, visual impairments, deaf-blindness, and autism each made up about 3 percent or less of students with disabilities. (See Table 3.1.)

Learning Disabilities

The Education for All Handicapped Children Act (see above) defined a learning disability (LD) as "…a disorder in one or more of the basic psychological processes involved in understanding or using language, spoken or written, which may manifest itself in an imperfect ability to listen, think, speak, read, write, or do mathematical calculations."

The law includes perceptual handicaps, brain injury, minimal brain dysfunction, dyslexia, and developmental aphasia (inability to use words) as learning disabilities. The LD category does not include learning problems that are primarily the result of visual, hearing, or motor handicaps; mental retardation; or environmental, cultural, or economic disadvantage. To be categorized as LD, a student must also show a severe discrepancy between potential, as measured by IQ (Intelligence Quotient), and current ability level, as measured by achievement tests. Unfortunately, a student who

TABLE 3.2

Gender of Elementary and Secondary-Aged Students with Disabilities, by Disability Category[a]

	Male	Female
Specific Learning Disability	69.3	30.8
Mental Retardation	59.0	41.6
Emotional Disturbance	79.4	21.0

a/ Percentages may not sum to 100 due to rounding or reporting errors.

Source: U.S. Department of Education, Office for Civil Rights, 1994 Elementary and Secondary School Compliance Reports.

Source: *To Assure the Free Appropriate Public Education of all Children with Disabilities*, U.S. Department of Education, Washington, DC, 1998

has problems in school but does not fit into any other category may be diagnosed as LD. This practice sometimes makes the LD category a "dumping ground" for students who need remedial education.

In 1996-97, 2.7 million students were classified with specific learning disabilities, three times the 796,000 students identified in 1976-77. In 1976-77, LD students made up fewer than one-quarter (22 percent) of all those with disabilities, compared to almost half (45 percent) in 1996-97 (Table 3.1). Better understanding and diagnosis of learning disabilities may explain much of the increase. The growth also may possibly reflect the "dumping ground" problem mentioned above.

Characteristics of Special Education Students

Males are disproportionately represented among students in special education programs. More than two-thirds of all special education students are male. The differences seem greatest in the learning disability and emotional disturbance categories. In 1994, according to the U.S. Department of Education, males constituted 79.4 percent of the emotional disturbance category, 69.3 percent of the learning disability category, and 59 percent of the mental retardation category (Table 3.2). Several theories have been proposed to explain the disproportion of males in various disability categories. Some evidence suggests that boys have a greater vulnerability than girls do to certain genetic maladies and are more prone to developmental lags because of physiological or maturational differences. Some researchers have reported a higher degree of reading disabilities in boys than in girls, although others failed to find similar problems among males in other countries. Still others have suggested sex bias in the diagnosis and classification of students with disabilities.

The racial proportion of children with learning disabilities is very similar. In 1994, White, Black, and Hispanic students (5.7 percent each) were equally likely to be classified as learning disabled. American Indian students (7.3 percent) were most likely to receive learning disabled services, while Asian/Pacific Islander students (2 percent) were least likely. However, discrepancies do occur in the mental retardation category. A total of 2.6 percent of Black students were identified as

TABLE 3.4

Percentage distribution of disabled persons 3 to 21 years old receiving education services for the disabled, by age group and educational environment: 1995–96

Type of disability	All environments	Regular class	Resource room	Separate class	Public separate school facility	Private separate school facility	Public residential facility	Private residential facility	Homebound/hospital environment
1	2	3	4	5	6	7	8	9	10
All persons, 3 to 21 years old	**100.0**	**45.4**	**26.8**	**23.2**	**2.2**	**1.0**	**0.4**	**0.2**	**0.7**
3 to 5 years old	100.0	50.7	9.3	31.7	4.1	1.5	0.1	0.1	2.5
6 to 21 years old	100.0	44.8	28.5	22.4	2.0	1.0	0.5	0.3	0.6
Mental retardation	100.0	9.9	26.9	56.0	5.2	1.0	0.4	0.2	0.5
Speech or language impairments	100.0	87.6	7.5	4.5	0.2	0.1	(1)	(1)	0.1
Visual impairments	100.0	46.8	20.1	17.4	2.9	1.9	9.4	0.9	0.5
Serious emotional disturbance	100.0	22.1	24.0	35.2	8.3	5.4	1.7	1.6	1.8
Orthopedic impairments	100.0	39.3	20.4	31.9	4.4	1.1	0.3	0.1	2.5
Other health impairments	100.0	42.8	28.8	18.5	1.1	0.6	0.1	0.2	7.9
Specific learning disabilities	100.0	41.3	39.3	18.4	0.3	0.3	0.1	(1)	0.2
Deaf-blindness	100.0	9.7	8.7	37.2	17.7	3.8	17.8	2.7	2.3
Multiple disabilities	100.0	9.1	11.9	51.5	15.4	6.7	2.0	1.5	1.9
Hearing impairments	100.0	35.4	19.1	28.5	3.8	2.7	9.3	1.0	0.2
Autism	100.0	10.8	9.4	54.7	15.2	6.6	0.7	2.2	0.5
Traumatic brain injury	100.0	26.1	24.2	30.3	3.1	11.3	0.3	2.0	2.7

1 Less than 0.05 percent.

NOTE.—There are some reporting variations, e.g., estimated or incomplete data and nonstandard definitions, from state to state. Data for 3- to 5-year-old children are no longer collected by type of disability. Because of rounding, details may not add to totals.

SOURCE: U.S. Department of Education, Office of Special Education and Rehabilitative Services, *Annual Report to Congress on the Implementation of The Individuals with Disabilities Education Act.* (This table was prepared February 1998.)

Source: *Digest of Education Statistics 1998*, National Center for Education Statistics, Washington, DC, 1999

having mental retardation, about twice the rate of American Indian and White students and a considerably higher rate than Hispanic and Asian/Pacific Islander students. Overall, less than 1 percent (0.8 percent) of the student population received services for emotional disturbance, although the rate for Black students (1.1 percent) was somewhat higher. (See Table 3.3.)

The charge that minority children are overrepresented among special education students has been an issue of national concern and debate for some time. Some observers maintain that poverty, rather than race/ethnicity, may account for some of the overrepresentation of minorities in special education programs. Others believe that school officials are more likely to place minority and poor children in special education because of low expectations regarding the performance of these children. Still others contend that poor, minority children are more likely to experience deficient prenatal and early childhood nutrition, which may result in learning disabilities.

Mainstreaming and Inclusion Programs

Over the past decade, a controversy has developed over where and how disabled students should be taught. For years, many disabled children were taught at home or in special classrooms or schools. Now, however, many parents, educators, and specialists believe that including disabled students in regular classrooms benefits both disabled and nondisabled students. In 1994, the U.S. General Accounting Office (GAO) reviewed these "inclusion programs," as they are called, in four states: California, Kentucky, New York, and Vermont (*Special Education Reform: Districts Grapple with Inclusion Programs*, Washington, DC, 1994).

The GAO study found that inclusion programs can give disabled students good peer role models, better social skills, and improvements in language development, behavior, and self-esteem, as well as academic progress. The benefits to nondisabled students included their becoming generally more compassionate, more helpful, and more accepting of the disabled as friends. The study warned, however, that inclusion programs were not for all disabled students and that there was a need for careful planning and funding. The success of the program depended on several conditions, as follows.

• An inclusion program calls for a collaborative learning environment; that is, the special education teacher and the regular classroom teacher must work together to ensure that each disabled student's special needs are met in the classroom.

- The school should serve only local disabled students, rather than having disabled students brought in from other parts of the district. In other words, the proportion of disabled to nondisabled students must be manageable.

- Classroom teachers must have adequate support, including large numbers of aides and special training for teaching disabled students.

During the 1995-96 school year, 95 percent of disabled students ages 3 through 21 received most of their educational and related services in school settings with nondisabled students. Over 45 percent were in regular classrooms, an additional 26.8 percent received special education and related services in resource rooms, and 23.2 percent were served in separate classrooms within a regular education building. Almost 9 of every 10 speech-impaired children (87.6 percent) were educated in regular classrooms, and 80.6 percent of those with learning disabilities received special education in resource rooms or in regular classes. (See Table 3.4.)

Trends in Special Education

Two important trends in special education have emerged over the past few years. First, children with handicaps are receiving educational services earlier, which lays a foundation for the learning skills they will need in elementary school. The Individuals with Disabilities Act (see above) includes the Grants for Infants and Families with Disabilities program for early intervention services to all children with disabilities ages birth through 2 years old and the Preschool Grants program to enable preschool children with disabilities to receive special education and related services. For many disabled children, early education programs can reduce or even eliminate the need for intensive services later.

TABLE 3.5

Students with disabilities exiting the educational system, by age, type of disability, and basis of exit: United States and outlying areas, 1993–94 and 1994–95

	Number						Percent					
Student characteristics	Graduated with diploma		Graduated with certificate		Reached maximum age [1]		Graduated with diploma		Graduated with certificate		Reached maximum age [1]	
	1993–94 [2]	1994–95	1993–94 [2]	1994–95	1993–94 [2]	1994–95	1993–94 [2]	1994–95	1993–94 [2]	1994–95	1993–94 [2]	1994–95
1	2	3	4	5	6	7	8	9	10	11	12	13
Age group												
14 to 21 (and over)	113,910	118,471	23,983	25,106	4,594	3,954	28.1	26.8	5.9	5.7	1.1	0.9
14	91	62	130	73	7	4	0.2	0.1	0.3	0.1	0.0	0.0
15	169	106	71	68	9	7	0.4	0.2	0.1	0.1	0.0	0.0
16	532	545	178	154	39	26	1.0	0.9	0.3	0.2	0.1	0.0
17	15,417	16,455	2,016	2,373	106	37	22.7	21.7	3.0	3.1	0.2	0.0
18	47,847	49,988	7,766	9,017	110	110	51.9	50.3	8.4	9.1	0.1	0.1
19	35,730	37,154	7,001	7,308	91	79	59.7	59.9	11.7	11.8	0.2	0.1
20	9,361	9,254	3,408	3,083	525	383	48.0	48.5	17.5	16.1	2.7	2.0
21 (and over)	4,763	4,907	3,413	3,030	3,707	3,308	30.9	33.3	22.1	20.5	24.0	22.4
Type of disability												
All disabilities, 14 to 21 and over	113,945	118,471	23,948	25,106	4,594	3,954	28.1	26.8	5.9	5.7	1.1	0.9
Specific learning disabilities	76,735	80,666	10,871	11,716	891	631	32.5	31.2	4.6	4.5	0.4	0.2
Mental retardation	13,900	13,817	9,117	9,045	2,307	2,101	26.3	25.5	17.2	16.7	4.4	3.9
Serious emotional disturbance	11,251	11,611	1,649	1,693	331	292	16.1	15.0	2.4	2.2	0.5	0.4
Speech or language impairments	3,423	3,492	473	485	121	70	18.3	17.6	2.5	2.4	0.6	0.4
Multiple disabilities	1,254	1,416	675	788	553	515	25.1	22.5	13.5	12.5	11.1	8.2
Other health impairments	2,250	2,222	191	260	44	40	21.7	20.1	1.8	2.3	0.4	0.4
Hearing impairments	2,209	2,110	391	454	48	33	44.1	40.5	7.8	8.7	1.0	0.6
Orthopedic impairments	1,557	1,619	285	339	133	107	33.5	31.2	6.1	6.5	2.9	2.1
Visual impairments	931	960	105	114	53	47	46.3	46.0	5.2	5.5	2.6	2.3
Autism	169	211	120	115	80	88	24.1	25.5	17.1	13.9	11.4	10.6
Deaf-blindness	34	33	26	34	8	9	23.9	20.5	18.3	21.1	5.6	5.6
Traumatic brain injury	232	314	45	63	25	21	35.4	36.9	6.9	7.4	3.8	2.5

[1] These figures reflect an estimate of those who were actually known to have dropped out and do not include youth who simply stopped coming to school or whose status was unknown.

[2] Upper age limits for service eligibility vary by state.

SOURCE: U.S. Department of Education, Office of Special Education and Rehabilitative Services, *Sixteenth, Seventeenth, and Nineteenth Annual Reports to Congress on the Implementation of The Individuals with Disabilities Education Act*, 1995 and 1996. (This table was prepared November 1998.)

Source: *Digest of Education Statistics 1998*, National Center for Education Statistics, Washington, DC, 1999

Second, special education has helped to eliminate the myth that disabled individuals, even the severely disabled, are unwilling or unable to work. Schools are assessing the abilities and talents of students with handicaps and matching them with potential occupations. Disabled students are receiving more training in vocational skills, as well as in making the transition from school to community life and work.

Exiting from Special Education

In 1984-85, the Office of Special Education Programs began collecting data on students ages 14 and older who had left the education system. In 1994-95, about one-fourth (26.8 percent) of exiting students with disabilities graduated with diplomas, and 5.7 percent graduated with certificates. About 1 percent reached the maximum age for services, which varies by state. The remainder left the educational system for other reasons (including death). (See Table 3.5.)

FIGURE 3.1

1972 Marland Definition
(Public Law 91–230, section 806)

Gifted and talented children are those identified by professionally qualified persons, who by virtue of outstanding abilities are capable of high performance. These are children who require differentiated educational programs and/or services beyond those normally provided by the regular school program in order to realize their contribution to self and society.

Children capable of high performance include those with demonstrated achievement and/or potential ability in any of the following areas, singly or in combination:

1. general intellectual ability,
2. specific academic aptitude,
3. creative or productive thinking,
4. leadership ability,
5. visual and performing arts,
6. psychomotor ability.

It can be assumed that utilization of these criteria for identification of the gifted and talented will encompass a minimum of 3 to 5 percent of the school population.

Source: *National Excellence: A Case for Developing America's Talent*, U.S. Department of Education, Office of Educational Research and Improvement, Washington, DC, 1993

Youth with disabilities were significantly more likely than youth in general and somewhat more likely than youth with similar demographic characteristics to drop out of school. Disabled students who receive inadequate educational preparation are even more seriously disabled when they leave school; they have reached the legal age for independence but probably have not developed marketable job skills. Despite their efforts, high school programs often fail to meet these students' needs.

GIFTED AND TALENTED STUDENTS

In America we often make fun of our brightest students, giving them such derogatory names as nerd, dweeb, or, in a former day, egghead. We have conflicting feelings about people who are smart, and we give conflicting signals to our children about how hard they should work to be smart. As a culture we seem to value beauty and brawn far more than brains. — Gregory Anrig, president of the Educational Testing Service, quoted in *National Excellence: A Case for Developing America's Talent (1993)*

Defining Giftedness

For more than a century, researchers, scientists, and educators have tried to define the term "gifted." Historically, the term was closely associated with the concept of genius. After intelligence (IQ) tests were developed, people who scored poorly were labeled retarded, and those who scored extremely well were considered geniuses. Currently, many observers criticize the use of IQ tests as a single measure of intelligence. They think the tests are biased in favor of the White middle and upper classes and penalize those from different cultural backgrounds. Also, many researchers and educators believe that giftedness is more than high intellectual ability. It also involves creativity, memory, motivation, physical dexterity, social adeptness, and aesthetic sensitivity — qualities needed to succeed in life but not measured by IQ tests.

Researchers and educators generally agree that intelligence takes many forms and that multiple criteria are necessary for measurement. Educators are learning to identify outstanding talent by evaluating student abilities in different settings, rather than relying solely on test scores. The following definition, based on the definition in the Jacob K. Javits Gifted and Talented Student Education Act of 1988 (PL 100-297), reflects the current knowledge and thinking.

Children and youth with outstanding talent perform or show the potential for performing at remarkably high levels of accomplishment when compared with others of their age, experience, or environment.

These children and youth exhibit high performance capability in intellectual, creative, and/or artistic areas, possess an unusual leadership capacity, or excel in specific academic fields. They require services or activities not ordinarily provided by the schools.

Outstanding talents are present in children and youth from all cultural groups, across all economic strata, and in all areas of human endeavor.

Identifying Gifted Students

Most states and localities have developed definitions of gifted and talented students based on the 1972 Marland Report to Congress (Figure 3.1). This definition identified a variety of abilities in addition to general intellectual ability and estimated that gifted students represent at least 3 to 5 percent of the student population. However, the methods used by most districts to identify gifted students lag far behind the Marland definition. In a national survey, 73 percent of the school districts said they

---

TABLE 3.6

State legislation on gifted and talented programs and number and percent of students receiving services in public elementary and secondary schools, by state: 1993–94 and 1995–96

State	State-mandated gifted and talented programs, 1995–96 [1]	Discretionary state-supported gifted and talented, 1995–96 [2]	Gifted and talented students receiving services, 1993–94	Gifted and talented students as a percent of enrollment, 1993–94	State	State-mandated gifted and talented programs, 1995–96 [1]	Discretionary state-supported gifted and talented, 1995–96 [2]	Gifted and talented students receiving services, 1993–94	Gifted and talented students as a percent of enrollment, 1993–94
1	2	3	4	5	1	2	3	4	5
Alabama	X		16,522	2.4	Montana	X		—	—
Alaska	X		4,696	4.0	Nebraska	X		18,600	10.0
Arizona	X		39,200	—	Nevada		X	8,343	2.0
Arkansas	X		34,710	8.0	New Hampshire		X	—	—
California		X	290,000	5.0	New Jersey	—	—	—	—
Colorado		X	—	—	New Mexico	X		—	—
Connecticut	X		16,871	[3]3.5	New York	X		135,000	6.0
Delaware		X	—	5.0	North Carolina	X		88,450	8.0
District of Columbia	—	—	—	9.0	North Dakota		X	1,107	1.0
Florida	X		74,572	3.5	Ohio	X		244,670	13.0
Georgia	—	—	—	5.0	Oklahoma	X		61,082	10.0
Hawaii	X		18,000	11.0	Oregon	X		—	8.5
Idaho	X		—	1.3	Pennsylvania	X		79,756	4.6
Illinois	X		[4]166,234	5.0	Rhode Island		X	—	3.5–5.0
Indiana		X	85,192	8.9	South Carolina	X		52,000	10.0
Iowa	X		—	4.0	South Dakota		X	6,515	4.4
Kansas	X		—	3.1	Tennessee	X		18,626	2.0
Kentucky	X		52,600	5.0	Texas	X		248,769	7.0
Louisiana	X		24,000	3.2	Utah	X		—	—
Maine	X		10,100	5.0	Vermont	—	—	—	—
Maryland		X	90,222	12.0	Virginia	X		121,598	9.2
Massachusetts		X	—	—	Washington		X	38,781	1.5
Michigan		X	225,154	14.0	West Virginia	X		—	3.5
Minnesota		X	55,467	7.2	Wisconsin	X		—	15.0
Mississippi	X		21,678	4.3	Wyoming		X	—	3.0
Missouri		X	24,877	5.0	Guam	X		—	—

[1] Mandate requiring identification of and/or services for gifted/talented students.
[2] No mandate requiring identification of or services for gifted/talented students.
[3] Grades 2 through 6 only.
[4] Data for 1991–92.
—Data not available.

SOURCE: Council of State Directors of Programs for the Gifted, *The 1994 and 1996 State of the States Gifted and Talented Education Reports.* (This table was prepared July 1997.)

Source: *Digest of Education Statistics 1998*, National Center for Education Statistics, Washington, DC, 1999

had adopted the Marland definition, but few reported using it to identify any area of giftedness other than general high intelligence and achievement. Most relied on tests and teacher recommendations to admit students into gifted and talented programs. This practice may well miss many students with other outstanding talents.

In *National Excellence: A Case for Developing America's Talent* (Washington, DC, 1993), the U.S. Department of Education reported that several categories of children are particularly neglected in programs for top students. These include

- Culturally different children (minority or economically disadvantaged students).

- Females (especially in mathematics and science programs).

- Students with disabilities.

- Students with artistic talent.

- High-potential students who underachieve in school.

Students who would otherwise be excluded can be tested for giftedness. Several culture-free instruments have been developed for identifying gifted minority and disadvantaged students. Coordination between the special-education teacher and the gifted-education teacher can help identify gifted disabled students. Gifted underachievers can be identified by comparing their intellectual aptitude (usually IQ scores) with their actual performance, such as grades or achievement test scores.

Mixed Messages

Again and again, it has been noticed that intellect in America is resented as a kind of excellence, as a claim to distinction, as a challenge to egalitarianism, as a quality which almost certainly deprives a man or woman of the common touch. — Richard

TABLE 3.7

Percent of high school dropouts (status dropouts) among persons 16 to 24 years old, by sex and race/ethnicity: April 1960 to October 1997

Year	Total				Men				Women			
	All races	White, non-Hispanic	Black, non-Hispanic	Hispanic origin	All races	White, non-Hispanic	Black, non-Hispanic	Hispanic origin	All races	White, non-Hispanic	Black, non-Hispanic	Hispanic origin
1	2	3	4	5	6	7	8	9	10	11	12	13
1960 [1]	27.2 —	— —	— —	— —	27.8 —	— —	— —	— —	26.7 —	— —	— —	— —
1967 [2]	17.0 —	15.4 —	28.6 —	— —	18.5 —	11.7 —	30.0 —	— —	17.6 —	16.1 —	20.5 —	— —
1968 [2]	16.2 —	14.7 —	27.4 —	— —	15.8 —	14.4 —	27.1 —	— —	16.5 —	15.0 —	27.6 —	— —
1969 [2]	15.2 —	13.6 —	26.7 —	— —	14.3 —	12.6 —	26.9 —	— —	16.0 —	14.6 —	26.7 —	— —
1970 [2]	15.0 —	13.2 —	27.9 —	— —	14.2 —	12.2 —	29.4 —	— —	15.7 —	14.1 —	26.6 —	— —
1971 [2]	14.7 —	13.4 —	23.7 —	— —	14.2 —	12.6 —	25.5 —	— —	15.2 —	14.2 —	22.1 —	— —
1972	14.6 (0.3)	12.3 (0.3)	21.3 (1.1)	34.3 (2.2)	14.1 (0.4)	11.6 (0.4)	22.3 (1.6)	33.7 (3.2)	15.1 (0.4)	12.8 (0.4)	20.5 (1.4)	34.8 (3.1)
1973	14.1 (0.3)	11.6 (0.3)	22.2 (1.1)	33.5 (2.2)	13.7 (0.4)	11.5 (0.4)	21.5 (1.5)	30.4 (3.2)	14.5 (0.4)	11.8 (0.4)	22.8 (1.5)	36.4 (3.2)
1974	14.3 (0.3)	11.9 (0.3)	21.2 (1.0)	33.0 (2.1)	14.2 (0.4)	12.0 (0.4)	20.1 (1.5)	33.8 (3.0)	14.3 (0.4)	11.8 (0.4)	22.1 (1.5)	32.2 (2.9)
1975	13.9 (0.3)	11.4 (0.3)	22.9 (1.1)	29.2 (2.0)	13.3 (0.4)	11.0 (0.4)	23.0 (1.6)	26.7 (2.8)	14.5 (0.4)	11.8 (0.4)	22.9 (1.4)	31.6 (2.9)
1976	14.1 (0.3)	12.0 (0.3)	20.5 (1.0)	31.4 (2.0)	14.1 (0.4)	12.1 (0.4)	21.2 (1.5)	30.3 (2.9)	14.2 (0.4)	11.8 (0.4)	19.9 (1.4)	32.3 (2.8)
1977	14.1 (0.3)	11.9 (0.3)	19.8 (1.0)	33.0 (2.0)	14.5 (0.4)	12.6 (0.4)	19.5 (1.5)	31.6 (2.9)	13.8 (0.4)	11.2 (0.4)	20.0 (1.4)	34.3 (2.8)
1978	14.2 (0.3)	11.9 (0.3)	20.2 (1.0)	33.3 (2.0)	14.6 (0.4)	12.2 (0.4)	22.5 (1.5)	33.6 (2.9)	13.9 (0.4)	11.6 (0.4)	18.3 (1.3)	33.1 (2.8)
1979	14.6 (0.3)	12.0 (0.3)	21.1 (1.0)	33.8 (2.0)	15.0 (0.4)	12.6 (0.4)	22.4 (1.5)	33.0 (2.8)	14.2 (0.4)	11.5 (0.4)	20.0 (1.3)	34.5 (2.8)
1980	14.1 (0.3)	11.4 (0.3)	19.1 (1.0)	35.2 (1.9)	15.1 (0.4)	12.3 (0.4)	20.8 (1.5)	37.2 (2.7)	13.1 (0.4)	10.5 (0.4)	17.7 (1.3)	33.2 (2.6)
1981	13.9 (0.3)	11.3 (0.3)	18.4 (0.9)	33.2 (1.8)	15.1 (0.4)	12.5 (0.4)	19.9 (1.4)	36.0 (2.6)	12.8 (0.4)	10.2 (0.4)	17.1 (1.2)	30.4 (2.5)
1982	13.9 (0.3)	11.4 (0.3)	18.4 (1.0)	31.7 (1.9)	14.5 (0.4)	12.0 (0.4)	21.2 (1.5)	30.5 (2.7)	13.3 (0.4)	10.8 (0.4)	15.9 (1.3)	32.8 (2.7)
1983	13.7 (0.3)	11.1 (0.3)	18.0 (1.0)	31.6 (1.9)	14.9 (0.4)	12.2 (0.4)	19.9 (1.5)	34.3 (2.8)	12.5 (0.4)	10.1 (0.4)	16.2 (1.3)	29.1 (2.6)
1984	13.1 (0.3)	11.0 (0.3)	15.5 (0.9)	29.8 (1.9)	14.0 (0.4)	11.9 (0.4)	16.8 (1.4)	30.6 (2.8)	12.3 (0.4)	10.1 (0.4)	14.3 (1.2)	29.0 (2.6)
1985	12.6 (0.3)	10.4 (0.3)	15.2 (0.9)	27.6 (1.9)	13.4 (0.4)	11.1 (0.4)	16.1 (1.4)	29.9 (2.8)	11.8 (0.4)	9.8 (0.4)	14.3 (1.2)	25.2 (2.7)
1986	12.2 (0.3)	9.7 (0.3)	14.2 (0.9)	30.1 (1.9)	13.1 (0.4)	10.3 (0.4)	15.0 (1.3)	32.8 (2.7)	11.4 (0.4)	9.1 (0.4)	13.5 (1.2)	27.2 (2.6)
1987	12.6 (0.3)	10.4 (0.3)	14.1 (0.9)	28.6 (1.8)	13.2 (0.4)	10.8 (0.4)	15.0 (1.3)	29.1 (2.6)	12.1 (0.4)	10.0 (0.4)	13.3 (1.2)	28.1 (2.6)
1988	12.9 (0.3)	9.6 (0.3)	14.5 (1.0)	35.8 (2.3)	13.5 (0.4)	10.3 (0.5)	15.0 (1.5)	36.0 (3.2)	12.2 (0.4)	8.9 (0.4)	14.0 (1.4)	35.4 (3.3)
1989	12.6 (0.3)	9.4 (0.3)	13.9 (1.0)	33.0 (2.2)	13.6 (0.5)	10.3 (0.5)	14.9 (1.5)	34.4 (3.1)	11.7 (0.4)	8.5 (0.4)	13.0 (1.3)	31.6 (3.1)
1990	12.1 (0.3)	9.0 (0.3)	13.2 (0.9)	32.4 (1.9)	12.3 (0.4)	9.3 (0.4)	11.9 (1.3)	34.3 (2.7)	11.8 (0.4)	8.7 (0.4)	14.4 (1.3)	30.3 (2.7)
1991	12.5 (0.3)	8.9 (0.3)	13.6 (0.9)	35.3 (1.9)	13.0 (0.4)	8.9 (0.4)	13.5 (1.4)	39.2 (2.7)	11.9 (0.4)	8.9 (0.4)	13.7 (1.3)	31.1 (2.7)
1992 [3]	11.0 (0.3)	7.7 (0.3)	13.7 (0.9)	29.4 (1.9)	11.3 (0.4)	8.0 (0.4)	12.5 (1.3)	32.1 (2.7)	10.7 (0.4)	7.4 (0.4)	14.8 (1.4)	26.6 (2.6)
1993 [3]	11.0 (0.3)	7.9 (0.3)	13.6 (0.9)	27.5 (1.8)	11.2 (0.4)	8.2 (0.4)	12.6 (1.3)	28.1 (2.5)	10.9 (0.4)	7.6 (0.4)	14.4 (1.3)	26.9 (2.5)
1994 [3]	11.4 (0.3)	7.7 (0.3)	12.6 (0.8)	30.0 (1.2)	12.3 (0.4)	8.0 (0.4)	14.1 (1.1)	31.6 (1.6)	10.6 (0.4)	7.5 (0.4)	11.3 (1.0)	28.1 (1.7)
1995 [3]	12.0 (0.3)	8.6 (0.3)	12.1 (0.7)	30.0 (1.1)	12.2 (0.4)	9.0 (0.4)	11.1 (1.0)	30.0 (1.6)	11.7 (0.4)	8.2 (0.4)	12.9 (1.1)	30.0 (1.7)
1996 [3]	11.1 (0.3)	7.3 (0.3)	13.0 (0.8)	29.4 (1.2)	11.4 (0.4)	7.3 (0.4)	13.5 (1.2)	30.3 (1.7)	10.9 (0.4)	7.3 (0.4)	12.5 (1.1)	28.3 (1.7)
1997 [3]	11.0 (0.3)	7.6 (0.3)	13.4 (0.8)	25.3 (1.1)	11.9 (0.4)	8.5 (0.4)	13.3 (1.2)	27.0 (1.6)	10.1 (0.4)	6.7 (0.4)	13.5 (1.1)	23.4 (1.6)

[1] Based on the April 1960 decennial census.
[2] White and black include persons of Hispanic origin.
[3] Because of changes in data collection procedures, data may not be comparable with figures for earlier years.
— Data not available.

NOTE.—"Status" dropouts are 16- to 24-year-olds who are not enrolled in school and who have not completed a high school program, regardless of when they left school. People who have received GED credentials are counted as high school completers. All data except for 1960 are based on October counts. Data are based upon sample surveys of the civilian noninstitutional population. Standard errors appear in parentheses.

SOURCE: U.S. Department of Commerce, Bureau of the Census, Current Population Survey, unpublished tabulations; and U.S. Department of Education, National Center for Education Statistics, *Dropout Rates in the United States*. (This table was prepared December 1998.)

Source: *Digest of Education Statistics 1998*, National Center for Education Statistics, Washington, DC, 1999

Hofstadter, *Anti-Intellectualism in American Life*, 1970

In *National Excellence: A Case for Developing America's Talent* (see above), the U.S. Department of Education argued that the nation is squandering the gifts and talents of many students. Compared to top students in other industrialized nations, American students achieve lower scores on international tests and are offered a less rigorous curriculum. They also read fewer demanding books, do less homework, and enter the labor force or college less well-prepared. In addition, not enough American students perform at the highest levels on the National Assessment of Educational Progress (NAEP) tests, which provide some indication of how well students are achieving. (See Chapter IV for a further discussion of international comparisons and NAEP results.)

Many observers argue that American society has always held low expectations of academic excellence and has shown ambivalence about high academic and artistic performance. While the nation prizes creativity and academic success, especially if it has practical application, it assigns negative names such as "nerd" or "dweeb" to those who excel academically. High-achieving minority students often face further scorn by being accused of "acting White" by their peers. While American students are encouraged to complete high school and earn good grades, they are seldom required to work hard or master challenging knowledge or skills. The message seems to be "aim for academic *adequacy*, not academic *excellence*."

Serving Gifted Students

Not all states and localities collect data in the same way, so it is difficult to determine the exact number of students served in gifted and talented programs. In school year 1995-96, 31 states had state-mandated gifted and talented programs, and 16 states had discretionary (not set by law) programs (Table 3.6). In 1993-1994, 6.4 percent of all public school students and 4.9 percent of private school students participated in gifted and talented programs.

Estimating the expenditures for gifted and talented students is also difficult because some states do not keep separate records of these funds. In 1990, 37 states and territories reported spending about $396 million in state and local funds on gifted and talented education. This figure represented only 2 cents per $100 spent on elementary and secondary education. However small this amount may seem, it marks an improvement from 20 years ago, when only seven states had legislation and funding for gifted and talented programs.

The Jacob K. Javits Gifted and Talented Student Act of 1988 (see above) established a small federal contribution. This program, modestly funded with $6.5 million in 1998, supports grants, research, and the development of national leadership abilities. The act gives funding priority to programs that support gifted and talented students who are economically disadvantaged, speak limited English, or have disabilities.

DISADVANTAGED STUDENTS

Children who are seriously disadvantaged economically and socially often lag behind their peers. Statistically, they start preschool education later or miss it entirely and thus are less ready to start school. They have more learning disabilities, are more likely to be held back a grade, and ultimately, have higher dropout rates. Among the disadvantaged groups defined by educators and observers are

- Children from families with very low incomes.

- Children who are linguistically isolated (LI) or have limited English proficiency (LEP), usually because they are members of immigrant families.

- Children who change schools frequently; for example, children of seasonal farmworkers or homeless parents.

These children may suffer from health or behavioral problems related to poor diet, or their lin-

TABLE 3.8

Appropriations for Title I and Title VI, Elementary and Secondary Education Act (ESEA)[1] of 1994, by state or other area: 1996–97 and 1997–98

[In thousands]

State or other area	Title I total, school year 1996–97 [2]	Title I,[3] school year 1997–98 [4]							Title VI [5]	
		Total	Local education grants			Neglected and delinquent children	Migrant children	Other [6]	1996 appropriations for 1996–97	1997 appropriations for 1997–98
			Total [7]	Basic grants	Concentration grants					
1	2	3	4	5	6	7	8	9	10	11
Total [8]	**$7,215,249**	**$7,783,127**	**$7,295,232**	**$6,207,799**	**$1,012,028**	**$39,311**	**$305,473**	**$143,111**	**$275,000**	**$310,000**
Alabama	128,784	131,409	125,698	106,699	18,999	617	3,381	1,714	4,220	4,684
Alaska	25,348	26,662	16,935	15,302	1,633	172	9,071	484	1,365	1,539
Arizona	105,959	121,119	112,826	95,305	17,521	803	5,774	1,716	4,312	5,032
Arkansas	78,937	80,476	75,042	64,318	10,724	385	3,995	1,054	2,541	2,866
California	830,700	924,684	820,147	694,666	125,481	3,640	84,472	16,425	31,703	35,956
Colorado	69,894	74,147	69,612	60,653	8,959	277	3,238	1,020	3,797	4,280
Connecticut	55,932	71,835	67,008	58,097	8,911	775	2,732	1,320	3,020	3,426
Delaware	17,074	19,069	17,723	15,250	2,473	202	398	746	1,365	1,539
District of Columbia	21,703	23,309	21,490	18,099	3,391	847	308	664	1,365	1,539
Florida	306,097	358,106	328,272	280,197	48,075	1,326	23,513	4,995	12,480	14,442
Georgia	175,799	200,419	191,891	164,749	27,141	1,377	4,596	2,556	7,289	8,247
Hawaii	19,751	20,746	20,124	17,290	2,835	120	0	502	1,365	1,539
Idaho	27,055	26,092	21,879	19,128	2,751	100	3,588	524	1,366	1,553
Illinois	327,388	334,055	324,606	278,804	45,802	1,719	2,048	5,682	11,763	13,249
Indiana	113,324	117,423	111,758	100,338	11,420	632	3,248	1,784	5,784	6,486
Iowa	52,283	53,355	51,587	47,050	4,537	237	608	923	2,937	3,249
Kansas	59,938	64,479	53,947	47,957	5,991	539	9,112	881	2,748	3,066
Kentucky	132,963	137,956	127,104	107,970	19,134	859	7,944	2,049	3,845	4,276
Louisiana	192,972	197,894	191,287	161,779	29,509	656	2,564	3,386	4,870	5,426
Maine	29,334	32,818	28,085	25,272	2,814	132	4,095	506	1,365	1,539
Maryland	88,763	101,037	97,405	85,142	12,263	1,113	320	2,199	4,795	5,432
Massachusetts	125,917	148,846	142,984	121,950	21,033	743	2,196	2,924	5,431	6,123
Michigan	319,188	340,649	321,769	276,704	45,065	958	12,852	5,070	9,893	11,037
Minnesota	85,557	90,942	86,178	76,809	9,369	197	2,562	2,005	4,957	5,557
Mississippi	126,428	127,989	124,675	106,146	18,529	279	1,137	1,898	2,978	3,325
Missouri	117,408	128,881	124,488	107,700	16,788	709	1,097	2,587	5,442	6,082
Montana	26,226	26,509	25,308	21,716	3,592	68	620	514	1,365	1,539
Nebraska	34,365	36,505	31,736	28,834	2,902	297	3,562	911	1,768	1,978
Nevada	19,543	22,897	21,881	19,364	2,517	170	348	499	1,417	1,679
New Hampshire	16,648	17,689	16,730	15,324	1,407	347	89	523	1,365	1,539
New Jersey	145,386	165,699	158,037	136,704	21,333	2,464	1,133	4,064	7,333	8,330
New Mexico	61,052	64,712	62,366	52,663	9,703	292	1,037	1,018	1,941	2,174
New York	627,760	691,343	665,779	568,981	96,799	2,786	7,094	15,684	16,973	19,091
North Carolina	136,057	144,469	137,011	119,980	17,031	1,001	4,636	1,820	6,759	7,723
North Dakota	17,773	18,866	17,675	15,393	2,282	46	571	574	1,365	1,539
Ohio	307,328	307,721	298,122	257,641	40,481	2,118	1,598	5,882	11,232	12,541
Oklahoma	85,198	89,482	86,346	73,844	12,502	359	1,608	1,170	3,486	3,892
Oregon	79,527	80,243	67,462	59,481	7,981	1,198	10,614	969	3,112	3,530
Pennsylvania	315,880	338,981	323,243	280,804	42,440	670	6,572	8,496	11,385	12,769
Rhode Island	21,939	25,482	24,175	21,094	3,081	357	122	829	1,365	1,539
South Carolina	93,480	95,786	93,292	79,932	13,360	871	433	1,190	3,680	4,095
South Dakota	19,921	20,536	19,289	16,676	2,613	191	536	519	1,365	1,539
Tennessee	123,385	130,600	128,056	108,973	19,083	620	173	1,750	5,049	5,677
Texas	625,538	682,084	627,681	532,726	94,955	2,034	42,739	9,630	20,300	22,947
Utah	34,293	35,270	33,044	29,508	3,536	445	1,274	508	2,661	2,949
Vermont	16,327	17,774	16,307	14,525	1,781	104	845	518	1,365	1,539
Virginia	102,822	111,611	108,448	95,505	12,944	932	661	1,570	6,151	6,903
Washington	113,393	123,404	107,699	93,183	14,515	778	13,339	1,588	5,499	6,204
West Virginia	70,426	74,226	72,921	61,857	11,064	228	110	967	1,742	1,895
Wisconsin	125,368	128,105	124,316	113,849	10,467	936	595	2,258	5,406	6,065
Wyoming	16,270	16,624	15,894	14,313	1,581	87	153	490	1,365	1,539
Other activities										
Bureau of Indian Affairs	41,609	45,458	45,458	0	0	0	0	0	0	0
Migrant coordination activities	5,999	5,998	0	0	0	0	5,998	0	0	0
Even Start Migrant, Indian, and Territory setaside	8,600	8,600	3,500	0	0	0	0	5,100	0	0
Even Start Evaluation/ Technical Assistance	1,374	1,369	0	0	0	0	0	1,369	0	0
Even Start/State Literacy Initiative	0	0	0	0	0	0	0	0	0	0
Competitive grants	5,000	5,000	5,000	0	0	0	0	0	0	0
Outlying areas										
American Samoa	4,978	5,141	5,141	0	0	0	0	0	330	373
Guam	4,846	4,819	4,819	0	0	0	0	0	771	869
Northern Marianas	2,362	2,734	2,734	0	0	0	0	0	188	212
Puerto Rico	261,604	274,238	262,487	221,557	40,929	497	4,164	7,090	4,624	5,122
Virgin Islands	8,474	8,753	8,753	0	0	0	0	0	635	716

[1] Elementary and Secondary Education Act was most recently revised through the Improving America's Schools Act (IASA) of 1994.

[2] Data are based on fiscal year 1997 budget authorizations. Excludes $3,359,000 for Title I evaluation.

[3] Formerly Chapter 1.

[4] Data are based on fiscal year 1998 budget authorizations. Excludes $6,977,000 for Title I evaluation.

[5] Formerly Chapter 2.

[6] Includes capital expenses, and Even Start grants.

[7] Includes other programs not shown separately.

[8] Total includes other activities and outlying areas.

NOTE.—Because of rounding, details may not add to totals.

SOURCE: U.S. Department of Education, Budget Service, Elementary, Secondary, and Vocational Education Analysis Division, unpublished data. (This table was prepared March 1998.)

Source: *Digest of Education Statistics 1998*, National Center for Education Statistics, Washington, DC, 1999

guistic disadvantages may severely limit their ability to keep up in school. They may be very bright, even gifted, but their school achievement lags behind due to interrupted attendance or lack of programs to support their development. Linguistically isolated (LI) children are those living in households in which no person over 13 years of age speaks only English or speaks English very well. Limited English proficiency (LEP) children live in households where members have difficulty reading, writing, or understanding English.

Table 3.7 shows the 1972-1997 dropout rates for 16- to 24-year-olds. (Status dropouts are those who were not enrolled in school but were not high school graduates.) Minority students (Black, 13.4 percent; Hispanic, 25.3 percent) were more likely than White students (7.6 percent) to drop out. (For more information about student dropouts, see Chapter VI.)

The Title I (formerly Chapter 1) education program is the major federal program designed to help states and schools meet the special educational needs of disadvantaged students. Title I originated as part of the Elementary and Secondary Education Act of 1965 (PL 89-10) and was amended by the Improving America's Schools Act of 1994 (PL 103-382). Title I provides about $8 billion per year to fund programs and resources so that schools can improve learning for at-risk students, particularly schools with high concentrations of low-income children.

States and school districts can apply for Title I funds for a variety of programs aimed at improving the performance of disadvantaged students. Table 3.8 gives the appropriations for Title I and Title VI (formerly Chapter 2*) programs by state for the 1996-97 and 1997-98 school years. Typi-

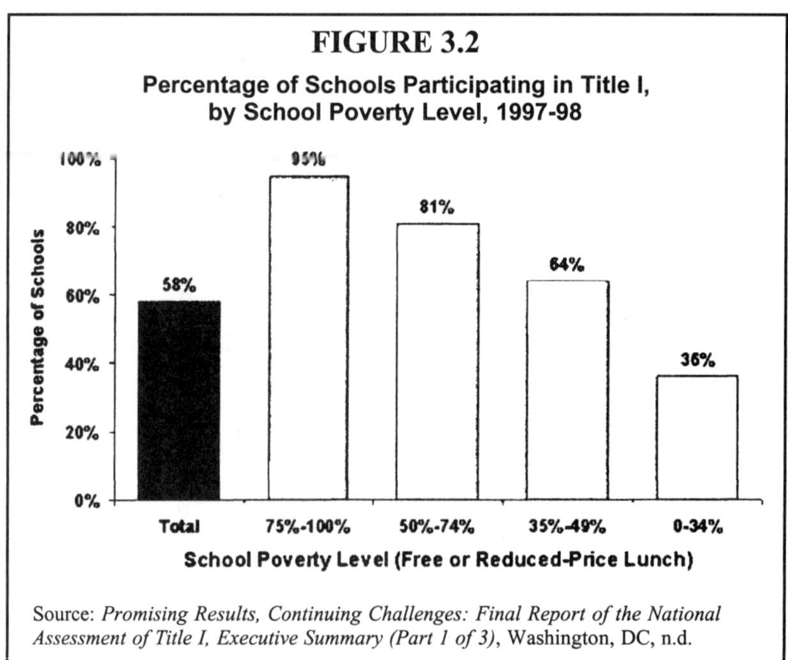

FIGURE 3.2

Percentage of Schools Participating in Title I, by School Poverty Level, 1997-98

Source: *Promising Results, Continuing Challenges: Final Report of the National Assessment of Title I, Executive Summary (Part 1 of 3)*, Washington, DC, n.d.

cally, states with higher rates of poor, immigrant, and/or migrant students, such as California, Florida, Illinois, Michigan, New York, Ohio, Pennsylvania, and Texas, apply for and receive more federal funds.

In 1997-1998, 95 percent of the highest-poverty schools — those with 75 percent or more students who are eligible for free or reduced price lunch — received Title I funds, compared to 36 percent of the lowest-poverty schools (Figure 3.2). Two-thirds of the 11 million students served by Title I were in elementary school (grades one through six).

Title I, Part A services were available to about 2 million students with limited English proficiency, 1 million students with disabilities, nearly 300,000 migrant students, and over 200,000 children identified as homeless. Minority students received Title I assistance at rates higher than their proportion of the student population. Twenty-eight percent of Title I participants were Black students, 30 percent were Hispanic, and 36 percent were non-Hispanic Whites. The remaining participants were from other ethnic/racial groups.

---

* Chapter 2 was established by Congress as part of the Education Consolidation and Improvement Act of 1981 (part of PL 97-35) to consolidate a number of education programs.

Students on the Move

Children who move frequently during their school years are more likely to have emotional or behavioral problems, to repeat a grade, or to be suspended or expelled from school. In "Geographic Mobility and Children's Emotional/Behavioral Adjustment and School Functioning" (*PEDIATRICS*, volume 93, number 2, 1994), Gloria A. Simpson and Mary Glenn Fowler evaluated the data from the 1988 *National Health Interview Survey of Child Health*. They reported that school-age children who moved three or more times were more than twice as likely to experience emotional or behavioral problems, while those who had moved only once or twice were not significantly affected.

Likewise, children who moved three or more times were 60 percent more likely to have repeated a grade and 80 percent more likely to have been expelled or suspended. Experts theorize that these children experience stress in the loss of old friends and familiar surroundings. Children may not understand the reasons for moving or may see the moves as a loss of autonomy. In addition, frequent moves may be a symptom of a stressed, chaotic family, a characteristic known to be related to emotional and school problems.

Migrant Children

With frequent moves, low incomes, and limited English skills, migrant children are at high risk for developing school problems. They often live

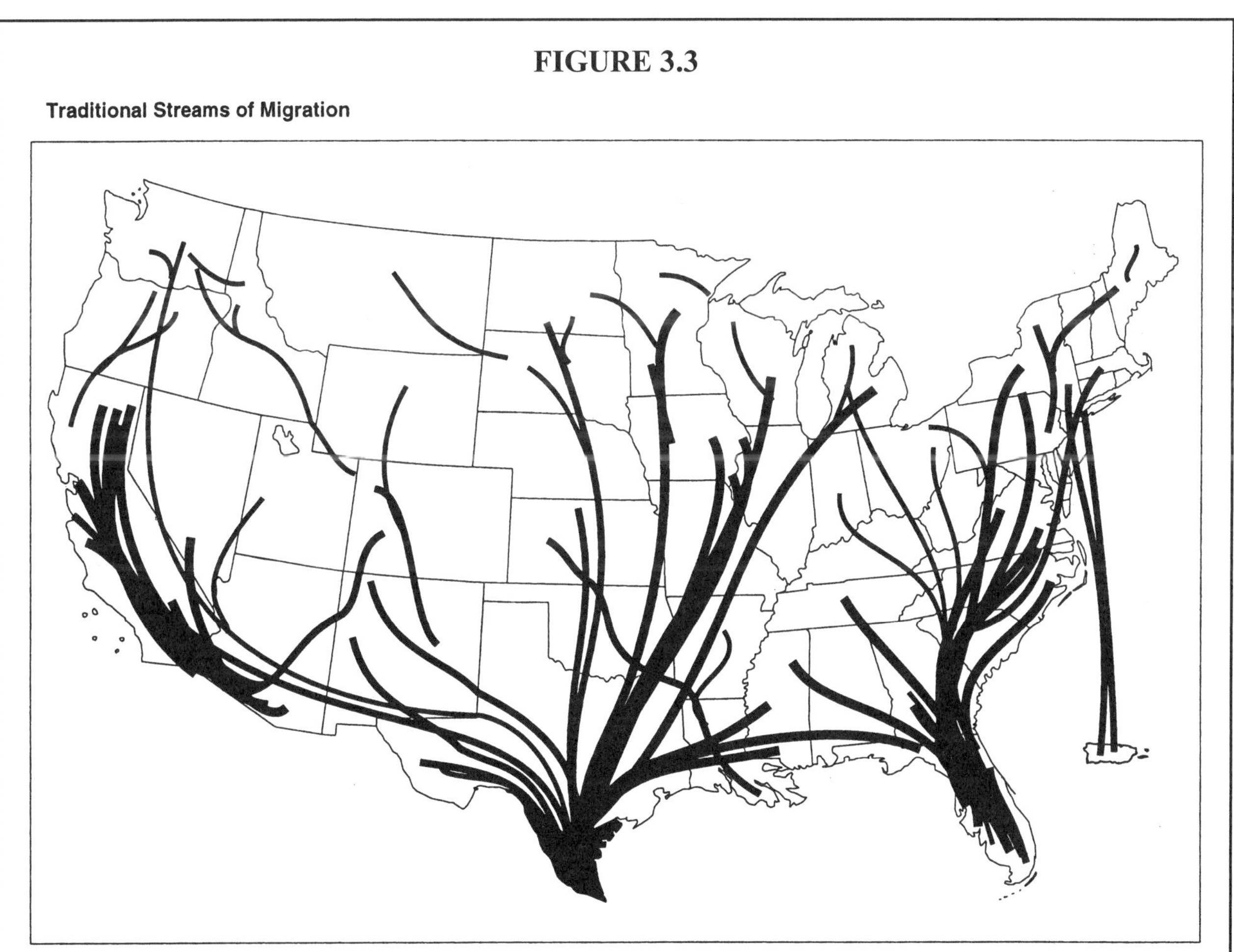

FIGURE 3.3

Source: GAO analysis of data from Joseph O. Prewitt Diaz, Robert T. Trottle II, and Vidal A. Rivera, Jr., The Effects of Migration on Children: An Ethnographic Study (Harrisburg: Pennsylvania Department of Education, Division of Migrant Education, 1989).

Source: *Migrant Children — Education and HHS Need to Improve the Exchange of Participant Information*, U.S. General Accounting Office, Washington, DC, 1999

in substandard housing and are frequently poverty-stricken and alienated from other children at school. They may experience exposure to harmful agricultural chemicals and receive inadequate health care. These factors can make getting an education very difficult. The Title I Migrant Education Program (MEP), authorized under the Hawkins-Stafford Elementary and Secondary School Improvement Amendments of 1968 (PL 100-297), provides funding for state education agencies to meet the special needs of migratory children.

The term "migrant children" may refer to independent children who move often, perhaps from family to family, or to children of migratory workers who move frequently to secure jobs in farming, fishing, timber, or dairy industries. The MEP serves current and former (for up to three years) migrant children ages 3 through 21. Most migrant education programs include preschool services, testing, regular academic or remedial instruction, bilingual education, vocational education, guidance and counseling, and health services. In 1997-98, the Title I appropriation for migrant children was $305.5 million (Table 3.8).

According to *The Federal Migrant Education Program: An Overview* (Patricia Osorio-O'Dea, Congressional Research Service, Washington, DC, 1998), about 83 percent of migrant students are Hispanic and include increasing numbers of immigrants. More than 40 percent are limited English proficient (LEP), and over two-thirds live in households with incomes below the poverty level. Migrant students experience more health problems, such as nutritional disease and respiratory infections, than other students.

California, Florida, Michigan, Texas, and Washington serve the majority of migrant students. Migrant families generally travel in three patterns of migration, called migrant streams (Figure 3.3).

• Texas and north through the Central Plains states.

• California to the Northwest and the western states.

• Florida and north along the East Coast states.

Until recently, the Migrant Student Record Transfer System (MSRTS), a national computer network, was used to transfer education and health records of migratory workers' children across state lines and school districts. MSRTS data were used to locate and determine children who might be eligible for MEP services. Criticized for its high cost and alleged ineffectiveness, the MSRTS was not reauthorized by the 1994 Improving America's Schools Act (PL 103-382). Currently, the Department of Education is measuring the effectiveness of the use of the World Wide Web (WWW) and Internet to link migrant student databases across the country.

Homeless Children

Title VII of the Stewart B. McKinney Homeless Assistance Act (PL 100-77; 1987) provides funding to facilitate the enrollment, attendance, and success in school of homeless children and youth. However, available resources have been limited. Although reports indicate increasing homelessness among children, funding for the McKinney programs in 1999 was $28.8 million, the same as the 1995 funding level.

TABLE 3.9

Estimates of Head Start Population and Percent Served, FY1997

Age	Population March 1997 (in 000s)	Economically eligible 1996 (in 000s)	Enrollment FY1997 (in 000s)	Percent served
Under 3	11,622	3,166	32	1%
Age 3	3,945	968	238	25%
Age 4	4,028	1,081	476	44%
Age 3-4	7,973	2,049	714	35%

Source: *Head Start: Background and Funding*, Congressional Research Service, Washington, DC, 1999

In 1994-1995, 33 state coordinators estimated that about 275,000 homeless children and youth were served through McKinney programs. That year, the average attendance rate for homeless students in grades one through 12 was 86 percent, a significant increase since 1987, when the Child Welfare League reported that 57 percent of the nation's homeless children did not attend school.

Families who become homeless are often forced to move frequently. Because of length-of-stay restrictions in shelters, short stays with relatives and friends, and/or necessary relocation to find a job, homeless children may have a difficult time attending school regularly. Lack of transportation may also keep them from getting to school. Children who miss school frequently fall behind academically, losing the opportunity to acquire the skills needed to help them escape poverty.

Since the passage of the McKinney Act, states have been successful in removing some of the obstacles to the enrollment of homeless children and youth. Residency and school records requirements have been relaxed so that homeless children can enroll in school. However, guardianship and immunization still remain barriers to enrollment. According to the National Law Center on Poverty and Homelessness, access to special education programs and services, participation in after-school events and extracurricular activities, availability of counseling and psychological services, and access to before- and after-school care programs are still problems.

Head Start

The Head Start program, established as part of the Economic Opportunity Act of 1964 (PL 88-452), has been one of the most durable federal programs for at-risk children. Because disadvantaged children tend to be less ready for school, the Head Start program operates where it is needed most — in early childhood, infancy to 5 years. Most children enter the program at ages 3 or 4. Until recently, not many children under age 3 were served by Head Start projects. However, the Early Head Start (EHS) program was established by the 1994 reauthorization of Head Start (PL 103-252). The EHS program serves infants and toddlers, and in 1999, 7.5 percent of the total Head Start appropriation was set aside to fund this program.

Head Start is designed to help low-income children improve their social competence, learning skills, health, and nutrition. Typically, parents are heavily involved in the Head Start programs for their children, both as volunteers and as paid workers. Head Start's guidelines for eligibility state that 90 percent or more of enrolled children must come from families at or below the poverty income level ($16,700 for a family of four in 1999). Also, at least 10 percent of the openings for service are reserved for disabled children. The services provided include

- Medical (including immunizations), dental, and mental health services.

- Nutritional and social services.

- Programs for cognitive and language development.

In addition, some parents receive formal training and certification as child-care workers.

TABLE 3.10

Percentage distribution of public high school graduates according to curriculum specialization in high school: 1982, 1990, and 1994

Curriculum specialization	1982	1990	1994
Total	**100.0**	**100.0**	**100.0**
College preparatory only	8.1	25.9	32.2
Vocational concentration only	33.1	25.0	20.9
Both vocational concentration and college preparatory	0.6	2.8	4.5
Other/general	58.2	46.3	42.4

SOURCE: U.S. Department of Education, National Center for Education Statistics. (forthcoming). *Vocational Education in the United States: Toward the Year 2000*, NCES 2000-029. Washington, DC.

Source: "Students Who Prepare for College and a Vocation," *Issue Brief*, National Center for Education Statistics, Washington, DC, 1999

Head Start appropriations have increased substantially in recent years. Between 1980 and 1990, federal funding grew by 111 percent. Since 1990, Head Start appropriations have tripled, from $1.5 billion to nearly $4.7 billion in 1999.

In 1997, Head Start projects served 746,809 children, including about 35 percent of poor children ages 3 and 4 (Table 3.9). Black children (38 percent) accounted for the highest proportion of enrollees. White children comprised another 33 percent, Hispanic children made up 25 percent, 4 percent were Native Americans, and another 4 percent were Asian or Pacific Islanders. About 13 percent of the enrollees were handicapped. Over half (56 percent) of Head Start participants were from single-parent families.

VOCATIONAL EDUCATION

Secondary Vocational Education

In the past, most high schools had a two-tiered educational system — a higher standards academic curriculum and a lower standards general track or vocational curriculum. Non-academic, vocational classes were for those who did not plan to attend college. However, today's high-skill job market requires all high school graduates to have both academic knowledge and workplace skills and training. Professional careers now demand technical skills and the ability to work in teams; technical careers require the ability to diagnose and analyze problems.

Recent Legislation

The 1990 Carl D. Perkins Vocational and Applied Technology Education Act (PL 101-392) mandated the integration of academic and vocational education, emphasizing a curriculum that makes connections between knowledge development and its application in the workplace. The 1998 renewal of the Perkins Act continued this commitment.

The School-to-Work Opportunities Act of 1994 (PL 103-239) further enhanced academic and vocational integration. School-to-work experiences prepare participants for both postsecondary education and employment and result in a variety of options following graduation from high school — four-year college, two-year college, technical training, skilled entry-level work on a career path, and pursuit of lifelong learning. Eight states were awarded school-to-work implementation grants in 1994, and 19 additional states received grants in 1995. Funding increased from $100 million in 1994 to $350 million in 1996. In 1998, $175 million was appropriated for school-to-work opportunities, with $313 million estimated for 1999 and $55 million for 2000.

Student Participation in Both Vocational Education and College Preparatory Curriculum

Though the percentage of high school graduates who complete both a vocational concentration and a college preparatory curriculum is small, it has increased significantly, from 0.6 percent in 1982 to 4.5 percent in 1994 (Table 3.10). A vocational concentration is three or more credits in a single occupational program area (such as business). In 1994, 12 percent of college preparatory high school graduates also completed a vocational concentration, and 18 percent of vocational concentrators also completed a college preparatory curriculum. High school graduates with vocational concentrations that use computers most extensively, such as business and technology/communications, were the most likely to have also completed a college preparatory curriculum.

Among 1992 public high school graduates, those who completed both a vocational concentration and a college preparatory curriculum were about as likely to have enrolled in a postsecondary institution in 1994 as those who completed college preparatory only (89.9 and 93.6 percent, respectively). Their postsecondary participation rates were generally higher than students who completed a vocational concentration only (51.8 percent). (See Table 3.11.)

Vocational Education Programs Changing

According to the Office of Vocational and Adult Education, a division of the Department of Education, vocational-technical education is changing in the following ways:

- Vocational-technical education now incorporates both school-based and work-based learning.

- Business partnerships are key to successful programs.

- For most occupations, postsecondary education is essential.

- Vocational-technical education now encompasses postsecondary institutions up to and including universities.

- Vocational-technical education uses more and higher technology.

- Vocational-technical education uses cyberspace as a resource.

Influenced by the School-to-Work Opportunities Act (see above), many states have developed a system of career clusters to serve as areas of major concentration for high school students. In *Toward a New Framework of Industry Programs for Vocational Education: Emerging Trends in Curriculum and Instruction* (MRA Associates, Inc., Berkeley, California, 1998), Gary Hoachlander surveyed each state regarding its efforts to develop industry or career clusters. Of the 47 states that responded, 38 had developed a new framework of clusters. At least 35 states had clusters in agriculture, business and administrative services, health and human services, manufacturing, and telecommunications. Twenty-six of the 38 states had a retail/wholesale cluster, and 16 states had a construction cluster. No other cluster was present in more than 15 states. Some clusters were unique to one or two states; for instance, mining was a separate cluster only in Kentucky and Nevada.

Hoachlander stressed that whatever framework is used to organize the delivery of work force preparation, it should satisfy the following three criteria.

- It should address the long-term employment prospects of students, emphasizing the knowledge and skill needed for a successful lifetime of work, not merely the requirement of entry-level jobs.

- It should encourage high levels of academic proficiency and mastery of sophisticated work-based knowledge and skill, contributing to the national agenda for improving education at all levels.

- It should preserve the full range of postsecondary options for program participants, eliminating any presumption that participating in work-related curricula at the elementary and secondary levels signals a lack of interest or an inability to pursue further education in four-year colleges and universities.

TABLE 3.11

Percentage of 1992 public high school graduates enrolled in a postsecondary institution by 1994, and of those enrolled, percentage distribution according to type of first institution, by curriculum specialization in high school

Curriculum specialization	Enrolled	Of those enrolled, type of first institution			
		Public 4-year	Private, not-for-profit 4-year	Public 2-year	Other*
Total	74.3	41.0	17.5	35.5	6.1
College preparatory only	93.6	53.8	26.7	17.3	2.1
Vocational concentration only	51.8	23.7	6.5	57.0	12.8
Both vocational concentration and college preparatory	89.9	57.1	15.5	23.7	3.6
Other/general	70.3	33.5	13.0	46.1	7.4

* Includes private, not-for-profit 2-year; public vocational-technical; and private, for-profit institutions.

NOTE: Percentages may not add to 100 due to rounding.

SOURCE: U.S. Department of Education, National Center for Education Statistics. (forthcoming). *Vocational Education in the United States: Toward the Year 2000*, NCES 2000-029. Washington, DC.

Source: "Students Who Prepare for College and a Vocation," *Issue Brief*, National Center for Education Statistics, Washington, DC, 1999

In a review of the 1994 *National Assessment of Educational Progress High School Transcript Studies*, K. Levesque et al. found that 97.2 percent of all public high school students took at least one vocational course, and 90.8 percent completed at least one specific occupational course (*Vocational Education in the United States: Toward the Year 2000*, National Center of Education Statistics, Washington, DC, June draft, 1999). Among high school graduates who had taken three or more specific occupational courses, the proportion that also completed a set of core academic courses increased from 5 percent in 1982 to 33 percent in 1994. In 1994, the average high school graduate had completed four Carnegie units (credits; see Chapter IV) in vocational education courses.

Tech Prep Education

The Perkins Act and the School-to-Work Opportunities Act (see above) both emphasized Tech Prep education, a 4+2, 3+2, or a 2+2 (depending on the number of years spent in the high school program) organized sequence of study in a technical field beginning as early as the ninth grade. The sequence, begun in high school, extends through two years of postsecondary occupational education or an apprenticeship program of at least two years past high school. The program culminates in an associate degree or certificate.

The Perkins Act requires the following seven elements in Tech Prep programs.

- A joint agreement between secondary and postsecondary consortium (association) participants.

- A common core of proficiency in math, science, communication and technology.

- A specifically developed Tech Prep curriculum.

- Joint in-service training of secondary and postsecondary teachers for effective curriculum implementation.

- Training of counselors to recruit students and to ensure program completion and appropriate employment.

- Equal access of special populations to the full range of Tech Prep programs.

- Preparatory services such as recruitment, occupational assessment, and career and personal counseling.

States receive federal funds to implement Tech Prep programs. In 1995, there were 1,029 consortia, but the number increases yearly. That same year, 737,635 students were involved in Tech Prep. In addition to receiving an associate degree or certificate, students will receive technical preparation in at least one field of engineering technology; applied science; mechanical, industrial, or practical art or trade; or agriculture, health or business. Outcomes also include employment.

Postsecondary Vocational Education

In *Vocational Education: 2-Year Colleges Improve Programs, Maintain Access for Special Populations* (1995), the GAO reviewed the ways in which colleges have enhanced the quality of their vocational programs. One method was the over-

---

TABLE 3.12

Percentages of Colleges Offering Certain Characteristics of Tech-Prep Programs, 1993-94

Characteristic	Percentage
Formal 2+2 (2 years in high school and 2 years in college) arrangement with high school	79.0
Postsecondary credit given for courses completed in high school	80.4
Curriculum includes applied academic courses	78.8
Tech-prep courses integrate academic and vocational instruction	79.4
Tech-prep involves high-tech courses	73.5
Work-based component, such as apprenticeships, co-ops, and internships	59.6

Source: *Vocational Education: 2-Year Colleges Improve Programs, Maintain Access for Special Populations*, U.S. General Accounting Office, Washington, DC, 1995

TABLE 3.13

Availability of Support Services for Special Population Students

Percentage of colleges with service available

Type of service	1990-91	1993-94
Curriculum/course modification for students with disabilities	83.7	85.6
Testing/assessment	97.6	98.4
Remediation of basic academic skills	97.9	98.2
Instructional aides	85.8	89.3
Tutoring	96.8	96.0
English-as-second-language courses	66.7	67.5
Interpreter service for the hearing-impaired	74.0	81.8[a]
Reader for vision-impaired	73.2	84.0[a]
Personal care attendant	28.5	29.4
Special/modified equipment to accommodate disabilities	79.7	88.8[a]
Removal of physical barriers	93.2	96.7[a]
Transportation services for students with disabilities	38.9	39.2
Liaison with social service agencies	96.0	97.3
Day care for children of students	62.7	63.7

[a]The difference between 1990-91 and 1993-94 is statistically significant at the 0.05 level.

Source: *Vocational Education: 2-Year Colleges Improve Programs, Maintain Access for Special Populations*, U.S. General Accounting Office, Washington, DC, 1995

whelming adoption of Tech Prep programs. By the 1993-94 school year, over 95 percent of the 475 two-year colleges and institutes surveyed either had or were developing such programs. Three out of 5 colleges offered work-based programs, such as co-ops (study one semester; work the next in one's major field), internships, and apprenticeships, as part of their Tech Prep programs (Table 3.12).

Colleges have been slower in integrating academic and vocational instruction than they have in establishing tech-prep programs. Only team-teaching by academic and vocational faculty showed a significant increase from 1990-91 to 1993-94. The use of other techniques, such as incorporating occupational concepts into academic curricula, were virtually unchanged.

To help vocational students with special needs, many of the surveyed colleges offered a number of support services. (See Table 3.13.) Interpreter services for hearing-impaired students and reader services for vision-impaired students have shown significant increases. The availability of special equipment and the removal of physical barriers for students with disabilities have also improved.

CHAPTER IV

TESTING AND ACHIEVEMENT

NATIONAL TESTS — PRO AND CON

In recent years, some critics of American education have proposed establishing standard achievement testing for the nation's students. The debate rages in Congress, in state and local education agencies, and among parents. In his March 1996 address to the National Education Summit, President Bill Clinton challenged the nation's governors to raise academic standards. In his February 1997 State of the Union address, the president proposed national testing programs for fourth graders in reading and eighth graders in mathematics.

Congress authorized the independent, bipartisan National Assessment Governing Board (NAGB) to develop these voluntary national tests. The NAGB has been directed to determine

- The extent to which test items chosen for use on the tests are free from racial, cultural, or gender bias.

- Whether the test development process and test items adequately assess student reading and mathematics comprehension and achievement.

- Whether the test development process and test items take into account the needs of disabled, disadvantaged, and limited English proficient students.

Approximately 4,800 students from grade 4 and 4,800 students from grade 8 will participate in this study.

Who Favors National Testing?

Many congressional Democrats support the tests, claiming they will help states and local communities measure and raise their academic standards. In general, many parents favor the testing program, believing that it will improve their children's scholastic achievement and give parents better information about how well their children are doing. (See Table 4.1.)

TABLE 4.1

President Clinton has proposed that the performance of the nation's public schools be assessed according to how well students score on achievement tests at two different grade levels. In general, do you favor or oppose this proposal?

	National Totals %	No Children In School %	Public School Parents %	Nonpublic School Parents %
Favor	57	56	59	53
Oppose	37	37	37	42
Don't know	6	7	4	5

Source: "The 29th Annual Phi Delta Kappa/Gallup Poll of The Public's Attitudes Toward The Public Schools," *Phi Delta Kappan*, September 1997

TABLE 4.2

President Clinton has proposed that the performance of the nation's public schools be assessed according to how well students score on achievement tests at two different grade levels. In general, do you favor or oppose this proposal?

	Teachers %	Public %
Favor	22	57
Oppose	69	37
No opinion	9	6

Source: "The Fourth Annual Phi Delta Kappa Poll of Teachers' Attitudes Toward the Public Schools," *Phi Delta Kappan*, November 1997

TABLE 4.3

Average number of Carnegie units earned by public high school graduates in various subject fields, by student characteristics: 1994

Student characteristics	Total	English	History/social studies	Mathematics			Science					Foreign languages	Arts	Vocational education [1]	Personal use [2]	Computer science [3]
				Total	Less than algebra	Algebra or higher	Total	General science	Biology	Chemistry	Physics					
1	2	3	4	5	6	7	8	9	10	11	12	13	14	15	16	17
1994 graduates	**24.16**	**4.20**	**3.57**	**3.37**	**0.85**	**2.53**	**3.04**	**0.87**	**1.26**	**0.62**	**0.28**	**1.76**	**1.66**	**3.87**	**2.92**	**0.65**
Male	23.98	4.16	3.54	3.36	0.93	2.44	3.02	0.90	1.20	0.60	0.32	1.54	1.43	4.07	3.18	0.65
Female	24.33	4.23	3.61	3.38	0.77	2.62	3.05	0.85	1.31	0.65	0.25	1.97	1.87	3.69	2.68	0.65
Race/ethnicity																
White	24.31	4.19	3.58	3.39	0.78	2.62	3.12	0.88	1.29	0.66	0.30	1.75	1.74	3.87	2.87	0.64
Black	23.60	4.31	3.54	3.26	1.15	2.12	2.80	0.91	1.21	0.50	0.18	1.37	1.36	4.24	3.00	0.65
Hispanic	24.07	4.22	3.49	3.39	1.09	2.30	2.69	0.83	1.19	0.50	0.18	2.10	1.51	3.70	3.36	0.76
Asian	24.50	4.04	3.68	3.76	0.81	2.95	3.35	0.79	1.22	0.82	0.52	2.62	1.31	2.88	2.92	0.73
American Indian	24.25	4.22	3.79	3.15	1.05	2.10	2.82	0.92	1.29	0.46	0.14	1.26	1.96	4.06	3.19	0.74
Academic track																
Academic [4]	24.30	4.30	3.75	3.62	0.69	2.93	3.33	0.84	1.34	0.78	0.37	2.11	1.88	2.56	2.89	0.61
Vocational [5]	22.77	3.67	2.77	2.19	1.38	0.81	1.87	0.87	0.91	0.06	0.02	0.54	0.97	8.33	2.97	0.65
Both [6]	24.95	4.22	3.50	3.27	1.07	2.20	2.80	1.00	1.20	0.45	0.16	1.16	1.08	6.49	2.67	0.84
Neither [7]	21.52	3.53	2.84	2.35	1.26	1.09	1.92	0.79	0.93	0.15	0.05	1.23	1.89	4.54	4.18	0.45

[1] Includes nonoccupational vocational education, vocational general introduction, agriculture, business, marketing, health, occupational home economics, trade and industry, and technical courses.

[2] Includes personal and social courses, religion and theology, and courses not included in the other subject fields.

[3] Computer courses are included in mathematics and vocational categories.

[4] Includes students who complete at least 12 Carnegie units in academic courses, but less than 3 Carnegie units in any specific labor market preparation field.

[5] Includes students who complete at least 3 Carnegie units in a specific labor market preparation field, but less than 12 Carnegie units in academic courses.

[6] Includes students who complete at least 12 Carnegie units in academic courses and at least 3 Carnegie units in a specific labor market preparation field.

[7] Includes students who complete less than 12 Carnegie units in academic courses and less than 3 Carnegie units in a specific labor market preparation field.

NOTE.—The Carnegie unit is a standard of measurement that represents one credit for the completion of a 1-year course.

SOURCE: U.S. Department of Education, National Center for Education Statistics, "High School and Beyond," First Followup survey; "1990 High School Transcript Study," "National Education Longitudinal Study of 1988," Second Followup survey, and the "1994 High School Transcript Study." (This table was prepared June 1997.)

Source: *Digest of Education Statistics 1998*, National Center for Education Statistics, Washington, DC, 1999

Who Opposes National Testing?

Opposition to the president's testing proposal has been growing among both Republicans and Democrats. Many conservatives in Congress think the testing program intrudes on the rights of states and local communities to direct their own educational programs. Others fear that the testing program is the first step in establishing a national curriculum. On the other hand, some liberal Democrats claim that the tests would be unfair to poor or minority schools, which would likely perform poorly on the tests and thus bear the stigma of failure.

Educators generally oppose national testing. (See Table 4.2.) Some fear that schools with already high academic standards may actually find that the testing program will reduce their standards to a lower national level. Many classroom teachers feel that their students are already overwhelmed with standardized testing. Others believe that designing and implementing fair, comprehensive tests is impossible without a national curriculum, which they generally oppose.

CARNEGIE UNITS*

In response to the recommendations of the National Education Goals Panel (see Chapter V), many state legislatures, local school boards, and departments of education have attempted to strengthen high school graduation requirements. While state-mandated standards cannot necessarily measure activities in the classroom, they tend to indicate a state's desire to improve its schools.

The District of Columbia and most states have established minimum Carnegie units required for high school graduation. By 1998, 32 states and the District of Columbia required 20 or more Carnegie units for graduation. The majority of units were in English, mathematics, sciences, social studies, computer science, and foreign languages. Table 4.3

---

* A Carnegie unit is a standardized measurement that represents one credit for the completion of a one-year high school course.

47

shows the average Carnegie units earned by high school graduates in 1994.

NATIONAL ASSESSMENT OF EDUCATIONAL PROGRESS

Created in 1969, the federally funded National Assessment of Educational Progress (NAEP) is the only regularly conducted national survey of educational achievement at the elementary, middle, and high school levels. The NAEP is authorized by Congress and administered by the National Center for Education Statistics (NCES). The National Assessment Governing Board (NAGP) determines which subjects will be assessed and how they will be assessed.

Designed as a measure of the nation's educational system, the NAEP is a series of reading, writing, mathematics, science, history, civics, and geography tests. The tests are given periodically to randomly selected samples of youth ages 9, 13, and 17 attending both public and private schools. Student performance in all grade levels is measured on a proficiency scale of 0 to 500. This allows a comparison of younger students with older ones, as well as an assessment of progress from year to year.

Beginning with the 1990 assessments, the NAGB also developed achievement levels for each subject at each grade level in an effort to measure

TABLE 4.4

Achievement Level Policy Definitions	
Basic:	Partial mastery of prerequisite knowledge and skills that are fundamental for proficient work at each grade.
Proficient:	Solid academic performance for each grade assessed. Students reaching this level have demonstrated competency over challenging subject matter, including subject-matter knowledge, application of such knowledge to real-world situations, and analytical skills appropriate to the subject matter.
Advanced:	Superior performance.

Source: *The Nation's Report Card — Focus on Mathematics*, National Center for Education Statistics, Washington, DC, 1999

TABLE 4.5

Levels of Reading Performance

Level 350:

Learn from Specialized Reading Materials

Readers at this level can extend and restructure the ideas presented in specialized and complex texts. Examples include scientific materials, literary essays, and historical documents. Readers are also able to understand the links between ideas, even when those links are not explicitly stated, and to make appropriate generalizations. Performance at this level suggests the ability to synthesize and learn from specialized reading materials.

Level 300:

Understand Complicated Information

Readers at this level can understand complicated literary and informational passages, including material about topics they study at school. They can also analyze and integrate less familiar material about topics they study at school as well as provide reactions to and explanations of the text as a whole. Performance at this level suggests the ability to find, understand, summarize, and explain relatively complicated information.

Level 250:

Interrelate Ideas and Make Generalizations

Readers at this level use intermediate skills and strategies to search for, locate, and organize the information they find in relatively lengthy passages and can recognize paraphrases of what they have read. They can also make inferences and reach generalizations about main ideas and author's purpose from passages dealing with literature, science, and social studies. Performance at this level suggests the ability to search for specific information, interrelate ideas, and make generalizations.

Level 200:

Partially Developed Skills and Understanding

Readers at this level can locate and identify facts from simple informational paragraphs, stories, and news articles. In addition, they can combine ideas and make inferences based on short, uncomplicated passages. Performance at this level suggests the ability to understand specific or sequentially related information.

Level 150:

Simple, Discrete Reading Tasks

Readers at this level can follow brief written directions. They can also select words, phrases, or sentences to describe a simple picture and can interpret simple written clues to identify a common object. Performance at this level suggests the ability to carry out simple, discrete reading tasks.

Source: J. R. Campbell et al., *NAEP 1996 Trends in Academic Progress*, National Center for Education Statistics, Washington, DC, 1997

the match between students' actual achievement and their desired achievement. A panel of teachers, education specialists, and other members of the general public categorized these levels into Basic, Proficient, and Advanced (Table 4.4). Achievement levels provide another way to report assessment results, allowing comparisons between percentages of students who achieve a level on one assessment with the percentage who achieve that level the next time that subject is assessed. They are also used to make comparisons between states and the nation. By federal law, the NAEP does not produce scores for individual students.

Reading Performance

The ability to read is fundamental to virtually all aspects of the education process. If students cannot read well, they usually cannot succeed in other subject areas. Eventually, they may have additional problems in a society that requires increasingly sophisticated job skills. The NAEP assesses reading proficiency on five levels, ranging from simple, discrete (separate) reading tasks to learning from specialized reading materials (Table 4.5). Performance is also described in terms of the percentage of students attaining the three achievement levels — Basic, Proficient, and Advanced.

In 1998, average reading scores increased for students in all three grade levels. For fourth- and twelfth-grade students, the national average scores were higher in 1998 than in 1994. For eighth-grade students, the national average score was higher than both 1994 and 1992. (See Figure 4.1.) Seven percent of fourth graders, 3 percent of eighth graders, and 6 percent of twelfth graders performed at the highest achievement level (Advanced). About one-third of fourth-, eighth-, and twelfth-grade students (31, 33, and 40 percent, respectively) performed at the Proficient level, while two-thirds to three-fourths (62 percent, 74 percent, and 77 percent) performed at the Basic level.

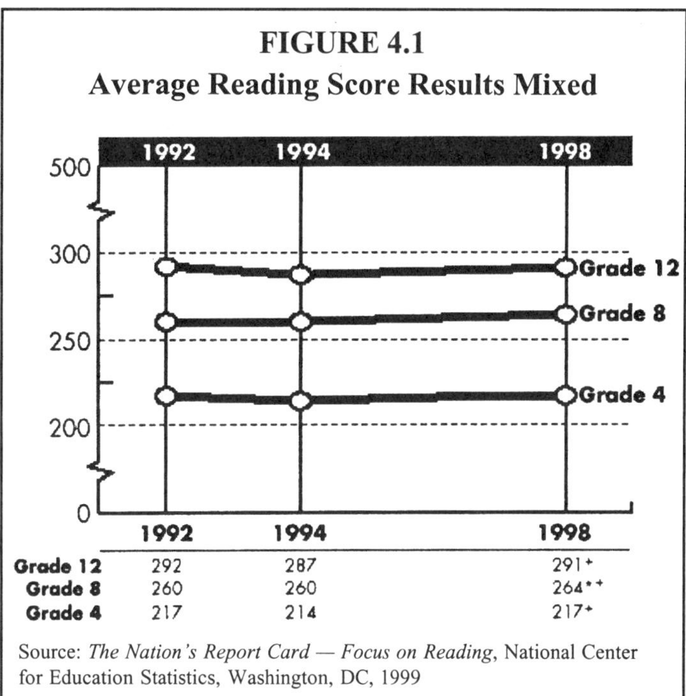

Source: *The Nation's Report Card — Focus on Reading*, National Center for Education Statistics, Washington, DC, 1999

Average Reading Proficiency Scores by Region and Type of School

Fourth and eighth graders in the Northeast and Central regions attained higher average scores than those in the Southeast and West. Twelfth graders in the Southeast had lower average reading scores than those in the other three regions.

At all three grade levels, public school students tended to have lower scores than nonpublic school students. In 1998, the scores for nonpublic school students were not significantly different from scores in 1994 and 1992. The average score of eighth-grade public school students was higher than in 1994 and 1992; for twelfth graders, the average score was higher than in 1994.

Average Reading Proficiency Scores by Race and Gender

For all three grade levels in 1998, the average reading scores for White and Asian/Pacific Islander students were higher than for Black, Hispanic, and American Indian students. Among fourth-grade students, the only significant increase among racial/ethnic groups was for Black students, whose

FIGURE 4.2
Reading Scale Scores by Race/Ethnicity

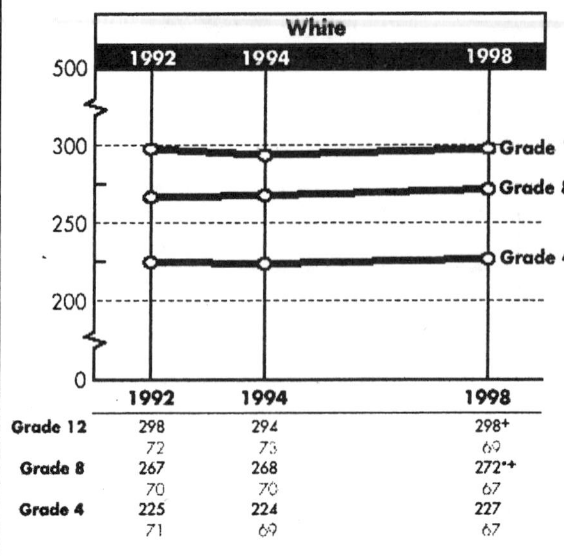

	1992	1994	1998
Grade 12	298	294	298+
	72	73	69
Grade 8	267	268	272*+
	70	70	67
Grade 4	225	224	227
	71	69	67

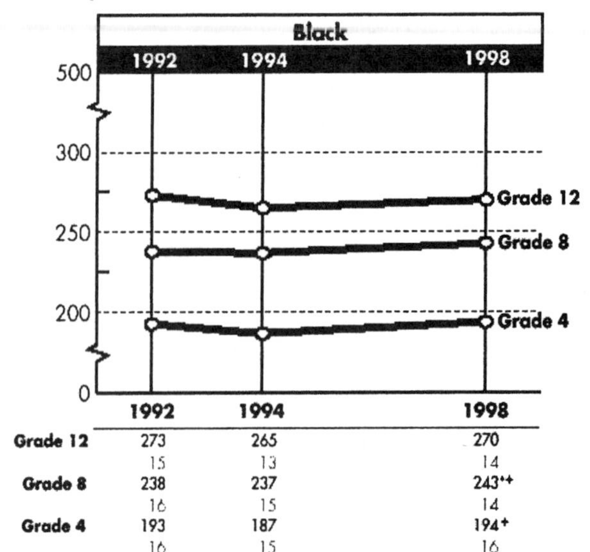

	1992	1994	1998
Grade 12	273	265	270
	15	13	14
Grade 8	238	237	243*+
	16	15	14
Grade 4	193	187	194+
	16	15	16

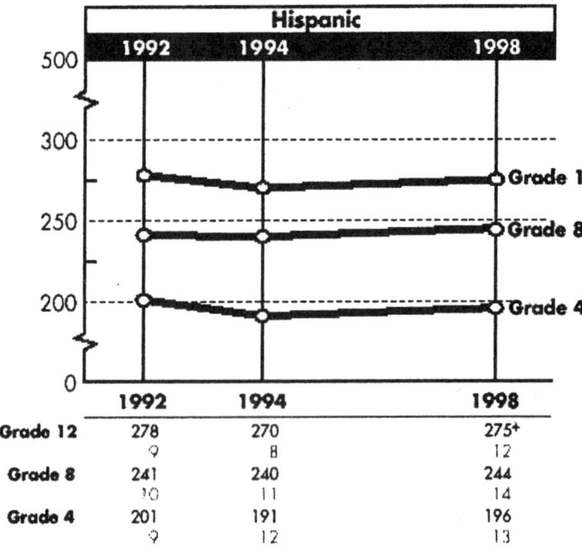

	1992	1994	1998
Grade 12	278	270	275+
	9	8	12
Grade 8	241	240	244
	10	11	14
Grade 4	201	191	196
	9	12	13

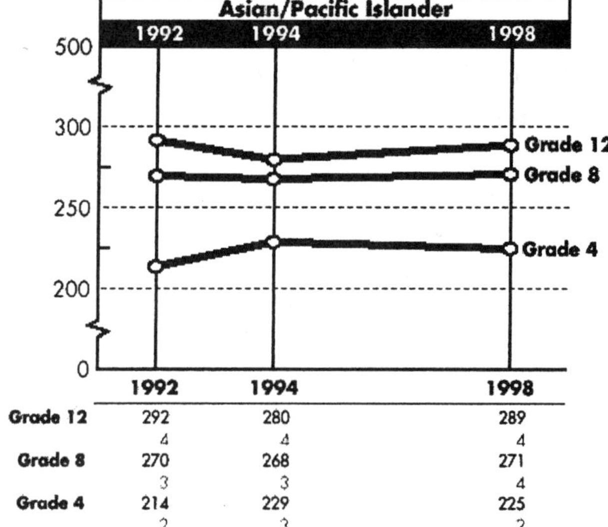

	1992	1994	1998
Grade 12	292	280	289
	4	4	4
Grade 8	270	268	271
	3	3	4
Grade 4	214	229	225
	2	3	2

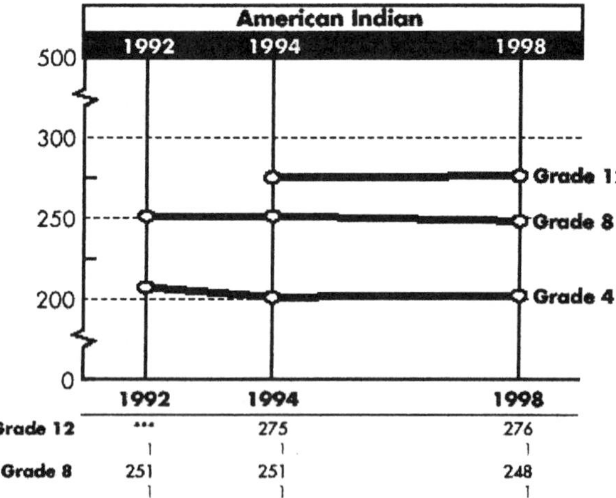

	1992	1994	1998
Grade 12	***	275	276
	1	1	1
Grade 8	251	251	248
	1	1	1
Grade 4	207	201	202
	2	2	2

* Indicates that the average scale score in 1998 is significantly different from that in 1992.

\+ Indicates that the average scale score in 1998 is significantly different from that in 1994.

Source: *The Nation's Report Card — Focus on Reading*, National Center for Education Statistics, Washington, DC, 1999

***Sample size is insufficient to permit a reliable estimate.

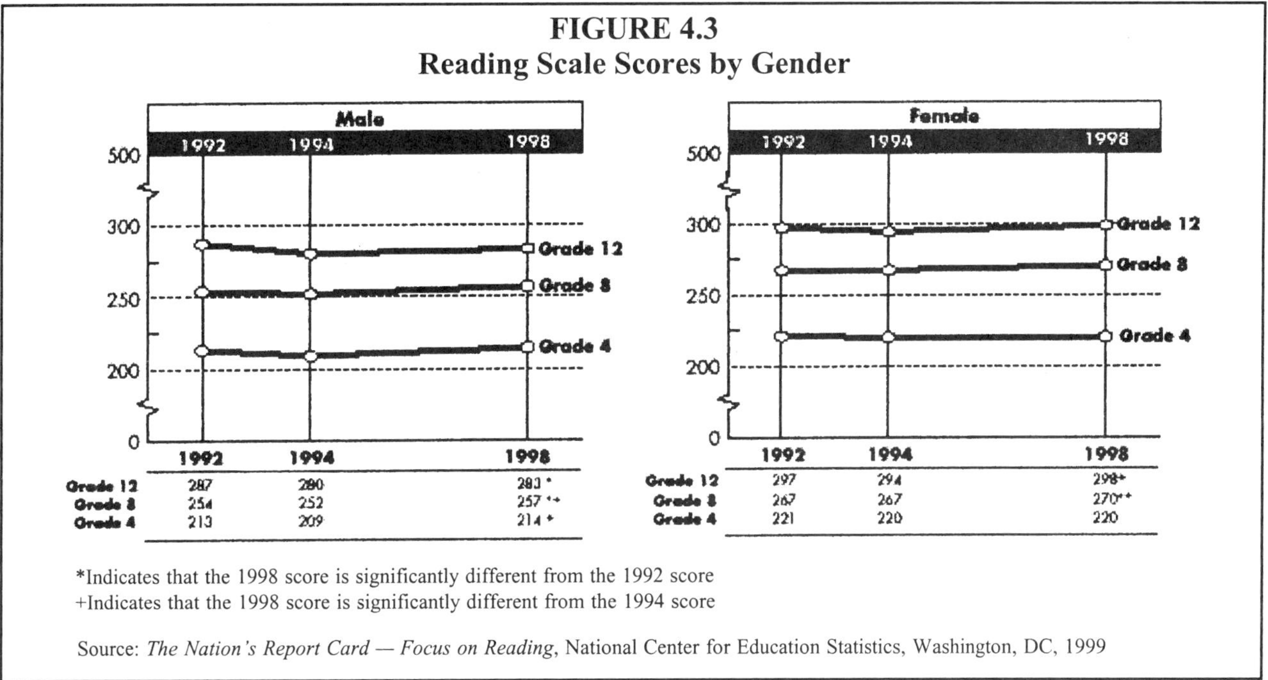

*Indicates that the 1998 score is significantly different from the 1992 score
+Indicates that the 1998 score is significantly different from the 1994 score

Source: *The Nation's Report Card — Focus on Reading*, National Center for Education Statistics, Washington, DC, 1999

average reading score increased 4 percent between 1994 and 1998. At the eighth-grade level, both White and Black students increased their average scores from 1992 to 1994 and again in 1998. Twelfth-grade White and Hispanic students raised their average reading scores between 1994 and 1998. (See Figure 4.2.)

Female students consistently scored higher reading proficiency averages than male students (Figure 4.3). Between 1994 and 1998, male fourth-grade students increased their average reading scores; female fourth graders showed no change. In grade 8, both male and female students had higher scores than in 1994 and in 1992. Female twelfth graders raised their reading scores between 1994 and 1998, while male twelfth graders made no significant change.

Mathematics Performance

Since 1978, the NAEP has assessed the mathematics performance of 9-, 13-, and 17-year-olds on five levels of achievement. Table 4.6 describes each level, from simple arithmetic facts to multistep problem solving and algebra.

Results from the 1996 NAEP assessment, the most recent math assessment, indicate that math-

ematics performance has improved nationally since 1978. In 1996, 99 percent of 9-year-olds had mastered simple arithmetic facts, compared to 97 percent in 1978. All 17-year-olds had mastered simple arithmetic facts and beginning skills and understanding (100 percent), while 97 percent of them could handle numerical operations and beginning problem solving, up from 92 percent in 1978.

Average math scores were higher in 1996 than in 1992 for all three grades and higher in 1992 than in 1990. In 1996, the average score for fourth graders was 224, a 5 percent increase from 1990. Both eighth and twelfth graders increased their math scores by 3 percent over the same period, to 272 and 304, respectively. (See Table 4.7.)

Average Mathematics Proficiency Scores by Region and Type of School

Fourth-grade students in the Northeast (236) averaged higher scores than their peers in other regions, while eighth- and twelfth-grade students (280 and 314, respectively) in the Central region scored higher averages. Students in all regions (except 17-year-olds in the Northeast) showed improvement and averaged at or above their 1973 and 1978 scores.

Public school students at all age levels tended to have somewhat lower scores than nonpublic school students. In 1996, twelfth-grade students in public schools scored an average of 303, compared to 315 for their private school peers. The scores of eighth graders were 271 and 284, respectively, and the scores of fourth graders were 222 and 237. (See Table 4.7.)

Average Mathematics Proficiency Scores by Race and Gender

Students of all races and ethnicity improved their average mathematics scores in the 1996 NAEP, compared to their scores in 1973 and 1978. Over the years, White and Asian/Pacific Islander students have consistently averaged higher mathematics scores than Black and Hispanic students. The scores of Black and Hispanic students, however, have increased significantly since 1973. For example, the average scores of Black 13-year-olds increased 10.5 percent between 1973 and 1996, and the average scores of Hispanic 13-year-olds rose 7 percent. Over the same period, the average scores for White 13-year-olds increased less than 3 percent. The gaps in scores between Black or Hispanic and White students remained similar between 1990 and 1996 (Table 4.7).

In 1990 and 1992, math scores for males and females were similar in the fourth and eighth grades; however, in the twelfth grade, males outscored females. In 1996, males outscored females in the fourth grade, while scores for the eighth and twelfth grades were the same or similar. (See Table 4.7.) The next NAEP math and science assessments are scheduled for the year 2000.

TABLE 4.6

Levels of Mathematics Performance

Level 350:

Multistep Problem Solving and Algebra

Students at this level can apply a range of reasoning skills to solve multistep problems. They can solve routine problems involving fractions and percents, recognize properties of basic geometric figures, and work with exponents and square roots. They can solve a variety of two-step problems using variables, identify equivalent algebraic expressions, and solve linear equations and inequalities. They are developing an understanding of functions and coordinate systems.

Level 300:

Moderately Complex Procedures and Reasoning

Students at this level are developing an understanding of number systems. They can compute with decimals, simple fractions, and commonly encountered percents. They can identify geometric figures, measure lengths and angles, and calculate areas of rectangles. These students are also able to interpret simple inequalities, evaluate formulas, and solve simple linear equations. They can find averages, make decisions based on information drawn from graphs, and use logical reasoning to solve problems. They are developing the skills to operate with signed numbers, exponents, and square roots.

Level 250:

Numerical Operations and Beginning Problem Solving

Students at this level have an initial understanding of the four basic operations. They are able to apply whole number addition and subtraction skills to one-step word problems and money situations. In multiplication, they can find the product of a two-digit and a one-digit number. They can also compare information from graphs and charts, and are developing an ability to analyze simple logical relations.

Level 200:

Beginning Skills and Understandings

Students at this level have considerable understanding of two-digit numbers. They can add two-digit numbers but are still developing an ability to regroup in subtraction. They know some basic multiplication and division facts, recognize relations among coins, can read information from charts and graphs, and use simple measurement instruments. They are developing some reasoning skills.

Level 150:

Simple Arithmetic Facts

Students at this level know some basic addition and subtraction facts, and most can add two-digit numbers without regrouping. They recognize simple situations in which addition and subtraction apply. They also are developing rudimentary classification skills.

Source: J. R. Campbell et al., *NAEP 1996 Trends in Academic Progress*, National Center for Education Statistics, Washington, DC, 1997

Science Performance

From 1977 to 1996, the NAEP has assessed the science performances of students ages 9, 13, and 17 on five levels of achievement. Table 4.8 describes each level, from "knows everyday science facts" to "integrates specialized scientific information." In general, the 1996 NAEP assessment indicated that science performance has improved slightly since 1977. Almost all students knew everyday science facts, and a large majority of all students understood simple scientific principals.

Average Science Proficiency Scores by Region and Type of School

Fourth-grade students in the Northeast averaged higher science scores than their peers in the other regions, while eighth- and twelfth-grade students scored higher averages in the Central region. Gains and losses in all regions were mixed. After declining in the 1970s and early 1980s, by 1996,

they had generally returned to their 1970 levels, except for older students in the Northeast.

As in reading and mathematics, public school students tended to score slightly lower averages than nonpublic school students did. For public school twelfth graders, the average was 295, compared to 303 for nonpublic school students. Public school eighth graders averaged 255, compared to 268 for nonpublic school students. Public school fourth graders averaged 229, compared to a 238 average for nonpublic school students.

Average Science Proficiency Scores by Race and Gender

White students have consistently performed well above Blacks and Hispanics in science. For Black, Hispanic, and White 17-year-olds, average science scores in 1996 were not significantly different from those of 1970 (1977 for Hispanic students). After declining during the 1970s, scores began to recover in the 1980s. White 9- and 13-year-olds scored slightly higher than the 1970 levels after declining in the 1970s. The scores of Black and Hispanic 9- and 13-year-olds, despite some fluctuations, rose between 1970 (1977 for Hispanics) and 1996. (See Table 4.9.)

Among both male and female 17-year-olds, average science scores declined between 1970 and 1982. Their average scores in 1996, while increasing slightly since 1982, were still below the 1970 averages. For 9- and 13-year-olds, scores showed a similar decline, although not as steep, between 1970 and 1982; however, their scores in 1996 had recovered to or above the 1970 levels. Male students at all age levels achieved higher average science proficiency scores than did female students. (See Table 4.10.)

Writing Performance

In 1998, NAEP administered a writing assessment to students at grades 4, 8, and 12, measuring performance on three types of writing: narrative, informative, and persuasive. Responses were evaluated using scoring guides developed for each grade level and purpose of writing. Student performance was reported in two ways: scale scores and achievement levels.

When the 1998 results were released, Gary W. Phillips, Acting Commissioner for the National Center for Education Statistics, said, "The average, or typical, American student is not a proficient writer. Instead, students show only partial mastery of the knowledge and skills needed for solid academic performance in writing." Only about one-fourth or less of the students in each grade level assessed performed at the "Proficient" level, and only 1 percent performed at the "Advanced" level (Figure 4.4).

Writing Performance by Race and Gender

Writing scores at each grade level range from 0 to 300, with a national average of 150. Fourth-grade Asian/Pacific Islander students had higher average writing scores than White students; White

---

TABLE 4.8

Levels of Science Performance

Level 350:

Integrates Specialized Scientific Information

Students at this level can infer relationships and draw conclusions using detailed scientific knowledge from the physical sciences, particularly chemistry. They also can apply basic principles of genetics and interpret the social implications of research in this field.

Level 300:

Analyzes Scientific Procedures and Data

Students at this level can evaluate the appropriateness of the design of an experiment. They have more detailed scientific knowledge and the skill to apply their knowledge in interpreting information from text and graphs. These students also exhibit a growing understanding of principles from the physical sciences.

Level 250:

Applies General Scientific Information

Students at this level can interpret data from simple tables and make inferences about the outcomes of experimental procedures. They exhibit knowledge and understanding of the life sciences, including a familiarity with some aspects of animal behavior and of ecological relationships. These students also demonstrate some knowledge of basic information from the physical sciences.

Level 200:

Understands Simple Scientific Principles

Students at this level are developing some understanding of simple scientific principles, particularly in the life sciences. For example, they exhibit some rudimentary knowledge of the structure and function of plants and animals.

Level 150:

Knows Everyday Science Facts

Students at this level know some general scientific facts of the type that could be learned from everyday experiences. They can read simple graphs, match the distinguishing characteristics of animals, and predict the operation of familiar apparatuses that work according to mechanical principles.

Source: J. R. Campbell et al., *NAEP 1996 Trends in Academic Progress*, National Center for Education Statistics, Washington, DC, 1997

TABLE 4.9

Average science performance (scale score), by race–ethnicity and age: 1970–96

	White			Black			Hispanic		
Year	Age 9	Age 13	Age 17	Age 9	Age 13	Age 17	Age 9	Age 13	Age 17
1970	236	263	312	179	215	258	—	—	—
1973	231	259	304	177	205	250	—	—	—
1977	230	256	298	175	208	240	192	213	262
1982	229	257	293	187	217	235	189	226	249
1986	232	259	298	196	222	253	199	226	259
1990	238	264	301	196	226	253	206	232	262
1992	239	267	304	200	224	256	205	238	270
1994	240	267	306	201	224	257	201	232	261
1996	239	266	307	202	226	260	207	232	269

— Not available.

NOTE: The science performance scale has a range from 0 to 500. See supplemental table 1-1 for detailed explanations of levels.

SOURCE: U.S. Department of Education, National Center for Education Statistics, National Assessment of Educational Progress, *NAEP 1996 Trends in Academic Progress*, revised 1998.

TABLE 4.10

Average science performance (scale score), by sex and age: 1970–96

	Total			Male			Female		
Year	Age 9	Age 13	Age 17	Age 9	Age 13	Age 17	Age 9	Age 13	Age 17
1970	225	255	305	228	257	314	223	253	297
1973	220	250	296	223	252	304	218	247	288
1977	220	247	290	222	251	297	218	244	282
1982	221	250	283	221	256	292	221	245	275
1986	224	251	289	227	256	295	221	247	282
1990	229	255	290	230	259	296	227	252	285
1992	231	258	294	235	260	299	227	256	289
1994	231	257	294	232	259	300	230	254	289
1996	230	256	296	232	261	300	228	252	292

Source of both tables: *The Condition of Education 1999*, National Center for Education Statistics, Washington, DC, 1999

fourth graders had higher scores than Black, Hispanic, and American Indian students. At grades 8 and 12, Asian/Pacific Islander and White students had higher scores than Black, Hispanic, and American Indian students. (See Table 4.11.) Around 10 percent of Black, Hispanic, and American Indian students reached or exceeded the "Proficient" level, compared to between one-fourth and one-third of White students and Asian/Pacific Islander students.

At all three grade levels, females had higher average writing scores than males (Table 4.12). Across the three grades, between 29 and 36 percent of female students were at or above the "Proficient" level, while between 14 and 17 percent of male students attained this level.

Planning Before Writing

A key factor in better writing performance was planning what to write before starting to write. A brochure that discussed how to plan for and how to revise writing was given to each student participating in the 1998 writing assessment. Space for planning was provided in the students' test booklets. Those students who gave visible evidence of planning for one or two tasks on the assessment outscored other students who did not plan.

Nearly half (47 percent) of fourth graders and two-thirds of eighth graders (66 percent) and twelfth graders (67 percent) planned their written response for at least one of the two tasks in the test

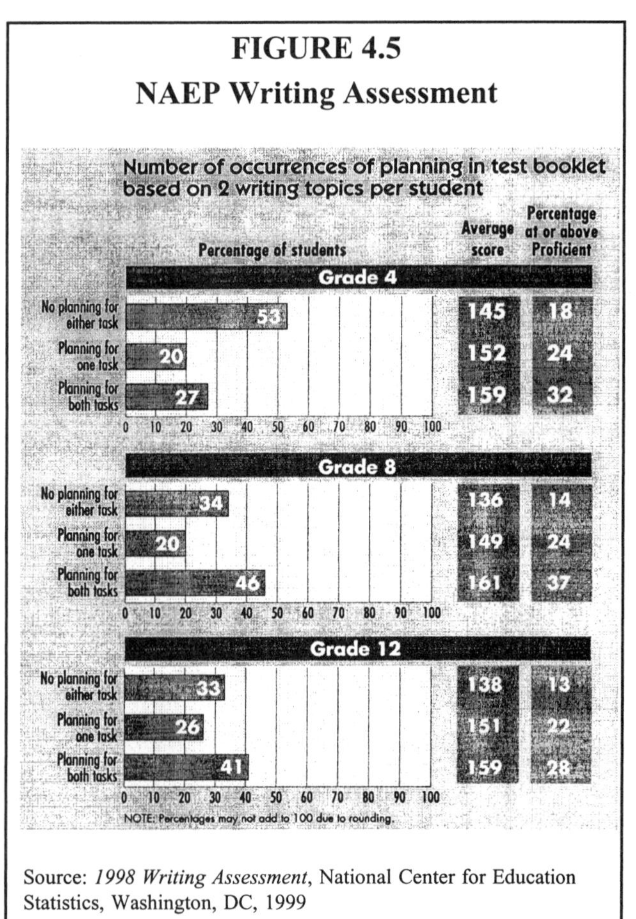

TABLE 4.11 Average Writing Scores by Race/Ethnicity	
Grade 4	
White	157
Black	131
Hispanic	134
Asian/Pacific Islander	164
American Indian	138
Grade 8	
White	158
Black	131
Hispanic	131
Asian/Pacific Islander	159
American Indian	132
Grade 12	
White	156
Black	134
Hispanic	135
Asian/Pacific Islander	152
American Indian	129

TABLE 4.12 Average Writing Scores by Gender	
Grade 4	
Male	142
Female	158
Grade 8	
Male	140
Female	160
Grade 12	
Male	140
Female	159

Source of figure and tables: *1998 Writing Assessment*, National Center for Education Statistics, Washington, DC, 1999

booklet. Students who planned their responses to both tasks had higher average scores than those who planned for only one task. Students who did not plan for either task had the lowest average scores. (See Figure 4.5.)

three grades, scores were higher among nonpublic school students than among public school students. Scores tended to increase with parents' level of education.

NAEP Assessment of Civics

In 1998, NAEP conducted an assessment of civics for fourth-, eighth-, and twelfth-grade students. It was based on a newly developed civics framework with the goal of measuring how well American youth are being prepared to meet their citizenship responsibilities. The assessment included both multiple-choice and essay items, which even critics agreed were not easy.

About two-thirds of the students at each grade performed at or above the "Basic" level, and about one-fourth performed at or above the "Proficient" level. Between 30 and 35 percent of the students performed below the Basic level.

In general, eighth- and twelfth-grade girls scored higher than boys in civics. White and Asian/Pacific Islander students outscored American Indian, Black, and Hispanic students. Students in the Northeast and Central regions generally scored higher than those in the Southeast and West. At all

Source: *1998 Writing Assessment*, National Center for Education Statistics, Washington, DC, 1999

Student Performance in Mathematics and Science

The Third International Mathematics and Science Study (TIMSS), completed in 1995, compared the mathematics and science skills of a half-million fourth-, eighth-, and twelfth-grade students in countries around the world. This comparison with students in other countries allows for the monitoring of progress toward the National Education Goal of being first in the world in mathematics and science achievement (see Chapter V).

The 21-nation mathematics and science averages of students in their last year of secondary school were 500 each. U.S. twelfth graders scored considerably below both averages. In mathematics, U.S. students scored lower than students in 14 countries, outperforming students in only two countries. Among the 21 TIMSS nations, U.S. students' mathematics scores were not significantly different from those in Italy, the Russian Federation, Lithuania, and the Czech Republic. In science, U.S. twelfth graders scored below students in their final year of secondary school in 11 countries and scored higher than students in two countries. Their science scores were not significantly different from those of seven countries, including France, Germany, Italy, and the Russian Federation. (See Table 4.13.)

The United States was one of three countries that did not have a significant gender gap in mathematics. In all but one of the TIMSS nations, there was a gender gap in science; however, the U.S. gender gap was one of the smallest.

U.S. student performance has improved in both mathematics and science, as evidenced by scores on the NAEP. However, other nations have also been improving. Therefore, the nation's relative international standing has not improved in spite of

TABLE 4.13

Average mathematics and science performance scores of students in the final year of secondary school, by sex and country: 1995

Country	Mathematics			Science		
	Overall	Male	Female	Overall	Male	Female
International average	**500**	**518**	**485**	**500**	**521**	**482**
Netherlands*	560	585	533	558	582	532
Sweden	552	573	531	559	585	534
Denmark*	547	575	523	509	532	490
Switzerland	540	555	522	523	540	500
Iceland*	534	558	514	549	572	530
Norway*	528	555	501	544	574	513
France*	523	544	506	487	508	468
Australia*	522	540	510	527	547	513
New Zealand	522	536	507	529	543	515
Canada*	519	537	504	532	550	518
Austria*	518	545	503	520	554	501
Slovenia*	512	535	490	517	541	494
Germany*	495	509	480	497	514	478
Hungary	483	485	481	471	484	455
Italy*	476	490	464	475	495	458
Russian Federation*	471	488	460	481	510	463
Lithuania*	469	485	461	461	481	450
Czech Republic	466	488	443	487	512	460
United States*	461	466	456	480	492	469
Cyprus*	446	454	439	448	459	439
South Africa*	356	365	348	349	367	333

* Country did not satisfy one or more of the sampling or other guidelines. See the supplemental note to this indicator for detailed explanations.

NOTE: Nations are sorted from highest to lowest by average mathematics score.

SOURCE: U.S. Department of Education, National Center for Education Statistics, *Pursuing Excellence: A Study of U.S. Twelfth-Grade Mathematics and Science Achievement in International Context*, 1998.

Source: *The Condition of Education 1999*, National Center for Education Statistics, Washington, DC, 1999

TABLE 4.14

Percentage of the population in large, industrialized countries who completed secondary and higher education, by age, sex, and country: 1996

| | 25–34 years old | | | | | | 25–64 years old | |
| | Total | | Male | | Female | | Total | |
Country	Secondary education[1]	Higher education	Secondary education[1]	Higher education	Secondary education[1]	Higher education	Secondary education[1]	Higher education
Canada	84.9	20.1	82.9	19.4	86.9	20.8	76.4	17.3
France[2]	74.3	12.4	73.6	11.7	74.9	12.9	60.2	9.7
Germany	86.4	12.9	88.3	14.1	84.4	11.6	81.5	13.1
Italy	52.1	8.3	50.0	8.0	54.3	8.7	38.2	8.1
Japan[3]	90.6	22.9	89.3	34.2	91.8	11.5	69.7	13.3
United Kingdom	86.6	15.2	87.5	16.5	85.6	13.8	76.3	12.8
United States	86.9	26.5	85.9	25.9	87.9	27.1	85.7	25.8

[1] Includes individuals who have completed at least secondary education.

[2] The allocation for individual education level for France was revised in 1996. The result is a reduction in the number of people with upper secondary level qualification and an increase in the number with lower secondary level qualification.

[3] Data are for 1989.

NOTE: In the United States, completing secondary education is defined as graduating from high school or earning a GED; completing higher education is defined as earning a bachelor's degree or higher. Individuals for whom educational attainment is unknown are excluded from the analysis.

SOURCE: Organisation for Economic Co-operation and Development, INES Project, International Indicators Project.

Source: *The Condition of Education 1999*, National Center for Education Statistics, Washington, DC, 1999

the increasing achievement of students since the 1980s.

Fourth- and Eighth-Grade Student Performance

U.S. eighth graders scored above the 41-nation average in science, outperforming students in 15 countries and scoring below those in nine countries. However, eighth graders were below the international average in mathematics. Their scores were lower than eighth graders in 20 countries and higher than those in seven countries. (See Figure 4.6.)

Fourth graders in the United States scored higher than the 26-nation average in both science and mathematics. Only Korean students outperformed U.S. fourth graders in science. In mathematics, U.S. fourth-grade students scored above their peers in 12 countries and below in seven countries. (See Figure 4.6.)

The relative standing of U.S. students compared to other TIMSS countries drops from fourth to eighth to twelfth grade. Some observers believe that this is because many students are getting limited exposure to rigorous mathematics and science content in middle and high school. For instance, 90 percent of all U.S. high school students stop taking challenging math courses before getting to calculus. Unlike most other countries, where algebra and geometry are introduced before high school, only 25 percent of American students take algebra in middle school. In addition, although state requirements for challenging math and science courses has increased in the last decade, there is still a great need for improvement. Another concern is the high percentage of high school math and science teachers who lack adequate preparation in the content areas they teach (see Chapter VIII).

Educational Attainment

Among persons ages 25 to 34 in other developed countries, only Japan (90.6 percent) had graduated a higher proportion of students from secondary school than the United States had (86.9 percent) in 1996. The proportion from Germany and the United Kingdom was statistically the same as that of the United States. Only Italy and France had not graduated more than 80 percent of their population in this age group. For those achieving higher education, only the United States, Japan, and Canada had graduated more than 20 percent of their populations. (See Table 4.14.)

In Japan, males were three times more likely than females to achieve higher education, but in Canada, France, Italy, and the United States, the proportion of females and males was similar. U.S. females ages 25 to 34 were more likely to complete higher education than their female and male counterparts in other large, industrial countries (with the exception of Japanese males). (See Table 4.14.)

HIGH SCHOOL EXIT EXAMS

In recent years, school accountability has been a major issue of school reform. Many states have mandated what children should learn in each grade, developed assessments to measure student achievement, designed school report cards, rated their schools and publicly identified failing schools, assisted low-performing schools with additional funding, and even closed or taken over failing schools. Included in the various accountability measures is the high school exit examination.

Currently, 26 states are either using high school exit exams or are in the process of developing such tests. In most states, students must pass an exit test to receive a high school diploma. A few states differentiate the diplomas, according to whether the test was passed or not. Most states initially administer the exit exam in tenth or eleventh grade. This allows time for remediation or other interventions to be provided for students who fail the test the first time. All states with high school exit exams allow students to take the test multiple times.

A number of high school graduation tests have been challenged in court. Florida was one of the first to face litigation, based on the state's disproportionate failure rate among Black students. In *Debra P. v. Turlington* 644 F.2d 397 (5th Cir. 1981), the Fifth Circuit Court of Appeals affirmed the district court's ruling in favor of the students. The decision was based on the opinion that the state had not "made any effort to make certain whether the test covered material actually studied in the classrooms of the state" and that students had a "property interest" in their diplomas since they had

attended school during the required years and passed the required courses.

When the case (83-3326, 11th Cir. C. App., 1984) was reheard, the court reversed the decision, ruling that the students had, in fact, had an opportunity to learn the material covered in the exit test. The court established the following legal standards for high school exit exams:

- The test must measure knowledge and skills that are taught in the state's schools, referred to as "curricular validity."

- Students must receive adequate notice of the test, the requirements for passing the test, and the consequences of not passing the test.

- The test must not intentionally discriminate against a protected group or class (such as disadvantaged students).

Proponents of high school exit exams believe that standardized tests are the best way to ensure high standards and accountability. They maintain that tests can communicate what is expected of students and teachers and assess whether progress is being made. If tests are aligned to a rigorous curriculum, they are the best chance that low-performing students have to get the education they need and to narrow the minority achievement gap.

Those who oppose the so-called "high-stakes" tests (for instance, using the results of a single standardized exam to determine high school graduation) point out that a single test is not an accurate measure of a student's performance. Opponents claim that these tests put poor and minority students at a disadvantage. A further criticism of "high-stakes" tests is that they push teachers to "teach to" the test, taking too much time away from classroom practices that support true learning.

SCORES ON
COLLEGE ENTRANCE TESTS

Students wishing to enter most colleges and universities in the United States generally take ei-

TABLE 4.15

Mean SAT/SAT I Scores for College-Bound Seniors, 1972-1999

Year	Verbal			Math		
	Male	Female	Total	Male	Female	Total
1972	531	529	530	527	489	509
1973	523	521	523	525	489	506
1974	524	520	521	524	488	505
1975	515	509	512	518	479	498
1976	511	508	509	520	475	497
1977	509	505	507	520	474	496
1978	511	503	507	517	474	494
1979	509	501	505	516	473	493
1980	506	498	502	515	473	492
1981	508	496	502	516	473	492
1982	509	499	504	516	473	493
1983	508	498	503	516	474	494
1984	511	498	504	518	478	497
1985	514	503	509	522	480	500
1986	515	504	509	523	479	500
1987	512	502	507	523	481	501
1988	512	499	505	521	483	501
1989	510	498	504	523	482	502
1990	505	496	500	521	483	501
1991	503	495	499	520	482	500
1992	504	496	500	521	484	501
1993	504	497	500	524	484	503
1994	501	497	499	523	487	504
1995	505	502	504	525	490	506
1996	507	503	505	527	492	508
1997	507	503	505	530	494	511
1998	509	502	505	531	496	512
1999	509	502	505	531	495	511

*For 1972-1986, a formula was applied to the original mean and standard deviation to convert the mean to the recentered scale. For 1987-1995, individual student scores were converted to the recentered scale and then the mean was recomputed. For 1996-1999 most students received scores on the recentered scale. (Any score on the original scale was converted to the recentered scale prior to recomputing the mean.)

ther the Scholastic Assessment Test (SAT®) or the American College Test (ACT) as part of their admission requirements. The SAT is the primary admissions test for 22 states, mostly in the East and on the West Coast. The ACT is more popular in 28 states in the Midwest, South, and West, where a large percentage of students attend public colleges and universities. Most colleges will accept either the SAT or the ACT. In addition, some schools require three SAT II subject tests.

These two college entrance tests are standardized, three-hour tests intended as an assessment of readiness for college. The SAT measures students' mathematical and verbal reasoning abilities. The ACT is curriculum-based and tests four areas: English, math, reading comprehension, and science reasoning. Students who elect to take these tests usually plan to continue their education beyond high school; therefore, these tests do not profile all high school students.

61

Performance on the SAT is measured on a scale of 200 to 800. The mean SAT scores for 1999 were 505 for the verbal section and 511 for the mathematics section (Table 4.15). The verbal score was well below the 1972 level, while the mathematics score was about the same as 1972. (Note that the score scale was recalculated in April 1995, so the data shown in Table 4.15 may differ from earlier reports of SAT scores. Scores for earlier years in Table 4.15 have been estimated on the new scale.)

The ACT results are measured on a scale of 1 to 36. The 1999 average composite ACT score was 21, unchanged since the 1994-95 school year. (See Table 4.16, which also includes average scores for English, mathematics, reading, and science reasoning.)

More than 1.2 million college-bound seniors took the SAT in 1999, and more than 1 million students took the ACT. The number of students taking both the SAT and ACT has grown steadily, especially over the past few years. In general, the more students taking the tests, the lower the scores will be. As more students take the tests, the number of test-takers will likely include students who are less academically accomplished.

Are Scores Rising?

As shown in Table 4.15, SAT test scores dropped in the 1970s, 1980s, and early 1990s. Observers have attributed the decline in college entrance examination scores to the increase in the number of students from lower scholastic achievement levels taking the tests in recent years. While that may explain the initial drop, a major part of the decrease resulted from a decline in performance among the kinds of students who had previously done well in these tests. Although verbal scores have remained unchanged, math scores have risen

---

TABLE 4.16

Average ACT scores for total group

Reference Year	Number	English	Mathematics	Reading	Science Reasoning	Composite
1994-95	945369	20.2	20.2	21.3	21.0	20.8
1995-96	924663	20.3	20.2	21.3	21.1	20.9
1996-97	959301	20.3	20.6	21.3	21.1	21.0
1997-98	995039	20.4	20.8	21.4	21.1	21.0
1998-99	1019053	20.5	20.7	21.4	21.0	21.0

Source: *1999 ACT National and State Scores.* Copyright © The American College Testing Program. Reprinted with permission.

TABLE 4.17

Average ACT Scores and Standard Deviations for Males and Females

	English	Mathematics	Reading	Science Reasoning	Composite
Males (N=437293)					
Average	20.0	21.4	21.1	21.5	21.1
Standard Deviation	5.5	5.2	6.1	4.8	4.9
Females (N=577828)					
Average	20.9	20.2	21.6	20.6	20.9
Standard Deviation	5.5	4.7	5.9	4.2	4.6

Source: *1999 ACT National and State Scores.* Copyright © The American College Testing Program. Reprinted with permission.

TABLE 4.18

Background Information

SAT I Mean Scores and Standard Deviations for Males, Females, and Total by Ethnic Group

| | SAT I Verbal | | | | | |
| | Mean Scores | | | Standard Deviations | | |
SAT I Test Takers Who Described Themselves as:	Male	Female	Total	Male	Female	Total
American Indian or Alaskan Native	486	481	484	106	105	105
Asian, Asian American, or Pacific Islander	502	495	498	125	126	126
African American or Black	432	435	434	100	99	100
Hispanic or Latino Background:						
Mexican or Mexican American	459	448	453	102	101	102
Puerto Rican	462	450	455	105	101	103
Latin American, South American, Central American, or Other Hispanic or Latino	471	457	463	109	107	108
White	531	524	527	103	99	101
Other	515	508	511	121	118	119
No Response	493	490	492	122	123	122

| | SAT I Math | | | | | |
| | Mean Scores | | | Standard Deviations | | |
SAT I Test Takers Who Described Themselves as:	Male	Female	Total	Male	Female	Total
American Indian or Alaskan Native	499	467	481	108	102	106
Asian, Asian American, or Pacific Islander	579	541	560	122	121	123
Black or African American	434	415	422	102	95	99
Hispanic or Latino Background:						
Mexican or Mexican American	476	441	456	102	95	100
Puerto Rican	470	433	448	105	97	102
Latin American, South American, Central American, or Other Hispanic or Latino	488	446	464	109	103	107
White	548	512	528	105	100	104
Other	537	494	513	118	112	117
No Response	519	488	505	122	120	122

slightly in the mid-1990s, leading some officials to be cautiously optimistic.

Gender of Test-Takers

In 1998-99, females accounted for the majority (54 percent) of students taking the SAT. Females have historically scored lower than males on college entrance examinations. This fact led FairTest, a Cambridge, Massachusetts, organization that analyzes tests, to blame bias, claiming that "SAT bias will illegally cheat thousands of young women out of college admissions and scholarship aid they have earned by superior classroom performance."

The SAT gender gap was at the highest level (43 points) since the SAT was revised, partly to reduce "gender-related prediction differences," in 1995. The SAT has historically overpredicted male college grades and underpredicted female grades. Howard T. Everson, a College Board spokesman, commenting on the gender gap, pointed out that "for a variety of reasons, young women are socialized and steered away from more rigorous math courses and that plays itself out in scores on standardized tests."

In 1999, females' mean verbal SAT score was 502, compared to 509 for males, and females' mathematics score was 495, compared to 531 for males (Table 4.15). Among ACT-takers, females' 1999 average composite score was 20.9, compared to 21.1 for males. While females scored slightly higher scores in English and reading, males scored higher averages on mathematics and science reasoning. (See Table 4.17.) The gender gap on the ACT equates to just 8 points on the SAT scale.

Race and Ethnicity of Test-Takers

In 1998-99, White students accounted for two-thirds (67 percent) of those taking the SAT, although the proportion of minority test-takers has risen steadily from 13 percent in 1973 to 33 percent in 1999. Black students made up 11 percent; Asian-American, 9 percent; Hispanic, 8 percent; and American Indian/Alaskan Native, 1 percent. Four percent classified themselves as "other." In all racial and ethnic categories, more women than men took the test.

Despite gains over the past two decades, overall SAT scores for minorities (with the exception of Asian-American students) still lagged behind the scores of White students (Table 4.18). Many educators and critics of standardized testing have maintained for some time that the SAT is culturally biased to favor students from middle- and upper-class backgrounds. The College Board disagrees and states that every attempt is made to make the test fair for all students.

For those taking the ACT in 1999, the racial and ethnic proportions were similar to those taking the SAT. Whites (Caucasians) made up 72 per-

---

TABLE 4.19

Average Racial/Ethnic Scores by Level of Academic Preparation

	African American Average	American Indian Average	Caucasian Average	Mexican American Average	Asian American Average	Puerto Rican/ Cuban Average
Total Group	(n= 103932)	(n= 10830)	(n= 732025)	(n= 38257)	(n= 33251)	(n= 15073)
English	16.4	18.1	21.3	17.6	20.5	18.8
Usage/Mech	7.8	8.8	10.7	8.6	10.4	9.3
Rhet Skills	8.5	9.4	11.0	9.1	10.5	9.7
Mathematics	16.9	18.5	21.3	18.7	23.1	19.6
Pre/Elem-Alg	8.3	9.4	11.4	9.6	12.1	10.2
Alg/Crd-Geom	8.3	9.0	10.4	9.1	11.5	9.6
Plane Geom/Trig	8.3	9.5	10.9	9.5	11.9	10.0
Reading	17.1	19.3	22.1	18.8	21.2	19.8
Soc Stu/Sci	8.4	9.7	11.2	9.3	10.7	9.8
Arts/Literature	8.6	9.8	11.4	9.7	10.9	10.3
Sci Reasoning	17.3	19.3	21.7	18.9	21.3	19.6
Composite	17.1	18.9	21.7	18.6	21.7	19.6

Source: *1999 ACT National and State Scores*. Copyright © The American College Testing Program. Reprinted with permission.

cent of ACT test-takers and Blacks, 10 percent. Smaller proportions of Hispanics (5 percent), Asian-Americans (3 percent), and American Indians (1 percent) took the ACT. The mean composite scores of White and Asian-American students were identical (21.7 for both), followed by Hispanics (18.6 to 19.6), American Indians (18.9), and Blacks (17.1). (See Table 4.19.)

The Black-White Gap

The greatest test score gaps have been documented between Black and White students. In *The Black-White Test Score Gap* (Brookings Institute, Washington, DC, 1998), editors Christopher Jencks and Meredith Phillips point out that gaps appear before kindergarten and persist into adulthood. In general, Black students score below 70 to 80 percent of White students of the same age.

Though the Black/White SAT test score gap narrowed between 1976 and the late 1980s, the gap has since widened again. In 1998-99, Black students' average score on the SAT verbal test was 93 points lower than White students' average. On the SAT math test, the average score for Black students was 106 points less than for Whites.

Surprisingly, the test score gap is wider at higher achievement levels than at lower levels. When compared with White students of comparable socioeconomic status, the academic achievement of Black middle-class and upper-income students falls behind. On some tests, Black students from middle-class or wealthier families have scored no better than White students from low-income families have.

Educators and other observers have attempted to discover the reasons for the disparity in the test scores. Possible explanations include

- Lingering racial inferiority complexes.

- Peer pressure (not wanting to appear "White").

- Low teacher expectations.

- Curriculum.

- Parental involvement.

- Access to information.

- Vestiges of racism in schools.

- Excessive pressure to do well because they are considered to represent their race.

Some researchers point to differences in home life. A study by Harvard researcher Ronald Ferguson found that Black children watch twice as much television as White children. A national study asked students to name the lowest grades they could bring home without incurring parental anger. Blacks consistently named lower grades than other groups. Lower expectations by parents, teachers, and Black students themselves seem to be a significant factor in poorer academic performance.

CHAPTER V

NATIONAL GOALS FOR IMPROVEMENT

A CALL TO REFORM

A Nation at Risk (Washington, DC, 1983), prepared by the National Commission on Excellence in Education, proved to be a "wake-up call" to the nation on the state of its educational system. It warned of a "rising tide of mediocrity that threatens our very future as a nation and as a people." As a result, educators, lawmakers, and governors began earnest efforts to improve schools. The report recommended, among other things, a longer school year, a tougher curriculum, and stronger teacher-training programs. It specifically expressed alarm at the deterioration of academics at the secondary school level.

To improve the situation, the report recommended that no student should graduate from high school without completing

- Four years of English.

- Three years each of mathematics, science, and social studies.

- One-half year of computer science.

- For college-bound students, two years of a foreign language.

NATIONAL EDUCATION GOALS

At the first Education Summit, held in Charlottesville, Virginia, in 1989, President George Bush and the nation's state governors established six National Education Goals to be achieved by the year 2000. The National Education Goals Panel was created in 1990 to oversee and report on the progress toward these national goals. Expressing the continued concern of the nation, Congress passed the Goals 2000: Educate America Act (PL 103-227), signed on March 31, 1994, by President Bill Clinton. The Act reemphasized the National Education Goals and added two more goals. Table 5.1 lists the goals and a brief explanation for each.

MODEST GAINS AND UNEVEN PROGRESS

While the National Education Goals have been widely supported, the public's awareness of them has been relatively low (Table 5.2). Some educators have questioned the ability of schools to achieve them. The 1994 Goals 2000 Act made additional funds available to support, accelerate, and sustain state and local improvement efforts. The federal budget obligations for Goals 2000 were $91 million in 1994, $294 million in 1995, and $480 million in 1996. In 1999, the Congress appropriated $491 million for Goals 2000.

How Close Are We to Reaching the Goals?

While many schools responded to the challenge, the Goals panel reported in its 1992 report that any gains had been modest. In its November 1995 report, the panel noted that the results had been disappointing. Although the nation was halfway to the target year (2000), it was far from reaching its education goals. In its 1999 report, the panel

The National Education Goals

Goal 1: Ready to Learn

By the year 2000, all children in America will start school ready to learn.

Goal 2: School Completion

By the year 2000, the high school graduation rate will increase to at least 90 percent.

Goal 3: Student Achievement and Citizenship

By the year 2000, all students will leave grades 4, 8, and 12 having demonstrated competency over challenging subject matter including English, mathematics, science, foreign languages, civics and government, economics, arts, history, and geography, and every school in America will ensure that all students learn to use their minds well, so they may be prepared for responsible citizenship, further learning, and productive employment in our Nation's modern economy.

Goal 4: Teacher Education and Professional Development

By the year 2000, the Nation's teaching force will have access to programs for the continued improvement of their professional skills and the opportunity to acquire the knowledge and skills needed to instruct and prepare all American students for the next century.

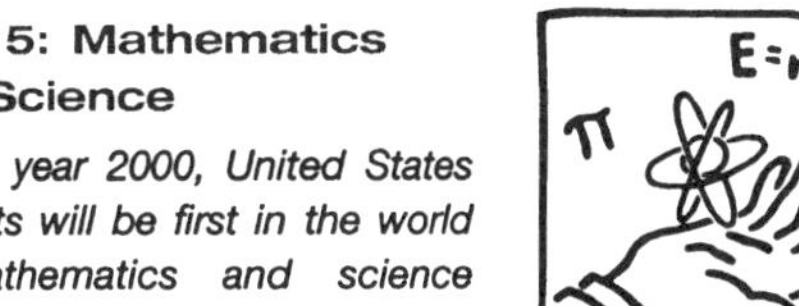

Goal 5: Mathematics and Science

By the year 2000, United States students will be first in the world in mathematics and science achievement.

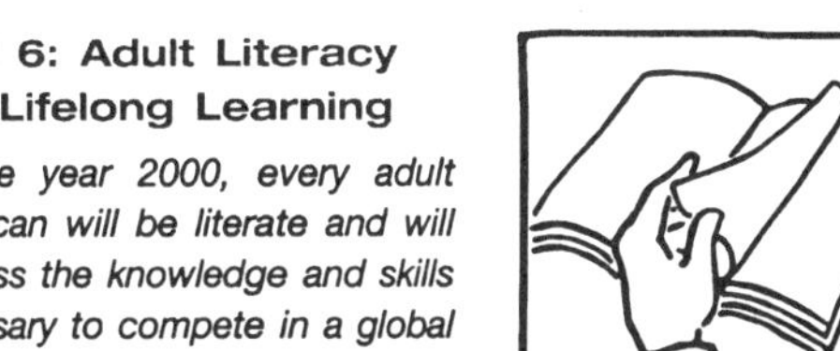

Goal 6: Adult Literacy and Lifelong Learning

By the year 2000, every adult American will be literate and will possess the knowledge and skills necessary to compete in a global economy and exercise the rights and responsibilities of citizenship.

Goal 7: Safe, Disciplined, and Alcohol- and Drug-free Schools

By the year 2000, every school in the United States will be free of drugs, violence, and the unauthorized presence of firearms and alcohol and will offer a disciplined environment conducive to learning.

Goal 8: Parental Participation

By the year 2000, every school will promote partnerships that will increase parental involvement and participation in promoting the social, emotional, and academic growth of children.

Source: *The National Education Goals Report: Building a Nation of Learners, 1999*, National Education Goals Panel, Washington, DC, 1999

---

found that, of the 27 indicators established to measure progress, 12 areas showed improvement, eleven were unchanged, and five had worsened. The remaining indicators were either not measured or had only had baseline (current status) measurements made.

Goal 1: Ready to Learn

Much improvement has been made in preparing youngsters to enter school ready to learn. Birth defects declined somewhat to 33 percent in 1997, compared to 37 percent in 1990. The proportion

TABLE 5.2

Awareness of and perceived importance of the National Goals for Education:[1] 1992 and 1993

National Goals, by the year 2000	Awareness of goals, 1992 (Percent)				Priority assigned, 1993 (Percent)				
	National totals	No children in school	Public school parents	Nonpublic school parents	Very high	High	Low	Very low	Don't know
	2	3	4	5	6	7	8	9	10
All children in America will start school ready to learn	28	25	33	31	41	48	8	1	2
The high school graduation rate will increase to at least 90%	27	24	31	26	54	38	6	1	1
American students will leave grades 4, 8, and 12 having demonstrated competency in challenging subject matter[2]	26	22	31	36	59	33	6	1	1
American students will be first in the world in mathematics and science achievement	23	23	22	32	45	43	9	2	1
Every adult American will be literate and will possess the skills necessary to compete in a global economy and to exercise the rights and responsibilities of citizenship	25	21	30	28	54	37	7	1	1
Every school in America will be free of drugs and violence and will offer a disciplined environment conducive to learning	24	21	28	22	71	19	7	2	1

[1] The National Goals were agreed upon by former President George Bush and the nation's governors in a 1989 education summit held in Charlottesville, Virginia.

[2] Subject matter includes English, mathematics, science, history, and geography. In addition, every school in America will insure that all students learn to use their minds in order to prepare them for responsible citizenship, further learning, and productive employment in a modern economy.

Phi Delta Kappan, "The Annual Gallup Poll of the Public's Attitudes Toward the Public Schools," September 1992 and October 1993. (This table was prepared April 1994.)

Source: *Digest of Education Statistics 1995*, National Center for Education Statistics, Washington, DC, 1995

of two-year-olds immunized against childhood diseases grew from 75 percent in 1994 to 78 percent in 1997. Reading to preschool children, an important aid to learning readiness, grew from 66 percent in 1993 to 72 percent in 1996, although it dropped to 69 percent in 1999. Between 1991 and 1999, improvement in preschool participation was particularly significant, reducing the gap between

TABLE 5.3

	Baseline	Update	Progress?
GOAL 1 **Ready to Learn**			
1. **Children's Health Index:** Has the U.S. reduced the percentage of infants born with 1 or more of 4 health risks? (1990 vs. 1997)	37%	33%	↑
2. **Immunizations:** Has the U.S. increased the percentage of 2-year-olds who have been fully immunized against preventable childhood diseases? (1994 vs. 1997)	75%	78%	↑
3. **Family-Child Reading and Storytelling:** Has the U.S. increased the percentage of 3- to 5-year-olds whose parents read to them or tell them stories regularly? (1993 vs. 1999)	66%	69%	↑
4. **Preschool Participation:** Has the U.S. reduced the gap (in percentage points) in preschool participation between 3- to 5-year-olds from high- and low-income families? (1991 vs. 1999)	28 points	13 points	↑

Source: *The National Education Goals Report: Building a Nation of Learners, 1999*, National Education Goals Panel, Washington, DC, 1999

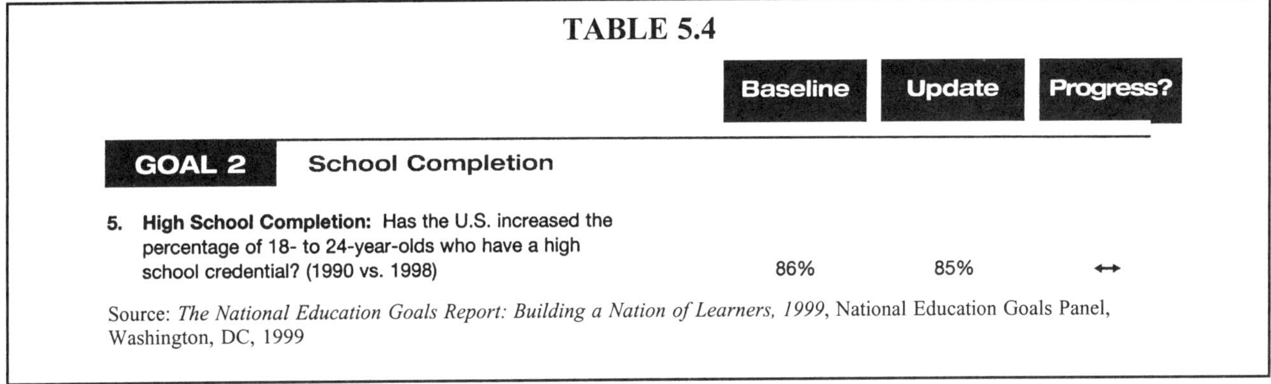

3- to 5-year-olds from high- and low-income families by more than half (53.6 percent). (See Table 5.3. Note the legend showing progress: an arrow pointing up indicates improvement, an arrow pointing down indicates a worse performance, and a horizontal arrow denotes no change.)

Goal 2: School Completion

The goal for high school completion among 18- to 24-year-olds is 90 percent by 2000. However, the proportion of high school graduates was virtually unchanged, from 86 percent in 1990 to 85 percent in 1998 (Table 5.4).

Goal 3: Student Achievement and Citizenship

Progress toward student achievement and citizenship has been disappointing. The percentage of fourth-grade and twelfth-grade students who met the panel's reading standards between 1992 and 1998 was statistically unchanged. On the other hand, the performance of eighth graders increased significantly. Math performance improved at all grades between 1990 and 1996. (The remaining areas were not updated.) Table 5.5 shows the updates and baseline measurements for these indicators.

Goal 4: Teacher Education and Development

Between 1991 and 1994, the percentage of teachers with a degree in their primary teaching assignment declined from 66 percent to 63 percent. The baseline measurement for professional development, 85 percent, was established in 1994,

and this area has not been updated since. (See Table 5.6.)

Goal 5: Mathematics and Science

The purpose of this goal is to provide future workers for the high-technology labor market. Many observers claim that, without an adequate supply of persons trained in mathematics and science, the United States will not be able to participate successfully in the global economy. Table 5.7 shows the status of the indicators that support this goal. It is encouraging to note that the proportion of college degrees in mathematics and science increased between 1991 and 1996.

In 1993-94, many classroom teachers of mathematics and science did not major in the teaching fields to which they were assigned. Figures 5.1 and 5.2 illustrate, by state, the magnitude of this problem.

The National Education Goals Panel strongly believes that these deficiencies can be addressed by toughening mathematics and science standards, improving curricula, and strengthening teacher preparation and knowledge. Their recommendations for raising mathematics and science achievement are listed in Table 5.8.

Goal 6: Adult Literacy and Learning

Adult literacy and lifelong learning is another area in which lack of progress has been disappointing. Level 3 prose literacy requires a person to make low-level inferences from text or to match infor-

TABLE 5.5

	Baseline	Update	Progress?

GOAL 3   Student Achievement and Citizenship

	Baseline	Update	Progress?
6. Reading Achievement: Has the U.S. increased the percentage of students scoring at or above Proficient in reading? (1992 vs. 1998)			
• Grade 4	29%	31%[ns]	↔
• Grade 8	29%	33%	↑
• Grade 12	40%	40%	↔
7. Writing Achievement: Has the U.S. increased the percentage of students scoring at or above Proficient in writing? (1998)			
• Grade 4	23%	—	
• Grade 8	27%	—	
• Grade 12	22%	—	
8. Mathematics Achievement: Has the U.S. increased the percentage of students scoring at or above Proficient in mathematics? (1990 vs. 1996)			
• Grade 4	13%	21%	↑
• Grade 8	15%	24%	↑
• Grade 12	12%	16%	↑
9. Science Achievement: Has the U.S. increased the percentage of students scoring at or above Proficient in science? (1996)			
• Grade 4	29%	—	
• Grade 8	29%	—	
• Grade 12	21%	—	
10. Civics Achievement: Has the U.S. increased the percentage of students scoring at or above Proficient in civics? (1998)			
• Grade 4	23%	—	
• Grade 8	22%	—	
• Grade 12	26%	—	
11. History Achievement: Has the U.S. increased the percentage of students scoring at or above Proficient in U.S. history? (1994)			
• Grade 4	17%	—	
• Grade 8	14%	—	
• Grade 12	11%	—	
12. Geography Achievement: Has the U.S. increased the percentage of students scoring at or above Proficient in geography? (1994)			
• Grade 4	22%	—	
• Grade 8	28%	—	
• Grade 12	27%	—	

—   Data not available.
[ns]   Interpret with caution. Change was not statistically significant.

Source: *The National Education Goals Report: Building a Nation of Learners, 1999*, National Education Goals Panel, Washington, DC, 1999

mation in text with task directions. In 1992, only 52 percent of adult Americans could successfully perform this task. The gap in adult education participation between those with a high school diploma or less and those who have postsecondary education has remained statistically unchanged. In addition, the ratio of White and minority college attendance and completion has not statistically improved. (See Table 5.9.)

TABLE 5.6

	Baseline	Update	Progress?
GOAL 4 Teacher Education and Professional Development			
13. Teacher Preparation: Has the U.S. increased the percentage of secondary school teachers who hold an undergraduate or graduate degree in their main teaching assignment? (1991 vs. 1994)	66%	63%	↓
14. Teacher Professional Development: Has the U.S. increased the percentage of teachers reporting that they participated in professional development programs on 1 or more topics since the end of the previous school year? (1994)	85%	—	

—   *Data not available.*
ns   *Interpret with caution. Change was not statistically significant.*

Source: *The National Education Goals Report: Building a Nation of Learners, 1999*, National Education Goals Panel, Washington, DC, 1999

Goal 7: Safe, Disciplined, and Alcohol- and Drug-Free Schools

Almost no progress has been made toward reaching the goal of safe, disciplined, and alcohol- and drug-free schools. The only encouraging sign is that fewer tenth graders (33 percent) reported being threatened or injured at school than did in 1991 (40 percent). On the other hand, more public-school teachers were threatened or injured in

TABLE 5.7

	Baseline	Update	Progress?
GOAL 5 Mathematics and Science			
15. International Mathematics Achievement: Has the U.S. improved its standing on international mathematics assessments? (1995)			
• Grade 4	7 out of 25 countries scored above the U.S.		
• Grade 8	20 out of 40 countries scored above the U.S.		
• Grade 12	14 out of 20 countries scored above the U.S.		
16. International Science Achievement: Has the U.S. improved its standing on international science assessments? (1995)			
• Grade 4	1 out of 25 countries scored above the U.S.		
• Grade 8	9 out of 40 countries scored above the U.S.		
• Grade 12	11 out of 20 countries scored above the U.S.		
17. Mathematics and Science Degrees: Has the U.S. increased mathematics and science degrees (as a percentage of all degrees) awarded to:			
• all students? (1991 vs. 1996)	39%	43%	↑
• minorities (Blacks, Hispanics, American Indians/ Alaskan Natives)? (1991 vs. 1996)	39%	40%	↑
• females? (1991 vs. 1996)	35%	41%	↑

—   *Data not available.*
ns   *Interpret with caution. Change was not statistically significant.*

Source: *The National Education Goals Report: Building a Nation of Learners, 1999*, National Education Goals Panel, Washington, DC, 1999

1994 (15 percent) than in 1991 (10 percent). All other indicators were either unchanged or worse. (See Table 5.10.)

Goal 8: Parental Participation

The Goals panel's 1998 report found that 78 percent of K-8 public schools had more than one-half of their parents involved in parent-teacher conferences in 1996. On the other hand, only 41 percent of K-8 public schools considered parent input when making policy decisions in three or more areas. The proportion of parents who had participated in two or more activities at their children's schools was unchanged from 1993 to 1999. (See Table 5.11.)

Goals Not Considered a Failure

In spite of the failure of America's schools to reach any of the eight National Education Goals, both Republican and Democratic politicians credited the goals with setting high standards. Following the release of the 1999 report, Education Secretary Richard Riley said, "The goals we have set are like a North Star. They give us a sense of direction, and they challenge us to keep moving forward."

The Goals panel recognized 12 states — Connecticut, Indiana, Maine, Maryland, Michigan, Minnesota, North Carolina, North Dakota, Oklahoma, Texas, Washington, and Wisconsin — for making outstanding progress toward the goals over the past decade. Wisconsin Governor Tommy Thompson commented, "Nothing drives a governor faster and better than a report that says you don't measure up."

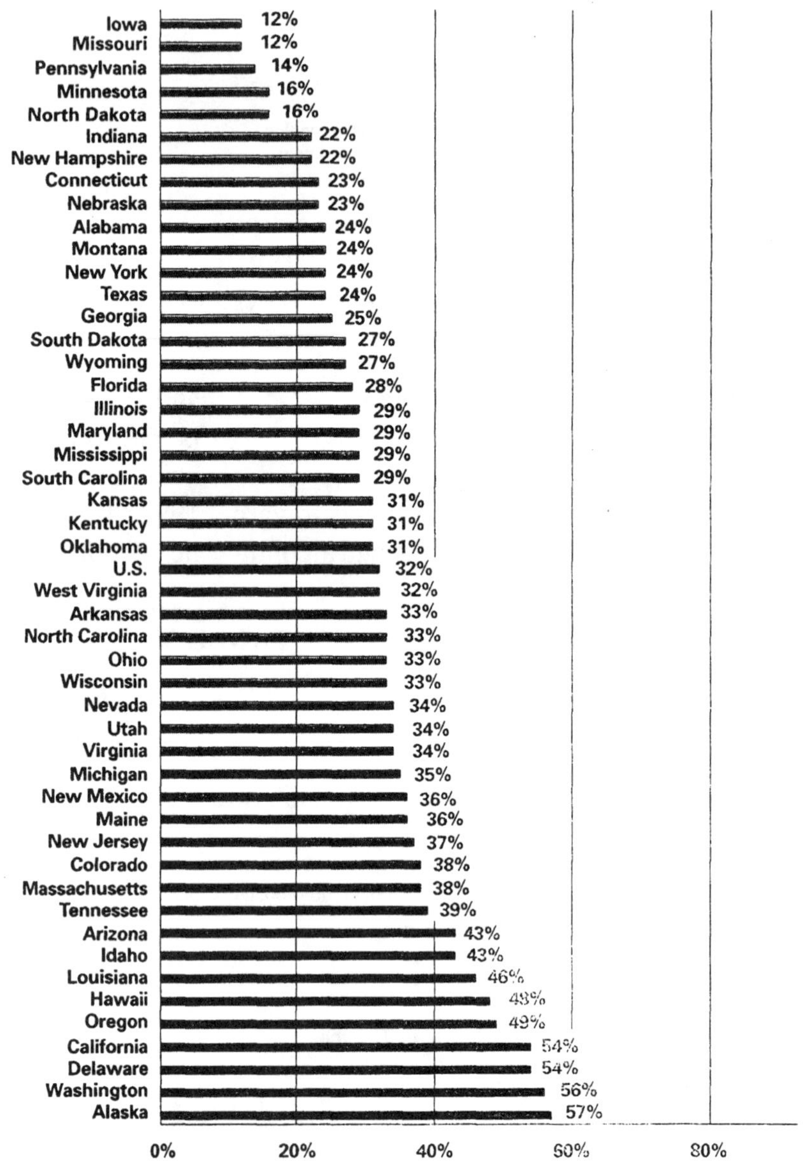

FIGURE 5.1

Percentage of public secondary teachers who taught one or more mathematics classes without at least a minor in mathematics, 1993-1994

Source: *The National Education Goals Report: Summary, 1997*, National Education Goals Panel, Washington, DC, 1997

NATIONAL URBAN EDUCATION GOALS

The Council of the Great City Schools (GCS), representing 57 of the nation's largest urban public school districts, revised and adapted the National Education Goals to the needs of urban schools. Michael Casserly, executive director, observed, "Cities have become so isolated racially, culturally and economically. And unfortunately most of the national leadership has either had an enormous sense of indifference or an overt hostility to the cities."

The National Urban Education Goals for the year 2000 are

1. Readiness to learn — All urban children will start school ready to learn.

2. Increased graduation rates — Urban schools will increase their graduation rates so they are at least comparable to the national average.

3. Improvement in academic achievement — Schools and communities will demonstrate high expectations for all learners so that urban students will attain a level of achievement that will allow them to successfully compete with students nationally and internationally in our global community.

4. Quality teachers — Urban schools will be adequately staffed with qualified teachers who are culturally and racially sensitive and who reflect the racial characteristics of their students.

5. Postsecondary opportunities — Urban school graduates will be fully prepared to enter and successfully complete higher education, expe-

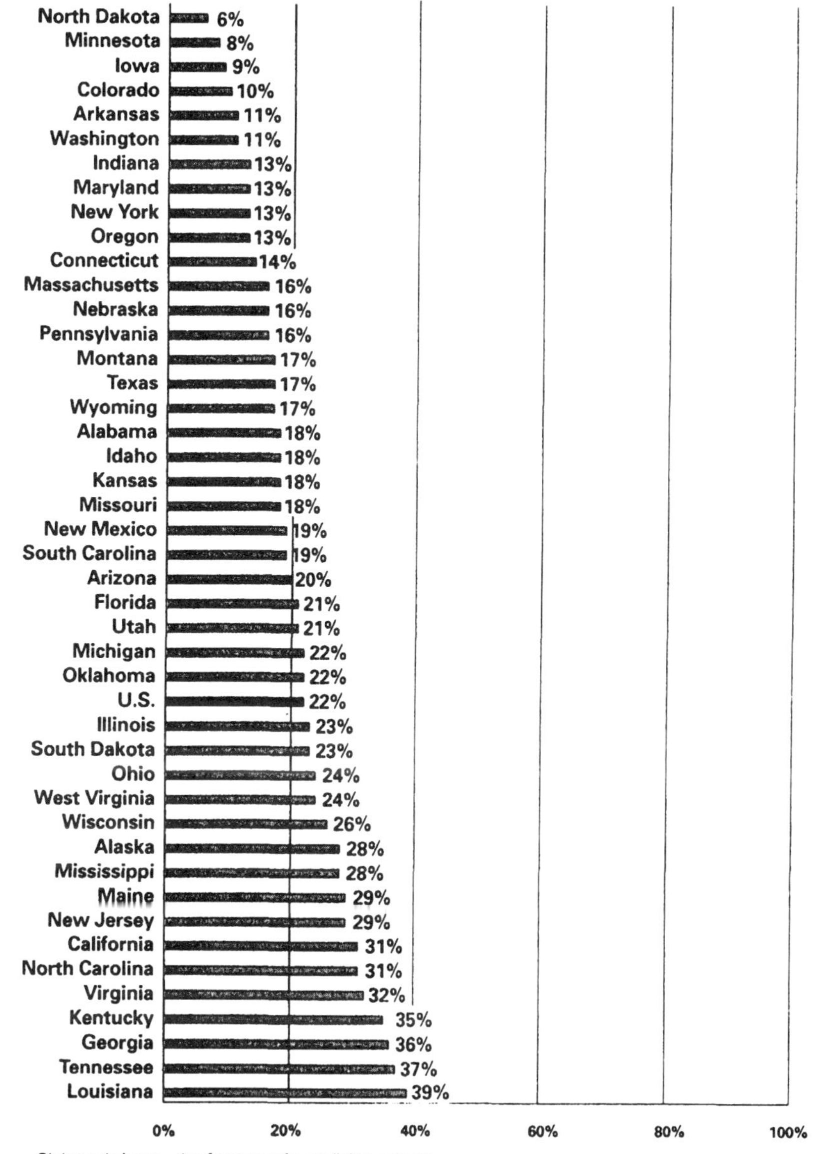

FIGURE 5.2

Percentage of public secondary teachers who taught one or more science classes without at least a minor in science, 1993-1994

Source: *The National Education Goals Report: Summary, 1997*, National Education Goals Panel, Washington, DC, 1997

rience successful employment, and exercise their responsibilities as citizens.

6. Safe and caring environment — Urban schools will be free of drugs and alcohol, students will be healthy and well-nourished, and schools will be well-maintained and safe.

7. Equitable and adequate funding — America's urban schools will be funded equitably and adequately by all levels of government to enable urban students to meet the urban goals.

8. Increased parental involvement — All parents/ guardians of urban school children will be involved in the education of their children, and urban schools will have programs to encourage and reinforce that activity.

The GCS believes the goals are realistic and attainable, but meeting them will require the in-

---

TABLE 5.8

How Can We Raise Mathematics and Science Achievement to World-Class Levels?

1. Set tougher standards for students in mathematics and science that are comparable to the best in the world.

2. Align other components of the education system with the standards, including curricula, instruction, textbooks, assessments, and school policies.

3. Strengthen teachers' subject-matter knowledge and teaching skills in mathematics and science, and move state teacher policies more in line with instructional goals embedded in state standards.

Source: *The National Education Goals Report: Summary, 1997*, National Education Goals Panel, Washington, DC, 1997

TABLE 5.9

	Baseline	Update	Progress?
GOAL 6 — Adult Literacy and Lifelong Learning			
18. Adult Literacy: Has the U.S. increased the percentage of adults who score at the three highest levels in prose literacy? (1992)	52%	—	
19. Participation in Adult Education: Has the U.S. reduced the gap (in percentage points) in adult education participation between adults who have a high school diploma or less, and those who have additional postsecondary education or technical training? (1991 vs. 1999)	27 points	29 points[ns]	↔
20. Participation in Higher Education: Has the U.S. reduced the gap (in percentage points) between White and Black high school graduates who:			
• enroll in college? (1990 vs. 1997)	14 points	9 points[ns]	↔
• complete a college degree? (1992 vs. 1998)	16 points	19 points[ns]	↔
Has the U.S. reduced the gap (in percentage points) between White and Hispanic high school graduates who:			
• enroll in college? (1990 vs. 1997)	11 points	13 points[ns]	↔
• complete a college degree? (1992 vs. 1998)	15 points	19 points[ns]	↔

— *Data not available.*
[ns] *Interpret with caution. Change was not statistically significant.*

Source: *The National Education Goals Report: Building a Nation of Learners, 1999*, National Education Goals Panel, Washington, DC, 1999

TABLE 5.10

	Baseline	**Update**	**Progress?**
GOAL 7 Safe, Disciplined, and Alcohol- and Drug-free Schools			
21. Overall Student Drug and Alcohol Use: Has the U.S. reduced the percentage of 10th graders reporting doing the following during the previous year:			
• using any illicit drug? (1991 vs. 1998)	24%	37%	↓
• using alcohol? (1993 vs. 1998)	63%	63%	↔
22. Sale of Drugs at School: Has the U.S. reduced the percentage of 10th graders reporting that someone offered to sell or give them an illegal drug at school during the previous year? (1992 vs. 1998)	18%	29%	↓
23. Student and Teacher Victimization: Has the U.S. reduced the percentage of students and teachers reporting that they were threatened or injured at school during the previous year?			
• 10th grade students (1991 vs. 1998)	40%	33%	↑
• public school teachers (1991 vs. 1994)	10%	15%	↓
24. Disruptions in Class by Students: Has the U.S. reduced the percentage of students and teachers reporting that student disruptions interfere with teaching and learning?			
• 10th grade students (1992 vs. 1998)	17%	16%[ns]	↔
• secondary school teachers (1991 vs. 1994)	37%	46%	↓

—   *Data not available.*
ns   *Interpret with caution. Change was not statistically significant.*

TABLE 5.11

	Baseline	**Update**	**Progress?**
GOAL 8 Parental Participation			
25. Schools' Reports of Parent Attendance at Parent-Teacher Conferences: Has the U.S. increased the percentage of K-8 public schools which reported that more than half of their parents attended parent-teacher conferences during the school year? (1996)	78%	—	
26. Schools' Reports of Parent Involvement in School Policy Decisions: Has the U.S. increased the percentage of K-8 public schools which reported that parent input is considered when making policy decisions in three or more areas? (1996)	41%	—	
27. Parents' Reports of Their Involvement in School Activities: Has the U.S. increased the percentage of students in Grades 3 to 12 whose parents reported that they participated in two or more activities in their child's school during the current school year? (1993 vs. 1999)	63%	62%[ns]	↔

—   *Data not available.*
ns   *Interpret with caution. Change was not statistically significant.*

Source of both tables: *The National Education Goals Report: Building a Nation of Learners, 1999*, National Education Goals Panel, Washington, DC, 1999

volvement of all segments of society — government, parents, educators, and taxpayers.

Urban Student Demographics

The Council compiled several important demographic details in *Key Facts: 1997-98 Data About Council Member Districts* (Washington, DC, 1999). For example, the 57 GCS districts made up only 0.3 percent of all school districts in the nation in 1997-98 but enrolled 14.3 percent of all K-12 public-school children. This proportion has stayed relatively constant since 1982-83.

The school systems were overwhelmingly minority. In 1992-93, the GCS schools enrolled 36 percent of the nation's public-school Black children, 30 percent of its Hispanic children, 21 percent of its Asian-American children, 7 percent of its Alaskan/Native American children, but only 5 percent of its White children. In 1997-98, 43 of the 57 districts gave enrollment totals by race/ethnicity. These districts enrolled 29.7 percent of the nation's public-school Black students, 24.5 percent of its Hispanic students, 21.7 percent of its Asian/Pacific Islander students, 7.3 percent of its Alaskan/Native American students, and only 3.8 percent of its White students. About 41 percent of all GCS students were Black, and 31.9 percent were Hispanic.

In 1997-98, 62.5 percent of GCS students were eligible to receive free/reduced-price lunches, and 21 percent were English language learners, with 120 languages spoken. Nearly 10 percent of the nation's schools were in GCS districts. Of the total number of teachers in the nation's 16,411 school districts, 12.5 percent were employed by GCS districts.

CHAPTER VI

STUDENTS AT RISK

WHAT DOES "AT RISK" MEAN?

In 1997, the U. S. Bureau of the Census identified the following six indicators of risk to children's welfare:

- Poverty.

- Welfare dependence.

- Absent parents.

- One-parent families.

- Unwed mothers.

- Parents who have not completed high school.

Children who grow up with one or more of these conditions may be statistically at greater risk of dropping out of school, being unemployed, or for girls, becoming teenage mothers. About 16 percent of 16- and 17-year-olds who experienced three or more risk factors were not in school. In contrast, only 1 percent of students with no risk factors, 4 percent with one risk factor, and 10 percent with two risk factors were not in school.

The relationship between these risk factors and teenage motherhood was similar. Fifteen percent of 16-

and 17-year-old girls who experienced three or more risk factors had given birth. Fewer than 1 percent for those with no risk factors, 2 percent with only one factor, and 4 percent with two factors had become mothers.

These factors and others do not, of course, totally predict a student's success or failure. Many adolescents overcome difficulties and become outstanding students and members of society. As Jack Frymier stated in *Growing Up Is Risky Business, and Schools Are Not to Blame* (Phi Delta Kappa,

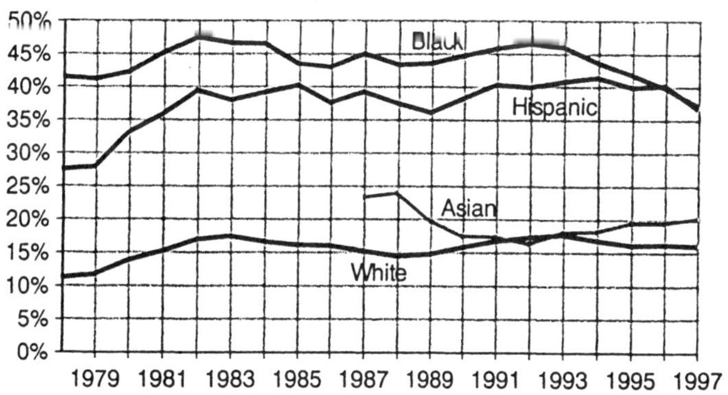

FIGURE 6.1

In 1997, the proportion of black juveniles living in poverty reached its lowest point in over two decades

- For whites and Hispanics, the proportion of juveniles in poverty has been relatively stable since 1982.

- Poverty rates among black juveniles exceeded Hispanic rates between 1978 and 1995 and were similar thereafter.

Note: Race proportions include persons of Hispanic ethnicity. Persons of Hispanic ethnicity can be of any race; however, most are white. American Indian data are not presented because of small sample size.

Source: Authors' analysis of Bureau of the Census' Poverty in the United States: 1997, *Current Population Reports: Consumer Income*.

Source: *Juvenile Offenders and Victims: 1999 National Report*, Office of Juvenile Justice and Delinquency Prevention, Washington, DC, 1999

TABLE 6.1

Early childhood education: Percentage of children ages 3 to 4[a] enrolled in
preschool by race, Hispanic origin, and poverty status, selected years 1980-97

Race and Hispanic origin, and income	1980	1985	1990[b]	1991	1992	1993	1994[b]	1995[b]	1996[b]	1997[b]
Total	30	32	41	34	34	34	44	45	45	48
Race and Hispanic origin										
White, non-Hispanic	32	35	44	39	38	38	48	49	48	52
Black, non-Hispanic	28	28	37	27	29	30	45	43	45	55
Hispanic[c]	24	20	26	20	18	17	26	29	33	31
Poverty status										
Below poverty	21	19	29	22	23	23	36	34	34	40
At or above poverty	34	37	45	39	38	38	47	49	48	51

[a] Estimates based on children who have yet to enter kindergarten.

[b] Data for 1990 and 1994-97 may not be comparable with other years because of changes in survey procedures.

[c] Persons of Hispanic origin may be of any race.

SOURCE: U.S. Bureau of the Census, October Current Population Surveys. Tabulated by the U.S. Department of Education, National Center for Education Statistics.

Source: *America's Children: Key National Indicators of Well-Being*, Federal Interagency Forum on Child and Family Statistics, Washington, DC, 1999

Bloomington, Indiana, 1992), Winston Churchill would have been considered an at-risk adolescent. Only his nanny loved him. He was ignored by his parents, bored by his studies, and isolated at his boarding school by his poor social skills and lack of athletic accomplishment.

Instead of turning to drugs or other destructive behaviors, Winston began to read books, became interested in the army and then in reporting, and finally turned to politics. Frymier said, "After more than 60 years of trying, he finally made it, and he made it big. But he was at risk as a child." However, it is harder to be successful when a child must first overcome challenges, such as poverty and an unhealthy environment or family situation. For many of today's children, life's experiences can crush hope, health, and ambition.

AT-RISK CHILDREN

In school, at-risk children are those who face significant obstacles, such as poverty or cultural and language barriers, that make it difficult for them to succeed academically. Children from at-risk groups — immigrant households, those with limited English-speaking abilities, and very low-income families — comprised about 4 to 5 percent of all school-age children in 1990.

In 1997, the poverty threshold for a family of four was $16,400. Though children under age 18 made up 26 percent of the population, they accounted for 40 percent of all persons living below the poverty level. The proportion of poor children varied by race and ethnicity. In 1997, the 37 percent poverty rate for Black and Hispanic children under age 18 was far greater than the rates for White (16 percent) and Asian (20 percent) children (Figure 6.1).

Parents, educators, and government officials generally agree that disadvantaged children often need special help to prepare them for school, and both public and private services are available. In 1997, however, most disadvantaged children were not enrolled in Head Start and other early childhood centers (Table 6.1).

78

Percentage of children aged 5–17 who spoke a language other than English at home and who spoke English with difficulty,* by race/ethnicity: 1979, 1989, 1992, and 1995

Race/ethnicity	1979	1989	1992	1995
Total	3	5	5	5
White	1	1	1	1
Black	—	1	2	1
Hispanic	29	28	30	31

— Too few sample observations for a reliable estimate.

* Respondents were asked to rate the child's ability to speak English using the following scale: "not at all," "not well," "well," or "very well." All those who reported less than "very well" were categorized as having difficulty speaking English.

Source: Thomas M. Smith et al., *The Condition of Education 1997*, National Center for Education Statistics, Washington, DC, 1997

Language Barriers

At-risk students with language barriers are classified either as "linguistically isolated" (LI) or as "limited English proficiency" (LEP). LI students are those in whose homes no person over 13 years of age speaks only English or speaks English very well. LEP indicates those who have difficulty reading, writing, or understanding English. The number of school-age children with limited English proficiency (LEP) doubled between 1986 and 1996. In 1996, nearly 3.5 million LEP children were enrolled in the nation's schools. Table 6.2 shows that the majority of LEP students are Hispanic.

MIDDLE SCHOOL AND JUNIOR HIGH — HIGH-RISK YEARS

As noted in *Great Transitions: Preparing Adolescents for a New Century* (Carnegie Council on Adolescent Development, New York, 1995), the middle grades (sixth, seventh, eighth, and sometimes ninth) are critical years for young adolescents. The Carnegie Council and other researchers have pointed out that the organization and curriculum of many middle-grade schools are often inconsistent with students' intellectual, emotional, and interpersonal needs. For many young people, entering middle school or junior high means leaving the neighborhood elementary school to be thrust into a much larger, possibly more impersonal environment some distance from home. Classmates and teachers change on an hourly basis, making it difficult to form relationships with both peers and adults. Both students and teachers observed that, at a time when adolescents want and need more self-determination, middle school and junior high students participate less in class decision-making than elementary students do.

The Carnegie Council concluded that the middle school curriculum does not encourage critical, complex thinking. This lack of intellectual stimulation is deliberate. Some educators feel that students this age are unable to concentrate on serious topics because of their rapid physical and emotional development. These educators believe that such learning experiences should be left to the high school years, although much research suggests this is not necessarily the case.

Once alienated, students can become more vulnerable to high-risk behavior. The *PRIDE* (National Parents' Resource Institute for Drug Education) Survey in 1997-1998 illustrated that the transition from fifth to sixth grade (from elementary to middle school) was a particularly vulnerable time when it comes to drug and alcohol use.

The survey found that students' use of alcohol, tobacco, and other drugs quadrupled from fourth to sixth grade. The survey also indicated that these students greatly overestimated how many of their peers used drugs when compared with actual reported use. This can have a significant effect because, according to the National Institute on Drug Abuse, drug use by peers is one of the strongest correlations in predicting adolescent drug use. (For more information on drug, alcohol, and tobacco use, see *Illegal Drugs — America's Anguish* and *Alcohol and Tobacco — America's Drugs of Choice*, Information Plus, Wylie, Texas, 1999.)

Recommendation

The Carnegie Council's recommendations were intended to help all middle-grade students, especially those at risk of being left behind. Major recommendations called for

TABLE 6.3

Percent of high school dropouts (status dropouts) among persons 16 to 24 years old, by sex and race/ethnicity: April 1960 to October 1997

Year	Total				Men				Women			
	All races	White, non-Hispanic	Black, non-Hispanic	Hispanic origin	All races	White, non-Hispanic	Black, non-Hispanic	Hispanic origin	All races	White, non-Hispanic	Black, non-Hispanic	Hispanic origin
1	2	3	4	5	6	7	8	9	10	11	12	13
1960 [1]	27.2 —	— —	— —	— —	27.8 —	— —	— —	— —	26.7 —	— —	— —	— —
1967 [2]	17.0 —	15.4 —	28.6 —	— —	16.5 —	14.7 —	30.6 —	— —	17.3 —	16.1 —	26.9 —	— —
1968 [2]	16.2 —	14.7 —	27.4 —	— —	15.8 —	14.4 —	27.1 —	— —	16.5 —	15.0 —	27.6 —	— —
1969 [2]	15.2 —	13.6 —	26.7 —	— —	14.3 —	12.6 —	26.9 —	— —	16.0 —	14.6 —	26.7 —	— —
1970 [2]	15.0 —	13.2 —	27.9 —	— —	14.2 —	12.2 —	29.4 —	— —	15.7 —	14.1 —	26.6 —	— —
1971 [2]	14.7 —	13.4 —	23.7 —	— —	14.2 —	12.6 —	25.5 —	— —	15.2 —	14.2 —	22.1 —	— —
1972	14.6 (0.3)	12.3 (0.3)	21.3 (1.1)	34.3 (2.2)	14.1 (0.4)	11.6 (0.4)	22.3 (1.6)	33.7 (3.2)	15.1 (0.4)	12.8 (0.4)	20.5 (1.4)	34.8 (3.1)
1973	14.1 (0.3)	11.6 (0.3)	22.2 (1.1)	33.5 (2.2)	13.7 (0.4)	11.5 (0.4)	21.5 (1.5)	30.4 (3.2)	14.5 (0.4)	11.8 (0.4)	22.8 (1.5)	36.4 (3.2)
1974	14.3 (0.3)	11.9 (0.3)	21.2 (1.0)	33.0 (2.1)	14.2 (0.4)	12.0 (0.4)	20.1 (1.5)	33.8 (3.0)	14.3 (0.4)	11.8 (0.4)	22.1 (1.5)	32.2 (2.9)
1975	13.9 (0.3)	11.4 (0.3)	22.9 (1.1)	29.2 (2.0)	13.3 (0.4)	11.0 (0.4)	23.0 (1.6)	26.7 (2.8)	14.5 (0.4)	11.8 (0.4)	22.9 (1.4)	31.6 (2.9)
1976	14.1 (0.3)	12.0 (0.3)	20.5 (1.0)	31.4 (2.0)	14.1 (0.4)	12.1 (0.4)	21.2 (1.5)	30.3 (2.9)	14.2 (0.4)	11.8 (0.4)	19.9 (1.4)	32.3 (2.8)
1977	14.1 (0.3)	11.9 (0.3)	19.8 (1.0)	33.0 (2.0)	14.5 (0.4)	12.6 (0.4)	19.5 (1.5)	31.6 (2.9)	13.8 (0.4)	11.2 (0.4)	20.0 (1.4)	34.3 (2.8)
1978	14.2 (0.3)	11.9 (0.3)	20.2 (1.0)	33.3 (2.0)	14.6 (0.4)	12.2 (0.4)	22.5 (1.5)	33.6 (2.9)	13.9 (0.4)	11.6 (0.4)	18.3 (1.3)	33.1 (2.8)
1979	14.6 (0.3)	12.0 (0.3)	21.1 (1.0)	33.8 (2.0)	15.0 (0.4)	12.6 (0.4)	22.4 (1.5)	33.0 (2.8)	14.2 (0.4)	11.5 (0.4)	20.0 (1.3)	34.5 (2.8)
1980	14.1 (0.3)	11.4 (0.3)	19.1 (1.0)	35.2 (1.9)	15.1 (0.4)	12.3 (0.4)	20.8 (1.5)	37.2 (2.7)	13.1 (0.4)	10.5 (0.4)	17.7 (1.3)	33.2 (2.6)
1981	13.9 (0.3)	11.3 (0.3)	18.4 (0.9)	33.2 (1.8)	15.1 (0.4)	12.5 (0.4)	19.9 (1.4)	36.0 (2.6)	12.8 (0.4)	10.2 (0.4)	17.1 (1.2)	30.4 (2.5)
1982	13.9 (0.3)	11.4 (0.3)	18.4 (1.0)	31.7 (1.9)	14.5 (0.4)	12.0 (0.4)	21.2 (1.5)	30.5 (2.7)	13.3 (0.4)	10.8 (0.4)	15.9 (1.3)	32.8 (2.7)
1983	13.7 (0.3)	11.1 (0.3)	18.0 (1.0)	31.6 (1.9)	14.9 (0.4)	12.2 (0.4)	19.9 (1.5)	34.3 (2.8)	12.5 (0.4)	10.1 (0.4)	16.2 (1.3)	29.1 (2.6)
1984	13.1 (0.3)	11.0 (0.3)	15.5 (0.9)	29.8 (1.9)	14.0 (0.4)	11.9 (0.4)	16.8 (1.4)	30.6 (2.8)	12.3 (0.4)	10.1 (0.4)	14.3 (1.2)	29.0 (2.6)
1985	12.6 (0.3)	10.4 (0.3)	15.2 (0.9)	27.6 (1.9)	13.4 (0.4)	11.1 (0.4)	16.1 (1.4)	29.9 (2.8)	11.8 (0.4)	9.8 (0.4)	14.3 (1.2)	25.2 (2.7)
1986	12.2 (0.3)	9.7 (0.3)	14.2 (0.9)	30.1 (1.9)	13.1 (0.4)	10.3 (0.4)	15.0 (1.3)	32.8 (2.7)	11.4 (0.4)	9.1 (0.4)	13.5 (1.2)	27.2 (2.6)
1987	12.6 (0.3)	10.4 (0.3)	14.1 (0.9)	28.6 (1.8)	13.2 (0.4)	10.8 (0.4)	15.0 (1.3)	29.1 (2.6)	12.1 (0.4)	10.0 (0.4)	13.3 (1.2)	28.1 (2.6)
1988	12.9 (0.3)	9.6 (0.3)	14.5 (1.0)	35.8 (2.3)	13.5 (0.4)	10.3 (0.5)	15.0 (1.5)	36.0 (3.2)	12.2 (0.4)	8.9 (0.4)	14.0 (1.4)	35.4 (3.3)
1989	12.6 (0.3)	9.4 (0.3)	13.9 (1.0)	33.0 (2.2)	13.6 (0.5)	10.3 (0.5)	14.9 (1.5)	34.4 (3.1)	11.7 (0.4)	8.5 (0.4)	13.0 (1.3)	31.6 (3.1)
1990	12.1 (0.3)	9.0 (0.3)	13.2 (0.9)	32.4 (1.9)	12.3 (0.4)	9.3 (0.4)	11.9 (1.3)	34.3 (2.7)	11.8 (0.4)	8.7 (0.4)	14.4 (1.3)	30.3 (2.7)
1991	12.5 (0.3)	8.9 (0.3)	13.6 (0.9)	35.3 (1.9)	13.0 (0.4)	8.9 (0.4)	13.5 (1.4)	39.2 (2.7)	11.9 (0.4)	8.9 (0.4)	13.7 (1.3)	31.1 (2.7)
1992 [3]	11.0 (0.3)	7.7 (0.3)	13.7 (0.9)	29.4 (1.9)	11.3 (0.4)	8.0 (0.4)	12.5 (1.3)	32.1 (2.7)	10.7 (0.4)	7.4 (0.4)	14.8 (1.4)	26.6 (2.6)
1993 [3]	11.0 (0.3)	7.9 (0.3)	13.6 (0.9)	27.5 (1.8)	11.2 (0.4)	8.2 (0.4)	12.6 (1.3)	28.1 (2.5)	10.9 (0.4)	7.6 (0.4)	14.4 (1.3)	26.9 (2.5)
1994 [3]	11.4 (0.3)	7.7 (0.3)	12.6 (0.8)	30.0 (1.2)	12.3 (0.4)	8.0 (0.4)	14.1 (1.1)	31.6 (1.6)	10.6 (0.4)	7.5 (0.4)	11.3 (1.0)	28.1 (1.7)
1995 [3]	12.0 (0.3)	8.6 (0.3)	12.1 (0.7)	30.0 (1.1)	12.2 (0.4)	9.0 (0.4)	11.1 (1.0)	30.0 (1.6)	11.7 (0.4)	8.2 (0.4)	12.9 (1.1)	30.0 (1.7)
1996 [3]	11.1 (0.3)	7.3 (0.3)	13.0 (0.8)	29.4 (1.2)	11.4 (0.4)	7.3 (0.4)	13.5 (1.2)	30.3 (1.7)	10.9 (0.4)	7.3 (0.4)	12.5 (1.1)	28.3 (1.7)
1997 [3]	11.0 (0.3)	7.6 (0.3)	13.4 (0.8)	25.3 (1.1)	11.9 (0.4)	8.5 (0.4)	13.3 (1.2)	27.0 (1.6)	10.1 (0.4)	6.7 (0.4)	13.5 (1.1)	23.4 (1.6)

[1] Based on the April 1960 decennial census.

[2] White and black include persons of Hispanic origin.

[3] Because of changes in data collection procedures, data may not be comparable with figures for earlier years.

—Data not available.

NOTE.—"Status" dropouts are 16- to 24-year-olds who are not enrolled in school and who have not completed a high school program, regardless of when they left school. People who have received GED credentials are counted as high school completers. All data except for 1960 are based on October counts. Data are based upon sample surveys of the civilian noninstitutional population. Standard errors appear in parentheses.

SOURCE: U.S. Department of Commerce, Bureau of the Census, Current Population Survey, unpublished tabulations; and U.S. Department of Education, National Center for Education Statistics, *Dropout Rates in the United States*. (This table was prepared December 1998.)

Source: *Digest of Education Statistics 1998*, National Center for Education Statistics, Washington, DC, 1999

TABLE 6.4

Status dropout rates and number and distribution of dropouts of 16-through 24-year-olds, by background characteristics: October 1998

Characteristic	Status dropout rate (percent)	Number of status dropouts (thousands)	Population (thousands)	Percent of all dropouts	Percent of population
Total	11.8	3,942	33,445	100.0	100.0
Sex					
Male	13.3	2,241	16,854	56.8	50.4
Female	10.3	1,701	16,592	43.2	49.6
Race–ethnicity[1]					
White, non-Hispanic	7.7	1,697	21,920	43.0	66.0
Black, non-Hispanic	13.8	675	4,893	17.1	14.6
Hispanic	29.5	1,487	5,034	37.7	15.1
Asian/Pacific Islander	4.1	55	1,356	1.4	4.1
Age					
16	3.3	133	4,000	3.4	12.0
17	6.7	266	3,938	6.7	11.8
18	13.2	524	3,955	13.3	11.8
19	14.7	580	3,947	14.7	11.8
20 through 24	13.9	2,440	17,605	61.9	52.6
Recency of immigration					
Born outside the 50 states and the District of Columbia					
Hispanic	44.4	961	2,167	24.4	6.5
Non-Hispanic	7.2	130	1,789	3.3	5.3
First generation[2]					
Hispanic	20.5	315	1,538	8.0	4.6
Non-Hispanic	5.2	94	1,787	2.4	5.3
Second generation or more[3]					
Hispanic	15.8	210	1,328	5.3	4.0
Non-Hispanic	9.0	2,233	24,385	56.6	74.3
Region					
Northeast	9.4	577	6,109	14.6	18.3
Midwest	8.0	622	7,772	15.8	23.2
South	13.1	1,522	11,597	38.6	34.7
West	15.3	1,221	7,967	31.0	23.8

[1]Due to relatively small sample sizes, American Indians/Alaskan Natives are included in the total but are not shown separately.

[2]Individuals defined as "first generation" were born in the 50 states or the District of Columbia, and one or both of their parents were born outside the 50 states or the District of Columbia.

[3]Individuals defined as "second generation or more" were born in the 50 states or the District of Columbia, as were both of their parents.

NOTE: Because of rounding, details may not add to totals.

Source: Phillip Kaufman et al., *Dropout Rates in the United States: 1998*, National Center for Education Statistics, Washington, DC, 1999

- The creation of small communities of learning in which teachers and students work as teams, with the assurance that every student is well known by at least one adult.

- A core academic program that helps students to think critically, behave ethically, and be prepared to assume responsibilities.

- The elimination of tracking by achievement level.

- Teachers who have been specially prepared to teach in the middle grades.

DROPPING OUT

Trends in Dropout Rates

Despite the public perception that dropout rates are increasing, the U.S. Department of Education reports that national dropout rates have generally declined over the past 30 years. The total status

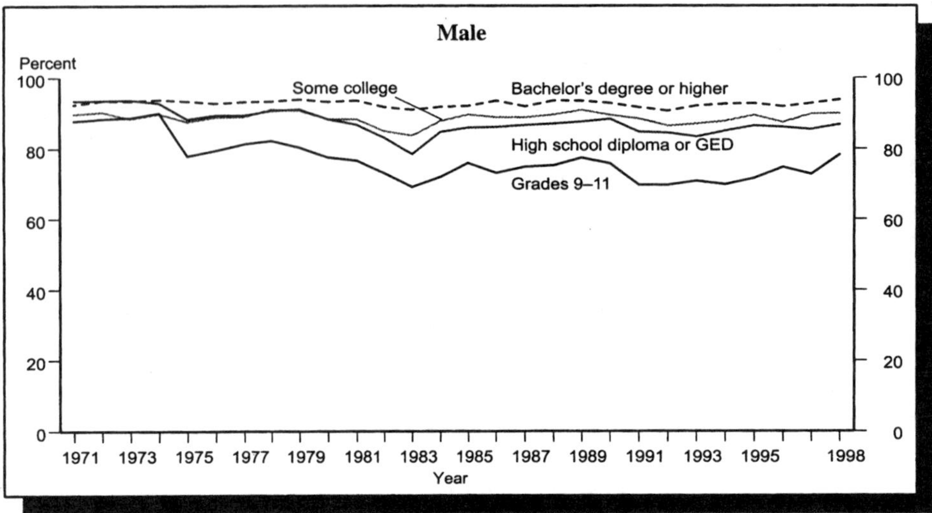

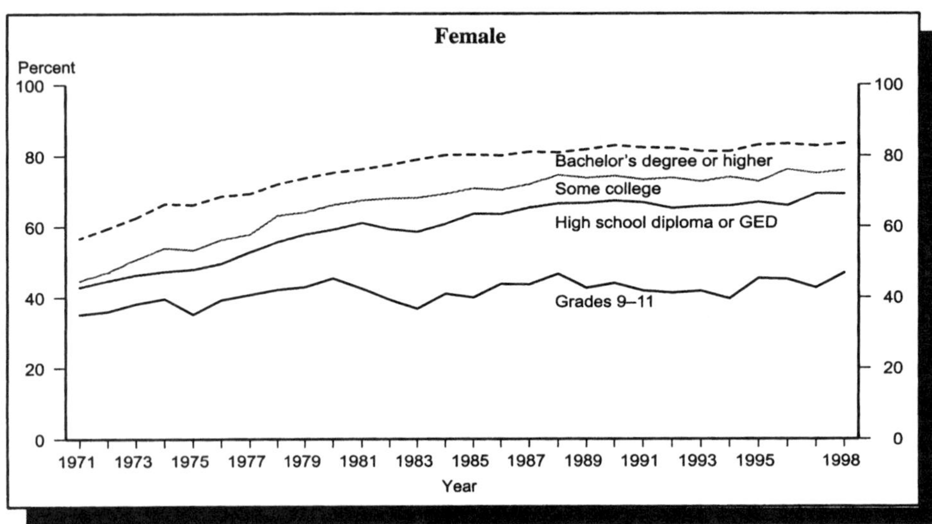

NOTE: The Current Population Survey (CPS) questions used to obtain educational attainment were changed in 1992. The employment rate represents the number of employed individuals as a percentage of the total population.

SOURCE: U.S. Department of Commerce, Bureau of the Census, March Current Population Surveys.

Source: *The Condition of Education 1999*, National Center for Education Statistics, Washington, DC, 1999

dropout rate for persons 16 through 24 years of age was 27.2 percent in 1960, 14.1 percent in 1980, and 11 percent in 1997 (Table 6.3). (Status dropouts are persons who are not enrolled in school and who are not high school graduates or holders of General Educational Development [GED] diplomas.)

Historically, Hispanic students have had significantly higher dropout rates than either White or Black non-Hispanics. In 1980, White students had a dropout rate of 11.4 percent; Black students, 19.1 percent; and Hispanic students, 35.2 percent. By 1997, the estimated White rate was 7.6 percent, the Black rate was 13.4 percent, and the Hispanic rate remained very high at an estimated 25.3 percent. (See Table 6.3.)

In 1998, dropout rates remained about the same for White students (7.7 percent) and Black students

(13.8 percent), but the rate for Hispanic students returned to the 1996 level of 29.5 percent. Nearly 2 in 5 (37.7 percent) of all dropouts were Hispanic. (See Table 6.4.) The high Hispanic dropout rate can be partly attributed to the fact that more Hispanics than non-Hispanics ages 16 to 24 were born outside the United States.

Among this foreign-born group, the dropout rate (44.4 percent) was considerably higher than it was among first- and later-generation Hispanics (20.5 percent and 15.8 percent, respectively) (Table 6.4). Data from *Dropout Rates in the United States: 1995* (National Center for Education Statistics, Washington, DC, 1997) show that more than half of the foreign-born Hispanic dropouts had never enrolled in a U.S. school. They may have entered the United States at an age beyond high school age or may have come to this country for employment, not education. In addition, 80 percent of foreign-born young Hispanics spoke little, if any, English.

The Costs of Dropping Out

Young people who drop out before finishing high school usually pay a high price. Dropouts have

---

TABLE 6.5

Unemployment rate of persons 16 years old and over, by age, sex, race/ethnicity, and highest degree attained: 1995, 1996, and 1997

Sex, race/ethnicity, and highest degree attained	Percent unemployed, 1995 [1]				Percent unemployed, 1996 [1]				Percent unemployed, 1997 [1]			
	16- to 24-year-olds [2]			25 years old and over	16- to 24-year-olds [2]			25 years old and over	16- to 24-year-olds [2]			25 years old and over
	Total	16 to 19 years	20 to 24 years		Total	16 to 19 years	20 to 24 years		Total	16 to 19 years	20 to 24 years	
1	2	3	4	5	6	7	8	9	10	11	12	13
All persons												
All education levels	12.1	17.3	9.1	4.3	12.0	16.7	9.3	4.2	11.3	16.0	8.5	3.8
Less than a high school graduate	20.2	20.8	18.6	9.0	19.7	19.7	19.4	8.7	18.4	18.9	17.1	8.1
High school graduate, no college	12.0	14.7	10.8	4.8	12.0	14.9	10.8	4.7	11.0	14.0	9.6	4.3
Some college, no degree	6.7	8.4	6.3	4.3	7.0	8.1	6.7	4.0	7.1	8.5	6.7	3.5
Associate degree	5.3	—	5.1	3.3	4.8	—	4.5	3.3	4.5	—	4.3	2.7
Bachelor's degree or higher	5.5	—	5.5	2.4	5.3	—	5.3	2.2	3.7	—	3.7	2.0
Men												
All education levels	12.5	18.4	9.2	4.3	12.6	18.1	9.5	4.1	11.8	16.9	8.9	3.6
Less than a high school graduate	19.9	21.6	15.9	8.8	19.8	21.2	16.4	7.8	18.3	19.7	15.1	7.2
High school graduate, no college	11.7	15.3	10.4	4.8	11.9	15.1	10.6	4.7	10.8	13.9	9.6	4.2
Some college, no degree	6.8	9.3	6.3	4.0	7.5	9.4	7.1	3.9	7.5	9.2	7.1	3.3
Associate degree	4.9	—	4.8	3.3	4.1	—	4.2	3.2	—	—	—	2.6
Bachelor's degree or higher	6.3	—	6.3	2.3	6.1	—	6.1	2.1	4.2	—	4.3	1.9
Women												
All education levels	11.7	16.1	9.0	4.4	11.3	15.2	9.0	4.3	10.7	15.0	8.1	3.9
Less than a high school graduate	20.8	18.0	21.4	9.0	19.6	18.1	25.3	10.1	18.6	17.9	21.2	9.6
High school graduate, no college	12.3	14.2	11.4	4.7	12.2	14.7	10.9	4.6	11.2	14.2	9.7	4.3
Some college, no degree	6.6	7.7	6.3	4.6	6.6	7.2	6.4	4.1	6.7	8.0	6.3	3.7
Associate degree	5.5	—	5.5	3.3	5.2	—	4.8	3.3	4.8	—	4.5	2.8
Bachelor's degree or higher	5.0	—	4.9	2.7	4.8	—	4.8	2.4	3.2	—	3.3	2.2
White [3]												
All education levels	10.2	14.5	7.7	3.9	10.2	14.2	7.8	3.7	9.4	13.6	6.9	3.3
Less than a high school graduate	17.2	17.7	15.9	8.3	16.7	17.0	16.0	8.0	15.5	16.2	13.5	7.2
High school graduate, no college	10.0	11.9	9.2	4.2	9.9	12.2	8.9	4.0	9.1	11.6	7.9	3.6
Some college, no degree	5.8	7.3	5.3	3.7	6.0	7.0	5.8	3.5	5.9	7.1	5.6	3.0
Associate degree	4.8	—	4.7	3.1	4.2	—	3.9	3.0	3.6	—	3.4	2.5
Bachelor's degree or higher	5.1	—	5.1	2.3	5.1	—	5.1	2.1	3.1	—	3.2	1.8
Black [3]												
All education levels	23.9	35.7	17.7	7.4	23.9	33.6	18.8	7.7	23.2	32.4	18.3	7.3
Less than a high school graduate	39.1	40.4	35.8	12.4	37.8	37.6	38.2	12.6	36.3	36.4	35.8	13.1
High school graduate, no college	22.5	31.8	19.3	8.2	23.0	31.5	20.0	9.1	20.9	28.1	18.4	8.1
Some college, no degree	13.0	18.7	12.2	7.5	13.7	17.1	13.1	6.7	15.1	21.0	14.0	6.1
Associate degree	10.7	—	8.5	4.6	9.7	—	10.0	5.5	—	—	—	—
Bachelor's degree or higher	8.7	—	8.6	3.2	6.1	—	6.0	3.1	6.5	—	6.4	3.6
Hispanic origin [4]												
All education levels	15.5	24.1	11.5	7.6	15.5	23.6	11.8	7.1	13.8	21.6	10.3	6.1
Less than a high school graduate	20.2	28.2	13.7	10.4	20.1	26.1	14.6	9.7	18.8	25.7	13.0	8.5
High school graduate, no college	14.1	18.7	12.3	6.8	13.6	20.7	11.5	6.6	11.4	15.7	9.9	5.7
Some college, no degree	10.4	14.1	9.4	6.1	10.5	13.2	9.8	4.9	8.9	11.3	8.4	4.1
Associate degree	—	—	—	5.5	—	—	—	4.9	—	—	—	—
Bachelor's degree or higher	—	—	—	3.5	—	—	—	3.8	—	—	—	3.5

[1] The unemployment rate is the percent of individuals in the labor force who are not working and who made specific efforts to find employment sometime during the prior 4 weeks. The labor force includes both employed and unemployed persons.
[2] Excludes persons enrolled in school.
[3] Includes persons of Hispanic origin.
[4] Persons of Hispanic origin may be of any race.

—Data not available.

SOURCE: U.S. Department of Labor, Bureau of Labor Statistics, Office of Employment and Unemployment Statistics, unpublished tabulations of annual everages from the Current Population Survey. (This table was prepared September 1998.)

Source: *Digest of Education Statistics 1998*, National Center for Education Statistics, Washington, DC, 1999

TABLE 6.6

Total annual money income and median income of persons 25 years old and over, by educational attainment and sex: 1996

Sex, earnings, and age	Total	Less than 9th grade	Some high school (no diploma)	High school graduate (includes equivalency)	Some college, no degree	Associate degree	College				
								Bachelor's degree or higher			
							Total	Bachelor's degree	Master's degree	Professional degree	Doctor's degree
1	2	3	4	5	6	7	8	9	10	11	12
Men, 25 years old and over					Number, in thousands						
Total	81,620	6,477	8,212	26,226	14,033	5,299	21,374	13,672	4,776	1,708	1,218
With income	79,423	6,139	7,671	25,510	13,756	5,210	21,136	13,510	4,709	1,702	1,215
					Percentage distribution of men with income						
Total	100.0	100.0	100.0	100.0	100.0	100.0	100.0	100.0	100.0	100.0	100.0
$1 to $4,999 or loss	4.3	8.9	8.3	4.5	3.5	3.1	2.2	2.5	2.1	1.3	1.4
$5,000 to $9,999	9.4	28.8	17.2	9.5	7.0	4.6	3.4	3.9	2.7	2.6	1.7
$10,000 to $14,999	11.2	24.8	20.8	11.9	9.0	7.1	5.2	6.2	3.6	2.5	3.5
$15,000 to $24,999	20.1	22.5	27.8	24.5	20.9	17.6	11.2	13.1	9.1	6.0	5.9
$25,000 to $34,999	17.3	8.9	14.6	20.1	20.6	20.8	14.2	16.3	12.4	8.0	7.0
$35,000 to $49,999	17.2	3.5	7.1	18.0	20.1	24.7	20.2	21.5	20.1	14.4	14.7
$50,000 to $74,999	12.4	1.7	3.0	8.7	13.2	16.4	21.8	21.3	23.7	17.2	26.3
$75,000 and over	8.2	0.9	1.1	2.8	5.6	5.7	21.7	15.1	26.3	48.1	39.3
Median income	$27,248	$12,174	$16,058	$24,814	$29,160	$33,065	$44,161	$39,624	$50,003	$71,869	$62,255
Women, 25 years old and over					Number, in thousands						
Total	88,961	6,836	9,000	31,360	15,335	7,107	19,323	13,685	4,356	739	543
With income	83,056	5,775	7,929	29,212	14,528	6,839	18,775	13,247	4,285	715	527
					Percentage distribution of women with income						
Total	100.0	100.0	100.0	100.0	100.0	100.0	100.0	100.0	100.0	100.0	100.0
$1 to $4,999 or loss	16.2	24.5	22.5	17.1	15.3	12.5	11.4	12.9	8.0	9.0	5.5
$5,000 to $9,999	20.1	45.8	36.1	21.8	16.5	12.1	8.5	9.5	6.1	4.6	5.7
$10,000 to $14,999	14.5	16.5	19.3	18.0	14.7	12.9	6.9	7.7	5.3	3.6	3.2
$15,000 to $24,999	21.2	9.5	15.7	24.9	24.8	23.8	17.4	19.3	13.3	9.4	13.5
$25,000 to $34,999	13.0	2.1	3.9	10.8	14.8	19.5	19.8	20.5	20.0	13.0	11.2
$35,000 to $49,999	8.9	0.8	1.6	5.0	9.2	13.1	18.7	16.5	25.6	16.6	20.3
$50,000 to $74,999	4.4	0.6	0.5	1.8	3.6	4.9	11.6	9.5	15.6	18.9	19.7
$75,000 and over	1.9	0.2	0.3	0.6	1.0	1.2	5.8	4.0	6.2	24.9	20.9
Median income	$14,682	$7,276	$8,544	$12,702	$16,255	$20,460	$27,556	$25,192	$33,302	$42,059	$42,431

NOTE.—Because of rounding, details may not add to totals.

SOURCE: U.S. Department of Commerce, Bureau of the Census, *Current Population Reports,* Series P-60, No. 197, "Money Income in the United States: 1996." (This table was prepared August 1998.)

Source: *Digest of Education Statistics 1998*, National Center for Education Statistics, Washington, DC, 1999

a much harder time making the transition from school to work and economic independence. In 1995, Senator Nancy Kassebaum (R-KS) observed

> The need to keep young people in school cannot be emphasized too strongly. Failure to receive a high school diploma spells tragedy for the individual dropout who operates at a permanent disadvantage in job prospects and lifetime earnings. It is a tragedy as well for our nation, which loses the productive capacity we so badly need from all our workers.

The employment rates of high school graduates and GED holders have consistently been higher than those of dropouts. In 1998, less than half (47.3 percent) of females who did not complete high school were employed, compared to 69.5 percent of high school graduates and 83.8 percent of college graduates. For male dropouts, 78.5 percent were employed, compared to 87 percent of high school graduates and 94 percent of college graduates. (See Figure 6.2.)

Minority students who drop out are at even higher economic risk. In 1997, 36.3 percent of Black dropouts and 18.8 percent of Hispanic dropouts ages 16 to 24 were unemployed. In comparison, 15.5 percent of White dropouts in the same age range were not working. (See Table 6.5.)

Persons without high school diplomas tend to earn considerably less than those with more education. In 1996, the median income (half earned more; half earned less) of males with less than a ninth-grade education was $12,174. Those who attended high school but did not graduate earned $16,058, 65 percent of the median earnings of male high school graduates ($24,814). Females with less than a ninth-grade education made $7,276. Those who attended high school but did not graduate earned $8,544, a median income just 67 percent of the earnings of their counterparts who graduated. (See Table 6.6.)

As might be expected from the unemployment and income data, non-graduates were more likely than graduates to be on welfare. In 1994, those without a high school diploma were more than twice as likely as high school graduates to receive food stamps, to be on Medicaid, and to receive housing assistance. (See Table 6.7.) Non-graduates were also more likely to stay on welfare programs longer. In 1994, non-graduates were on major assistance programs for a median of 11.0 months, compared to 7.2 months for graduates.

Many significant consequences of dropping out of school cannot be measured statistically. Some of those who drop out may likely experience life-long poverty. Some who are poorly prepared to compete in society may turn to crime or substance abuse. Some become teenage parents without the ability to offer their children more than they had, possibly contributing to a cycle of dependence. Furthermore, the U.S. economy is deprived of the literate, technically trained, and dedicated workers it needs to compete internationally. Finally, those without a high school diploma generally do not have the opportunities to enjoy their lives as much as they could.

Reasons for Dropping Out

Prepared by the National Center for Education Statistics, the *National Education Longitudinal Study of 1988* (NELS:88) studied students from the eighth grade through their high school years and beyond. Follow-up surveys were done in 1990, 1992, and 1994. A fourth follow-up survey will be conducted in 2000.

The 1992 survey revealed that students in the NELS:88 survey who dropped out of school were more likely to give school-related than job-related

TABLE 6.7

Average Monthly Participation Rates and Median Family Benefits by Selected Characteristics: 1993 and 1994

| Characteristic | Program participation rates (percent) | | | | | | | | | | | | Monthly family benefits[2] (dollars) | | | |
| | Any means-tested program[1] | | AFDC/GA | | SSI | | Food stamps | | Medicaid | | Housing assistance | | 1993 | | 1994 | |
	1993	1994	1993	1994	1993	1994	1993	1994	1993	1994	1993	1994	Median	Stand-ard error	Median	Stand-ard error
Total number of recipients[3]	39,162	39,514	14,675	14,438	4,841	5,106	25,713	25,383	27,984	29,332	13,044	12,206	(X)	(X)	(X)	(X)
As percent of the population.	15.2	15.2	5.7	5.5	1.9	2.0	10.0	9.7	10.9	11.3	5.1	4.7	485	4.0	476	3.0
Sex																
Male.	13.0	13.0	4.5	4.3	1.4	1.4	8.4	8.2	8.8	9.2	4.4	3.9	490	7.5	479	5
Female.	17.2	17.3	6.8	6.7	2.4	2.5	11.5	11.2	12.8	13.2	5.7	5.4	483	5	473	5.5
Educational Attainment (people 18 years old and over)																
Less than 4 years of high school.	25.8	25.6	6.5	5.9	7.5	7.7	15.3	14.8	17.5	17.8	9.0	8.4	432	7	433	5.5
High school graduate, no college.	10.5	10.5	2.9	3.0	1.9	2.0	6.2	6.1	6.4	6.7	3.6	3.5	396	10	386	10.5
1 or more years of college	4.6	4.5	1.2	1.2	0.8	0.9	2.4	2.3	2.7	2.8	1.9	1.7	420	13	433	11

Source: *Dynamics of Economic Well-Being: Program Participation, Who Gets Assistance?, 1993 to 1994*, Bureau of the Census, Washington, DC, 1999

or family-related reasons. Forty-three percent of those who dropped out between the tenth and twelfth grades reported that they "did not like school." Nearly as many (39 percent) reported that they were failing in school. Almost equal proportions of female and male students complained that they left because they "could not get along with teachers." Male students were more likely than females to report school expulsion and suspension as reasons for leaving school.

Female dropouts were more likely than males to cite family-related reasons. About 21 percent of females left school because they became parents, compared to only 8 percent of males. More than one-quarter of female dropouts said they left school because of pregnancy — 31 percent of Hispanics, 34.5 percent of Blacks, and 26 percent of Whites. Black dropouts were the least likely to mention "got married" as a reason for leaving school prematurely — 2 percent compared to 13 percent of Hispanic and 15 percent of White dropouts. Over one-fourth (28.5 percent) of dropouts left school because they "found a job." A much larger proportion of males (36 percent) than females (22 percent) gave this reason.

"DETACHED YOUTH"

Unfortunately, some young people drop out not only from school, but also from work. The Federal Interagency Forum on Child and Family Statistics applies the term "detached youth" to persons ages 16 to 19 "who are neither enrolled in school nor working." Over the past two decades, this has been a persistent problem; however, the proportion has been declining since 1991, when 11 percent of youth ages 16 to 19 were not enrolled in school or working. The proportion fell to 9 percent in 1996 and 1997 and to 8 percent in 1998. Black youths (12.7 percent) were more likely than White youths (7.2 percent) to fall in this category. Females (8.7 percent) and males (7.5 percent) were about equally likely to be "detached." (See Figure 6.3.) Nearly 14 percent of Hispanic youths were not in school and not working. Studies suggest that the longer a young person remains "detached," the greater the chances are that his or her future prospects will be limited.

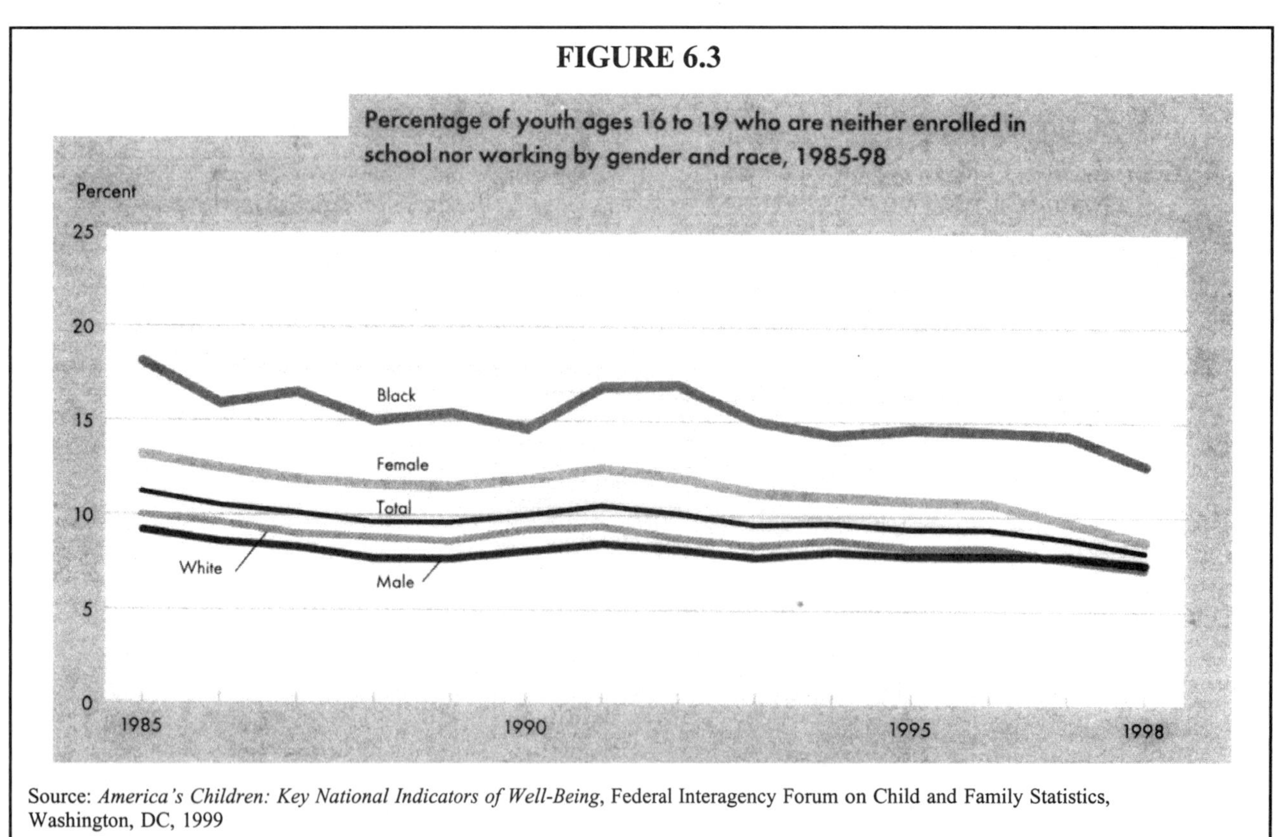

FIGURE 6.3

Source: *America's Children: Key National Indicators of Well-Being*, Federal Interagency Forum on Child and Family Statistics, Washington, DC, 1999

NATIONAL LONGITUDINAL STUDY ON ADOLESCENT HEALTH

The behavioral choices teens make can put their health and success in life at risk. Both the Adolescent Health Program at the University of Minnesota (Minneapolis) and the Centers for Disease Control and Prevention (CDC) monitor teen risk behaviors. The Adolescent Health Program conducts the *National Longitudinal Study on Adolescent Health* (Add Health), and the CDC prepares the annual *Youth Risk Behavior Surveillance* (see below).

The Add Health study, reported in the *Journal of the American Medical Association* (Michael D. Resnick et al., "Protecting Adolescents from Harm," vol. 278, no. 10, September 10, 1997), measured the following risks:

- Emotional distress.

- Suicidal thoughts and behaviors.

- Violence.

- Use of cigarettes, alcohol, and marijuana.

- Age at which sexual activity began.

- Pregnancy history.

The Add Health study interviewed 12,118 adolescents in grades 7 through 12 and found certain home conditions statistically associated with risk behaviors. For example, access to guns in the home was linked to suicidal tendancies and violence, and access to substances at home was related to teens' use of cigarettes, alcohol, and marijuana. Working 20 hours or more a week was linked to emotional distress and use of cigarettes, alcohol, and marijuana.

On the other hand, adolescents who felt strongly connected to family and school were protected to some extent against health-risk behaviors. Parental disapproval of early sexual activity was associated with later onset of sexual activity, and parental expectations of school achievement were linked to lower levels of risk behavior. The presence of parents before school, after school, at dinner, and at bedtime was associated with lower levels of emotional distress, suicidal thoughts, and suicide attempts. Feeling "connected" at school also was associated with lower levels of these behaviors.

THE *MONITORING THE FUTURE* STUDY

Funded by the National Institute on Drug Abuse (NIDA) in Washington, DC, the Institute for Social Research at the University of Michigan conducts an annual survey of substance use among students. The 1999 *Monitoring the Future* study found that the use of illegal drugs remained the same as the past year, the third consecutive year that overall drug use either declined or stayed level. Dr. Lloyd Johnston, director of the study, observed that illegal drug use is down some from the peak levels in the mid-1990s, "But not much of that improvement occurred this year. I am hopeful that this is just a pause in a longer-term decline. In fact, we saw such a pause in the 80s, in the middle of what turned out to be a continuing decline in drug use."

Attitudes Toward Drugs

In 1999, far fewer students considered substance use extremely dangerous than did in 1991. The proportions of those who saw great risk in the use of marijuana decreased significantly in all grades between 1991 and 1999; only 15.7 percent of 1999 seniors considered trying marijuana once or twice very risky, down from 27.1 percent in 1991. The perceived risk of crack and powdered cocaine dropped more among twelfth graders than among eighth and tenth graders, dropping 4 percentage points for perceived crack risk in just the past year. The percentage of seniors who saw great risk in smoking one or more packs of cigarettes a day was about the same in 1991 (69.4 percent) and 1999 (70.8 percent). In 1999, students perceived daily drinking and binge drinking as slightly less

TABLE 6.8

Trends in <u>Harmfulness</u> of Drugs as Perceived by Eighth, Tenth, and Twelfth Graders, 1991–99

Percentage saying "great risk"[a]

How much do you think people risk harming themselves (physically or in other ways), if they . . .	8th Grade 1991	1992	1993	1994	1995	1996	1997	1998	1999	'98–'99 change	10th Grade 1991	1992	1993	1994	1995	1996	1997	1998	1999	'98–'99 change	12th Grade 1991	1992	1993	1994	1995	1996	1997	1998	1999	'98–'99 change
Try marijuana once or twice	40.4	39.1	36.2	31.6	28.9	27.9	25.3	28.1	28.0	0.0	30.0	31.9	29.7	24.4	21.5	20.0	18.8	19.6	19.2	-0.4	27.1	24.5	21.9	19.5	16.3	15.6	14.9	16.7	15.7	-1.0
Smoke marijuana occasionally	57.9	56.3	53.8	48.6	45.9	44.3	43.1	45.0	45.7	+0.7	48.6	48.9	46.1	38.9	35.4	32.8	31.9	32.5	33.5	+1.0	40.6	39.6	35.6	30.1	25.6	25.9	24.7	24.4	23.9	-0.5
Smoke marijuana regularly	83.8	82.0	79.6	74.3	73.0	70.9	72.7	73.0	73.3	+0.3	82.1	81.1	78.5	71.3	67.9	65.9	65.9	65.8	65.9	+0.2	78.6	76.5	72.5	65.0	60.8	59.9	58.1	58.5	57.4	-1.1
Try inhalants once or twice[b]	35.9	37.0	36.5	37.9	36.4	40.8	40.1	38.9	40.8	+1.9	37.8	38.7	40.9	42.7	41.6	47.2	47.5	45.8	48.2	+2.3s	—	—	—	—	—	—	—	—	—	—
Try inhalants regularly[b]	65.6	64.4	64.6	65.5	64.8	68.2	68.7	67.2	68.8	+1.6	69.8	67.9	69.6	71.5	71.8	75.8	74.5	73.3	76.3	+3.0ss	—	—	—	—	—	—	—	—	—	—
Take LSD once or twice[c]	—	—	42.1	38.3	36.7	36.5	37.0	34.9	34.1	-0.8	—	—	48.7	46.5	44.7	45.1	44.5	43.5	45.0	+1.5	46.6	42.3	39.5	38.8	36.4	36.2	34.7	37.4	34.9	-2.5
Take LSD regularly[c]	—	—	68.3	65.8	64.4	63.6	64.1	59.6	58.8	-0.8	—	—	78.9	75.9	75.5	75.3	73.8	72.3	73.9	+1.6	84.3	81.8	79.4	79.1	78.1	77.8	76.6	76.5	76.1	-0.4
Try crack once or twice[b]	62.8	61.2	57.2	54.4	50.8	51.0	49.9	49.3	48.7	-0.6	70.4	69.6	66.6	64.7	60.9	60.9	59.2	58.0	57.8	-0.1	60.6	62.4	57.6	58.4	54.6	56.0	54.0	52.2	48.2	-4.0s
Take crack occasionally[b]	82.2	79.6	76.8	74.4	72.1	71.6	71.2	70.6	70.6	0.0	87.4	86.4	84.4	83.1	81.2	80.3	78.7	77.5	79.1	+1.7	76.5	76.3	73.9	73.8	72.8	71.4	70.3	68.7	67.3	-1.4
Try cocaine powder once or twice[b]	55.5	54.1	50.7	48.4	44.9	45.2	45.0	44.0	43.3	-0.6	59.1	59.2	57.5	56.4	53.5	53.6	52.2	50.9	51.6	+0.7	53.6	57.1	53.2	55.4	52.0	53.2	51.4	48.5	46.1	-2.4
Take cocaine powder occasionally[b]	77.0	74.3	71.8	69.1	66.4	65.7	65.8	65.2	65.4	+0.1	82.2	80.1	79.1	77.8	75.6	75.0	73.9	71.8	73.6	+1.8	69.8	70.8	68.6	70.6	69.1	68.8	67.7	65.4	64.2	-1.2
Try heroin once or twice without using a needle[c]	—	—	—	—	60.1	61.3	63.0	62.8	63.0	+0.2	—	—	—	—	70.7	72.1	73.1	71.7	73.7	+2.0	—	—	—	—	55.6	58.6	60.5	59.6	58.5	-1.1
Take heroin occasionally without using a needle[c]	—	—	—	—	76.8	76.6	79.2	79.0	78.9	-0.1	—	—	—	—	85.1	85.8	86.5	84.9	86.5	+1.6	—	—	—	—	71.2	71.0	74.3	73.4	73.6	+0.2
Try one or two drinks of an alcoholic beverage (beer, wine, liquor)	11.0	12.1	12.4	11.6	11.6	11.8	10.4	12.1	11.6	-0.5	9.0	10.1	10.9	9.4	9.3	8.9	9.0	10.1	10.5	+0.4	9.1	8.6	8.2	7.6	5.9	7.3	6.7	8.0	8.3	+0.3
Take one or two drinks nearly every day	31.8	32.4	32.6	29.9	30.5	28.6	29.1	30.3	29.7	-0.6	36.1	36.8	35.9	32.5	31.7	31.2	31.8	31.9	32.9	+0.9	32.7	30.6	28.2	27.0	24.8	25.1	24.8	24.3	21.8	-2.5
Have five or more drinks once or twice each weekend	59.1	58.0	57.7	54.7	54.1	51.8	55.6	56.0	55.3	-0.8	54.7	55.9	54.9	52.9	52.0	50.9	51.8	52.5	51.9	-0.6	48.6	49.0	48.3	46.5	45.2	49.5	43.0	42.8	43.1	+0.3
Smoke one or more packs of cigarettes per day[d]	51.6	50.8	52.7	50.8	49.8	50.4	52.6	54.3	54.8	+0.5	60.3	59.3	60.7	59.0	57.0	57.9	59.9	61.9	62.7	+0.8	69.4	69.2	69.5	67.6	65.6	68.2	68.7	70.8	70.8	0.0
Use smokeless tobacco regularly	35.1	35.1	36.9	35.5	33.5	34.0	35.2	36.5	37.1	+0.6	40.3	39.6	44.2	42.2	38.2	41.0	42.2	42.8	44.2	+1.4	37.4	35.5	38.9	36.6	33.2	37.4	38.6	40.9	41.1	+0.2
Take steroids[e]	64.2	69.5	70.2	67.6	—	—	—	—	—		67.1	72.7	73.4	72.5	—	—	—	—	—		65.6	70.7	69.1	66.1	66.4	67.6	67.2	68.1	62.1	-5.9sss
Approx. N (in thousands) =	*17.4*	*18.7*	*18.4*	*17.4*	*17.5*	*17.9*	*18.8*	*18.1*	*16.7*		*14.7*	*14.8*	*15.3*	*15.9*	*17.0*	*15.7*	*15.6*	*15.0*	*13.6*		*2.5*	*2.7*	*2.8*	*2.6*	*2.6*	*2.4*	*2.6*	*2.5*	*2.3*	

NOTES: Level of significance of difference between the two most recent classes: s = .05, ss = .01, sss = .001. '—' indicates data not available.
SOURCE: The Monitoring the Future Study, the University of Michigan.

[a]Answer alternatives were: (1) No risk, (2) Slight risk, (3) Moderate risk, (4) Great risk, and (5) Can't say, drug unfamiliar.
[b]8th and 10th grade: Beginning in 1997, data based on two-thirds of N indicated due to changes in questionnaire forms.
[c]8th and 10th grade: Data based on one of two forms in 1993–96; N is one-half of N indicated. Beginning in 1997, data based on one-third of N indicated due to changes in questionnaire forms.
[d]8th and 10th grade: Beginning in 1999, data based on two-thirds of N indicated due to changes in questionnaire forms.
[e]8th and 10th grade: Data based on two forms in 1991 and 1992. Data based on one of two forms in 1993 and 1994; N is one-half of N indicated.

Source: The *Monitoring the Future* Study, Institute for Social Research, University of Michigan, Ann Arbor, MI, 1999

TABLE 6.9

Trends in Annual and 30-Day Prevalence of Use of Various Drugs for Eighth, Tenth, and Twelfth Graders

	Annual										30-Day									
	1991	1992	1993	1994	1995	1996	1997	1998	1999	'98–'99 change	1991	1992	1993	1994	1995	1996	1997	1998	1999	'98–'99 change
Any Illicit Drug[a]																				
8th Grade	11.3	12.9	15.1	18.5	21.4	23.6	22.1	21.0	20.5	-0.5	5.7	6.8	8.4	10.9	12.4	14.6	12.9	12.1	12.2	+0.1
10th Grade	21.4	20.4	24.7	30.0	33.3	37.5	38.5	35.0	35.9	+0.9	11.6	11.0	14.0	18.5	20.2	23.2	23.0	21.5	22.1	+0.6
12th Grade	29.4	27.1	31.0	35.8	39.0	40.2	42.4	41.4	42.1	+0.7	16.4	14.4	18.3	21.9	23.8	24.6	26.2	25.6	25.9	+0.3
Any Illicit Drug Other Than Marijuana[a]																				
8th Grade	8.4	9.3	10.4	11.3	12.6	13.1	11.8	11.0	10.5	-0.5	3.8	4.7	5.3	5.6	6.5	6.9	6.0	5.5	5.5	0.0
10th Grade	12.2	12.3	13.9	15.2	17.5	18.4	18.2	16.6	16.7	+0.1	5.5	5.7	6.5	7.1	8.9	8.9	8.8	8.6	8.6	0.0
12th Grade	16.2	14.9	17.1	18.0	19.4	19.8	20.7	20.2	20.7	+0.5	7.1	6.3	7.9	8.8	10.0	9.5	10.7	10.7	10.4	-0.3
Any Illicit Drug Including Inhalants[a,b]																				
8th Grade	16.7	18.2	21.1	24.2	27.1	28.7	27.2	26.2	25.3	-0.9	8.8	10.0	12.0	14.3	16.1	17.5	16.0	14.9	15.1	+0.2
10th Grade	23.9	23.5	27.4	32.5	35.6	39.6	40.3	37.1	37.7	+0.6	13.1	12.6	15.5	20.0	21.6	24.5	24.1	22.5	23.1	+0.6
12th Grade	31.2	28.8	32.5	37.6	40.2	41.9	43.3	42.4	43.1	+0.7	17.8	15.5	19.3	23.0	24.8	25.5	26.9	26.6	26.5	-0.1
Marijuana/Hashish																				
8th Grade	6.2	7.2	9.2	13.0	15.8	18.3	17.7	16.9	16.5	-0.4	3.2	3.7	5.1	7.8	9.1	11.3	10.2	9.7	9.7	0.0
10th Grade	16.5	15.2	19.2	25.2	28.7	33.6	34.8	31.1	32.1	+1.0	8.7	8.1	10.9	15.8	17.2	20.4	20.5	18.7	19.4	+0.7
12th Grade	23.9	21.9	26.0	30.7	34.7	35.8	38.5	37.5	37.8	+0.3	13.8	11.9	15.5	19.0	21.2	21.9	23.7	22.8	23.1	+0.3
Inhalants[b,c]																				
8th Grade	9.0	9.5	11.0	11.7	12.8	12.2	11.8	11.1	10.3	-0.8	4.4	4.7	5.4	5.6	6.1	5.8	5.6	4.8	5.0	+0.2
10th Grade	7.1	7.5	8.4	9.1	9.6	9.5	8.7	8.0	7.2	-0.8	2.7	2.7	3.3	3.6	3.5	3.3	3.0	2.9	2.6	-0.3
12th Grade	6.6	6.2	7.0	7.7	8.0	7.6	6.7	6.2	5.6	-0.6	2.4	2.3	2.5	2.7	3.2	2.5	2.5	2.3	2.0	-0.3
Nitrites[d]																				
8th Grade	—	—	—	—	—	—	—	—	—		—	—	—	—	—	—	—	—	—	
10th Grade	—	—	—	—	—	—	—	—	—		—	—	—	—	—	—	—	—	—	
12th Grade	0.9	0.5	0.9	1.1	1.1	1.6	1.2	1.4	0.9	-0.5	0.4	0.3	0.6	0.4	0.4	0.7	0.7	1.0	0.4	-0.6s
Hallucinogens[c]																				
8th Grade	1.9	2.5	2.6	2.7	2.6	4.1	3.7	3.4	2.9	-0.5	0.8	1.1	1.2	1.3	1.7	1.9	1.8	1.4	1.3	-0.1
10th Grade	4.0	4.3	4.7	5.8	7.2	7.8	7.6	6.9	6.9	0.0	1.6	1.8	1.9	2.4	3.3	2.8	3.3	3.2	2.9	-0.3
12th Grade	5.8	5.9	7.4	7.6	9.3	10.1	9.8	9.0	9.4	+0.4	2.2	2.1	2.7	3.1	4.4	3.5	3.9	3.8	3.5	-0.3
LSD																				
8th Grade	1.7	2.1	2.3	2.4	3.2	3.5	3.2	2.8	2.4	-0.4	0.6	0.9	1.0	1.1	1.4	1.5	1.5	1.1	1.1	0.0
10th Grade	3.7	4.0	4.2	5.2	6.5	6.9	6.7	5.9	6.0	+0.1	1.5	1.6	1.6	2.0	3.0	2.4	2.8	2.7	2.3	-0.4
12th Grade	5.2	5.6	6.8	6.9	8.4	8.8	8.4	7.6	8.1	+0.5	1.9	2.0	2.4	2.6	4.0	2.5	3.1	3.2	2.7	-0.5
Hallucinogens Other Than LSD																				
8th Grade	0.7	1.1	1.0	1.3	1.7	2.0	1.8	1.6	1.5	-0.1	0.3	0.4	0.5	0.7	0.8	0.9	0.7	0.7	0.6	-0.1
10th Grade	1.3	1.4	1.9	2.4	2.8	3.3	3.3	3.4	3.2	-0.2	0.4	0.5	0.7	1.0	1.0	1.0	1.2	1.4	1.2	-0.2
12th Grade	2.0	1.7	2.2	3.1	3.8	4.4	4.6	4.6	4.3	-0.3	0.7	0.5	0.8	1.2	1.3	1.6	1.7	1.6	1.6	0.0

(Table continued on next page)

TABLE 6.9 (Continued)

Trends in Annual and 30-Day Prevalence of Use of Various Drugs for Eighth, Tenth, and Twelfth Graders

	Annual										30-Day									
	1991	1992	1993	1994	1995	1996	1997	1998	1999	'98–'99 change	1991	1992	1993	1994	1995	1996	1997	1998	1999	'98–'99 change
PCP[d]																				
8th Grade	—	—	—	—	—	—	—	—	—	—	—	—	—	—	—	—	—	—	—	—
10th Grade	—	—	—	—	—	—	—	—	—	—	—	—	—	—	—	—	—	—	—	—
12th Grade	1.4	1.4	1.4	1.6	1.8	2.6	2.3	2.1	1.8	-0.3	0.5	0.6	1.0	0.7	0.6	1.3	0.7	1.0	0.8	-0.2
MDMA (Ecstasy)[d]																				
8th Grade	—	—	—	—	—	2.3	2.3	1.8	1.7	-0.1	—	—	—	—	—	1.0	1.0	0.9	0.8	-0.1
10th Grade	—	—	—	—	—	4.6	3.9	3.3	4.4	+1.1s	—	—	—	—	—	1.8	1.3	1.3	1.8	+0.5
12th Grade	—	—	—	—	—	4.6	4.0	3.6	5.6	+2.0ss	—	—	—	—	—	2.0	1.6	1.5	2.5	+1.0s
Cocaine																				
8th Grade	1.1	1.5	1.7	2.1	2.6	3.0	2.8	3.1	2.7	-0.4	0.5	0.7	0.7	1.0	1.2	1.3	1.1	1.4	1.3	-0.1
10th Grade	2.2	1.9	2.1	2.8	3.5	4.2	4.7	4.7	4.9	+0.2	0.7	0.7	0.9	1.2	1.7	1.7	2.0	2.1	1.8	-0.3
12th Grade	3.5	3.1	3.3	3.6	4.0	4.9	5.5	5.7	6.2	+0.5	1.4	1.3	1.3	1.5	1.8	2.0	2.3	2.4	2.6	+0.2
Crack																				
8th Grade	0.7	0.9	1.0	1.3	1.6	1.8	1.7	2.1	1.8	-0.4s	0.3	0.5	0.4	0.7	0.7	0.8	0.7	0.9	0.8	-0.1
10th Grade	0.9	0.9	1.1	1.4	1.8	2.1	2.2	2.5	2.4	-0.1	0.3	0.4	0.5	0.6	0.9	0.8	0.9	1.1	0.8	-0.3s
12th Grade	1.5	1.5	1.5	1.9	2.1	2.1	2.4	2.5	2.7	+0.2	0.7	0.6	0.7	0.8	1.0	1.0	0.9	1.0	1.1	+0.1
Other Cocaine[e]																				
8th Grade	1.0	1.2	1.3	1.7	2.1	2.5	2.2	2.4	2.3	-0.1	0.5	0.5	0.6	0.9	1.0	1.0	0.8	1.0	1.1	+0.1
10th Grade	2.1	1.7	1.8	2.4	3.0	3.5	4.1	4.0	4.4	+0.4	0.6	0.6	0.7	1.0	1.4	1.3	1.6	1.8	1.6	-0.2
12th Grade	3.2	2.6	2.9	3.0	3.4	4.2	5.0	4.9	5.8	+0.9	1.2	1.0	1.2	1.3	1.3	1.6	2.0	2.0	2.5	+0.5
Heroin[f]																				
8th Grade	0.7	0.7	0.7	1.2	1.4	1.6	1.3	1.3	1.4	+0.1	0.3	0.4	0.4	0.6	0.6	0.7	0.6	0.6	0.6	0.0
10th Grade	0.5	0.6	0.7	0.9	1.1	1.2	1.4	1.4	1.4	0.0	0.2	0.2	0.3	0.4	0.6	0.5	0.6	0.7	0.7	0.0
12th Grade	0.4	0.6	0.5	0.6	1.1	1.0	1.2	1.0	1.1	+0.1	0.2	0.3	0.2	0.3	0.6	0.5	0.5	0.5	0.5	0.0
Other Narcotics[g]																				
8th Grade	—	—	—	—	—	—	—	—	—	—	—	—	—	—	—	—	—	—	—	—
10th Grade	—	—	—	—	—	—	—	—	—	—	—	—	—	—	—	—	—	—	—	—
12th Grade	3.5	3.3	3.6	3.8	4.7	5.4	6.2	6.3	6.7	+0.4	1.1	1.2	1.3	1.5	1.8	2.0	2.3	2.4	2.6	+0.2
Amphetamines[g]																				
8th Grade	6.2	6.5	7.2	7.9	8.7	9.1	8.1	7.2	6.9	-0.3	2.6	3.3	3.6	3.6	4.2	4.6	3.8	3.3	3.4	+0.1
10th Grade	8.2	8.2	9.6	10.2	11.9	12.4	12.1	10.7	10.4	-0.3	3.3	3.6	4.3	4.5	5.3	5.5	5.1	5.1	5.0	-0.1
12th Grade	8.2	7.1	8.4	9.4	9.3	9.5	10.2	10.1	10.2	+0.1	3.2	2.8	3.7	4.0	4.0	4.1	4.8	4.6	4.5	-0.1
Ice[h]																				
8th Grade	—	—	—	—	—	—	—	—	—	—	—	—	—	—	—	—	—	—	—	—
10th Grade	—	—	—	—	—	—	—	—	—	—	—	—	—	—	—	—	—	—	—	—
12th Grade	1.4	1.3	1.7	1.8	2.4	2.8	2.3	3.0	1.9	-1.1ss	0.6	0.5	0.6	0.7	1.1	1.1	0.8	1.2	0.8	-0.4

(Table continued on next page)

Table 6.9 (Continued)

Table 6.9 (Continued)

Trends in Annual and 30-Day Prevalence of Use of Various Drugs for Eighth, Tenth, and Twelfth Graders

	Annual										30-Day									
	1991	1992	1993	1994	1995	1996	1997	1998	1999	'98–'99 change	1991	1992	1993	1994	1995	1996	1997	1998	1999	'98–'99 change
Barbiturates[g]																				
8th Grade	—	—	—	—	—	—	—	—	—	—	—	—	—	—	—	—	—	—	—	—
10th Grade	—	—	—	—	—	—	—	—	—	—	—	—	—	—	—	—	—	—	—	—
12th Grade	3.4	2.8	3.4	4.1	4.7	4.9	5.1	5.5	5.8	+0.3	1.4	1.1	1.3	1.7	2.2	2.1	2.1	2.6	2.6	0.0
Tranquilizers[g]																				
8th Grade	1.8	2.0	2.1	2.4	2.7	3.3	2.9	2.6	2.5	-0.1	0.8	0.8	0.9	1.1	1.2	1.5	1.2	1.2	1.1	-0.1
10th Grade	3.2	3.5	3.3	3.3	4.0	4.6	4.9	5.1	5.4	+0.3	1.2	1.5	1.1	1.5	1.7	1.7	2.2	2.2	2.2	0.0
12th Grade	3.6	2.8	3.5	3.7	4.4	4.6	4.7	5.5	5.8	+0.3	1.4	1.0	1.2	1.4	1.8	2.0	1.8	2.4	2.5	+0.1
Alcohol[i]																				
Any use																				
8th Grade	54.0	53.7	51.6	—	—	—	—	—	—	—	25.1	26.1	26.2	—	—	—	—	—	—	—
				45.4	46.8	45.3	46.5	45.5	43.7	43.5	-0.2			24.3	25.5	24.6	26.2	24.5	23.0	24.0	+1.0
10th Grade	72.3	70.2	69.3	—	—	—	—	—	—	—	42.8	39.9	41.5	—	—	—	—	—	—	—
				63.4	63.9	63.5	65.0	65.2	62.7	63.7	+1.0			38.2	39.2	38.8	40.4	40.1	38.8	40.0	+1.2
12th Grade	77.7	76.8	76.0	—	—	—	—	—	—	—	54.0	51.3	51.0	—	—	—	—	—	—	—
				72.7	73.0	73.7	72.5	74.8	74.3	73.8	-0.5			48.6	50.1	51.3	50.8	52.7	52.0	51.0	-1.0
Been Drunk[h]																				
8th Grade	17.5	18.3	18.2	18.2	18.4	19.8	18.4	17.9	18.5	+0.6	7.6	7.5	7.8	8.7	8.3	9.6	8.2	8.4	9.4	+1.0
10th Grade	40.1	37.0	37.8	38.0	38.5	40.1	40.7	38.3	40.9	+2.6s	20.5	18.1	19.8	20.3	20.8	21.3	22.4	21.1	22.5	+1.4
12th Grade	52.7	50.3	49.6	51.7	52.5	51.9	53.2	52.0	53.2	+1.2	31.6	29.9	28.9	30.8	33.2	31.3	34.2	32.9	32.9	0.0
Cigarettes																				
Any use																				
8th Grade	—	—	—	—	—	—	—	—	—	—	14.3	15.5	16.7	18.6	19.1	21.0	19.4	19.1	17.5	-1.6s
10th Grade	—	—	—	—	—	—	—	—	—	—	20.8	21.5	24.7	25.4	27.9	30.4	29.8	27.6	25.7	-1.9
12th Grade	—	—	—	—	—	—	—	—	—	—	28.3	27.8	29.9	31.2	33.5	34.0	36.5	35.1	34.6	-0.5
Smokeless Tobacco[d]																				
8th Grade	—	—	—	—	—	—	—	—	—	—	6.9	7.0	6.6	7.7	7.1	7.1	5.5	4.8	4.5	-0.3
10th Grade	—	—	—	—	—	—	—	—	—	—	10.0	9.6	10.4	10.5	9.7	8.6	8.9	7.5	6.5	-1.0
12th Grade	—	—	—	—	—	—	—	—	—	—	—	11.4	10.7	11.1	12.2	9.8	9.7	8.8	8.4	-0.4
Steroids[h]																				
8th Grade	1.0	1.1	0.9	1.2	.0	0.9	1.0	1.2	1.7	+0.5sss	0.4	0.5	0.5	0.5	0.6	0.4	0.5	0.5	0.7	+0.2s
10th Grade	1.1	1.1	1.0	1.1	.2	1.2	1.2	1.2	1.7	+0.5ss	0.6	0.6	0.5	0.6	0.6	0.5	0.7	0.6	0.9	+0.3s
12th Grade	1.4	1.1	1.2	1.3	.5	1.4	1.4	1.7	1.8	+0.1	0.8	0.6	0.7	0.9	0.7	0.7	1.0	1.1	0.9	-0.2

(Table continued on next page)

91

TABLE 6.9 (Continued)

NOTES: Level of significance of difference between the two years: s = .05, ss = .01, sss = .001.

'-' indicates data not available. '*' indicates less than .05 percent but greater than 0 percent.

Any apparent inconsistency between the change estimate and the prevalence of use estimates for the two years is due to rounding error.

SOURCE: The Monitoring the Future Study, the University of Michigan.

Approximate Weighted Ns	1991	1992	1993	1994	1995	1996	1997	1998	1999
8th Grade	17,500	18,600	18,300	17,300	17,500	17,800	18,600	18,100	16,700
10th Grade	14,800	14,800	15,300	15,800	17,000	15,600	15,500	15,000	13,600
12th Grade	15,000	15,800	16,300	15,400	15,400	14,300	15,400	15,200	13,600

[a]For 12th graders only: Use of "any illicit drug" includes any use of marijuana, LSD, other hallucinogens, crack, other cocaine, or heroin, or any use of other narcotics, amphetamines, barbiturates, or tranquilizers not under a doctor's orders. For 8th and 10th graders: The use of other narcotics and barbiturates has been excluded, because these younger respondents appear to overreport use (perhaps because they include the use of nonprescription drugs in their answers).

[b]For 12th graders only: Data based on five of six forms in 1991-1998; N is five-sixths of N indicated. Data based on three of six forms beginning in 1999; N is one-half of N indicated.

[c]Inhalants are unadjusted for underreporting of amyl and butyl nitrites; hallucinogens are unadjusted for underreporting of PCP.

[d]For 8th and 10th graders only: Smokeless tobacco data based on one of two forms for 1991-96 and on two of four forms beginning in 1997; N is one-half of N indicated. MDMA data based on one-third of N indicated due to changes on the questionnaire forms. For 12th graders only: Data based on one form; N is one-sixth of N indicated.

[e]For 12th graders only: Data based on four of six forms; N is four-sixths of N indicated.

[f]In 1995, the heroin question was changed in three of six forms for 12th graders and in one of two forms for 8th and 10th graders. Separate questions were asked for use with injection and without injection. Data presented here represent the combined data from all forms. In 1996, the heroin question was changed in the remaining 8th and 10th grade form.

[g]Only drug use which was not under a doctor's orders is included here.

[h]For 12th graders only: Data based on two of six forms; N is two-sixths of N indicated.

[i]For all grades: In 1993, the question text was changed slightly in half of the forms to indicate that a "drink" meant "more than a few sips." The data in the upper line for alcohol came from forms using the original wording, while the data in the lower line came from forms using the revised wording. In 1993, each line of data was based on one of two forms for the 8th and 10th graders and on three of six forms for the 12th graders. N is one-half of N indicated for all groups. Data for 1994-99 were based on all forms for all grades.

[j]Daily use is defined as use on twenty or more occasions in the past thirty days except for 5+ drinks, cigarettes, and smokeless tobacco, for which actual daily use is measured.

Source: The *Monitoring the Future* Study, Institute for Social Research, University of Michigan, Ann Arbor, MI, 1999

TABLE 6.10

Long-Term Trends in Prevalence of Cigarettes for Eighth, Tenth, and Twelfth Graders

	1975	1976	1977	1978	1979	1980	1981	1982	1983	1984	1985	1986	1987	1988	1989	1990	1991	1992	1993	1994	1995	1996	1997	1998	1999	'98–'99 change
Lifetime																										
8th Grade																	44.0	45.2	45.3	46.1	46.4	49.2	47.3	45.7	44.1	-1.6
10th Grade																	55.1	53.5	56.3	56.9	57.6	61.2	60.2	57.7	57.6	-0.1
12th Grade	73.6	75.4	75.7	75.3	74.0	71.0	71.0	70.1	70.6	69.7	68.8	67.6	67.2	66.4	65.7	64.4	63.1	61.8	61.9	62.0	64.2	63.5	65.4	65.3	64.6	-0.7
Thirty-Day																										
8th Grade																	14.3	15.5	16.7	18.6	19.1	21.0	19.4	19.1	17.5	-1.6s
10th Grade																	20.8	21.5	24.7	25.4	27.9	30.4	29.8	27.6	25.7	-1.9
12th Grade	36.7	38.8	38.4	36.7	34.4	30.5	29.4	30.0	30.3	29.3	30.1	29.6	29.4	28.7	28.6	29.4	28.3	27.8	29.9	31.2	33.5	34.0	36.5	35.1	34.6	-0.5
Daily																										
8th Grade																	7.2	7.0	8.3	8.8	9.3	10.4	9.0	8.8	8.1	-0.7
10th Grade																	12.6	12.3	14.2	14.6	16.3	18.3	18.0	15.8	15.9	+0.1
12th Grade	26.9	28.8	28.8	27.5	25.4	21.3	20.3	21.1	21.2	18.7	19.5	18.7	18.7	18.1	18.9	19.1	18.5	17.2	19.0	19.4	21.6	22.2	24.6	22.4	23.1	+0.7
1/2 pack+ per day																										
8th Grade																	3.1	2.9	3.5	3.6	3.4	4.3	3.5	3.6	3.3	-0.3
10th Grade																	6.5	6.0	7.0	7.6	8.3	9.4	8.6	7.9	7.6	-0.3
12th Grade	17.9	19.2	19.4	18.8	16.5	14.3	13.5	14.2	13.8	12.3	12.5	11.4	11.4	10.6	11.2	11.3	10.7	10.0	10.9	11.2	12.4	13.0	14.3	12.6	13.2	+0.6
Approx. Ns																										
8th Grade																	*17500*	*18600*	*18300*	*17300*	*17500*	*17800*	*18600*	*18100*	*16700*	
10th Grade																	*14800*	*14800*	*15300*	*15800*	*17000*	*15600*	*15500*	*15000*	*13600*	
12th Grade	*9400*	*15400*	*17100*	*17800*	*15500*	*15900*	*17500*	*17700*	*16300*	*15900*	*16000*	*15200*	*16300*	*16300*	*16700*	*15200*	*15000*	*15800*	*16300*	*15400*	*15400*	*14300*	*15400*	*15200*	*13600*	

NOTE: Level of significance of difference between the two years indicated: s = .05, ss = .01, sss = .001.
SOURCE: The Monitoring the Future Study, The University of Michigan.

Source: The *Monitoring the Future* Study, Institute for Social Research, University of Michigan, Ann Arbor, MI, 1999

risky than they did in 1991. However, 1999 seniors considered daily drinking far less risky than 1991 seniors. One encouraging sign was that a slightly higher proportion of eighth-grade students considered using heroin dangerous in 1999 than in 1995, when heroin was first added to the survey. (See Table 6.8.)

Generally, with a few exceptions, personal disapproval of drug use also declined from 1991 to 1999. In 1999, only half (48.8 percent) of seniors disapproved of trying marijuana once or twice, compared to 68.7 percent in 1991. Only three-fifths (62.5 percent) disapproved of occasional use, while 79.4 percent of seniors in 1991 did. In general, students disapproved most strongly of heroin (90 percent), crack (87.6 percent) and cocaine (84.3 percent), and LSD (83 percent) and disapproved least of occasional use of alcohol (24.6 percent).

Researchers fear that these changes in attitudes and beliefs could lead to an increase in use. It is important to keep in mind, however, that an overwhelming majority of students disapprove of drug (with the exception of marijuana) and cigarette use. Use of marijuana once or twice and alcohol use were the only categories for which fewer than half of students expressed disapproval.

Marijuana

In 1999, 16.5 percent of eighth graders, 32.1 percent of tenth graders, and 37.8 percent of twelfth graders reported having used marijuana at least once during the 12 months before the survey. These rates represented increases from 1991 when 6.2 percent of eighth graders, 16.5 percent of tenth graders, and 23.9 percent of twelfth graders said they had used marijuana at least once in the past year. Among seniors, current use of marijuana (any use within 30 days of the survey) was down from a peak of 37 percent in 1979 to 23.1 percent in 1999, but the rate had been as low as 11.9 percent in 1992. (See Table 6.9.) About 6 percent of se-

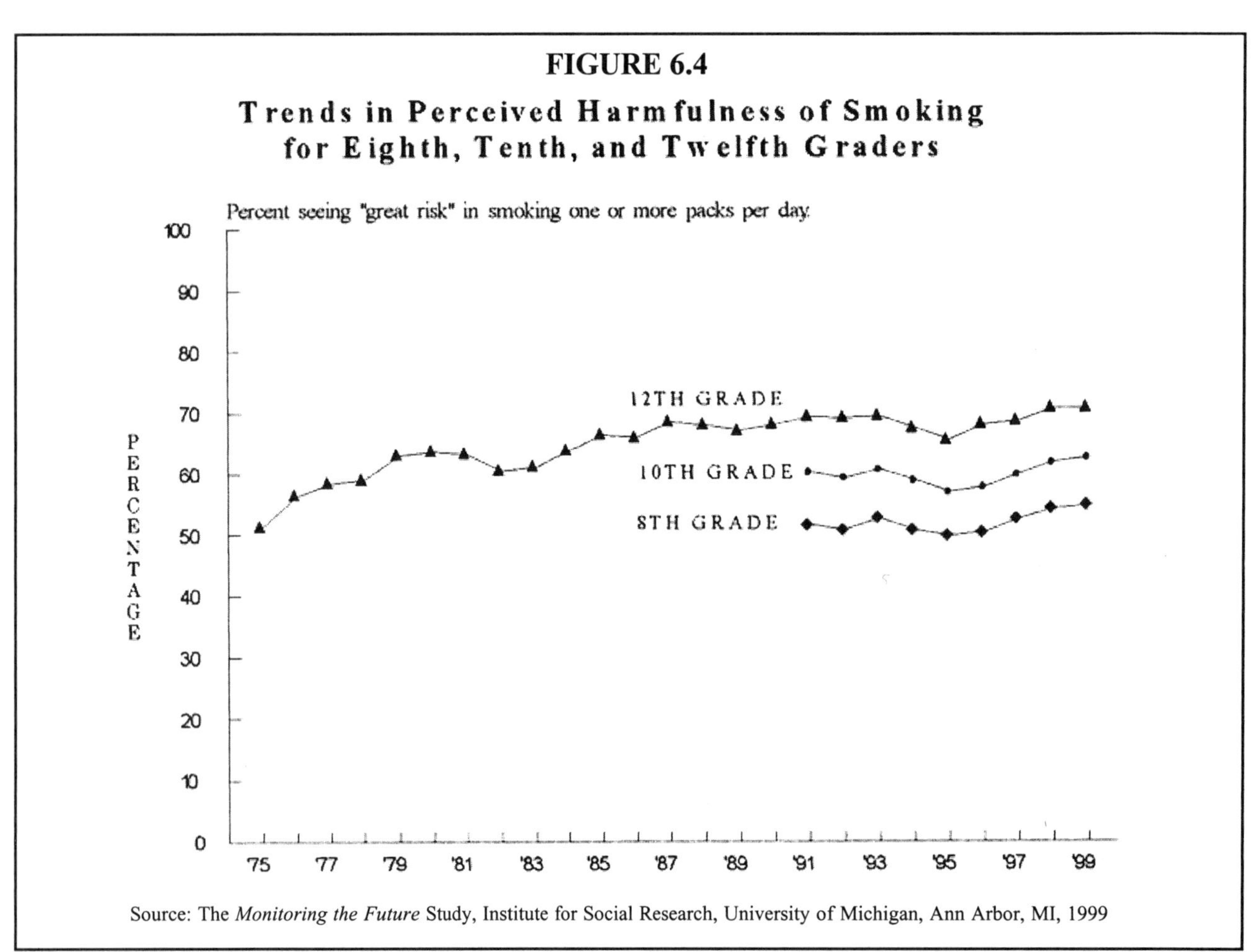

FIGURE 6.4

Trends in Perceived Harmfulness of Smoking for Eighth, Tenth, and Twelfth Graders

Source: The *Monitoring the Future* Study, Institute for Social Research, University of Michigan, Ann Arbor, MI, 1999

niors reported using marijuana daily in 1999, up significantly from 1991 (2 percent), but still far below the almost 11 percent in 1978.

The most alarming news is that the proportion of eighth graders using marijuana in the month preceding the survey more than tripled, from 3.2 percent in 1991 to 9.7 percent in 1999. At the same time, the proportion of tenth-grade users more than doubled, from 8.7 percent in 1991 to 19.4 percent in 1999, and twelfth-grade users increased from 13.8 percent in 1991 to 23.1 percent in 1999. (See Table 6.9.) Daily use of marijuana also grew alarmingly, although proportions were still low. The proportion of eighth graders using marijuana daily increased sevenfold, from 0.2 percent in 1991 to 1.4 percent in 1999. The proportion of tenth graders grew fourfold, from less than 1 percent in 1991 to almost 4 (3.8) percent in 1999, and the percentage of seniors who used marijuana daily tripled, from 2 percent in 1991 to nearly 6 percent in 1999.

Inhalants

During the 1990s, the proportion of eighth, tenth, and twelfth graders who used inhalants, such as glues, solvents, and aerosols, peaked in 1995 and then began to decline. Inhalants are most often used in the earlier grade levels. For example, 10.3 percent of eighth graders reported using an inhalant during the previous year, compared to 7.2 percent of tenth graders and 5.6 percent of twelfth graders (Table 6.9). Inhalant use has risen fairly steadily from the mid-1970s. Dr. Johnson warns that because most inhalants are common household products, young people may not understand that they are potentially lethal.

Alcohol and Cigarettes

In 1999, 52.1 percent of eighth graders, 70.6 percent of tenth graders, and 80 percent of twelfth graders reported having tried alcohol in their life-

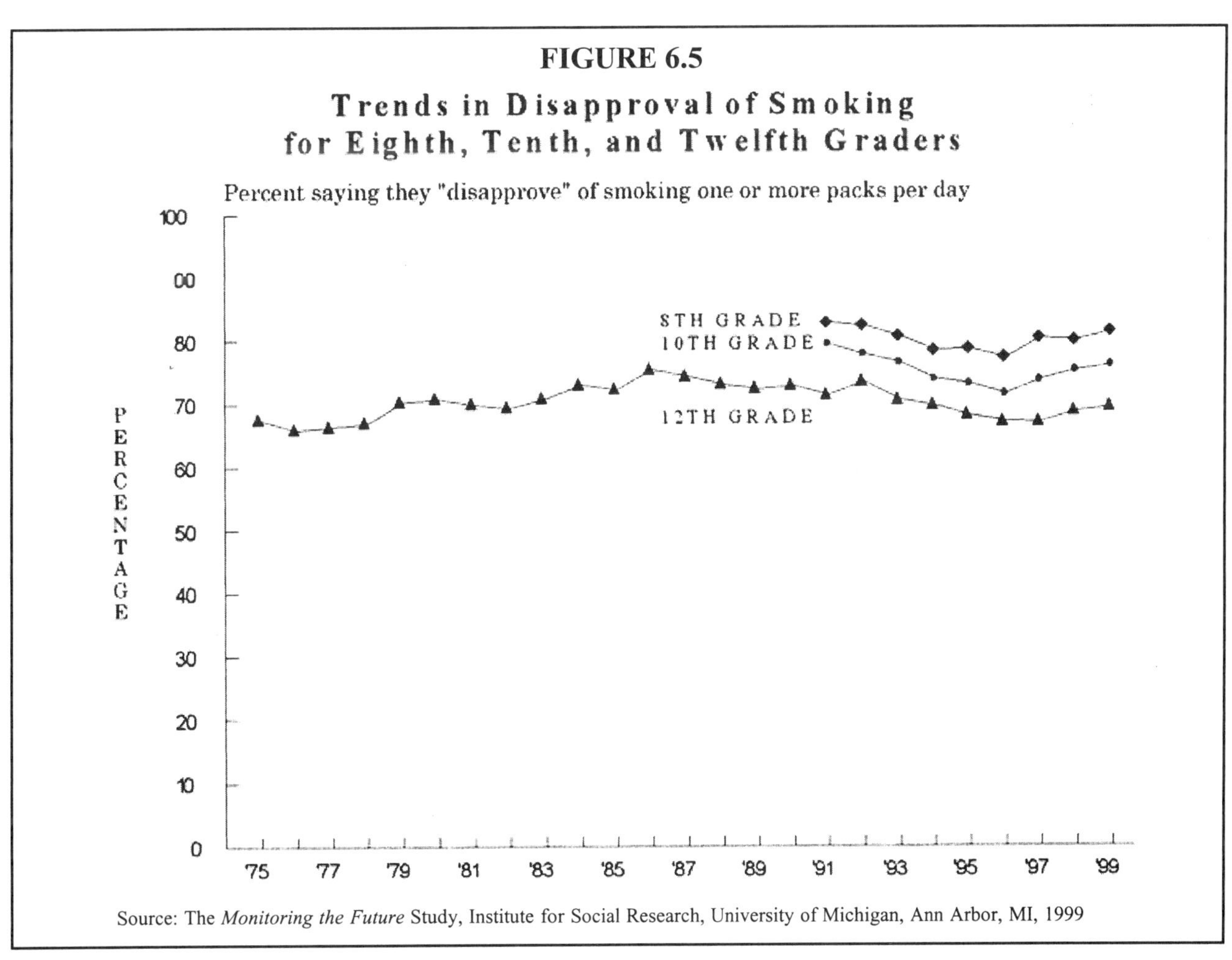

FIGURE 6.5

Trends in Disapproval of Smoking for Eighth, Tenth, and Twelfth Graders

Source: The *Monitoring the Future* Study, Institute for Social Research, University of Michigan, Ann Arbor, MI, 1999

times. Twenty-four percent of eighth graders, 40 percent of tenth graders, and 51 percent of twelfth graders had used alcohol within the month prior to the survey (Table 6.9). Students also reported that episodes of heavy drinking ("binge" drinking) were quite common. When asked if they had five or more drinks in a row on at least one occasion in the previous two weeks, 15 percent of eighth graders, 26 percent of tenth graders, and 31 percent of twelfth graders admitted that they had.

Cigarette smoking among seniors declined slowly but steadily from 1975 to the early 1990s, but the rates grew slightly between 1991 and 1996 and have since leveled out. In 1999, 3.3 percent of eighth graders, 7.6 percent of tenth graders, and 13.2 percent of twelfth graders reported smoking at least half a pack a day. (See Table 6.10.)

In 1999, about one-half to two-thirds of students believed that smoking one or more packs of cigarettes a day represented a great risk, virtually unchanged since 1991 (Figure 6.4). Students in the younger grades (81 percent and 76 percent, respectively) were somewhat more likely than seniors (70 percent) to disapprove of daily cigarette smoking (Figure 6.5).

Dr. Johnson has often warned that the increases in adolescent smoking pose serious consequences for the nation's future health and productivity. "As we and many others have observed previously," he stated, "cigarettes will kill far more of today's children than all other drugs combined, including alcohol." However, the nation feels less concern because many of the health consequences do not show up for 30 years. "If cigarette smoking killed quickly, like drunk driving does," said Dr. Johnston, "the country would be treating the current rates of adolescent smoking as an extreme emergency."

TABLE 6.11

Percentage of students in middle school (grades 6–8) and high school (grades 9–12) currently* using tobacco products, by type of tobacco product, sex, and race/ethnicity — United States, National Youth Tobacco Survey, 1999

| Type of tobacco product | Sex | | | | Race/Ethnicity | | | | | | | |
| | Male | | Female | | White | | Black | | Hispanic | | Total | |
	%	(95% CI[†])	%	(95% CI)	%	(95% CI)	%	(95% CI)	%	(95% CI)	%	(95% CI)
Any use[§]												
Middle school	14.2	(± 2.2)	11.3	(± 2.2)	11.6	(± 2.3)	14.4	(± 2.7)	15.2	(± 5.2)	**12.8**	(± 2.0)
High school	38.1	(± 3.2)	31.4	(± 3.1)	39.4	(± 3.2)	24.0	(± 4.2)	30.7	(± 4.4)	**34.8**	(± 2.7)
Cigarette												
Middle school	9.6	(± 1.7)	8.8	(± 1.7)	8.8	(± 2.0)	9.0	(± 1.8)	11.0	(± 4.1)	**9.2**	(± 1.6)
High school	28.7	(± 2.8)	28.2	(± 3.3)	32.8	(± 3.1)	15.8	(± 3.8)	25.8	(± 4.7)	**28.4**	(± 2.7)
Smokeless												
Middle school	4.2	(± 1.3)	1.3	(± 0.5)	3.0	(± 1.1)	1.9	(± 0.9)	2.2	(± 0.9)	**2.7**	(± 0.7)
High school	11.6	(± 2.8)	1.5	(± 0.6)	8.7	(± 2.1)	2.4	(± 1.3)	3.6	(± 1.6)	**6.6**	(± 1.6)
Cigar												
Middle school	7.8	(± 1.3)	4.4	(± 1.3)	4.9	(± 1.0)	8.8	(± 2.3)	7.6	(± 2.9)	**6.1**	(± 1.1)
High school	20.3	(± 1.9)	10.2	(± 1.6)	16.0	(± 1.6)	14.8	(± 3.5)	13.4	(± 2.9)	**15.3**	(± 1.4)
Pipe												
Middle school	3.5	(± 0.8)	1.4	(± 0.6)	2.0	(± 0.6)	2.0	(± 0.9)	3.8	(± 1.7)	**2.4**	(± 0.5)
High school	4.2	(± 0.9)	1.4	(± 0.5)	2.6	(± 0.6)	1.8	(± 0.9)	3.8	(± 1.4)	**2.8**	(± 0.5)
Bidi												
Middle school	3.1	(± 0.8)	1.8	(± 0.6)	1.8	(± 0.5)	2.8	(± 1.3)	3.5	(± 1.6)	**2.4**	(± 0.6)
High school	6.1	(± 1.0)	3.8	(± 1.0)	4.4	(± 0.9)	5.8	(± 2.1)	5.6	(± 2.1)	**5.0**	(± 0.8)
Kretek												
Middle school	2.2	(± 0.6)	1.7	(± 0.7)	1.7	(± 0.7)	1.7	(± 0.8)	2.1	(± 0.6)	**1.9**	(± 0.5)
High school	6.2	(± 1.1)	5.3	(± 1.5)	6.5	(± 1.5)	2.8	(± 1.5)	5.5	(± 1.9)	**5.8**	(± 1.2)

* Used tobacco on one or more of the 30 days preceding the survey.
† Confidence interval.
§ Use of cigarettes, smokeless tobacco, cigars, pipes, bidis, or kreteks.

Source: "Tobacco Use Among Middle and High School Students — United States, 1999," *Morbidity and Mortality Weekly Report,* vol. 49, no. 3, January 28, 2000

TABLE 6.12

Percentage of high school students who used tobacco, by sex, race/ethnicity, and grade — United States, Youth Risk Behavior Survey, 1997

Category	Lifetime cigarette use*			Current cigarette use[†]			Frequent cigarette use[§]			Smokeless tobacco use[¶]		
	Female	Male	Total	Female	Male	Total	Female	Male	Total	Female	Male	Total
Race/Ethnicity												
White**	70.3	70.4	**70.4**	39.9	39.6	**39.7**	20.1	19.8	**19.9**	1.6	20.6	**12.2**
	(±3.3)[††]	(±2.4)	(±2.3)	(±3.2)	(±3.8)	(±2.4)	(±3.2)	(±3.3)	(±2.2)	(±0.9)	(±4.0)	(±2.5)
Black**	66.8	70.1	**68.4**	17.4	28.2	**22.7**	4.3	10.1	**7.1**	1.3	3.2	**2.2**
	(±5.2)	(±4.7)	(±4.4)	(±3.9)	(±5.5)	(±3.8)	(±1.8)	(±3.1)	(±1.8)	(±1.2)	(±1.7)	(±1.1)
Hispanic	72.7	76.9	**75.0**	32.3	35.5	**34.0**	8.1	13.2	**10.9**	1.2	8.3	**5.1**
	(±3.9)	(±3.6)	(±2.7)	(±3.7)	(±3.6)	(±2.7)	(±2.7)	(±3.7)	(±2.6)	(±1.0)	(±3.3)	(±2.3)
Grade												
9	69.1	66.5	**67.7**	32.6	34.2	**33.4**	11.6	14.5	**13.1**	2.1	16.6	**9.7**
	(±5.5)	(±5.9)	(±5.1)	(±4.9)	(±7.3)	(±5.1)	(±3.4)	(±6.3)	(±3.8)	(±1.7)	(±5.1)	(±2.7)
10	68.9	70.8	**70.0**	35.1	35.6	**35.3**	14.1	15.7	**15.0**	0.9	11.6	**6.8**
	(±5.1)	(±3.9)	(±3.9)	(±7.8)	(±2.9)	(±4.1)	(±2.9)	(±2.7)	(±1.9)	(±0.6)	(±3.2)	(±1.7)
11	67.1	70.2	**68.8**	31.7	40.7	**36.6**	17.7	19.9	**18.9**	2.1	16.5	**10.0**
	(±4.5)	(±3.5)	(±3.1)	(±5.2)	(±4.7)	(±3.6)	(±4.2)	(±3.3)	(±2.8)	(±1.7)	(±4.5)	(±2.5)
12	71.7	75.1	**73.7**	38.8	40.0	**39.6**	19.0	19.7	**19.4**	0.6	18.3	**10.5**
	(±4.4)	(±4.6)	(±4.1)	(±6.8)	(±5.0)	(±4.9)	(±3.3)	(±4.3)	(±3.1)	(±0.6)	(±6.2)	(±3.6)
Total	**69.3**	**70.9**	**70.2**	**34.7**	**37.7**	**36.4**	**15.7**	**17.6**	**16.7**	**1.5**	**15.8**	**9.3**
	(±2.6)	(±1.9)	(±1.9)	(±2.8)	(±2.7)	(±2.3)	(±2.1)	(±2.7)	(±1.9)	(±0.7)	(±3.7)	(±2.2)

*Ever tried cigarette smoking, even one or two puffs.
[†]Smoked cigarettes on ≥1 of the 30 days preceding the survey.
[§]Smoked cigarettes on ≥20 of the 30 days preceding the survey.
[¶]Used chewing tobacco or snuff on ≥1 of the 30 days preceding the survey.
**Non-Hispanic.
[††]Ninety-five percent confidence interval.

Source: "Youth Risk Behavior Surveillance — United States, 1997," *Morbidity and Mortality Weekly Report*, vol. 47, no. SS-3, August 14, 1998

For more information about substance use among adolescents, see *Illegal Drugs — America's Anguish* and *Alcohol and Tobacco — America's Drugs of Choice*, both from Information Plus, Wylie, Texas, 1999.

TOBACCO USE AMONG AMERICAN MIDDLE AND HIGH SCHOOL STUDENTS

The *National Youth Tobacco Survey* (NYTS), conducted in 1999 by the American Legacy Foundation and the Centers for Disease Control and Prevention (CDC) Foundation, reported on the prevalence of tobacco use among middle school and high school students across the country. In 1999, nearly 13 percent of middle school students and 35 percent of high school students used some type of tobacco (Table 6.11).

Among middle school students (grades 6 through 8), cigarettes (9.2 percent) and cigars (6.1 percent) were the most prevalent type of tobacco used. Cigarette smoking rates were similar among males and females and among racial/ethnic groups. Black students (8.8 percent) were significantly more likely than White students (4.9 percent) to smoke cigars. Boys were more likely than girls to use smokeless tobacco, smoke cigars, and smoke tobacco in a pipe. (See Table 6.11.)

Not surprisingly, high school students (grades 9 through 12) were also more likely to smoke cigarettes (28.4 percent) and cigars (15.3 percent). White (32.8 percent) and Hispanic (25.8 percent) students were significantly more likely than Black students (15.8 percent) to smoke cigarettes. White students (8.7 percent) were significantly more likely than Black (2.4 percent) and Hispanic (3.6 percent) students to use smokeless tobacco. Boys were far more likely to use smokeless tobacco, smoke cigars, and smoke tobacco in a pipe than girls. (See Table 6.11.)

In 1999, 2.4 percent of middle school students and 5 percent of high school students smoked bidis (Table 6.11). A bidi, imported primarily from India, is a small, hand-rolled cigarette wrapped in herb leaves. The tobacco is available in a variety of flavors, such as strawberry, chocolate, and mint. The CDC reported that bidis contain as much as seven times the nicotine as regular cigarettes.

TABLE 6.13

Percentage of high school students who drank alcohol or used marijuana, by sex, race/ethnicity, and grade — United States, Youth Risk Behavior Survey, 1997

Category	Lifetime alcohol use*			Current alcohol use[†]			Episodic heavy drinking[§]			Lifetime marijuana use[¶]			Current marijuana use**		
	Female	Male	Total	Female	Male	Total	Female	Male	Total	Female	Male	Total	Female	Male	Total
Race/Ethnicity															
White[††]	79.9 (±2.9)[§§]	82.4 (±2.0)	**81.3** (±2.1)	51.6 (±4.8)	56.0 (±2.8)	**54.0** (±3.0)	32.9 (±3.2)	41.6 (±3.1)	**37.7** (±2.3)	41.9 (±4.4)	48.3 (±3.8)	**45.4** (±3.9)	21.2 (±2.8)	28.0 (±3.6)	**25.0** (±3.1)
Black[††]	73.8 (±3.4)	72.2 (±2.8)	**73.0** (±2.4)	34.9 (±3.5)	39.2 (±4.5)	**36.9** (±2.9)	11.5 (±2.8)	21.0 (±3.0)	**16.1** (±2.0)	45.4 (±4.4)	59.3 (±4.2)	**52.2** (±3.7)	21.4 (±3.6)	35.6 (±4.4)	**28.2** (±3.3)
Hispanic	82.1 (±3.8)	83.9 (±3.6)	**83.1** (±2.3)	50.7 (±3.9)	56.7 (±6.5)	**53.9** (±3.8)	28.8 (±4.2)	40.0 (±6.1)	**34.9** (±3.4)	43.2 (±5.5)	54.7 (±6.1)	**49.5** (±4.9)	23.3 (±4.4)	33.1 (±4.9)	**28.6** (±4.0)
Grade															
9	73.6 (±5.0)	70.5 (±5.6)	**72.0** (±4.9)	43.7 (±6.6)	44.7 (±7.4)	**44.2** (±6.1)	25.8 (±4.9)	25.5 (±5.6)	**25.7** (±4.0)	36.1 (±6.2)	41.3 (±5.5)	**38.8** (±4.5)	20.1 (±4.3)	26.8 (±5.3)	**23.6** (±3.8)
10	76.9 (±5.7)	77.9 (±3.5)	**77.4** (±4.0)	45.3 (±7.5)	48.7 (±3.9)	**47.2** (±4.3)	26.3 (±7.2)	32.7 (±2.9)	**29.9** (±3.7)	43.3 (±6.0)	48.1 (±4.9)	**45.9** (±4.7)	20.9 (±4.7)	28.5 (±2.9)	**25.0** (±2.5)
11	80.1 (±2.7)	83.4 (±2.0)	**81.9** (±1.6)	47.8 (±6.2)	57.8 (±2.9)	**53.2** (±2.9)	28.2 (±4.2)	45.2 (±4.5)	**37.5** (±2.9)	43.8 (±5.0)	55.6 (±3.8)	**50.3** (±3.8)	22.9 (±4.5)	34.7 (±4.4)	**29.3** (±3.6)
12	82.3 (±3.4)	85.3 (±3.0)	**84.0** (±2.6)	53.7 (±5.5)	60.2 (±5.6)	**57.3** (±4.9)	33.6 (±5.0)	44.0 (±5.6)	**39.3** (±4.6)	47.7 (±6.8)	56.1 (±5.9)	**52.4** (±5.1)	21.9 (±5.1)	30.3 (±5.8)	**26.6** (±4.1)
Total	78.4 (±2.2)	79.7 (±2.0)	79.1 (±2.0)	47.8 (±3.9)	53.3 (±2.4)	50.8 (±2.8)	28.6 (±2.8)	37.3 (±2.4)	33.4 (±2.1)	42.9 (±3.6)	50.7 (±2.8)	47.1 (±2.9)	21.4 (±2.0)	30.2 (±2.9)	26.2 (±2.2)

*Ever had at least one drink of alcohol.
[†]Drank alcohol on ≥1 of the 30 days preceding the survey.
[§]Drank five or more drinks of alcohol on at least one occasion on ≥1 of the 30 days preceding the survey.
[¶]Ever used marijuana.
**Used marijuana one or more times during the 30 days preceding the survey.
[††]Non-Hispanic.
[§§]Ninety-five percent confidence interval.

Source: "Youth Risk Behavior Surveillance — United States, 1997," *Morbidity and Mortality Weekly Report*, vol. 47, no. SS-3, August 14, 1998

About 2 percent of middle school students and 5.8 percent of high school students smoked Kreteks (Table 6.11). Kreteks are clove cigarettes, a mixture of tobacco and clove spice rolled into a cigarette. Most are imported from Indonesia. Many clove cigarettes have a mint flavor added to the paper around the filter. Some people suspect that clove cigarettes have more nicotine than regular cigarettes, while others believe they have less.

YOUTH RISK
BEHAVIOR SURVEILLANCE

The CDC periodically surveys risk behaviors among youths. In the "Youth Risk Behavior Surveillance — United States, 1997" (supplement to *Morbidity and Mortality Weekly Report*, August 14, 1998), the CDC reported that Black high school students were less likely than White or Hispanic students to use tobacco, alcohol, and cocaine/crack. With the exception of smokeless tobacco, females were about as likely as males to smoke cigarettes and use alcohol.

Using Tobacco

In 1997, White students (39.7 percent) and Hispanic students (34 percent) were more likely than Black teens (22.7 percent) to have smoked cigarettes at least once in the 30 days preceding the survey. White students were also more likely to be frequent cigarette smokers (19.9 percent) and to use smokeless tobacco products (12.2 percent). (See Table 6.12)

Not surprisingly, seniors were most likely to be current (39.6 percent) and frequent (19.4 percent) smokers. Males and females were almost equally likely to be frequent smokers at all grade levels. Males (15.8 percent) were far more likely than females (1.5 percent) to use smokeless tobacco. (See Table 6.12.)

Using Alcohol and Marijuana

In 1997, Black high school students (36.9 percent) reported lower levels of current alcohol use

98

TABLE 6.14

Percentage of high school students who reported engaging in sexual behaviors, by sex, race/ethnicity, and grade — United States, Youth Risk Behavior Survey, 1997

Category	Ever had sexual intercourse			First sexual intercourse before age 13			Four or more sex partners during lifetime			Currently sexually active*			Currently abstinent[†]		
	Female	Male	Total	Female	Male	Total	Female	Male	Total	Female	Male	Total	Female	Male	Total
Race/Ethnicity															
White[§]	44.0	43.3	**43.6**	3.2	4.6	**4.0**	12.1	11.3	**11.6**	35.1	29.6	**32.0**	20.2	31.7	**26.6**
	(±5.7)[¶]	(±3.9)	(±4.2)	(±1.0)	(±1.0)	(±0.8)	(±1.9)	(±1.5)	(±1.5)	(±4.4)	(±3.0)	(±3.1)	(±2.3)	(±3.4)	(±2.4)
Black[§]	65.6	80.3	**72.7**	11.0	33.3	**21.7**	25.4	52.8	**38.5**	47.3	60.5	**53.6**	27.9	24.6	**26.1**
	(±4.4)	(±2.8)	(±2.8)	(±3.4)	(±4.6)	(±2.3)	(±5.9)	(±3.9)	(±3.6)	(±4.2)	(±4.1)	(±3.2)	(±3.8)	(±4.2)	(±2.7)
Hispanic	45.7	57.7	**52.2**	3.4	11.4	**7.7**	10.2	20.1	**15.5**	33.2	37.3	**35.4**	27.2	35.2	**32.0**
	(±3.9)	(±6.3)	(±3.6)	(±1.4)	(±2.5)	(±1.4)	(±3.0)	(±3.2)	(±2.4)	(±3.8)	(±5.6)	(±3.9)	(±5.5)	(±5.4)	(±4.1)
Grade															
9	34.0	41.8	**38.0**	6.5	14.7	**10.8**	7.9	16.2	**12.2**	22.4	25.9	**24.2**	33.3	37.5	**35.7**
	(±4.0)	(±6.1)	(±3.8)	(±2.0)	(±3.2)	(±2.0)	(±2.4)	(±3.2)	(±2.5)	(±3.5)	(±4.8)	(±3.3)	(±5.9)	(±6.3)	(±4.4)
10	43.5	41.7	**42.5**	5.1	9.7	**7.6**	11.7	15.5	**13.8**	31.2	27.6	**29.2**	28.4	33.9	**31.3**
	(±5.2)	(±4.6)	(±4.3)	(±1.2)	(±3.0)	(±1.8)	(±3.2)	(±2.8)	(±2.7)	(±5.2)	(±3.0)	(±2.9)	(±8.3)	(±6.4)	(±5.7)
11	50.3	49.3	**49.7**	3.5	8.2	**6.1**	15.8	17.4	**16.7**	41.5	34.8	**37.8**	17.5	29.2	**23.8**
	(±5.8)	(±5.5)	(±5.2)	(±1.3)	(±2.3)	(±1.6)	(±3.9)	(±3.4)	(±2.9)	(±5.7)	(±4.9)	(±4.8)	(±4.9)	(±4.5)	(±3.7)
12	61.9	60.1	**60.9**	2.9	6.0	**4.7**	20.6	20.6	**20.6**	49.5	43.1	**46.0**	20.0	28.2	**24.5**
	(±7.4)	(±6.8)	(±6.5)	(±1.3)	(±2.0)	(±1.4)	(±4.4)	(±3.8)	(±3.5)	(±5.9)	(±5.4)	(±5.0)	(±4.7)	(±3.5)	(±3.1)
Total	**47.7**	**48.9**	**48.4**	**4.5**	**9.4**	**7.2**	**14.1**	**17.6**	**16.0**	**36.5**	**33.4**	**34.8**	**23.4**	**31.5**	**27.8**
	(±3.7)	(±3.4)	(±3.1)	(±0.7)	(±1.8)	(±0.9)	(±2.0)	(±1.5)	(±1.4)	(±2.7)	(±2.6)	(±2.2)	(±2.9)	(±2.3)	(±1.8)

* Sexual intercourse during the 3 months preceding the survey.
[†] Among those who have ever had sexual intercourse, no sexual intercourse during the 3 months preceding the survey.
[§] Non-Hispanic.
[¶] Ninety-five percent confidence interval.

Source: "Youth Risk Behavior Surveillance — United States, 1997," *Morbidity and Mortality Weekly Report*, vol. 47, no. SS-3, August 14, 1998

than either White (54 percent) or Hispanic students (53.9 percent). Black teenagers (16.1 percent) were also less likely to report binge drinking (five or more drinks in a row) than were White (37.7 percent) or Hispanic students (34.9 percent). Female students were slightly less likely than males to be current drinkers and considerably less likely to be binge drinkers. (See Table 6.13.)

White youth (45.4 percent) were only slightly less likely to report lifetime marijuana use than either Black (52.2 percent) or Hispanic (49.5 percent) students. Students of all races were about equally likely to have used marijuana in the past 30 days — Whites, 25 percent; Blacks, 28.2 percent; and Hispanics, 28.6 percent. A lower percentage of females (21.4 percent) than males (30.2 percent) were current users in 1997. (See Table 6.13.)

Sexual Activity

In *Great Transitions* (see above), the Carnegie Council on Adolescent Development pointed out that the age of first intercourse has declined over the past 30 years. In its 1997 "Youth Risk Behavior Surveillance" (see above), the CDC reported that about 4.5 percent of females and 9.4 percent of males had first experienced sexual intercourse before age 13. Over one-third (36.5 percent) of high school females and one-third (33.4 percent) of males claimed they were currently sexually active. Fourteen percent of females and 17.6 percent of males had had four or more sexual partners. Nearly one-quarter (23.4 percent) of high school females and one-third (31.5 percent) of high school males reported that they were currently abstinent. (See Table 6.14.)

Not surprisingly, older students tended to be more sexually active than younger students. Black students (53.6 percent) were more likely than White (32 percent) or Hispanic (35.4 percent) students to be sexually active. More than one-fifth (21.7 percent) of Black students had first experienced sexual intercourse before age 13, and nearly two-fifths (38.5 percent) had had four or more partners. (See Table 6.14.)

In 1997, more than half (56.8 percent) of sexually active students reported using condoms during their last sexual encounters, and one-fifth (20.5 percent) of the female students used birth control pills. Black students (64 percent) were significantly more likely than White (55.8 percent) and Hispanic

99

TABLE 6.15

Percentage of high school students who reported engaging in violence or in behaviors resulting from violence on school property, by sex, race/ethnicity, and grade — United States, Youth Risk Behavior Survey, 1997

Category	Felt too unsafe to go to school*			Carried a weapon on school property*[†]			Threatened or injured with a weapon on school property[§]			In a physical fight on school property[§]			Property stolen or deliberately damaged on school property[§]		
	Female	Male	Total	Female	Male	Total	Female	Male	Total	Female	Male	Total	Female	Male	Total
Race/Ethnicity															
White[¶]	2.5 (±0.8)**	2.3 (±0.7)	**2.4** (±0.6)	2.1 (±0.7)	12.3 (±4.0)	**7.8** (±2.3)	3.7 (±1.1)	8.2 (±1.7)	**6.2** (±1.1)	5.9 (±1.1)	19.1 (±2.9)	**13.3** (±1.7)	28.6 (±5.6)	35.7 (±3.4)	**32.6** (±3.7)
Black[¶]	6.1 (±2.2)	7.5 (±2.1)	**6.8** (±1.5)	7.8 (±1.9)	10.7 (±2.9)	**9.2** (±1.9)	5.8 (±1.4)	14.0 (±3.3)	**9.9** (±1.8)	17.0 (±4.3)	24.6 (±3.3)	**20.7** (±2.4)	30.6 (±3.2)	37.5 (±3.9)	**34.0** (±3.1)
Hispanic	7.7 (±2.6)	6.8 (±2.1)	**7.2** (±1.7)	4.3 (±1.5)	15.6 (±3.0)	**10.4** (±1.9)	4.6 (±1.8)	12.7 (±1.9)	**9.0** (±1.2)	12.3 (±2.7)	24.7 (±5.3)	**19.0** (±2.9)	30.6 (±2.8)	33.4 (±4.9)	**32.1** (±3.3)
Grade															
9	5.8 (±1.5)	5.2 (±1.5)	**5.5** (±1.0)	5.4 (±1.4)	14.5 (±3.7)	**10.2** (±1.8)	6.1 (±1.6)	13.7 (±3.6)	**10.1** (±2.0)	12.4 (±2.7)	29.3 (±5.3)	**21.3** (±2.5)	33.7 (±4.5)	39.8 (±4.8)	**36.9** (±2.6)
10	3.9 (±1.2)	4.0 (±1.3)	**4.0** (±1.0)	3.5 (±1.3)	11.1 (±3.1)	**7.7** (±1.9)	5.2 (±1.9)	10.1 (±3.1)	**7.9** (±2.2)	11.3 (±3.9)	21.6 (±3.6)	**17.0** (±3.3)	30.0 (±4.2)	39.7 (±4.4)	**35.4** (±3.5)
11	3.2 (±1.3)	5.0 (±2.9)	**4.2** (±1.7)	3.1 (±1.3)	14.6 (±4.9)	**9.4** (±2.6)	2.3 (±0.8)	9.0 (±2.4)	**5.9** (±1.4)	6.2 (±2.0)	17.8 (±2.4)	**12.5** (±1.7)	27.5 (±6.7)	36.2 (±4.2)	**32.3** (±4.9)
12	3.0 (±1.2)	2.3 (±0.8)	**2.6** (±0.8)	3.0 (±1.3)	10.1 (±2.8)	**7.0** (±1.8)	2.5 (±1.2)	8.4 (±2.3)	**5.8** (±1.6)	4.9 (±2.2)	13.1 (±2.6)	**9.5** (±1.4)	25.4 (±4.8)	30.0 (±3.8)	**27.9** (±3.6)
Total	**3.9** (±0.7)	**4.1** (±0.8)	**4.0** (±0.6)	**3.7** (±0.7)	**12.5** (±2.9)	**8.5** (±1.5)	**4.0** (±0.6)	**10.2** (±1.4)	**7.4** (±0.9)	**8.6** (±1.5)	**20.0** (±2.0)	**14.8** (±1.3)	**29.0** (±3.7)	**36.1** (±2.6)	**32.9** (±2.6)

*On ≥1 of the 30 days preceding the survey.
[†]Such as a gun, knife, or club.
[§]One or more times during the 12 months preceding the survey.
[¶]Non-Hispanic.
**Ninety-five percent confidence interval.

Source: "Youth Risk Behavior Surveillance — United States, 1997," *Morbidity and Mortality Weekly Report*, vol. 47, no. SS-3, August 14, 1998

(48.3 percent) students to report using condoms. Over 8 percent of the females surveyed reported having been pregnant, and 4.7 percent of the males stated that they had gotten someone pregnant.

Violence, Fear, and Weapons in Schools

Experiencing violence, feeling unsafe, and carrying weapons at school — all have increased over the past two decades. Nonetheless, most students and teachers still report that they feel safe at school. In its 1997 *Youth Risk Behavior Surveillance*, the CDC found that 4 percent of the students surveyed had missed at least one school day during the 30 days before the survey because they felt too unsafe to go to school. Only 2.4 percent of White students felt too unsafe to go to school, compared to 6.8 percent of Black and 7.2 percent of Hispanic students. Ninth graders (5.5 percent) were more than twice as likely as twelfth graders (2.6 percent) to fear going to school. (See Table 6.15.)

Getting into Fights

The CDC asked high school students whether they had been in a fight on school property. In 1997,

14.8 percent of the students surveyed were in at least one physical fight on school property during the 12 months preceding the survey. Male students (20 percent) were twice as likely as females (8.6 percent) to have been in a fight. Black (20.7 percent) and Hispanic (19 percent) students were more likely than White students (13.3 percent) to have been in a fight. (See Table 6.15.)

Carrying a Weapon

Weapons brought to school have included guns, knives, clubs, brass knuckles, razor blades, spiked jewelry, and other objects capable of inflicting harm. The 1997 *Youth Risk Behavior Surveillance* found that about 8.5 percent of students reported carrying a weapon of some type on school property during the 30 days before the survey. Males (12.5 percent) were far more likely than females (3.7 percent) to carry weapons at school. (See Table 6.15.)

In 1997, 7.4 percent of the students surveyed reported that they had been threatened or injured with a weapon at school one or more times in the past 12 months. Males (10.2 percent) were more

TABLE 6.16

Teen Birth Rate (Births per 1,000 Females Ages 15-19, 15-17, and 18-19)

Ages:	1960	1970	1980	1986	1990	1991	1992	1993	1994	1995	1996	1997	1998
15-19	89.1	68.3	53.0	50.2	59.9	62.1	60.7	59.6	58.9	56.8	54.4	52.3	51.1
15-17	43.9	38.8	32.5	30.5	37.5	38.7	37.8	37.8	37.6	36.0	33.8	32.1	30.4
18-19	166.7	114.7	82.1	79.6	88.6	94.4	94.5	92.1	91.5	89.1	86.0	83.6	82.0

Source: *Facts at a Glance 1999*, Child Trends, Washington, DC, 1999

likely than females (4 percent) to report this behavior. More ninth graders (10.1 percent each) than tenth graders (7.9 percent), eleventh graders (5.9 percent), and twelfth graders (5.8 percent) reported threats and injuries with weapons. (See Table 6.15.)

PERCEPTIONS OF SCHOOL SAFETY

On April 20, 1999, 12 students were murdered by two of their classmates at Columbine High School in Littleton, Colorado. In May 1999, following this tragic school shooting, the *Gallup Youth Survey* asked 403 teenagers ages 13 through 17 about a number of issues related to school shootings and school safety. Thirty-four percent of the girls and 13 percent of the boys said they had been fearful of going to school since the Columbine shootings. In a survey completed just before the shootings, 15 percent reported feeling fearful about school safety.

In the May 1999 survey, nearly half (48 percent) of the teenagers said they had had bomb threats in their schools, and 5 percent had a school closing on one day following the Columbine shootings. Nearly two-thirds (64 percent) of the respondents reported that their schools had held discussions or taken other steps to prevent tragedies like the one in Littleton. Most students (71 percent) felt their schools were doing enough to prevent such happenings.

In October 1999, a *New York Times*/CBS News poll asked 1,038 teenagers about school safety. Though half (52 percent) of the teenagers surveyed said they thought a Columbine-type shooting could happen at their school, 45 percent considered their school safe or extremely safe, and 42 percent felt it was somewhat safe. Many experts think that may reflect some good solid sense. "It is not that kids are in denial — I think they probably have better perspective than many parents," observed James Alan Fox, Lipman Professor of Criminal Justice at Northeastern University. "In the last couple of years, there have been about four dozen school shootings each year. But there are 50 million schoolchildren, so the chances are literally one in a million."

In a 1999 state-by-state survey, the Department of Education found that far fewer students were expelled for taking guns to school in 1997-1998 than in the previous school year. Expulsions dropped by nearly 30 percent, from 5,724 in 1996-1997 to 3,930 in 1997-1998. Just over half of the expulsions were at high schools, 33 percent were at junior high schools, and 10 percent were at elementary schools.

TEENAGE PREGNANCY

From 1960 through 1986, the number of live births per 1,000 females ages 15 to 17 generally

TABLE 6.17

Teen Birth Rate (Births per 1,000 Females Ages 15-19) by Race/Ethnicity

Race/Ethnicity:	1990	1991	1992	1993	1994	1995	1996	1997	1998
Hispanics	100	107	107	107	108	107	102	97	94
Blacks	113	116	112	109	105	96	91	88	85
Non-Hispanic Whites	43	43	42	41	40	39	38	36	35

Source: *Facts at a Glance 1999*, Child Trends, Washington, DC, 1999

TABLE 6.18										
Marital and Non-marital Birth Rate (Births per 1,000 Females)										
Rate by Marital Status and Age:	1970	1980	1990	1991	1992	1993	1994	1995	1996	1997	1998
Marital, ages 15-19	444	350	420	410	398	388	351	362	344	323	--
Non-marital, ages 15-19	22	28	43	45	45	45	46	44	43	42	--
Non-marital, ages 20-24	38	41	65	68	69	69	72	70	71	71	--
Non-marital, ages 15-44	26	29	44	45	45	45	47	45	45	44	44

Source: *Facts at a Glance 1999*, Child Trends, Washington, DC, 1999

declined, but the rate increased during the late 1980s and early 1990s. The National Center for Health Statistics reported that, in 1998, there were 30.4 live births per 1,000 females ages 15 to 17 (Table 6.16).

In 1998, mothers ages 15 through 19 accounted for a total of 484,976 live births. Non-Hispanic White teenagers had a birth rate of 35 births per 1,000 females ages 15 through 19, while non-Hispanic Black teenagers experienced a birth rate of 85 births per 1,000 females in the same age group. The birth rate for Hispanic teenage mothers was 94 births per 1,000 females ages 15 through 19. (See Table 6.17.)

Most teenage mothers are unmarried and lack the resources to give their children adequate care. The National Center for Health Statistics reported that in 1998, 79 percent of all teen births occurred outside of marriage. In 1997, the non-marital birth rate of females ages 15 through 19 was 42 per 1,000 females (Table 6.18).

AIDS AND OTHER SEXUALLY TRANSMITTED DISEASES

The Centers for Disease Control and Prevention (CDC) identifies certain diseases as "notifiable," meaning that state and local medical authorities must report each occurrence to the CDC. Sexually transmitted diseases (STDs) are included in the notifiable disease list. Human immunodeficiency virus (HIV, the virus that causes AIDS [acquired immunodeficiency syndrome]) is probably the best known STD, but it is not the most common. Syphilis, chlamydia, and gonorrhea are the three most common STDs reported to the CDC.

In 1998, there were 198,558 cases of chlamydia among persons ages 15 through 19, the highest number of cases for all age groups. This age group also had the highest number of gonorrhea cases, 103,428 in 1998. There were 605 cases of primary and secondary syphilis among teenagers ages 15 through 19. Although antibiotics can cure many STDs, they can still have serious health consequences, including an increase in a victim's risk of contracting HIV if exposed.

Adolescents are at a higher risk for acquiring STDs for the following reasons:

- They may be more likely to have multiple sexual partners rather than a single, long-term relationship.

- They may be more likely to engage in unprotected intercourse.

- They may select partners at higher risk.

- The age of initiation of sexual activity has steadily decreased.

- Adolescents face multiple barriers to quality STD prevention services, such as lack of insurance or concerns about confidentiality.

HIV/AIDS remains the most dangerous STD. Young people who are sexually active and/or inject drugs are at great risk of contracting the virus. Through June 1999, the CDC reported that a cumulative total of 3,564 AIDS cases had been diagnosed in youths 13 to 19 years of age. More males (2,134 cases) were diagnosed than were females (1,430 cases). (See Table 6.19.) Countless more

TABLE 6.19

AIDS cases by sex, age at diagnosis, and race/ethnicity, reported through June 1999, United States

Male Age at diagnosis (years)	White, not Hispanic		Black, not Hispanic		Hispanic		Asian/Pacific Islander		American Indian/ Alaska Native		Total[1]	
	No.	(%)	No.	(%)	No.	(%)	No.	(%)	No.	(%)	No.	(%)
Under 5	513	(0)	2,064	(1)	755	(1)	16	(0)	12	(1)	3,364	(1)
5-12	334	(0)	438	(0)	277	(0)	9	(0)	4	(0)	1,064	(0)
13-19	829	(0)	792	(0)	469	(0)	23	(1)	19	(1)	2,134	(0)
20-24	7,452	(3)	6,586	(3)	3,973	(4)	156	(3)	73	(4)	18,266	(3)
25-29	37,007	(13)	23,902	(12)	15,511	(15)	562	(12)	307	(18)	77,384	(13)
30-34	66,541	(23)	40,769	(21)	25,274	(24)	985	(22)	447	(27)	134,150	(23)
35-39	64,874	(23)	44,016	(23)	23,520	(22)	983	(22)	374	(22)	133,954	(23)
40-44	47,251	(17)	34,527	(18)	16,466	(16)	780	(17)	254	(15)	99,416	(17)
45-49	28,426	(10)	19,971	(10)	9,203	(9)	477	(11)	103	(6)	58,257	(10)
50-54	15,336	(5)	10,242	(5)	4,865	(5)	251	(6)	41	(2)	30,779	(5)
55-59	8,320	(3)	5,630	(3)	2,700	(3)	156	(3)	26	(2)	16,860	(3)
60-64	4,622	(2)	3,084	(2)	1,468	(1)	65	(1)	16	(1)	9,267	(2)
65 or older	3,826	(1)	2,573	(1)	1,179	(1)	61	(1)	9	(1)	7,657	(1)
Male subtotal	**285,331**	**(100)**	**194,594**	**(100)**	**105,660**	**(100)**	**4,524**	**(100)**	**1,685**	**(100)**	**592,552**	**(100)**
Female **Age at diagnosis (years)**												
Under 5	476	(2)	2,052	(3)	748	(3)	14	(2)	13	(4)	3,308	(3)
5-12	176	(1)	463	(1)	211	(1)	7	(1)	—	—	860	(1)
13-19	236	(1)	943	(1)	241	(1)	7	(1)	2	(1)	1,430	(1)
20-24	1,543	(6)	3,922	(6)	1,406	(6)	35	(6)	29	(8)	6,944	(6)
25-29	4,332	(17)	9,878	(15)	3,824	(16)	79	(13)	51	(15)	18,179	(15)
30-34	5,908	(23)	14,948	(22)	5,579	(23)	113	(19)	82	(24)	26,679	(22)
35-39	5,185	(20)	14,865	(22)	4,900	(21)	110	(18)	68	(20)	25,164	(21)
40-44	3,374	(13)	10,221	(15)	3,167	(13)	90	(15)	43	(12)	16,916	(14)
45-49	1,800	(7)	4,982	(7)	1,713	(7)	61	(10)	29	(8)	8,606	(7)
50-54	1,007	(4)	2,454	(4)	953	(4)	26	(4)	15	(4)	4,460	(4)
55-59	662	(3)	1,371	(2)	584	(2)	21	(3)	9	(3)	2,648	(2)
60-64	442	(2)	821	(1)	302	(1)	24	(4)	4	(1)	1,595	(1)
65 or older	903	(3)	803	(1)	267	(1)	22	(4)	3	(1)	2,000	(2)
Female subtotal	**26,044**	**(100)**	**67,723**	**(100)**	**23,895**	**(100)**	**609**	**(100)**	**348**	**(100)**	**118,789**	**(100)**
Total[2]	**311,377**		**262,317**		**129,555**		**5,133**		**2,034**		**711,344**	

[1] Includes 758 males and 170 females whose race/ethnicity is unknown.
[2] Includes 3 persons whose sex is unknown.

Source: *HIV/AIDS Surveillance Report*, Midyear edition, vol. 11, no. 1, 1999

are infected with HIV, the virus that causes AIDS. Because of the long incubation period from the time of infection and the onset of symptoms, many people who develop AIDS in their early twenties were probably infected with HIV as teenagers.

JUVENILE OFFENDERS AND VICTIMS

Juvenile Arrests

Serious violent crimes committed by at least one juvenile offender declined 33 percent between 1993 and 1997. In 1997, according to the *National Crime Victimization Survey*, juveniles under age 18 were involved in 27 percent of all serious violent crimes, including 30 percent of robberies, 27 percent of aggravated assaults, and 14 percent of sexual assaults.

In 1997, about 95 percent of all arrests involved persons between ages 10 and 49. Juveniles ages 10 through 17 made up 19 percent of all arrests. Based on their proportion, juveniles were disproportionately involved in arrests for arson (50 per-

TABLE 6.20

Juveniles accounted for 37% of all burglary arrests in 1997, 30% of robbery arrests, 24% of weapon arrests, 14% of murder arrests, and 14% of drug arrests

	Juvenile arrests as a percent of total arrests						
Most serious offense charged	All persons	Males	Females	Whites	Blacks	American Indians	Asians
Total	**19%**	**18%**	**23%**	**20%**	**16%**	**19%**	**28%**
Violent Crime Index	17	17	17	16	19	15	23
Murder and nonnegligent manslaughter	14	14	8	13	14	9	23
Forcible rape	17	17	27	17	18	13	13
Robbery	30	30	28	31	29	31	47
Aggravated assault	14	14	16	14	15	13	18
Property Crime Index	35	35	34	38	29	40	45
Burglary	37	37	32	39	30	43	48
Larceny-theft	34	34	33	37	27	39	44
Motor vehicle theft	40	39	43	41	38	54	42
Arson	50	52	37	54	39	44	50
Other assaults	17	16	24	17	17	16	22
Forgery and counterfeiting	7	7	7	8	4	9	10
Fraud	3	3	2	3	3	4	6
Embezzlement	8	8	7	8	8	10	10
Stolen property (buying, receiving, possessing)	25	26	21	27	23	36	37
Vandalism	43	44	34	47	30	39	52
Weapons (carrying, possessing, etc.)	24	24	26	26	20	30	35
Prostitution and commercialized vice	1	2	1	1	1	2	1
Sex offenses (except forcible rape and prostitution)	18	18	17	17	21	12	14
Drug abuse violations	14	15	11	14	13	19	18
Gambling	17	18	6	6	22	4	4
Offenses against family and children	7	5	10	8	4	5	8
Driving under the influence	1	1	1	1	1	2	1
Liquor laws	25	22	35	27	11	26	29
Drunkenness	3	3	4	4	2	2	5
Disorderly conduct	27	25	31	27	25	18	35
Vagrancy	11	12	7	14	7	4	16
All other offenses (except traffic)	12	11	14	14	9	10	19

■ Persons between ages 10 and 49 commit most crimes: in 1997, 95% of all arrests involved persons in this age range. Persons ages 10–17 make up about 19% of this segment of the population. Therefore, based on their representation in this population, juveniles were disproportionately involved in arrests for arson, vandalism, motor vehicle theft, burglary, larceny-theft, robbery, and weapons law violations. In contrast, juveniles were underrepresented in arrests for murder, aggravated assault, forcible rape, driving under the influence, drunkenness, and drug abuse violations.

■ A greater portion of female arrests involved a juvenile (23%) than did male arrests (18%). Juveniles were involved in a larger proportion of female arrests than male arrests for liquor law violations (35% vs. 22%) and simple assaults (24% vs. 16%). Juveniles were involved in a larger proportion of male arrests than female arrests for arson (52% vs. 37%), vandalism (44% vs. 34%), murder (14% vs. 8%), and drug abuse violations (15% vs. 11%). There was little gender difference in juvenile proportions of arrests for most other crimes.

■ A greater proportion of white arrests involved a juvenile (20%) than did black arrests (16%). Juveniles accounted for a larger proportion of white arrests than black arrests for burglary (39% vs. 30%), weapons law violations (26% vs. 20%), vandalism (47% vs. 30%), larceny-theft (37% vs. 27%), and liquor law violations (27% vs. 11%).

Source: *Juvenile Offenders and Victims: 1999 National Report*, Office of Juvenile Justice and Delinquency Prevention, Washington, DC, 1999

cent), vandalism (43 percent), motor vehicle theft (40 percent), burglary (37 percent), larceny-theft (34 percent), robbery (30 percent), and weapons law violations (24 percent). (See Table 6.20.)

More female arrests involved a juvenile than did male arrests. More female teenagers were arrested for liquor law violations and simple assault. More males teenagers were arrested for arson, vandalism, murder, and drug abuse violations. More White and Asian arrests involved a juvenile than Black arrests. (See Table 6.20.)

Young people who commit violent crimes are likely to be sent to juvenile detention facilities or even adult prisons and jails. In any of these facilities, they are much less likely to complete their high school education. (For more information, see *Prisons and Jails — A Deterrent to Crime?*, Information Plus, Wylie, Texas, 1999.)

Juvenile Victims

Youth ages 16 to 19 are in the highest risk categories for becoming victims of violent crimes. In 1998, persons in this age range were twice as likely as those ages 25 to 34 to be victims and three times as likely as persons ages 35 to 49. The Bureau of Justice publication *Criminal Victimization 1998* (Washington, DC, 1999) reported that 82.4 of every 1,000 12- to 15-year-olds were victims of violent crimes (excluding murder and manslaughter), as were 91.1 of every 1,000 16- to 19-year-olds, significantly higher than older age groups (Table 6.21). About 1 in 8 murder victims were under the age of 18.

TABLE 6.21

Rates of violent crime and personal theft, by gender, age, race, and Hispanic origin, 1998

Characteristic of victim	Population	Victimizations per 1,000 persons age 12 or older						Per-sonal theft
		Violent crimes						
		All crimes of violence*	Rape/ Sexual assault	Robbery	Assault			
					Total	Aggra-vated	Simple	
Gender								
Male	107,595,530	43.1	0.2	4.6	38.3	10.5	27.8	1.2
Female	114,285,430	30.4	2.7	3.5	24.3	4.7	19.5	1.5
Age								
12-15	15,781,590	82.4	3.5	7.7	71.2	12.2	58.9	2.0
16-19	15,620,290	91.1	5.0	11.4	74.7	19.0	55.7	2.3
20-24	17,663,220	67.3	4.6	7.9	54.8	16.0	38.8	1.8
25-34	39,263,480	41.5	1.7	4.2	35.6	8.4	27.3	1.0
35-49	63,428,180	29.9	0.7	3.2	26.1	6.8	19.3	1.2
50-64	37,939,800	15.4	0.2	1.7	13.5	3.3	10.2	1.6
65 or older	32,184,400	2.8	0.0	0.5	2.3	0.5	1.8	0.8
Race								
White	185,831,440	36.3	1.5	3.7	31.1	7.0	24.2	1.2
Black	27,020,600	41.7	2.0	5.9	33.7	11.9	21.8	2.1
Other	9,028,930	27.6	0.7	4.4	22.5	6.6	15.9	1.4
Hispanic origin								
Hispanic	21,699,490	32.8	0.8	6.3	25.6	6.1	19.5	1.7
Non-Hispanic	197,506,660	36.8	1.6	3.7	31.5	7.6	23.9	1.3

*The National Crime Victimization Survey includes as violent crime rape/sexual assault, robbery, and assault, but not murder and manslaughter.

Source: *Criminal Victimization 1998: Changes 1997-98 with Trends 1993-98*, Bureau of Justice Statistics, Washington, DC, 1999

CHAPTER VII

ISSUES IN EDUCATION

Schools, like other institutions, face various issues as they grow and attempt to meet the needs of an ever-changing population. In frontier days, the problem was finding a teacher and furnishing her with little more than room and board in payment. During the post-World War II "baby boom," it was building enough schools and educating enough teachers to fill the need. During the 1960s and beyond, schools dealt with integration and busing. Later came sex and drug education and the role of religion in the classroom. Today, our schools continue to face many of these long-term problems, as well as new challenges: school vouchers, the education of a more diverse population, school-based social services, and aging or inadequate school facilities.

There is no clear consensus on how to solve these and other problems. According to Public Agenda, an online source for public opinion and policy analysis, in the fall 1999, 4 in 5 Americans (83 percent) say education will be a "very important" consideration in voting for a president in 2000. Some of the topics under discussion are school facilities, higher standards, assessment, accountability, school-choice programs, school funding, discipline, and safety.

SCHOOL-REFORM MOVEMENTS

In 1957, the "space race" began when the Soviet Union launched Sputnik I, its first satellite. To prevent the nation from supposedly lagging behind in the technology competition, American leaders called for improved educational techniques and student performance. In 1983, the (Ronald) Reagan Administration released *A Nation at Risk*, a report on education in the United States. Instead of responding to the earlier challenge, the report claimed, American education had produced students who actually were scoring lower on performance tests than in 1957. The writers of the report feared that the nation would become less competitive in world markets, causing the economy to suffer.

The report recommended that American education, especially in high school, should primarily focus on academic achievement, with students spending more time in school and working on homework. As a result, most states raised graduation requirements, revised programs of testing and evaluation, and improved teacher preparation standards.

Demands for reform continued in 1986 with eight new reports on the state of American education, including *Time for Results* (National Governors' Association, Washington, DC), *A Nation Prepared: Teachers for the 21st Century* (Carnegie Forum on Education and the Economy, Washington, DC), and *What Next? More Leverage for Teachers* (Education Commission of the States, Denver, Colorado). These publications focused on teacher training and salaries, state initiatives to reform education, and school choice (see below) as strategies to improve education. The states followed many of the reports' recommendations, especially in the areas of recruiting and preparing teachers and in restructuring the organization and management of their school systems.

At the Education Summit held in Charlottesville, Virginia, in 1989, President George Bush and the state governors established six National Education Goals to be met by the year 2000. In 1994, Congress passed the Goals 2000: Educate America Act (PL 103-227), reemphasizing the National Education Goals and adding two more goals. These goals presented a broad approach to education reform, including more parental involvement, improvement in nutrition and health care for preschool children, and adult education, among other things. To date, the nation has made little progress toward reaching the education goals. (See Chapter V for more information on the National Education Goals and the progress made toward reaching them.)

More recently, Congress passed the Charter School Expansion Act of 1998 (PL 105-278). The act authorizes a state educational agency (SEA) to use federal funds for planning, designing, and implementing public charter schools and requires local education agencies (LEAs) to use innovative assistance funds for the same purpose. Funding priorities are based on a state's progress in increasing its number of high quality and accountable charter schools. The act extends the authorization of appropriations for fiscal years (FY) 1999 through 2003. (See below for more information on charter schools.)

The Education Flexibility Partnership Act of 1999 (PL 106-25) gives states more freedom in how they spend federal education dollars. To participate in the Ed-Flex Partnership program, states must apply to the Secretary of Education for a waiver from the normal requirements for obtaining federal funds. They may then set up their own programs under which they would be held accountable for improved educational results in order to receive continued funding. For example, schools could use federal money intended for science and math teachers on reading programs to boost progress in that area. The following sections describe some of the approaches intended to improve education that have developed in recent years.

SITE-BASED MANAGEMENT

Site-based management (SBM; also called school-based management) moves control and decision-making from those in the central offices of a school system to those most closely involved with a school and its students — principals, teachers, parents, and other interested citizens. Acting as a school council, these individuals can develop their school's goals, allocate funds received from the system's budget, hire personnel, and set curriculum and discipline policies. SBM advocates claim that SBM can eliminate the cost and inefficiency of excessive bureaucracy, as well as increase accountability.

According to *Education Week on the WEB* (August 24, 1999), at least five states — Colorado, Florida, Kentucky, North Carolina, and Texas — require some type of participatory, collaborative decision-making at every school. Individual districts in other states, as well as several large urban school systems, are also involved in site-based management.

Proponents of SBM maintain the system improves teacher morale and permits more parent and community involvement in schools. Critics worry that SBM removes the decision-making power from capable administrators and gives it to a group of inexperienced, often adversarial members. The real measure is whether or not site-based management actually improves school performance.

The *Assessment of School-Based Management*, a 1996 report funded by the U.S. Department of Education, reported that there was "scant evidence that schools get better just because decisions are made by those closer to the classroom." However, SBM can be a successful part of other reforms that produce local school efforts to improve teaching and learning.

Researchers Priscilla Wohlstetter and Susan Albers Mohrman conducted an in-depth study of

27 schools in three U.S. school districts (Jefferson County, Kentucky; Prince William County, Virginia; and San Diego, California), one Canadian district (Edmonton, Canada), and one Australian state (Victoria). Wohlstetter and Mohrman found that more than half the schools studied were "actively restructuring" — their efforts had successfully produced changes in curriculum and instructional practices. The rest were struggling; though these schools were practicing SBM, little change had occurred. According to the researchers, successful SBM schools

- Establish multiple, teacher-led decision-making subcommittees.

- Focus on continuous improvement through professional development in process skills (such as management and group decision-making), as well as in areas related to curriculum and instruction.

- Create a well-developed system for sharing school-related information within the school and out to the community.

- Develop ways to more effectively reward staff behavior directed toward achieving school goals.

- Select principals who can facilitate and manage change.

- Use district, state and/or national guidelines to focus reform efforts and to target changes in curriculum and instruction.

In early 1997, the late Albert Shanker, then-president of the American Federation of Teachers, observed that SBM might not be the panacea (universal cure) for education that its proponents claimed. In the 1960s, the New York City school system was decentralized into 32 community school districts. Critics of the former system felt that centralization had created a bureaucracy that was more interested in the system than in the students, and it was hoped that decentralization would foster better response to local education needs.

After 25 years, decentralization in New York

TABLE 7.1

Estimated Percentage of Charter Schools by Source of Primary Control for Various School Decisions and Operations

Area of control	Source of primary control			
	School	District/charter granting agency	Both	Other
	Percentage of schools (%)			
Budget	72.9	19.4	0.3	7.4
Purchase of supplies/equipment	87.7	7.6	0.2	4.5
School calendar	76.8	19.6	0.1	3.5
Daily schedule	94.8	2.9	0.2	2.2
Student assessment policies	71.5	19.7	0.6	8.2
Student admissions policies	59.4	27.8	0.7	12.0
Student discipline	87.3	9.0	0.1	3.6
Establishment of curriculum	83.2	11.3	0.2	5.3
Hiring of teaching staff	87.5	7.4	0.3	4.8

NOTE: These data are based on responses from between 972 and 975 of the 975 open charter schools that responded to the survey. Schools were asked to rate each of these items separately, resulting in the range of responses. Up to three schools answered "don't know" for certain items. Most responses in the "other" category include the management company, the state legislature, and parents. The data presented in columns 3 through 5 of the table on the facing page represent the percentage of the total number of each type of school and includes responses from 173 open pre-existing public schools, 98 open pre-existing private schools, and between 702 and 704 open newly created schools (some newly created schools responded "don't know").

Source: *The State of Charter Schools 2000 — National Study of Charter Schools*, Office of Educational Research and Improvement, U.S. Department of Education, Washington, DC, 2000

1991	1992	1993	1994	1995	1996	1997	1998	1999
Minnesota	California	Colorado	Arizona	Alaska	Connecticut	Mississippi	Idaho	New York
		Georgia	Hawaii	Arkansas	District of Col.	Nevada	Missouri	Oklahoma
		Massachusetts	Kansas	Delaware	Florida	Ohio	Utah	Oregon
		Michigan		New Hampshire	Illinois	Pennsylvania	Virginia	
		New Mexico		Louisiana	New Jersey			
		Wisconsin		Rhode Island	North Carolina			
				Wyoming	South Carolina			
					Texas			

Source: *The State of Charter Schools 2000 — National Study of Charter Schools*, Office of Educational Research and Improvement, U.S. Department of Education, Washington, DC, 2000

appeared to have failed: student performance had not improved, and some schools became corrupt and filled positions based on patronage rather than ability. In 1996, the New York state legislature returned much of the formerly local authority to the chancellor of the New York City schools. Shanker believed that decentralization could not be successful without state or national academic standards, standardized testing, and financial accountability.

CHARTER SCHOOLS

In charter schools, teachers, parents, administrators, community groups, or private corporations design and operate a local school under charter (written contract) from a school district, state education agency, or other public institution. These local schools often have a specific focus, such as mathematics, arts, or science. In some cases, charter schools are nearly autonomous (self-directing) and are exempt from many state and district education rules. In other cases, the schools operate much like traditional public schools and must apply for certain exemptions, which may or may not be granted.

In 1998-99, according to *The State of Charter Schools 2000* (U.S. Department of Education, Washington, DC, 2000), most charter schools had primary control over administrative operations, such as purchase of supplies and equipment (87.7 percent), hiring of teachers (87.5 percent), and budget (72.9 percent). In addition, the majority had primary control over their education programs: daily schedule (94.8 percent), discipline (87.3 per-

cent), curriculum (83.2 percent), school calendar (76.8 percent), and student assessment policies (71.5 percent). A lower percentage of charter schools (59.4 percent), yet still a majority, reported primary control over their student admissions policies. When charter schools were not given primary control, the district, the charter-granting agency, or another source had primary authority. (See Table 7.1.)

Many states find charter schools appealing for several reasons. Overcrowded classrooms, district mismanagement or disorganization, low scores on standardized tests, and number of students at risk of dropping out of school are four common reasons noted for considering alternatives such as charter schools. In Arizona, charter schools on Indian reservations use the system to maintain their native languages and customs.

In 1991, there was only one charter school in the United States. By September 1999, according to the Center for Education Reform (CER), a national independent, non-profit advocacy organization for education reform, 1,674 charter schools were in operation. Thirty-six states and the District of Columbia have authorized charter schools (Table 7.2), but five of those states — Arkansas, New Hampshire, Oklahoma, Virginia, and Wyoming — did not have any charter schools in 1999.

The CER reported that 80 percent of the more than 50 reports on the progress and achievement of charter schools show that charter schools are achieving their goals. By the end of 1999, 39 charter schools (2.3 percent) had closed, either volun-

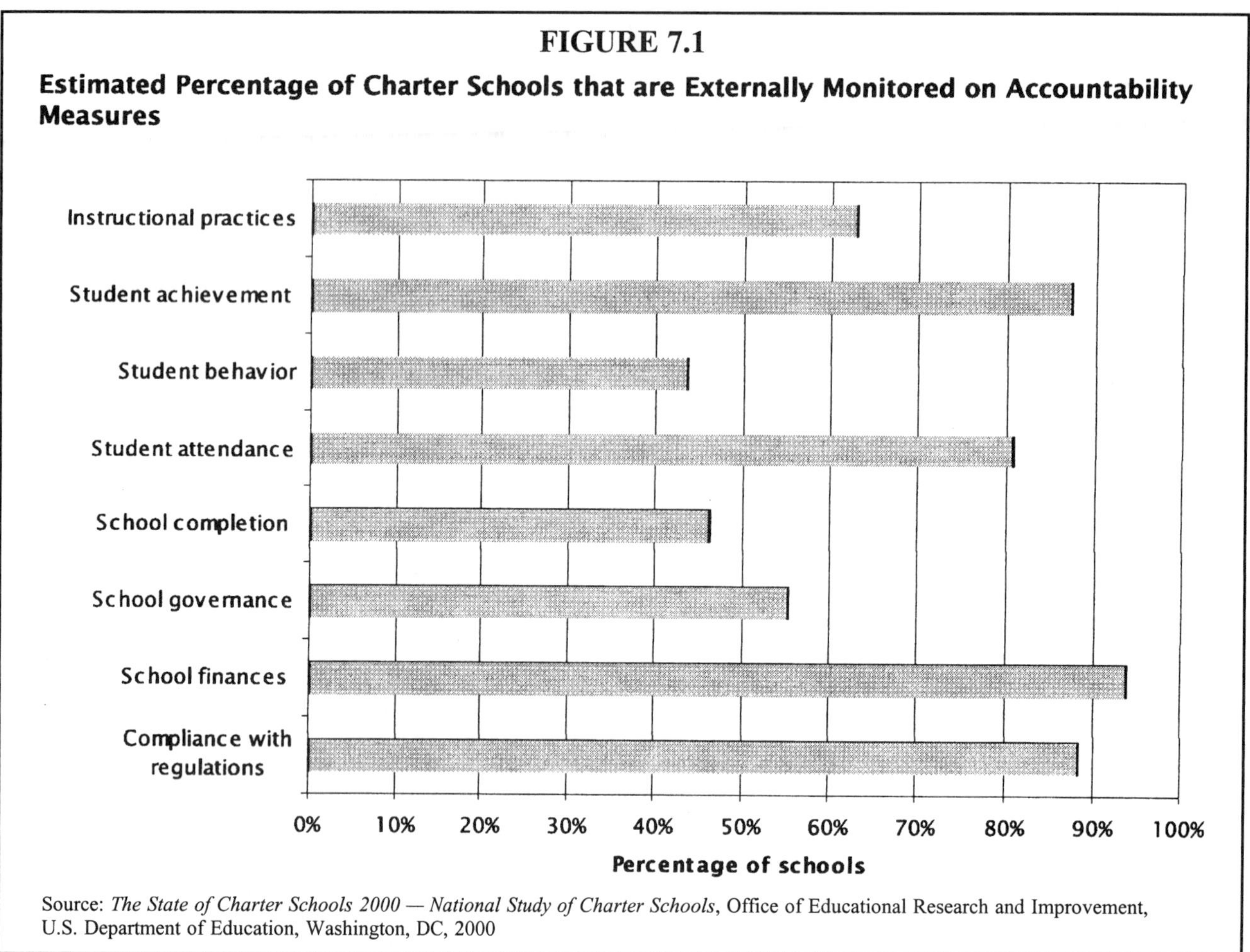

Source: *The State of Charter Schools 2000 — National Study of Charter Schools*, Office of Educational Research and Improvement, U.S. Department of Education, Washington, DC, 2000

tarily or due to low enrollment, inadequate programs, or financial or administrative problems. CER believes the closures do not indicate failure but rather an "evidence of accountability, one of the greatest strengths of the charter school movement."

Charter schools are held accountable for school and student outcomes. Because state legislation and regulatory practices differ greatly by state, charter schools report varying amounts of external monitoring. According to *The State of Charter Schools 2000* (see above), the schools surveyed received external monitoring in the areas of school finance (94 percent), compliance with state or federal regulations (88 percent), student achievement (87 percent), and school attendance (81 percent). In other areas, such as student behavior and school governance, there was a wider variation in monitoring among the states. (See Figure 7.1.)

Charter schools that target special populations, such as at-risk students, are increasingly popular. These schools may focus on nontraditional teaching and learning experiences, such as combining academics with work experience or changing the class structure. The National Conference of State Legislatures (NCSL) reports that many states, in approving charter schools, give preference to schools that serve at-risk students — those who lack essential skills, school failures, students with behavioral or attendance problems, pregnant students or those who are parents, or students who have a variety of socio-economic predictors. Some states require a specific number of charter schools to serve this special population. (See Figure 7.2.)

Charter Schools in Action (Hudson Institute, Indianapolis, Indiana, 1997) reported high parent, teacher, and student satisfaction levels following a two-year study of 60 charter schools in 14 states. The following are among its major findings:

110

- Charter schools are havens for children who had bad educational experiences elsewhere. Among students performing "poorly" in their previous school (as judged by their parents), nearly half are now doing "excellent" or "above average" work.

- Charter schools are very popular with students, parents, and teachers.

- Families and teachers are seeking out charter schools primarily for education reasons, such as curriculum, teaching, and class size.

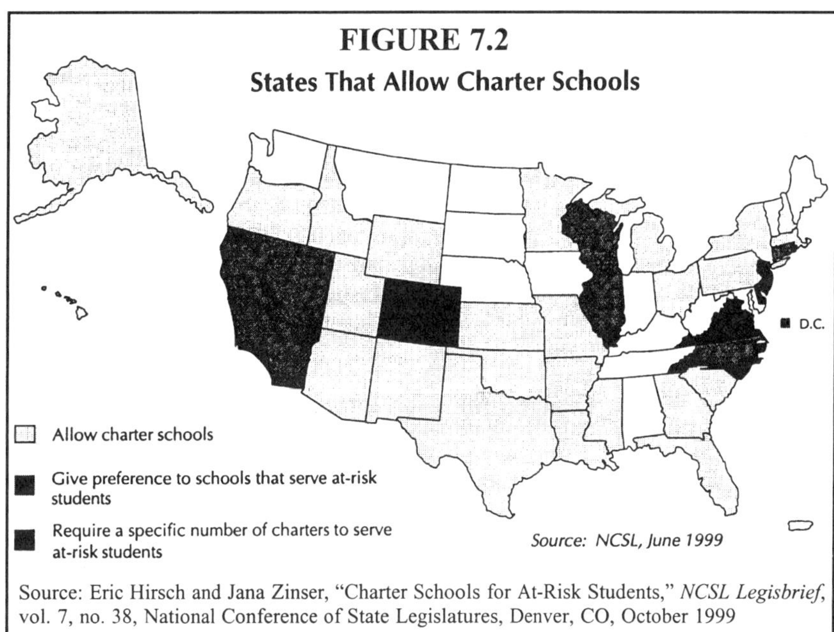

Source: Eric Hirsch and Jana Zinser, "Charter Schools for At-Risk Students," *NCSL Legisbrief*, vol. 7, no. 38, National Conference of State Legislatures, Denver, CO, October 1999

- Charter school teachers are diverse, but nearly all are finding personal fulfillment and professional reward, largely because they feel empowered (able to make their own decisions).

In 1998, University of California at Los Angeles (UCLA) researchers studied 10 California school districts with charter schools. They found that

- In most instances, charter schools are not yet held accountable for improved academic achievement.

- Charter schools vary widely in the amount of operating control they need or want and in the demands they make on school districts.

- School boards are ambivalent about their responsibilities to monitor charter schools; many are reluctant to become involved.

- Teachers in charter schools value their freedom, their collegiality (relationships with fellow teachers), and the smaller classes, but heavy workloads are an issue.

- No mechanisms are in place for charter schools and regular public schools to learn from one another.

- Public school educators believe charter schools have an unfair advantage.

Funding for charter schools varies widely, ranging from direct state funding to funding through the local school district. In fiscal year 1998, the federal budget appropriated $80 million for charter schools. In his 2000 State of the Union address, President Bill Clinton pledged continued support, stating, "We know charter schools provide real public school choice.... I ask you to help us meet our goal of 3,000 [charter schools] by next year."

For-Profit Schools

In some cases, beleaguered school boards and state education offices have turned to "privatizing" their schools, contracting with private corporations to administer one or more local schools. Contracts are usually awarded based on bids submitted by the education companies. In general, teachers' unions, such as the American Federation of Teachers, oppose privatizing schools. They, as well as other critics, fear that if it comes to a contest between the company's profits and the students' needs, the profit motive will likely win out.

An estimated 10 percent of all charter schools are run by private, for-profit companies, such as the Edison Project, Advantage Schools, Inc., TesseracT, and Beacon Education Management. By the end of 1999, the Edison Project, the leader in this group, operated 51 schools in 12 states, with an enrollment of over 24,000 students. Its program is based on extensive use of high technology, a longer school day and year, and a full-day kindergarten that has an academic program. While many educators support Edison's program, the company's record in reducing costs and improving scores has been mixed and inconclusive.

In the 1998 AFT (American Federation of Teachers) *Report on Student Achievement in the Edison Schools,* researchers reported discrepancies between the record of Edison schools and the company's sales presentations and marketing materials. The executive summary from the report contended that "Edison has exaggerated test score gains and emphasized favorable comparisons in order to show Edison schools in the most positive light. In fact, if public schools were to use some of Edison's evaluation methods and modes of presenting data, they would look a lot better, too." The National Education Association (NEA) contends that in the Edison Project's claims of "dramatic two-year gains" in achievement, it reported the results of only one — its highest performing — school, while public school districts report achievement for all of their schools.

However, Dr. Paul E. Peterson, a Harvard University professor, conducted an independent review of Edison's *Annual Report on School Performance,* as well as the AFT report. Peterson claims that "after taking into account all the information available, the evidence indicates that, in general, Edison students are learning more than comparable students in other public schools in the communities in which Edison operates."

SCHOOL CHOICE AND VOUCHERS

"School choice" allows students to attend schools other than the designated neighborhood school. Families who can afford to move to an area with high-performing schools or send their children to private schools already have school choice; less wealthy families generally do not. The major debate over school choice is whether or not parents should receive some kind of financial assistance from the state or local government to pay school fees if they elect to send their children to private schools.

Should Parents Choose Schools?

Parents generally influence which schools their children attend, often locating in an area known for excellent schools. The U.S. Supreme Court, in *Pierce v. Society of Sisters* (286 U.S. 510, 1925), upheld parents' constitutional right to select a church-affiliated or private school. Because "the child is not the mere creature of the state," parents cannot be forced to send their children to public schools. A family is free to choose private education or to leave one school district for another in which it believes the public schools are better. In reality, many people are limited by financial and social restrictions, and moving to another district or enrolling their children in private school may not be possible without financial help.

Minnesota introduced the first school-choice program in 1987. Since then, about three-fifths of the states have instituted "choice" plans of one sort or another. The plans usually follow one of three models.

- The *district-wide* model allows parents to select a public school within their district. Often, the district establishes specialty or "magnet" schools (those offering an emphasis on a particular subject area, such as business, science, or the arts) to attract students to different schools.

- The *statewide* model permits students to attend public schools outside their home districts, depending on available space, desegregation requirements, and the students' ability to travel. Typically, when a school district loses students, it also loses state funding, so this plan may not appeal to many school districts.

- The *private school* model, known as the voucher or scholarship plan, is the most controversial. This model allows parents to use public funds to send their children to private schools. Presently, only a few school districts offer a voucher plan.

Vouchers — Pro and Con

In the past decade, voucher plans have become a hotly debated political issue. Those favoring voucher programs consider them an equitable means of helping low-income families provide their children with better education. Voucher programs emphasize educational choices rather than requirements dictated by the government. In addition, many believe increased competition will cause public schools to improve or face closure.

Those opposing vouchers believe the plans would only help a few students, leaving most low-income students behind in schools with reduced community commitment. Critics maintain that vouchers weaken public schools by diverting resources from them. The debate becomes even more heated when voucher supporters include allowing students to elect to attend religious schools with public voucher funds. A major dimension of that debate concerns whether the use of vouchers at religiously affiliated private schools would violate the First Amendment by directly supporting religious institutions or would avoid such violations by supporting only the children.

In a September 1999 speech, Secretary of Education Richard Riley declared that vouchers

... undermine our public schools — which educate about 90 percent of our children — by draining badly needed public tax dollars into private and parochial schools. If we are serious about strengthening our public schools, we need a sustained commitment to improve them — to raise standards, to have accurate assessments linked to standards, and to adopt the strong accountability measures we've proposed, but not try to solve a public school problem by abandoning public schools.

A Rocky Political Road

Shortly before leaving office in 1992, President George Bush, a strong supporter of parental choice of schools, asked Congress for $230 million to support choice programs for private or parochial schools. Another Bush initiative, known as the "G.I. Bill* for Children," would have given $1,000 vouchers, redeemable at either public and private schools, for up to half a million low-income families. Neither proposal ever became law. Congress has continued to debate the issue. Both the House and the Senate approved a voucher plan as part of the fiscal year (FY) 1999 appropriations bill for the District of Columbia, but President Bill Clinton vetoed it.

In 1999, Florida became the first state to provide vouchers on a state-wide basis. Tax money, at least $4,000 per student per year, will go to students at the worst public schools so that they can get a private or parochial education. Two state court challenges have been filed.

Other recent development in the voucher debate are as follows:

- Wisconsin, 1998 — The Wisconsin Supreme Court, in *Jackson v. Benson* (218 Wis.2d 835, 578 N.W.2d 602), ruled that inclusion of religious schools in the Milwaukee Parental Choice Program does not violate the U.S. fed-

---

* The G.I. Bill was a federal program that provided money for education for World War II and other veterans.

eral or the Wisconsin state constitutional prohibitions against government support of religion. The U.S Supreme Court declined to review the case (119 S. Ct. 467, 1998).

- Ohio, 1999 — In August 1999, the U.S. District Court for the Northern District of Ohio concluded there was probable cause that the Cleveland voucher program, which gives low-income students scholarships to attend private secular or religious schools, violated the constitutional separation of church and state and would be found unconstitutional. The court issued an injunction halting the program, but allowed students who used the vouchers the previous year to remain in their private schools. New students may not participate in the program. An appeal of the injunction has been filed, and a decision as to the constitutionality of the Cleveland program is pending in federal district court. This case is expected to be eventually reviewed by the Supreme Court.

- Maine, 1999 — In two related cases (*Bagley v. Raymond School Department,* 1999 Me. 60 and *Strout v. Albanese,* No. 98-1986, 1999) brought by parents who wanted reimbursement for the cost of religious schools, the court ruled that inclusion of religious schools in the tuitioning program would be unconstitutional. Maine's "tuitioning" law allows reimbursements to families that send their children from districts lacking public schools to secular private schools. Appeals to the U.S. Supreme Court were filed in both cases. In October 1999, without comment or a recorded vote, the Court declined to review either case.

- Arizona, 1999 — The Arizona Supreme Court, in *Kotterman v. Killian* (972 P.2d 606), upheld the state program allowing a tax credit of up to $500 for individuals making charitable contributions

to "school tuition organizations" that provide scholarships to private schools, including religious schools. In October 1999, the U.S. Supreme Court denied review (68 LW 3232).

Do Americans Support School Choice?

The 1999 Phi Delta Kappa/Gallup poll found growing support for allowing parents to choose private schools and to receive financial assistance from public funds in order to do this. In 1999, 41 percent of the survey respondents favored publicly supported school choice, up from 33 percent in 1995. Nonetheless, over half (55 percent) still opposed this choice. (See Table 7.3.) Nonwhites (49 percent), respondents in the 18- to 29-year-old age group (48 percent), and urban residents (48 percent) were more likely to favor school choice. When asked if they favored or opposed the adoption of the voucher system in their state, opinions

---

TABLE 7.3

Do you favor or oppose allowing students and parents to choose a private school to attend at public expense?

	National Totals					No Children In School					Public School Parents				
	'99 %	'98 %	'97 %	'96 %	'95 %	'99 %	'98 %	'97 %	'96 %	'95 %	'99 %	'98 %	'97 %	'96 %	'95 %
Favor	41	44	44	36	33	38	41	44	33	30	45	48	45	39	38
Oppose	55	50	52	61	65	58	54	54	63	68	50	46	50	59	59
Don't know	4	6	4	3	2	4	5	2	4	2	5	6	5	2	3

TABLE 7.4

In the voucher system, a parent is given a voucher which can be used to pay all the tuition for attendance at a private or church-related school. Parents can then choose any private school, church-related school, or public school for their child. If a parent chooses a public school, the voucher would not apply. Would you favor or oppose the adoption of the voucher system in your state?

	National Totals		No Children In School		Public School Parents	
	'99 %	'98 %	'99 %	'98 %	'99 %	'98 %
Favor	47	48	43	44	54	55
Oppose	48	46	52	50	42	42
Don't know	5	6	5	6	4	3

Source of both tables: "The 31st Annual Phi Delta Kappa/Gallup Poll of the Public's Attitudes Toward the Public Schools," *Phi Delta Kappan,* September 1999

tended to differ based on whether or not they had children in school. Those with no children in school opposed the voucher system (52 percent to 43 percent), while public school parents favored vouchers (54 percent to 42 percent). (See Table 7.4.)

HOME SCHOOLING

About 25 years ago, a number of parents, unhappy with public schools, began teaching their children at home. In 1990, the Home School Legal Defense Association (HSLDA) in Paeonian Springs, Virginia, estimated that about 474,000 school-aged children were being taught at home. (The HSLDA provides legal counsel for home-schooling families.) The National Home Education Research Institute (NHERI) estimated that between 1.3 million and 1.7 million students (grades kindergarten through 12) in the United States were being home-schooled during the 1999-2000 school year. According to the NHERI, home schooling is growing at a rate of 7 percent to 15 percent per year.

State Requirements

Home schools are now legal in all 50 states, but states vary widely in the way they relate to home schooling. Because all states' laws require school attendance, the states have jurisdiction over home schools. Some states have set up elaborate requirements for home schools, while others have taken a "hands off" approach. Three states — New York, Ohio, and Texas — illustrate the wide variance in home school requirements.

New York

New York has established extensive requirements for home schools. Elementary-age students must spend 900 hours per year in class, and those in grades seven through 12 must be in class 990 hours per year. The teacher must be "competent" (no specific credentials required), and each year, the superintendent of local schools must receive advance notice of the intent to home-school. Records of attendance and assessment (including standardized tests) must be filed with the superintendent at specified times. Curriculum is specified by grade level and includes the basics, plus eight other subjects, such as American and New York history, music and art, health, and physical education. Students instructed at home are not awarded high school diplomas.

Ohio

Ohio requires students to spend 900 hours per year in class, and the home-school teacher must have a high school diploma or equivalent. Each year, advance notice of intent to home-school and assessment of student performance must be filed with the superintendent of schools. The assessment can be standardized test scores, a written description of progress, or another approved form of assessment. No attendance records are required. The state specifies which subjects must be taught, including the basics and other topics, such as first aid, fine arts, health, and government.

Texas

Texas has very few requirements for home schools, considering them private schools (which are not regulated by the state). The state requires no teacher certification, no advance notice, and no testing or attendance records. The only specified subjects are reading, spelling, grammar, mathematics, and good citizenship. Texas does not award diplomas to students that are home-schooled.

1998 Survey and Testing
of Home School Students

In *Scholastic Achievement and Demographic Characteristics of Home School Students in 1998* (*Education Policy Analysis Archives*, vol. 7, no. 8, 1999), Lawrence M. Rudner, University of Maryland professor, reported the results of the largest survey and testing program for students in home schools to date. He cautioned that home school students and their families are not a cross-section of the American population. Families who home school have an exceptionally strong commitment to education and children. The demographics of the students and their families show they are a select population.

- Home-school parents had more education beyond high school than parents in the general population — 88 percent, compared to 50 percent.

- Home-school families reported higher median incomes than the general American family with children — $52,000, compared to $36,000.

- Nearly all home-school students (98 percent) were in married couple families. Most home-school mothers (77 percent) did not participate in the labor force.

- Almost 1 of every 4 home-school students (23.6 percent) had at least one parent who was a certified teacher.

- Home-school students watch considerably less television than students nationwide — 65 percent watched one hour or less per day, compared to 25 percent nationally.

The survey's achievement testing of home-school students revealed substantially better scores than for their peers in public and private schools. In elementary grades, home-schooled students scored one grade level higher, and by eighth grade performed four grade levels higher. They achieved a composite score of 170 for five subjects in first grade, compared to 150 nationwide. By eighth grade, home-schooled students scored an average of 288, compared to 250 nationally. (See Table 7.5.) Figure 7.3 shows the relationship between median composite scale scores for home-schooled students, Catholic/private school students, and the nation's students as a whole.

According to Lawrence Rudner,

These comparisons between home-school students and students nationwide must be interpreted with a great deal of caution. This was not a controlled experiment. Students were not randomly assigned public, private or home schools. As a result, the

TABLE 7.5

Median Scaled Scores (corresponding Grade Equivalent Scores) by Subtest and Nominal Grade for Home School Students

Grade	Composite	Reading	Language	Math	Soc. Stud.	Science	National Median
1	170 (2.9)	174 (3.1)	166 (2.6)	164 (2.6)	166 (2.7)	164 (2.6)	150 (1.8)
2	192 (4.1)	196 (4.5)	186 (3.8)	188 (4.0)	189 (4.0)	195 (4.5)	168 (2.8)
3	207 (5.1)	210 (5.5)	195 (4.4)	204 (5.2)	205 (5.1)	214 (5.8)	185 (3.8)
4	222 (6.2)	228 (6.9)	216 (5.9)	220 (6.4)	216 (5.9)	232 (7.3)	200 (4.8)
5	243 (8.3)	244 (8.3)	237 (7.6)	238 (7.7)	236 (7.6)	260 (9.8)	214 (5.8)
6	261 (10.1)	258 (9.6)	256 (9.4)	254 (9.1)	265 (10.4)	273 (11.6)	227 (6.8)
7	276 (11.9)	277 (12.0)	276 (11.9)	272 (11.3)	276 (11.9)	282 (12.5)	239 (7.8)
8	288 (12.9)	288 (12.9)	291 (-)	282 (12.5)	290 (-)	289 (-)	250 (8.8)
9	292 (-)	294 (-)	297 (-)	281 (12.4)	297 (-)	292 (-)	260 (9.8)
10	310 (-)	314 (-)	318 (-)	294 (-)	318 (-)	310 (-)	268 (10.8)
11	310 (-)	312 (-)	322 (-)	296 (-)	318 (-)	314 (-)	275 (11.8)
12	326 (-)	328 (-)	332 (-)	300 (-)	334 (-)	331 (-)	280 (12.8)

(The - sign indicates the scaled scores are beyond the effective range for GES conversion.)

Source: Rudner, Lawrence N. (1999). *Scholastic Achievement and Demographic Characteristics of Home School Students in 1998. Education Policy Analysis Archives,* vol. 8, no. 7 (Entire issue). Available online at http://epaa.asu.edu/epaa/v7n8/

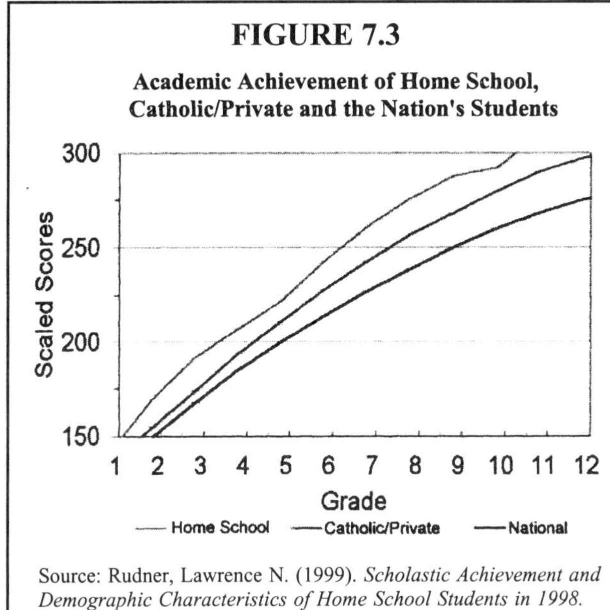

Source: Rudner, Lawrence N. (1999). *Scholastic Achievement and Demographic Characteristics of Home School Students in 1998. Education Policy Analysis Archives*, vol. 8, no. 7 (Entire issue). Available online at http://epaa.asu.edu/epaa/v7n8/

When Home Schoolers Apply to College

In "Home-Schooled Pupils Are Making Colleges Sit Up and Take Notice" (*Wall Street Journal*, February 11, 2000), Daniel Golden reported that, in 1999, home schoolers averaged 22.7 on the ACT college entrance exam, compared to 21 for public school students. Though home schoolers performed slightly lower in math, their scores in English and reading were 3 points higher than their public school counterparts. On the SAT, they scored an average of 1,083, compared to the national average of 1,016. (See Chapter IV for information on college entrance exams.) A recent survey by the National Center for Home Education found that 68 percent of colleges now accept parent-prepared transcripts or portfolios in place of an accredited diploma.

reported achievement differences between groups do not control for background differences in the home school and general United States population and, more importantly, cannot be attributed to the type of school a child attends. This study does not demonstrate that home schooling is superior to public or private schools. It should not be cited as evidence that our public schools are failing. It does not indicate that children will perform better academically if they are home-schooled.

The design of this study and the data do not warrant such claims. All the comparisons of home school students with the general population and with the private school population in this report fail to consider a myriad of differences between home school and public school students. We have no information as to what the achievement levels of home school students would be had they been enrolled in public or private schools. This study simply shows that those parents choosing to make a commitment to home schooling are able to provide a very successful academic environment.

Public Opinion About Home Schools

Americans are somewhat uncertain about home schools, although opposition has decreased slowly over the past decade. The Phi Delta Kappa/Gallup poll first asked about home schools in 1985 and found that 73 percent of those polled felt home schools were a bad thing. By 1997, opposition had declined to 57 percent. In 1999, 92 percent of those polled believed that home schooled students should take all the state and national assessment tests that public school students are required to take (Table 7.6).

TABLE 7.6

Would you favor or oppose requiring children who are schooled at home to take all the state and national assessment tests that public school students are required to take?

	National Totals %	No Children In School %	Public School Parents %
Favor	92	92	92
Oppose	7	6	8
Don't know	1	2	*

*Less than one-half of 1%.

Source of both tables: "The 31st Annual Phi Delta Kappa/Gallup Poll of the Public's Attitudes Toward the Public Schools," *Phi Delta Kappan*, September 1999

BILINGUAL EDUCATION

When first adopted, bilingual education was intended to offer better education to students (usually poor and recently immigrated to this country) who did not speak English. By instructing these students in their native languages — and teaching them English at the same time — they would overcome the language barriers to successful school achievement. Many observers still believe that children in bilingual programs acquire English at least as well as, and usually better than, children in all-English programs. However, in recent years, bilingual education has come under fire for failing to deliver the expected benefits.

While it is difficult to measure the effectiveness of bilingual education, some observers suggest that students in bilingual classes do not learn English more quickly and do not achieve better test scores. Some students do not participate in bilingual education, even when it is offered. And in many school districts, there is a shortage of bilingual teachers. In California, only 30 percent of its LEP (limited English proficient) students were in bilingual classes due to a shortage of bilingual teachers.

California Ends Bilingual Education Programs

The debate as to the effectiveness of bilingual education has led many critics to propose ending bilingual programs. In June 1998, California voters passed Proposition 227, which requires that public school students who cannot speak English be placed in a one-year English immersion course instead of in bilingual education. About 1.4 million of California's 5 million public school students are limited English proficient (LEP), nearly half (45 percent) the total number of LEP students in the United States.

Los Angeles teachers soon began reporting that their LEP students were learning English more quickly than anticipated after the ban on bilingual education. However, they questioned whether these students had acquired the language skills necessary to understand math, reading, or history lessons taught in English. They also worried that these students would not be ready to enter mainstream English classes within one year.

When California reported its standardized testing scores in August 1999, the scores of English learners had risen 18 percent in reading, 21 percent in mathematics, 15 percent in language, 21 percent in spelling, and 19 percent overall during the past year. In a few school districts, some of the score improvements had been as much as 93 percent.

Kenji Hakuta, professor of education at Stanford University, compared 1998 and 1999 scores in districts that had implemented Proposition 227 to districts that maintained bilingual programs. Both showed gains. When reading scores were considered in light of the overall gains in state scores for all students, scores for LEP students rose, as did non-LEP students. Scores for LEP students in English-only programs rose, as did scores for LEP students in bilingual programs. Hakuta hopes "this experience with trying to interpret the most recent release of SAT-9 (Stanford Achievement Test, Ninth Edition) data will convince the public that we should stop pointing the finger at bilingual programs and get into a serious discussion of improving schools, whether they be English-only or bilingual."

Successful Bilingual Programs

Disputing the claims that bilingual education is a failure, Stephen Krashen, professor of education at the University of Southern California, stated, "Serious research done in a scientifically respectable way (controlled studies) consistently shows that children in quality bilingual programs outperform comparison children in all-second-language (immersion) classes on tests of second language literacy." At the Georgetown University Roundtable on Languages and Linguistics in May 1999, Krashen presented the following characteristics he believed were necessary for successful bilingual programs.

- They must provide background knowledge through the first language.

- They must provide literacy in the first language.

- They must provide comprehensible input in English, through ESL (English as a Second Language) and sheltered subject matter teaching.

In sheltered classes, subject matter is taught to intermediate second-language acquirers. Beginners should be in regular ESL, and advanced students should be mainstreamed. Table 7.7 shows a sample bilingual program that utilizes the characteristics. Krashen concludes that bilingual education is a winner in all published studies if the program is properly organized. Commenting specifically on the success reported by the Los Angeles teachers, he claims that the immersion success is overstated and inconsistent.

Public Opinion on Teaching English to Immigrant Children

In the week following the California vote to ban bilingual education, the Gallup Organization asked Americans whether they preferred bilingual education or immersion to teach non-English speaking students in public schools. Sixty-three percent of respondents favored the idea of immersion, compared to 33 percent who favored bilingual education. (See Table 7.8.) This was very close to the 61 percent to 39 percent margin favoring Proposition 227 in California.

According to Public Agenda, a nonpartisan, nonprofit source for public opinion and policy analysis, 67 percent of parents favored teaching English to immigrants as quickly as possible (the immersion method), even if this means they fall behind in other subjects. A higher percentage of foreign-born parents (75 percent) believed this method was the best, while 66 percent of Hispanic parents agreed. The second option, rejected by most respondents, was to teach immigrants other subjects in their native language (the bilingual program), even if this means it takes them longer to learn English. According to Stephen Krashen, this option presumes that teaching subjects in the na-

---

TABLE 7.7

A sample bilingual program

	Mainstream	ESL/Sheltered	First Language
Beginning	Art, Music, PE	ESL	All core subjects
Intermediate	Art, Music, PE	ESL, Math, Science	Social Studies, Language Arts
Advanced	Art, Music, PE, Math, Science	ESL, Social Studies	Language Arts
Mainstream	All subjects		Heritage Language Development

Source: Stephen Krashen, *Bilingual Education: Arguments for and (Bogus) Arguments Against*, paper presented at the Georgetown Round Table on Languages and Linguistics, May 1999

TABLE 7.8

When there are a large number of non-English speaking students in a public school, these students are usually taught using one of the following two methods. After I read both methods, please tell me which one you prefer -- bilingual education, which means teaching these students their core subjects such as math and history in their native language, while providing them gradual training in how to read and speak English, or, immersion, which means teaching these students all of their subjects in English, while giving them intensive training in how to read and speak English. (ROTATED)

Immersion	63%
Bilingual	33
Both/depends (vol.)	1
Neither/other (vol.)	14
No opinion	2
	100%

Source: The Gallup Organization, Princeton, NJ, 2000

tive language delays English. He maintains that bilingual education taught properly (see above) accelerates, rather than delays, English language development and furthers both English and subject matter learning.

RELIGION IN PUBLIC SCHOOLS

The First Amendment issue of the separation of church and state is one of the most widely debated constitutional issues. During the past two decades, controversy has swirled around school prayer, religious baccalaureate services, and other exercises of religious belief within public schools. A number of religious and civil liberties groups (the American Jewish Committee, the American Muslim Council, the Baptist Joint Committee, the Anti-Defamation League, the Christian Legal Society, and the National Council of Churches, among many others) tried to clarify these issues in the handbook *Religion in the Public Schools: A Joint Statement of Current Law*. In May 1998, the Department of Education issued a letter and statement of principles regarding religious expression and activity in public schools to American educators. The guidelines were basically the same as originally issued in 1995.

According to the handbook, the church/state separation clause in the First Amendment was intended to prohibit the establishment of a state religion or the coercion of citizens to belong to a particular group, either religious or anti-religious. Contrary to popular belief, the Supreme Court's interpretations of First Amendment rights do not prohibit the private expression of religion in the public school. They do not prevent students from praying at school or in the classroom, so long as these activities do not disrupt the school's normal order or instruction. A student may pray either silently or quietly aloud whenever he or she is not actively participating in school activities, such as recitation in class. For example, students may not decide to pray aloud just as the teacher calls on them for an answer in class.

On the other hand, a student may not attempt to turn a class or meeting into a captive audience for a religious service. Public school officials may not legally require prayers during the school day, make them a part of graduation exercises, or organize religious baccalaureate services. Teachers and school administrators may not participate in, encourage, or insist upon student religious or anti-religious activities while they are acting in their capacities as representatives of the state. Doing so could be interpreted as coercion or as the establishment of a particular group as a state-sanctioned religion, something that violates the First Amendment. Teachers and other school personnel may exercise private religious activity, within the boundaries of the First Amendment, in faculty lounges or private offices.

Public schools may teach *about* religion, but they cannot give religious instruction. The study of the Bible and other religious scriptures is permissible as part of literature, history, and social studies classes so that students can understand the contribution of religious ideas and groups to the nation's culture. Students may express their personal religious beliefs in reports, homework, or artwork so long as these meet the goals of the assignments and are appropriate to the topics assigned.

The separation of church and state is very clear in some areas, but can be very ambiguous in others. For example, one of the biggest issues surrounding school vouchers is whether or not state funds, generated from taxes, can be used to pay tuition at parochial schools. The Wisconsin State Supreme Court, among others, has ruled that doing so would be an unconstitutional mingling of church and state. Recently, however, the U.S. Supreme Court seems to have changed its stance on the necessity for a rigid barrier between public schools and parochial schools. Five of the current justices criticized the 1985 finding in *Aguilar v. Felton* (473 U.S. 402), which ruled that sending public school teachers to parochial schools to conduct remedial classes was unconstitutional.

In 1997, the Court reheard the case, a most unusual procedure. A 5-4 divided U.S. Supreme Court, in *Agostini v. Felton* (65 LW 4524, 1997), ruled that "*Aguilar* [is] no longer good law." In reversing *Aguilar*, the court declared that

A federally funded program providing supplemental, remedial instruction to disadvantaged children on a neutral basis is not invalid under the Establishment Clause when such instruction is given on the premises of sectarian schools by government employees pursuant to a program containing safeguards ... this carefully constrained program also cannot reasonably be viewed as an endorsement of religion.... The mere circumstance that [an aid recipient] has chosen to use neutrally available state aid to help pay for [a] religious education [does not] confer any message of state endorsement of religion.

Specifically, the Court decided that Title I instructional services may be provided by public school teachers in private schools. Some observers believe the decision may help define future cases concerning state and religion, especially those involving vouchers that could be used to pay for tuition at religion-oriented schools.

TABLE 7.9

Allowing daily prayer to be spoken in the classroom

Favor	70%
Oppose	28
No opinion	2
	100%

TABLE 7.10

Allowing students to say prayers at graduation ceremonies as part of the official program

Favor	83%
Oppose	17
No opinion	*
	100%

Source of both tables: The Gallup Organization, Princeton, NJ, 2000

A Constitutional Amendment on School Prayer?

In the past several years, many U.S. Congressmen have proposed legislation to amend the constitution specifically to allow prayer in public schools. To date, none of the proposals has passed, but many legislators continue trying. In June 1998, the U.S. House voted for the first time since 1971 on a constitutional amendment to restore voluntary school prayer. The measure, the Religious Freedom Amendment, had a majority of voters but not the two-thirds needed to amend the Constitution.

Most Americans appear to support the idea of a constitutional amendment. In a 1997 Kaiser-Howard opinion poll, 69 percent favored a constitutional amendment to permit prayer in the public schools. According to a 1999 Gallup poll, 70 percent favored allowing daily prayer to be spoken in the classroom (Table 7.9) and 83 percent favored allowing students to say prayers at graduation ceremonies as part of the official program (Table 7.10).

SCHOOL-BASED SERVICE PROGRAMS

In recent years, many people have questioned whether or not school sites should be used as centers for other types of services, such as health care, family counseling, child care, transportation, and parent education. Those opposed to these nontraditional uses of school facilities fear that offering health or social services at school-based centers may distract teachers and students from their primary focus — education. They generally believe that providing these services is not the function of the school. Furthermore, the service center may present information (for example, about contraception and abortion) with which they do not agree.

Those in favor of school-based centers believe that social, emotional, and health problems affect students' academic performance. Sometimes the only visible sign that a family is in distress is the failing performance of a child in school. Close cooperation between school and service-center personnel can help to identify the problem and provide the necessary assistance. School-based centers are more accessible to both students and parents because the local school is sometimes the only place where parents actually come in contact with community officials.

According to *Making the Grade: State and Local Partnerships to Establish School-Based Health Centers* (George Washington University Medical Center, Washington, DC, 1998), in the 1997-98 school year, there were 1,157 school-based health programs in 45 states and the District of Columbia providing in-school care to students. This number is almost double the 607 centers in 1994. Most centers (63 percent) are located in urban schools, primarily in high schools, though the numbers in rural areas and in elementary and middle schools are increasing. Some believe that the numbers of students who enter high school sexually active or even pregnant would decrease with such programs in the earlier grades.

Most funding for school-based health centers comes from private sources and from local, state, and federal grants. However, these funding sources are limited and uncertain, so the centers are turning to third-party payers, such as Medicaid managed care organizations or the State Children's Health Insurance Program (SCHIP).

The Centers for Disease Control and Prevention (CDC; Atlanta, Georgia) has identified eight main components of coordinated, comprehensive school health programs.

- Complete health education.

- Family and community involvement.

- Healthy environment.

- Physical education.

- Counseling, psychological, and social services.

- Health services.

- Nutrition services.

- Healthy staff.

Fifteen states have received funds from the CDC to develop a statewide support system for school-based health programs. The CDC believes bad habits — tobacco use, poor nutrition, substance abuse, violence, physical inactivity, and sexual activities that result in sexually transmitted diseases or pregnancy — are often established in childhood and could be prevented with early intervention.

AN AGING INFRASTRUCTURE

The poor physical condition of American schools is a growing national problem. The average age of the country's K-12 schools is 43 years. In *School Facilities: America's Schools Report Differing Conditions* (Washington, DC, 1996), the General Accounting Office (GAO) reported that about one-third of all schools nationwide had at least one building in need of extensive repair, renovation, or replacement. About 58 percent of the schools had at least one environmental problem (asbestos, poor lighting, inadequate building security, etc.).

Elementary and secondary education is the nation's largest public enterprise, including more than 88,223 schools in 14,841 districts serving about 45.6 million students in 1996-1997. No one really knows the total replacement value of the nation's school buildings, but researchers frequently use an estimate of $422 billion. Whatever the actual number, school buildings represent an enormous investment of the nation's collective capital.

Are School Buildings Safe?

Are America's school buildings safe places for its students? In about one-third of all public schools, the answer appears to be no. In *School Facilities: Condition of America's Schools* (Wash-

TABLE 7.11

Estimated Percent of Schools and Number of Students Attending Schools with Inadequate Building Features, by Community Type

Building feature	Central city	Urban fringe/ large town	Rural/ small town
Roofs			
Percent of schools	32.8	26.9	23.9
Number of students (000s)	4,907	3,421[a]	3,575
Framing, floors, and foundations			
Percent of schools	22.2	15.1	16.7
Number of students (000s)	3,207[b]	1,868[c]	2,160[a]
Exterior walls, finishes, windows, and doors			
Percent of schools	34.3	24.8	22.4
Number of students (000s)	5,148	3,116[a]	3,246[a]
Interior finishes			
Percent of schools	29.8	23.4	20.8
Number of students (000s)	4,604[a]	2,959[b]	2,833[a]
Plumbing			
Percent of schools	34.2	27.0	28.6
Number of students (000s)	5,014	3,274[a]	3,952
HVAC			
Percent of schools	41.7	36.0	33.1
Number of students (000s)	6,022	4,516	4,900
Electrical power			
Percent of schools	31.8	26.7	22.7
Number of students (000s)	4,626	3,234[a]	3,166
Electrical lighting			
Percent of schools	29.4	26.3	21.7
Number of students (000s)	4,379[a]	3,320[a]	3,125[b]
Life safety codes			
Percent of schools	21.9	20.0	16.4
Number of students (000s)	3,032[b]	2,361[b]	2,221[a]
At least one inadequate building feature			
Percent of schools	66.6	56.8	51.7
Number of students (000s)	9,653	7,137	7,790

Note: Sampling errors for estimates based on percent of schools are less than ±4 percentage points. Sampling errors for estimates based on number of students are less than ±11 percentag points unless otherwise noted.

[a]Sampling errors are equal to or greater than 11 percentage points but less than 13 percentage points.

[b]Sampling errors are equal to or greater than 13 percentage points but less than 16 percentage points.

[c]Sampling errors are equal to or greater than 16 percentage points but less than 20 percentage points.

Source: *School Facilities: America's Schools Report Differing Conditions*, U.S. General Accounting Office, Washington, DC, 1996

Of all the major urban schools, the New York City schools are most in need. Repair and maintenance have been generally neglected since the financial crises of the 1970s. The estimated cost of returning New York's schools to good condition is $7.8 billion, but the city's five-year budget for school construction and renovation authorizes only $2.8 billion.

About 60 percent of the schools in the GAO survey reported that their buildings had at least one major feature needing repair, overhaul, or replacement. Problems with heating and air-conditioning plants; exterior walls, windows, and doors; plumbing; and roofs were most common. These conditions occurred in all kinds of communities, but were somewhat more prevalent in central city schools. (See Table 7.11.) Many of these problems, of course, are related; for example, a leaking roof causes wall, ceiling, and floor damage if it goes unrepaired for long.

More than half the schools reported at least one substandard environmental condition, such as heating, lighting, ventilation, or noise control. The most common problems involved heating, ventilation, and air conditioning systems. Central city schools were somewhat more likely to report problems than were schools in other areas. (See Table 7.12.) Unfortunately, the quality of the educational facility often tells the student how much the society values their education.

ington, DC, 1995) and in its 1996 report (see above), the GAO estimated the cost of repairing or upgrading aging and crumbling school facilities at $112 billion. Over the next three years, $11 billion will be needed to comply with federal mandates for providing physical access to all programs for all students and removing or correcting hazardous substances (asbestos, radon, lead, etc.).

Why are repairs and maintenance not performed in a timely manner? District officials cited lack of funds as the major cause of delaying vital repairs and maintenance from one year to the next (or beyond). About 1 in 3 districts reported an average of two bond-issue failures in the past 10 years; others reported that bond proceeds often did not bring in enough revenues to cover the full cost of repairs. Other districts said that state property tax limitations had reduced their state funding by as much as 40 percent over the past few years.

Some local school authorities reported that it was easier to defer school repairs than to cut academic programs or teaching staff. In many cases, funds are redirected from repair and maintenance to federally mandated projects. Also, for better or worse, it is often easy to ignore not-so-visible repair needs until the condition becomes critical. The GAO estimated that an average of $1.7 million per school would be needed to bring each facility up to good condition. Table 7.13 shows the distribution of amounts needed by school type.

As one school official told the GAO, the problem is basically too little money and too many demands.

Our school facilities are not energy efficient or wired for modern technology. Our floor tile is worn out and the furniture is in poor shape. Our taxpayers don't want to put any more [money] in schools. Our teachers want better pay. Our students and parents want more programs and technology. HELP!

Cost of School Construction

In 1998, 8,243 contracts were awarded for public school construction projects, which included both new schools and renovations of existing schools. Elementary schools accounted for about half of these awards. Costs amounted to about $18 billion in 1998. By the year 2001, school construction is projected to cost more than $20 billion.

TABLE 7.12

Estimated Percent of Schools and Number of Students Attending Schools with Unsatisfactory Environmental Conditions by Community Type

Environmental condition	Central city	Urban fringe/ large town	Rural/ small town
Lighting			
Percent of schools	20.4	17.3	11.4
Number of students (000s)	2,980[a]	2,072[b]	1,621[a]
Heating			
Percent of schools	22.8	19.0	17.0
Number of students (000s)	3,185[c]	2,249[a]	2,440[c]
Ventilation			
Percent of schools	31.5	28.2	23.6
Number of students (000s)	4,663	3,502[c]	3,380
Indoor air quality			
Percent of schools	22.5	19.0	17.2
Number of students (000s)	3,441[a]	2,421[a]	2,482
Acoustics for noise control			
Percent of schools	31.6	26.3	26.8
Number of students (000s)	4,250[c]	3,024[a]	3,755
Energy efficiency			
Percent of schools	46.1	40.3	38.6
Number of students (000s)	6,412	4,944	5,531
Physical security			
Percent of schools	26.5	22.8	23.5
Number of students (000s)	4,023[c]	3,038[a]	3,562[c]
At least one unsatisfactory environmental condition			
Percent of schools	65.1	58.5	53.9
Number of students (000s)	9,400	7,322	8,007

Note: Sampling errors for estimates based on percent of schools are less than ±4 percentage points. Sampling errors for estimates based on number of students are less than ±11 percentage points unless otherwise noted.

[a]Sampling errors are equal to or greater than 13 percentage points but less than 16 percentage points.

[b]Sampling errors are equal to or greater than 16 percentage points but less than 20 percentage points.

[c]Sampling errors are equal to or greater than 11 percentage points but less than 13 percentage points.

Source: *School Facilities: America's Schools Report Differing Conditions*, U.S. General Accounting Office, Washington, DC, 1996

TABLE 7.13

**Frequency Distribution of Amounts Reported Needed to Repair
or Upgrade Schools to Good Overall Condition**

Amount reported needed	Elementary schools	Secondary schools	Combined	Total (percent)[a]
$0	9,290	3,056	597	12,943 (16)
$1 to less than $100	22			22 (0)
$100 to less than $1,000	643	213	24	879 (1)
$1,000 to less than $100,000	10,179	3,276	500	13,955 (18)
$100,000 to less than $1 million	18,882	5,477	952	25,311 (32)
$1 million to less than $6 million	15,760	6,048	689	22,497 (28)
$6 million to less than $15 million	1,394	1,379	92	2,865 (4)
$15 million to less than $50 million	312	588	42	943 (1)
$50 million to less than $100 million		12	4	16 (0)
$100 million or more	19	5		23 (0)
Total (percent)[a]	**56,500 (71)**	**20,053 (25)**	**2,900 (4)**	**79,454 (100)**

[a]Slight discrepancies in row and column totals are due to rounding.

Source: *School Facilities: America's Schools Report Differing Conditions*, U.S. General Accounting Office, Washington, DC, 1996

More than one-third of the schools reported that their electrical wiring was insufficient for computers and other communications technology. One school reported that there were only two electrical outlets per classroom and that if four teachers plugged in equipment at the same time, they blew a circuit breaker.

By 1996, 98 percent of all schools owned computers, with the student-to-computer ratio at 10 to 1. The Educational Testing Service, in *Computers and Classrooms: The Status of Technology in U.S. Schools* (Policy Information Center, Princeton, New Jersey, 1997), reported that the cost of the technology present in the schools in 1996 was about $3 billion, or $70 per pupil. According to estimates, $15 billion will likely be needed to make schools "technology rich." This would be about $300 per student, or 5 percent of total educational spending.

During 1998, 30 state legislators proposed 73 bills, primarily directed at K-12 facilities. Forty-two failed, 20 passed, and 11 were pending. The Department of Education recommended that, when finances are lacking, incremental improvements be made one at a time and as costs allow.

TECHNOLOGY IN AMERICAN SCHOOLS

In 1994 and 1995, the GAO surveyed about 10,000 schools on their capacity for and use of technology (*School Facilities: America's Schools Not Designed or Equipped for 21st Century*, Washington, DC, 1995). Nearly three-quarters of the surveyed schools reported they had enough computers and television sets but lacked the building facilities to fully use their computers. Over half the schools lacked the modems, phone lines, conduits for cables, and fiber-optic cables that would enable them to network their school computers or link them to network service providers.

Internet Access

In 1998, according to the National Center for Education Statistics, 89 percent of public schools were connected to the Internet. However, perhaps a better way to evaluate how many students have access to the Internet is to look at how many instructional rooms (classrooms, computer labs, and library/media centers) are connected to the Internet. In 1998, 51 percent of instructional rooms in public schools were connected to the Internet, nearly double (27 percent) the percentage in 1997. The ratio of students per instructional computer in 1998 was 6 to 1.

CHAPTER VIII

TEACHERS

Teachers are the foundation of the education process. A well-designed, challenging curriculum, a first-class facility, and state-of-the-art equipment mean little without motivated and well-trained teachers to complete the equation. However, teachers are usually the first to come under fire when test scores and achievement are less than satisfactory and among the last to be rewarded when things go well. Overall, their salaries are considerably lower than those of similarly educated professionals.

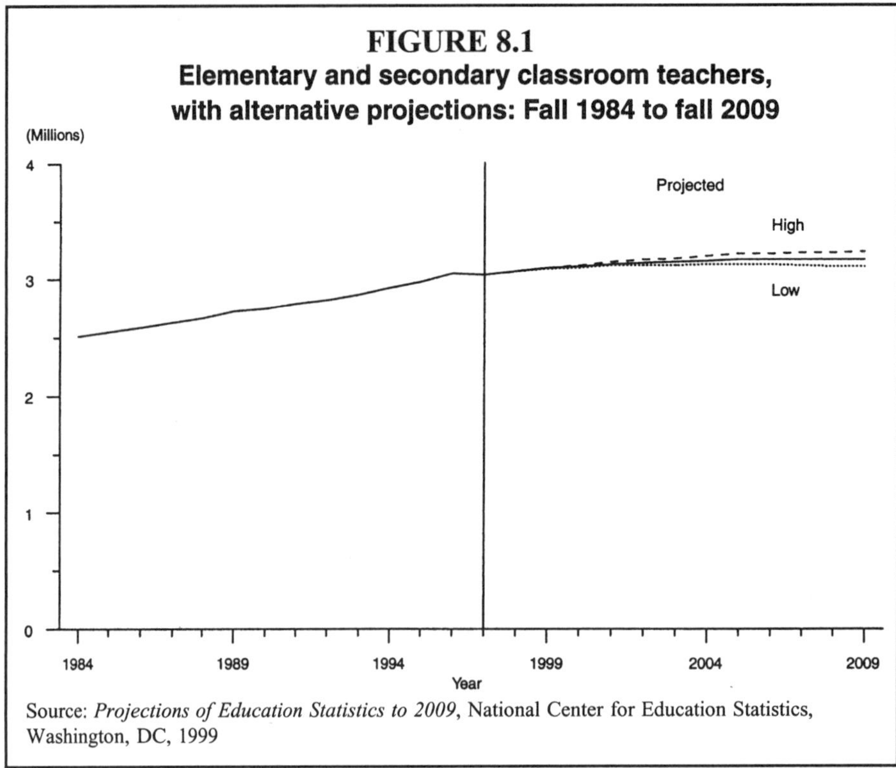

FIGURE 8.1
Elementary and secondary classroom teachers, with alternative projections: Fall 1984 to fall 2009

Source: *Projections of Education Statistics to 2009*, National Center for Education Statistics, Washington, DC, 1999

A growing number of teachers face situations that would have been inconceivable a generation ago, ranging from lack of respect from students to outright physical attacks. Teachers in inner-city schools particularly bear the brunt of many "school" problems that are often a reflection of society's problems. Despite the problems, the number of teachers is increasing, and a clear majority of teachers are pleased with what they do.

TRENDS IN TEACHER SUPPLY AND DEMAND

The number of classroom teachers in elementary and secondary schools has increased steadily, reaching 3.04 million in 1997, an increase of 21 percent from 1984. Based on the middle alternative projection, the National Center for Education Statistics (NCES) expects the number of classroom teachers to increase to 3.17 million by the year 2009, a 4 percent increase from 1997. (See Figure 8.1 and Table 8.1.)

A Teacher Shortage?

For several years, some observers have asked, "Is there a teacher shortage in the United States?" According to the Department of Education, 2 million more teachers will need to be hired over the next decade, including both beginning teachers and former teachers coming back into the profession. Following a survey of personnel officers in the nation's 200 largest school districts, the American Federation of Teachers (AFT) reported that more than two-thirds of respondents indicated a shortage of teacher applicants in 1998-99. Barely 29 percent reported an adequate supply, and only 3 percent indicated an oversupply of teachers. (See Figure 8.2.)

Teacher supply and demand, however, varies by region. While some states, such as California, Florida, Nevada, and Texas, are experiencing considerable shortages, others — Connecticut, Minnesota, New York, Pennsylvania, and Wisconsin — produce more certified teachers than they can hire. Significant differences exist even within states. Though some school districts have hundreds of applicants for every job, others — in less desirable areas and with lower pay scales — may have none. For instance, while only about one-quarter of the teachers licensed in the state of New York in 1996-97 were hired to teach in that state, New York City had to use 9,000 unlicensed teachers because of shortages. Suburban districts in New York pay far more, enticing teachers away from the city's schools.

Supply and demand also varies by field of instruction. Teacher shortage is most severe in special education, bilingual/ESL (English as a Second Language), math, and speech therapy. In the AFT survey, districts also reported shortages in foreign language, science, computer, school psychology, and occupational and physical therapy. While some surplus was reported in the elementary and social studies areas, no teaching area rated in the category of "considerable surplus." (See Table 8.2.)

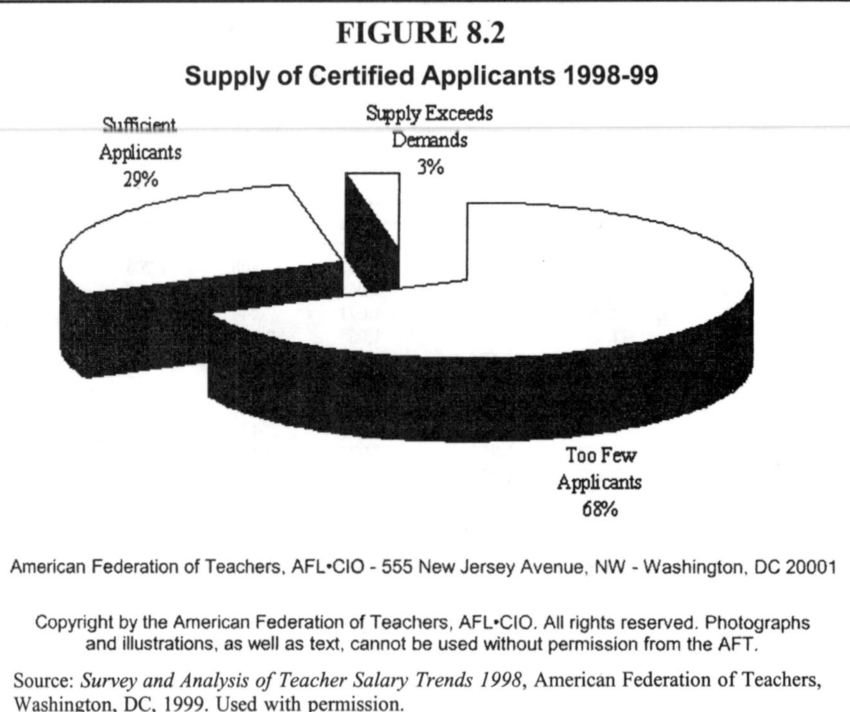

American Federation of Teachers, AFL•CIO - 555 New Jersey Avenue, NW - Washington, DC 20001

Source: *Survey and Analysis of Teacher Salary Trends 1998*, American Federation of Teachers, Washington, DC, 1999. Used with permission.

One consequence of teacher shortages is the increased hiring of uncertified teachers. According to the National Commission on Teaching and America's Future, more than one-fourth of newly hired teachers have not fully met the state licensing standards. Twelve percent were hired with no license at all, and an additional 15 percent hold temporary, provisional, or emergency licenses. Moreover, many teachers are teaching "out-of-field." Among public school teachers in grades 9 through 12, 21.5 percent of English teachers, 28.1 percent math teachers, 18.2 percent science teachers, and 17.8 percent social studies teachers were teaching with neither a major nor a minor in that subject.

Pupil-Teacher Ratio

Educators prefer a low ratio of students per teacher, which allows teachers to spend more time with each pupil. From 1984 to 1997, the pupil-teacher ratio in elementary schools declined slightly from 19.3 to 18.9 students per teacher. The NCES projects that this ratio will remain stable from 1998 to 2009. The pupil-teacher ratio in secondary schools also declined from 16.0 in 1984 to 14.5 in 1997. This ratio is projected to remain relatively constant over the next decade. (See Table 8.3.)

Table 8.4 shows the number of teachers and students and the average pupil-teacher ratios in public elementary and secondary schools by state. In fall 1996, New Jersey, Maine, and Vermont reported the lowest average pupil-teacher ratio (13.6 or 13.7), while Utah and California reported the highest (24.4 and 22.9, respectively). Some states have laws limiting class sizes,* especially in elementary schools. Several other states are involved in or considering similar laws. In 1998, Congress passed the 1999 Omnibus Appropriations Act (PL 105-277), allocating $1.1 billion for reducing class sizes and hiring more teachers in grades one through three.

---

*Pupil-teacher ratio and class size are not equivalent terms. Pupil-teacher ratio is calculated by dividing the number of students in a school by the number of instructors holding teaching certificates whose primary responsibility is to teach. These instructors include specialists who teach far more students, such as physical education teachers, or far fewer students, such as special education teachers. Average class size is calculated by surveying classroom teachers and asking how many students are in their classes.

TABLE 8.2

Teacher Supply and Demand by Field

		AAEE National Survey of School Districts		AFT Survey of Big Cities
		1997 Index	**3 Year Trend***	**1999 Index**
Considerable Shortage (5.00-4.21)				
	Special Education	4.08-4.29	Increased Shortage	4.64
	Math	3.81	No Change	4.51
	Speech Therapists	4.34	No Change	4.42
	Bilingual/ESL	4.34	Decreased Shortage	4.23
Some Shortage (4.20-3.41)				
	OT/PT Therapists	n.a.	n.a.	4.11
	Foreign Language	3.07-3.72	No Change	4.06
	Physical Sciences	3.70	Increased Shortage	4.06
	Computer	3.70	Increased Shortage	3.96
	Psychologists	3.58	No Change	3.78
	Vocational Ed.	n.a.	n.a.	3.73
	Life Sciences	3.62	Increased Shortage	3.6
	Reading	3.19	No Change	3.42
Balanced (3.40-2.61)				
	Art & Music	2.53-3.10	Increased Shortage	3.38
	Counselors	3.25	No Change	3.17
	English	2.64	Increased Shortage	2.89
	Social Workers	3.13	No Change	2.78
	Physical Education	2.11	No Change	2.74
	Pre-K/Kindergarten	2.56	Increased Shortage	2.71
Some Surplus (2.60-1.81)				
	Elementary	2.44	Increased Shortage	2.40
	Social Studies	2.05	Increased Shortage	2.07
Considerable Surplus (1.80-1.00)				
	No Teaching Areas			

*Three year trend in teacher shortage reported by AAEE.

Sources: American Association of Employment in Education (AAEE), "Teacher Supply and Demand in the United States 1997 Report," 1998. American Federation of Teachers, survey of school personnel directors in school districts serving the 200 U.S. largest cities.

American Federation of Teachers, AFL•CIO - 555 New Jersey Avenue, NW - Washington, DC 20001

Source: *Survey and Analysis of Teacher Salary Trends 1998*, American Federation of Teachers, Washington, DC, 1999. Used with permission.

SELECTED CHARACTERISTICS OF TEACHERS

Table 8.5 shows selected characteristics of both public- and private-school teachers in the 1993-94 school year. Women continued to make up the overwhelming majority of teachers in both public (73 percent) and private (75 percent) elementary and secondary schools. However, male teachers in public schools were more likely than women to have a master's degree (45.7 percent versus 40.6 percent), a doctorate (1.3 percent versus 0.5 percent), and more than 20 years of full-time teaching experience (39.6 percent versus 26.1 percent). Similar ratios of men's and women's degrees and teaching experience existed among private-school teachers.

Most public school teachers (86.5 percent in 1993-94) are White. In 1993-94, about 7.4 percent of public school teachers were Black, 4.2 percent were Hispanic, 1 percent were Asian or Pacific Islander, and fewer than 1 percent were American Indian or Alaskan Native. Even smaller proportions of minorities teach in private schools. (See Table 8.5.) Many public school systems, especially in larger cities, make deliberate efforts to recruit minority teachers as role models for minority stu-

TABLE 8.3

Pupil/teacher ratios in elementary and secondary schools, by control of institution and organizational level, with alternative projections: Fall 1984 to fall 2009

Year	Total		Public		Private	
	Elementary	Secondary	Elementary	Secondary	Elementary	Secondary
1984	19.3	16.0	19.7	16.1	[1]17.7	[1]14.4
1985	19.1	15.6	19.5	15.8	17.1	14.0
1986	18.8	15.5	19.3	15.7	[1]16.5	[1]13.6
1987	18.8	15.0	19.3	15.2	[2]16.5	[2]13.1
1988	18.6	14.7	19.0	14.9	[2]16.1	[2]12.8
1989	18.4	14.3	19.0	14.6	[2]15.1	[2]11.7
1990	18.5	14.3	18.9	14.6	[2]16.1	[2]11.3
1991	18.4	14.6	18.8	15.0	[2]16.0	[2]11.1
1992	18.4	14.8	18.8	15.2	[2]16.2	[2]11.3
1993	18.5	14.7	18.9	15.1	[3]16.3	[3]11.5
1994	18.6	14.4	19.0	14.8	[3]16.4	[3]11.4
1995	18.9	14.0	19.3	14.4	[3]16.6	[3]10.8
1996	18.5	14.2	18.9	14.4	16.4	11.5
1997[3]	18.9	14.5	19.4	14.8	16.6	11.6
Middle alternative projections						
1998	19.0	14.5	19.4	14.8	16.6	11.6
1999	19.0	14.5	19.4	14.8	16.6	11.6
2000	19.0	14.5	19.5	14.8	16.6	11.6
2001	19.0	14.6	19.4	14.9	16.6	11.6
2002	19.0	14.6	19.4	14.9	16.7	11.6
2003	18.9	14.7	19.3	15.0	16.7	11.7
2004	18.9	14.7	19.3	15.0	16.6	11.8
2005	18.9	14.8	19.3	15.1	16.6	11.9
2006	18.8	14.9	19.2	15.2	16.5	12.0
2007	18.8	14.9	19.2	15.2	16.5	12.0
2008	18.8	14.8	19.2	15.1	16.5	12.0
2009	18.8	14.7	19.2	15.0	16.5	11.9

[1] Estimated on the basis of past data.
[2] Estimate is from the survey on *Early Estimates*.
[3] Projected.

NOTE: The pupil-teacher ratios were derived from tables 2 and 32. Historical numbers may differ from those in previous editions. Projections are based on data through 1995. Data for 1996 are actual numbers.

SOURCE: U.S. Department of Education, National Center for Education Statistics, *Statistics of Public Elementary and Secondary Schools*; Common Core of Data surveys; *NCES Bulletin*, December 1984; 1985 Private School Survey; "Key Statistics for Private Elementary and Secondary Education: School Year 1988–89," *Early Estimates*; "Key Statistics for Private Elementary and Secondary Education: School Year 1990–91," *Early Estimates*; "Public and Private Elementary and Secondary Education Statistics: School Year 1991–92," *Early Estimates*; "Public and Private Elementary and Secondary Education Statistics: School Year 1992–93," *Early Estimates*; National Elementary and Secondary Enrollment Model; and Elementary and Secondary Teachers Model. (This table was prepared August 1998.)

Source: *Projections of Education Statistics to 2009*, National Center for Education Statistics, Washington, DC, 1999

dents, who have become the majority in most inner-city schools. (See below for more information about minority teachers.)

In 1996, women continued to make up about three-quarters (74.4 percent) of public school teachers. The vast majority (90.7 percent) of teachers were White. Most teachers (75.9 percent) were married. The median age (half were over, half were under) was 44, and the median years of teaching experience were 15 years. Over half (54.5 percent) of public school teachers had a master's or specialist degree, while less than 2 percent had a doctorate degree. (See Table 8.6.)

SALARIES

The past two decades have been marked by fluctuations in teachers' salaries. From the late 1970s through the early 1980s, as school enrollments fell, average teachers' salaries (in constant 1997-98 dollars, adjusted for inflation) also declined slightly. In 1979-80 and 1980-81, teachers' salaries averaged $33,272 and $32,944, respectively. Then, from 1982-83 to 1989-90, salaries rose steadily and relatively rapidly — to $39,956, a 17 percent increase. From 1990-91 to 1997-98, salaries remained comparatively stable (between $39,000 and $39,500). (See Figure 8.3.) Private

TABLE 8.4

Teachers, enrollment, and pupil/teacher ratios in public elementary and secondary schools, by state: Fall 1991 to fall 1996

State or other area	Pupil/ teacher ratio, fall 1991	Pupil/ teacher ratio, fall 1992	Pupil/ teacher ratio, fall 1993	Fall 1994			Fall 1995			Fall 1996		
				Teachers	Enrollment	Pupil/ teacher ratio	Teachers	Enrollment	Pupil/ teacher ratio	Teachers	Enrollment	Pupil/ teacher ratio
1	2	3	4	5	6	7	8	9	10	11	12	13
United States	17.3	17.4	17.4	2,551,875	44,111,482	17.3	2,598,220	44,840,481	17.3	2,666,034	45,592,213	17.1
Alabama	17.8	17.4	17.1	42,791	736,531	17.2	44,056	746,149	16.9	45,040	748,156	16.6
Alaska	16.7	16.8	17.5	7,205	127,057	17.6	7,379	127,618	17.3	7,418	129,919	17.5
Arizona	19.3	18.7	18.9	38,132	737,424	19.3	38,017	743,566	19.6	40,521	799,250	19.7
Arkansas	17.0	17.0	17.1	26,181	447,565	17.1	26,449	453,257	17.1	26,680	457,349	17.1
California	22.8	24.0	24.0	225,016	5,407,475	24.0	230,849	5,536,406	24.0	248,857	5,687,901	22.9
Colorado	17.9	18.3	18.6	34,894	640,521	18.4	35,388	656,279	18.5	36,398	673,438	18.5
Connecticut	14.0	14.3	14.4	35,316	506,824	14.4	36,070	517,935	14.4	36,551	527,129	14.4
Delaware	16.8	16.7	16.5	6,416	106,813	16.6	6,463	108,461	16.8	6,642	110,549	16.6
District of Columbia	12.7	13.3	13.3	6,110	80,450	13.2	5,305	79,802	15.0	5,288	78,648	14.9
Florida	17.6	18.4	18.4	110,674	2,111,188	19.1	114,938	2,176,222	18.9	120,471	2,242,212	18.6
Georgia	18.5	18.0	16.7	77,914	1,270,948	16.3	79,480	1,311,126	16.5	79,091	1,346,761	17.0
Hawaii	18.5	17.6	17.8	10,240	183,795	17.9	10,500	187,180	17.8	10,576	187,653	17.7
Idaho	19.4	19.6	19.7	12,582	240,448	19.1	12,784	243,097	19.0	13,078	245,252	18.8
Illinois	16.8	16.8	17.1	110,830	1,916,172	17.3	113,538	1,943,623	17.1	116,274	1,973,040	17.0
Indiana	17.6	17.6	17.5	55,496	969,022	17.5	55,821	977,263	17.5	56,708	983,415	17.3
Iowa	15.7	15.8	15.8	31,726	500,440	15.8	32,318	502,343	15.5	32,593	502,941	15.4
Kansas	15.2	15.2	15.1	30,579	460,838	15.1	30,729	463,008	15.1	30,875	466,293	15.1
Kentucky	17.2	17.3	17.6	38,784	657,642	17.0	39,120	659,821	16.9	39,331	656,089	16.7
Louisiana	16.6	17.0	17.1	47,599	797,933	16.8	46,980	797,366	16.6	47,334	793,296	16.6
Maine	14.0	14.1	14.1	15,404	212,601	13.8	15,392	213,569	13.9	15,551	213,593	13.7
Maryland	16.9	16.9	17.5	46,565	790,938	17.0	47,819	805,544	16.8	47,943	818,583	17.1
Massachusetts	15.1	15.0	14.9	60,489	893,727	14.8	62,710	915,007	14.6	64,574	933,898	14.5
Michigan	19.2	19.5	19.9	80,522	1,614,784	20.1	83,179	1,641,456	19.7	88,051	1,684,386	19.1
Minnesota	17.2	17.6	17.3	46,958	821,693	17.5	46,971	835,166	17.8	48,245	847,204	17.6
Mississippi	17.9	18.2	17.8	28,866	505,962	17.5	28,997	506,272	17.5	29,293	503,967	17.2
Missouri	16.0	16.2	15.8	56,606	878,541	15.5	57,951	889,881	15.4	59,436	900,042	15.1
Montana	15.8	15.8	16.4	10,079	164,341	16.3	10,076	165,547	16.4	10,268	164,627	16.0
Nebraska	14.7	14.6	14.5	19,774	287,100	14.5	20,028	289,744	14.5	20,174	291,967	14.5
Nevada	18.6	18.7	18.7	13,414	250,747	18.7	13,878	265,041	19.1	14,805	282,131	19.1
New Hampshire	15.5	15.6	15.5	12,109	189,319	15.6	12,346	194,171	15.7	12,692	198,308	15.6
New Jersey	13.8	13.6	13.6	85,258	1,174,206	13.8	86,706	1,197,381	13.8	[1]88,903	[1]1,208,179	[1]13.6
New Mexico	17.6	17.6	17.5	19,025	327,248	17.2	19,398	329,640	17.0	19,971	332,632	16.7
New York	15.4	15.2	15.2	182,273	2,766,208	15.2	181,559	2,813,230	15.5	185,104	2,843,131	15.4
North Carolina	16.8	16.7	16.3	71,592	1,156,767	16.2	73,201	1,183,090	16.2	75,239	1,210,108	16.1
North Dakota	15.3	15.2	15.4	7,796	119,288	15.3	7,501	119,100	15.9	7,892	120,123	15.2
Ohio	17.3	16.9	16.8	109,085	1,814,290	16.6	107,347	1,836,015	17.1	108,602	1,844,389	17.0
Oklahoma	15.6	15.5	15.5	39,406	609,718	15.5	39,364	616,393	15.7	39,491	620,695	15.7
Oregon	18.6	19.2	19.5	26,208	521,945	19.9	26,680	527,914	19.8	26,757	537,854	20.1
Pennsylvania	16.8	17.0	17.2	102,988	1,764,946	17.1	104,921	1,787,533	17.0	106,432	1,804,256	17.0
Rhode Island	14.6	14.3	14.8	10,066	147,487	14.7	10,482	149,799	14.3	10,656	151,324	14.2
South Carolina	16.9	17.2	16.7	39,437	648,725	16.4	39,922	645,586	16.2	41,463	653,011	15.7
South Dakota	14.8	15.3	14.9	9,985	143,482	14.4	9,641	144,685	15.0	9,625	143,331	14.9
Tennessee	19.4	19.6	18.8	47,406	881,425	18.6	53,403	893,770	16.7	54,790	905,089	16.5
Texas	15.8	16.1	16.0	234,213	3,677,171	15.7	240,371	3,748,167	15.6	247,650	3,828,975	15.5
Utah	24.9	24.2	24.7	19,524	474,675	24.3	20,039	477,121	23.8	19,734	481,812	24.4
Vermont	13.8	13.1	14.0	7,566	104,533	13.8	7,676	105,565	13.8	7,751	106,341	13.7
Virginia	15.7	15.1	14.8	72,505	1,060,809	14.6	74,731	1,079,854	14.4	74,523	1,096,093	14.7
Washington	20.2	20.2	20.1	46,439	938,314	20.2	46,907	956,572	20.4	48,307	974,504	20.2
West Virginia	15.3	15.2	14.9	21,024	310,511	14.8	21,073	307,112	14.6	20,888	304,052	14.6
Wisconsin	15.7	15.5	16.0	54,054	860,581	15.9	55,033	870,175	15.8	54,769	879,259	16.1
Wyoming	15.6	17.2	15.4	6,754	100,314	14.9	6,734	99,859	14.8	6,729	99,058	14.7
Outlying areas												
American Samoa	19.9	19.3	22.1	698	14,445	20.7	728	14,576	20.0	734	14,766	20.1
Guam	18.9	18.5	18.8	1,826	32,185	17.6	1,802	32,960	18.3	1,552	33,393	21.5
Northern Marianas	16.5	19.0	19.0	406	8,429	20.8	422	8,809	20.9	441	9,041	20.5
Puerto Rico	17.2	16.6	15.9	39,933	621,121	15.6	39,328	627,620	16.0	39,743	618,861	15.6
Virgin Islands	14.1	14.3	14.5	1,528	23,126	15.1	1,622	22,737	14.0	1,580	22,385	14.2

[1] Data imputed by the National Center for Education Statistics based on previous year's data.

NOTE.—Some data have been revised from previously published figures. Teachers reported in full-time equivalents.

SOURCE: U.S. Department of Education, National Center for Education Statistics, Common Core of Data surveys. (This table was prepared May 1998.)

Source: *Digest of Education Statistics 1998*, National Center for Education Statistics, Washington, DC, 1999

TABLE 8.5

Teachers in public elementary and secondary schools, by selected characteristics: 1993-94

Selected characteristics	Total [1]	Percent of teachers, by highest degree earned						Percent of teachers, by years of full-time teaching experience			
		No degree	Associate	Bachelor's	Master's	Education specialist	Doctor's	Less than 3	3 to 9	10 to 20	Over 20
1	2	3	4	5	6	7	8	9	10	11	12
Public schools											
Total	2,561,294	0.6	0.2	52.0	42.0	4.6	0.7	9.7	25.5	35.0	29.8
Men	694,098	1.3	0.4	46.2	45.7	5.1	1.3	8.9	21.6	29.9	39.6
Women	1,867,195	0.3	0.1	54.1	40.6	4.4	0.5	10.0	26.9	37.0	26.1
Race/ethnicity											
White	2,216,605	0.5	0.1	51.8	42.5	4.4	0.7	9.4	25.5	35.1	30.0
Black	188,371	0.5	0.2	48.4	44.6	5.4	0.9	8.5	20.8	35.5	35.2
Hispanic	108,744	0.9	0.5	62.8	29.8	4.6	1.4	16.7	32.1	34.1	17.1
Asian or Pacific Islander	27,510	0.9	0.4	49.3	34.7	13.1	1.7	14.9	29.7	29.2	26.2
American Indian or Alaskan	20,064	0.8	0.3	54.9	39.1	4.3	0.6	11.3	27.6	34.5	26.6
Age											
Less than 30	280,342	0.5	0.1	83.9	14.5	1.0	0.1	47.8	52.2	(2)	(2)
30 to 39	573,444	0.5	0.2	59.4	36.6	3.0	0.3	10.5	48.7	40.8	(2)
40 to 49	1,070,459	0.4	0.1	46.3	47.0	5.4	0.7	4.3	16.9	47.5	31.3
50 to 59	540,491	0.7	0.2	40.6	51.2	6.1	1.2	1.4	7.8	25.0	65.7
60 or more	96,557	1.5	0.1	43.1	46.2	6.6	2.5	0.8	4.4	19.9	74.9
Level											
Elementary	1,331,281	0.2	(2)	55.5	39.7	4.1	0.4	9.7	27.1	35.5	27.7
General	938,636	0.3	(2)	58.0	38.0	3.5	0.3	9.2	26.5	34.9	29.4
English	2,093	(2)	(2)	46.0	52.3	1.0	0.8	12.5	11.2	17.9	58.4
Mathematics	3,372	(2)	(2)	74.6	24.4	(2)	1.0	11.6	13.1	40.9	34.3
Special education	127,877	(2)	(2)	45.1	46.9	7.2	0.9	11.1	34.1	39.9	15.0
Other elementary	259,304	0.3	0.1	51.3	42.6	4.9	0.8	11.1	25.8	35.6	27.5
Secondary	1,230,013	0.9	0.3	48.2	44.4	5.1	1.1	9.7	23.8	34.5	32.0
English	172,603	0.1	(2)	48.3	44.8	5.5	1.3	9.2	22.9	33.6	34.3
Mathematics	141,051	0.1	(2)	50.2	45.5	3.4	0.8	9.4	24.3	31.7	34.5
Science	132,179	0.2	(2)	47.9	45.8	4.8	1.2	9.5	26.1	31.2	33.2
Social studies	130,045	0.1	(2)	47.8	46.0	4.9	1.2	10.3	20.5	28.7	40.5
Special education	111,215	0.1	0.1	42.1	49.1	7.2	1.3	9.3	28.8	45.1	16.8
Vocational/technical	113,269	7.3	2.3	45.2	39.9	4.7	0.5	6.8	23.0	35.7	34.5
Other secondary	429,653	0.5	0.2	50.1	43.0	5.1	1.1	10.7	23.1	35.6	30.7
Private schools											
Total	378,365	5.2	1.5	59.0	29.8	2.9	1.7	20.9	33.9	29.6	15.6
Men	93,130	4.4	0.9	47.3	40.6	2.6	4.3	21.7	28.2	28.7	21.4
Women	285,235	5.4	1.7	62.8	26.3	3.0	0.8	20.6	35.8	29.9	13.7
Race/ethnicity											
White	347,811	4.8	1.3	59.4	30.2	2.6	1.6	20.4	33.6	30.0	16.0
Black	11,664	8.3	3.7	55.8	26.4	4.8	1.0	26.9	34.9	27.9	10.3
Hispanic	12,221	11.1	4.9	57.4	19.9	4.4	2.3	25.5	41.8	21.6	11.1
Asian or Pacific Islander	5,167	6.8	0.9	46.1	36.8	5.7	3.6	26.1	34.6	26.6	12.7
American Indian or Alaskan	1,502	3.4	6.0	49.4	16.1	25.1	(2)	29.4	42.8	17.9	9.9
Age											
Less than 30	65,168	7.7	1.6	78.8	10.8	1.0	0.2	54.9	44.9	0.1	(2)
30 to 39	93,999	5.9	1.2	63.1	25.7	2.6	1.4	21.7	51.2	27.1	(2)
40 to 49	131,492	3.9	1.6	54.0	35.1	3.4	2.0	12.6	29.8	45.5	12.1
50 to 59	65,691	4.0	1.8	49.7	38.4	3.5	2.5	7.4	15.7	35.7	41.2
60 or more	22,015	5.6	0.9	39.4	46.6	4.4	2.9	6.6	6.5	13.8	73.1
Level											
Elementary	221,036	7.0	1.7	65.9	21.8	2.8	0.8	21.9	36.0	29.0	13.1
General	153,691	6.1	1.3	69.4	19.5	3.2	0.4	17.7	37.4	31.0	14.0
Special education	7,652	5.0	0.2	46.4	45.0	3.4	0.0	18.2	46.8	26.5	8.5
Other elementary	59,692	9.3	2.9	59.3	24.7	1.6	2.0	33.3	31.2	24.2	11.3
Secondary	157,329	2.6	1.2	49.2	41.1	3.0	2.8	19.5	30.9	30.4	19.2
English	24,335	1.6	(2)	51.3	43.1	1.5	2.5	16.3	30.8	31.3	21.7
Mathematics	23,238	1.3	0.9	50.1	42.6	3.0	2.2	14.7	31.1	29.3	24.8
Science	18,399	0.1	(2)	49.5	42.3	4.2	4.0	21.3	27.7	31.2	19.9
Social studies	20,059	0.2	0.4	53.5	38.7	4.1	3.1	21.0	27.8	30.8	20.4
Special education	6,048	0.1	3.7	56.5	33.7	5.1	0.9	17.8	42.8	29.0	10.4
Vocational/ technical	2,834	14.0	4.6	40.8	40.6	(2)	(2)	12.7	22.6	42.1	22.6
Other secondary	62,415	4.8	2.0	46.3	40.9	2.9	3.1	22.0	32.1	29.7	16.2

[1] Data are based upon a sample survey and may not be strictly comparable with data reported elsewhere.

[2] Less than .05 percent.

NOTE.—Excludes prekindergarten teachers. Data are based on a head count of all teachers rather than on the number of full-time-equivalent teachers reported on other tables. Details may not add to totals because of survey item nonresponse and rounding.

Source: *Digest of Education Statistics 1998*, National Center for Education Statistics, Washington, DC, 1999

TABLE 8.6

Selected characteristics of public school teachers: Spring 1961 to spring 1996

Item	1961	1966	1971	1976	1981	1986	1991	1996
1	2	3	4	5	6	7	8	9
Number of teachers, in thousands	**1,408**	**1,710**	**2,055**	**2,196**	**2,185**	**2,206**	**2,398**	**2,164**
Sex (percent)								
Men	31.3	31.1	34.3	32.9	33.1	31.2	27.9	25.6
Women	68.7	68.9	65.7	67.1	66.9	68.8	72.1	74.4
Median age (years)								
All teachers	41	36	35	33	37	41	42	44
Men	34	33	33	33	38	42	43	46
Women	46	40	37	33	36	41	42	44
Race (percent)								
White	—	—	88.3	90.8	91.6	89.6	86.8	90.7
Black	—	—	8.1	8.0	7.8	6.9	8.0	7.3
Other	—	—	3.6	1.2	0.7	3.4	5.2	2.0
Marital status (percent)								
Single	22.3	22.0	19.5	20.1	18.5	12.9	11.7	12.4
Married	68.0	69.1	71.9	71.3	73.0	75.7	75.7	75.9
Widowed, divorced, or separated	9.7	9.0	8.6	8.6	8.5	11.4	12.6	11.8
Highest degree held (percent) [1]								
Less than bachelor's	14.6	7.0	2.9	0.9	0.4	0.3	0.6	0.3
Bachelor's	61.9	69.6	69.6	61.6	50.1	48.3	46.3	43.6
Master's or specialist degree	23.1	23.2	27.1	37.1	49.3	50.7	52.6	54.5
Doctor's	0.4	0.1	0.4	0.4	0.3	0.7	0.5	1.7
College credits earned in last 3 years								
Percent who earned credits	—	—	60.7	63.2	56.1	53.1	50.3	50.2
Mean number of credits earned [2]	—	—	14	—	9	4	4	—
Median years of teaching experience	11	8	8	8	12	15	15	15
Teaching for first year (percent)	8.0	9.1	9.1	5.5	2.4	3.1	3.0	2.1
Average number of pupils per class								
Elementary teachers, not departmentalized	29	28	27	25	25	24	24	24
Elementary teachers, departmentalized	—	—	25	23	22	—	—	—
Secondary teachers	28	26	27	25	23	25	26	31
Mean number of students taught per day by secondary teachers	138	132	134	126	118	94	93	97
Average number of hours in required school day	7.4	7.3	7.3	7.3	7.3	7.3	7.2	7.3
Average number of hours per week spent on all teaching duties								
All teachers	47	47	47	46	46	49	47	49
Elementary teachers	49	47	46	44	44	47	44	47
Secondary teachers	46	48	48	48	48	51	50	52
Average number of days of classroom teaching in school year	—	181	181	180	180	180	180	180
Average number of nonteaching days in school year	—	5	4	5	6	5	5	6
Average annual salary as classroom teacher	[3] $5,264	$6,253	$9,261	$12,005	$17,209	$24,504	$31,790	$35,549
Total income, including spouse's (if married)	—	—	$15,021	$19,957	$29,831	$43,413	$55,491	$63,171
Willingness to teach again (percent)								
Certainly would	49.9	52.6	44.9	37.5	21.8	22.7	28.6	32.1
Probably would	26.9	25.4	29.5	26.1	24.6	26.3	30.5	30.5
Chances about even	12.5	12.9	13.0	17.5	17.6	19.8	18.5	17.3
Probably would not	7.9	7.1	8.9	13.4	24.0	22.0	17.0	15.8
Certainly would not	2.8	2.0	3.7	5.6	12.0	9.3	5.4	4.3

[1] Figures for curriculum specialist or professional diploma based on six years of college study are not included.
[2] Measured in semester hours.
[3] Includes extra pay for extra duties.
—Data not available.

NOTE.—Data are based upon sample surveys of public school teachers. Data differ from figures appearing in other tables because of varying processing procedures and time period coverages. Because of rounding, percents may not add to 100.0.

SOURCE: National Education Association, "Status of the American Public School Teacher, 1995–96." (Copyright © 1997 by the National Education Association. All rights reserved.) (This table was prepared October 1997.)

Source: *Digest of Education Statistics 1998*, National Center for Education Statistics, Washington, DC, 1999

schools tend to pay their teachers less than public schools.

In 1997-98, the average teacher salary was $39,385 — $39,075 for elementary teachers and $39,889 for secondary teachers. Alaska, at $51,738, had the highest average salary in the nation. Other states with the highest average teacher salaries were Connecticut ($50,730), New Jersey ($50,442), Michigan ($49,277), and New York ($49,034). The

133

lowest average salaries were paid in South Dakota ($27,341), North Dakota, ($28,230), Mississippi ($29,547), and Louisiana ($29,650). (See Table 8.7.)

Comparisons to Other Selected White-Collar Workers

The average teacher's salary tends to be considerably less than the salaries of other professionals with comparable years of education and experience (American Federation of Teachers, *Survey and Analysis of Teacher Salary Trends: 1998*, Washington, DC, 1998). Table 8.8 compares average teachers' salaries to the average salaries of other selected white-collar professionals. In 1998, the American Federation of Teachers (AFT) found that, in inflation-adjusted 1998 dollars, teachers earned

- 86 percent of accountants' earnings.

- 72 percent of the salaries of buyers and contract specialists.

- 62 percent of the earning of computer systems analysts.

- 61 percent of engineers' salaries.

- 55 percent of the earnings of attorneys.

In 1996, the average salary of all working persons with bachelor's degrees was 19 percent higher than the average teacher's salary.

TEACHER TURNOVER

In a Center for the Study of Teaching and Policy (CTP) Working Paper, *Teacher Turnover, Teacher Shortages, and the Organization of Schools* (University of Washington, Seattle, Washington, 1999), Richard M. Ingersoll, a University of Georgia professor, reported on his research into teacher turnover. After studying data from the National Center for Education Statistics' (NCES) *Schools and Staffing Survey* and its supplement, the *Teacher Follow-up Survey*, Ingersoll concluded

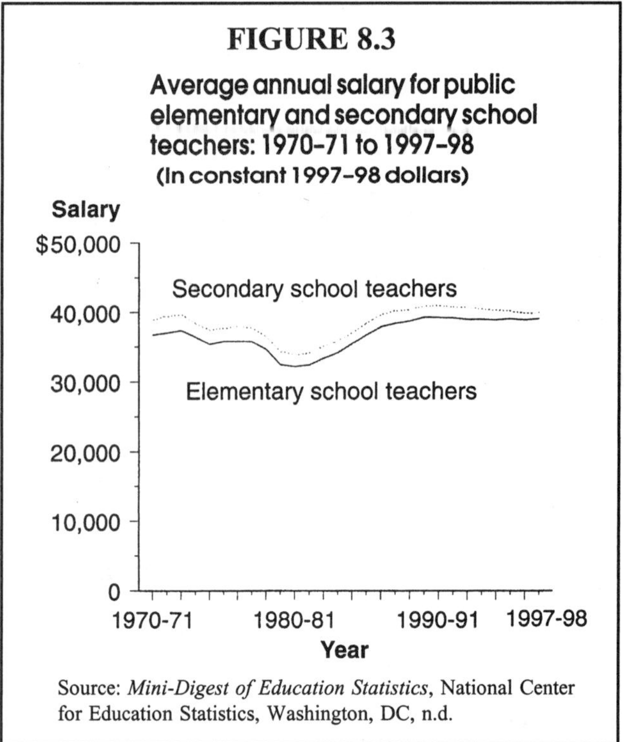

FIGURE 8.3

Average annual salary for public elementary and secondary school teachers: 1970–71 to 1997–98
(In constant 1997–98 dollars)

Source: *Mini-Digest of Education Statistics*, National Center for Education Statistics, Washington, DC, n.d.

that the teacher shortage problem (see above) is primarily a retention problem, directly related to high levels of pre-retirement turnover. Ingersoll found that nearly one-fourth of new teachers leave their jobs within three years. Teacher turnover, including both migration (moving to another school) and attrition (leaving the profession), averages 13 percent to 15 percent a year, compared to an average of 11 percent general employee turnover.

Migration and Attrition — Movers and Leavers

Teachers who move to other schools do not represent a loss to the profession, but they are a loss to the schools from which they move. Their departures cause a decrease in staff, which usually must be replaced. In 1994-95, migration accounted for about half of the total teacher turnover (7 percent of the total 14.3 percent). Attrition accounted for the remaining 7.3 percent of teachers who had departed the teaching profession. Twenty-seven percent of those who left teaching retired from the profession, rather than leaving because of dissatisfaction, personal reasons, or school staffing actions.

TABLE 8.7

Estimated average annual salary of teachers in public elementary and secondary schools, by state: 1969-70 to 1997-98

State	Current dollars							Constant 1997–98 dollars [1]						Percent change, 1979–80 to 1997–98 in constant dollars
	1969–70	1979–80	1989–90	1994–95	1995–96	1996–97	1997–98	1969–70	1979–80	1989–90	1994–95	1995–96	1996–97	
1	2	3	4	5	6	7	8	9	10	11	12	13	14	15
United States	**$8,626**	**$15,970**	**$31,367**	**$36,685**	**$37,716**	**$38,554**	**$39,385**	**$36,934**	**$33,272**	**$39,956**	**$39,449**	**$39,484**	**$39,242**	**18.4**
Alabama	6,818	13,060	24,828	31,144	31,313	32,549	32,818	29,193	27,209	31,626	33,491	32,781	33,129	20.6
Alaska	10,560	27,210	43,153	47,951	49,171	50,647	51,738	45,215	56,690	54,969	51,564	51,476	51,550	-8.7
Arizona	8,711	15,054	29,402	32,574	33,300	33,300	33,850	37,298	31,364	37,453	35,029	34,861	33,894	7.9
Arkansas	6,307	12,299	22,352	28,934	29,533	30,319	30,578	27,005	25,624	28,472	31,114	30,917	30,860	19.3
California	10,315	18,020	37,998	41,078	42,259	42,992	43,725	44,166	37,543	48,402	44,173	44,240	43,759	16.5
Colorado	7,761	16,205	30,758	34,571	35,364	36,271	37,052	33,230	33,762	39,180	37,176	37,022	36,918	9.7
Connecticut	9,262	16,229	40,461	50,045	50,254	50,426	50,730	39,657	33,812	51,540	53,816	52,610	51,325	50.0
Delaware	9,015	16,148	33,377	39,076	40,533	41,436	42,439	38,600	33,643	42,516	42,021	42,433	42,175	26.1
District of Columbia	10,285	22,190	38,402	43,700	43,700	45,012	46,350	44,037	46,231	48,917	46,993	45,748	45,815	0.3
Florida	8,412	14,149	28,803	32,588	33,330	33,889	34,475	36,018	29,478	36,690	35,044	34,892	34,493	17.0
Georgia	7,276	13,853	28,006	32,291	34,002	35,596	37,378	31,154	28,862	35,674	34,724	35,596	36,231	29.5
Hawaii	9,453	19,920	32,047	38,518	35,807	35,842	38,377	40,475	41,502	40,822	41,421	37,485	36,481	-7.5
Idaho	6,890	13,611	23,861	29,783	30,891	31,818	32,775	29,501	28,357	30,394	32,027	32,339	32,385	15.6
Illinois	9,569	17,601	32,794	39,431	40,919	42,125	43,873	40,972	36,670	41,773	42,402	42,837	42,876	19.6
Indiana	8,833	15,599	30,902	36,785	37,675	38,845	39,682	37,820	32,499	39,363	39,557	39,441	39,538	22.1
Iowa	8,355	15,203	26,747	31,511	32,372	33,272	34,040	35,774	31,674	34,071	33,886	33,889	33,865	7.5
Kansas	7,612	13,690	28,744	34,652	35,023	35,739	36,811	32,592	28,522	36,614	37,263	36,665	36,376	29.1
Kentucky	6,953	14,520	26,292	32,257	33,080	33,797	34,525	29,771	30,251	33,491	34,688	34,631	34,400	14.1
Louisiana	7,028	13,760	24,300	26,461	27,530	29,025	29,650	30,092	28,668	30,954	28,455	28,820	29,543	3.4
Maine	7,572	13,071	26,881	31,972	32,869	33,676	34,349	32,421	27,232	34,241	34,381	34,410	34,277	26.1
Maryland	9,383	17,558	36,319	40,661	41,160	41,148	41,739	40,175	36,581	46,263	43,725	43,089	41,882	14.1
Massachusetts	8,764	17,253	34,712	40,718	41,408	42,650	43,930	37,525	35,945	44,216	43,786	43,349	43,411	22.2
Michigan	9,826	19,663	37,072	41,895	46,832	48,238	49,277	42,072	40,966	47,223	45,052	49,027	49,098	20.3
Minnesota	8,658	15,912	32,190	35,948	36,937	38,281	39,106	37,071	33,151	41,004	38,657	38,668	38,964	18.0
Mississippi	5,798	11,850	24,292	26,818	27,692	27,720	29,547	24,825	24,689	30,943	28,839	28,990	28,214	19.7
Missouri	7,799	13,682	27,094	31,189	32,322	33,155	33,975	33,393	28,505	34,513	33,539	33,837	33,746	19.2
Montana	7,606	14,537	25,081	28,785	29,364	29,958	30,617	32,567	30,287	31,948	30,954	30,740	30,492	1.1
Nebraska	7,375	13,516	25,522	30,922	31,496	31,768	32,668	31,578	28,159	32,510	33,252	32,972	32,335	16.0
Nevada	9,215	16,295	30,590	34,836	36,167	37,340	37,093	39,456	33,949	38,966	37,461	37,862	38,006	9.3
New Hampshire	7,771	13,017	28,986	34,720	35,792	36,029	36,640	33,273	27,120	36,923	37,336	37,470	36,672	35.1
New Jersey	9,130	17,161	35,676	47,038	48,751	49,786	50,442	39,092	35,754	45,444	50,583	51,036	50,674	41.1
New Mexico	7,796	14,887	24,756	28,493	29,074	30,131	30,152	33,380	31,016	31,534	30,640	30,437	30,668	-2.8
New York	10,336	19,812	38,925	47,612	48,115	48,000	49,034	44,256	41,277	49,583	51,200	50,370	48,856	18.8
North Carolina	7,494	14,117	27,883	30,793	30,411	31,167	33,315	32,087	29,412	35,518	33,113	31,836	31,723	13.3
North Dakota	6,696	13,263	23,016	26,327	26,969	27,711	28,230	28,670	27,632	29,318	28,311	28,233	28,205	2.2
Ohio	8,300	15,269	31,218	36,802	37,835	38,676	38,977	35,538	31,812	39,766	39,575	39,608	39,366	22.5
Oklahoma	6,882	13,107	23,070	28,172	28,404	30,369	30,606	29,467	27,307	29,387	30,295	29,735	30,911	12.1
Oregon	8,818	16,266	30,840	38,555	39,706	40,960	42,150	37,756	33,889	39,284	41,460	41,567	41,690	24.4
Pennsylvania	8,858	16,515	33,338	44,510	46,087	47,147	47,650	37,927	34,408	42,466	47,864	48,247	47,988	38.5
Rhode Island	8,776	18,002	36,057	40,729	41,765	43,019	44,300	37,576	37,506	45,930	43,798	43,723	43,786	18.1
South Carolina	6,927	13,063	27,217	30,279	31,622	32,830	33,608	29,659	27,216	34,669	32,561	33,104	33,415	23.5
South Dakota	6,403	12,348	21,300	25,994	26,346	26,764	27,341	27,416	25,726	27,132	27,953	27,581	27,241	6.3
Tennessee	7,050	13,972	27,052	32,477	33,126	34,222	35,340	30,186	29,110	34,459	34,924	34,679	34,832	21.4
Texas	7,255	14,132	27,496	31,223	32,000	33,038	33,648	31,064	29,443	35,025	33,576	33,500	33,627	14.3
Utah	7,644	14,909	23,686	29,082	30,588	31,867	32,950	32,729	31,062	30,171	31,273	32,022	32,435	6.1
Vermont	7,968	12,484	29,012	35,406	36,295	36,053	36,299	34,117	26,009	36,956	38,074	37,996	36,696	39.6
Virginia	8,070	14,060	30,938	33,987	34,792	35,691	36,654	34,553	29,293	39,409	36,548	36,423	36,328	25.1
Washington	9,225	18,820	30,457	36,151	37,853	37,815	38,788	39,499	39,210	38,796	38,875	39,627	38,489	-1.1
West Virginia	7,650	13,710	22,842	31,944	32,155	33,257	33,398	32,755	28,564	29,096	34,351	33,662	33,850	16.9
Wisconsin	8,963	16,006	31,921	37,746	38,182	39,057	39,899	38,377	33,347	40,661	40,590	39,972	39,754	19.6
Wyoming	8,232	16,012	28,141	31,285	31,571	31,715	32,022	35,247	33,360	35,846	33,642	33,051	32,281	-4.0

[1] Based on the Consumer Price Index prepared by the Bureau of Labor Statistics, U.S. Department of Labor. Price index does not account for different rates of change in the cost of living among states.

NOTE.—Some data have been revised from previously published figures.

SOURCE: National Education Association, *Estimates of School Statistics;* and unpublished data. (Latest edition 1997–98. Copyright © 1998 by the National Education Association. All rights reserved.) (This table was prepared October 1998.)

Source: *Digest of Education Statistics 1998*, National Center for Education Statistics, Washington, DC, 1999

Reasons for Teacher Turnover

Ingersoll (see above) focused on two particular types of schools thought to be very different in the rates of and reasons for teacher migration and attrition. Table 8.9 shows rates for all schools; for high-poverty, urban public schools; and for small private schools. The overall turnover rate was 13.2 percent. The rate for high-poverty, urban public schools (14.4 percent) was just slightly higher than the overall rate, while the rate for small private schools (22.8 percent) was significantly higher. This rate gap is almost entirely the result of differing levels of attrition rather than migration.

TABLE 8.8

Trends in Teacher Salaries Compared to the Average Annual Salaries of Selected White-Collar Occupations

	Mean Teacher Salary	Accountant III	Buyer/Contract Specialist III	Attorney III	Computer Systems Analyst III	Engineer IV	Full Prof. Public Doctoral	Assistant Prof. Public Comprehensive
1998	$39,347	$45,919	$54,625	$71,530	$63,072	$64,489	$75,154	$40,762
1997	38,415	42,921	51,323	67,980	59,031	62,259	72,220	40,177
1996	37,594	42,172	46,592	66,560	57,772	60,684	69,760	39,000
1995	36,766	41,444	45,500	64,948	56,784	59,748	67,560	38,360
1994	35,764	39,884	44,616	64,532	54,548	56,368	64,860	37,220
1992	34,027	37,648	41,392	65,884	53,300	53,404	61,950	35,730
1990	31,347	35,489	38,385	59,087	47,958	49,365	57,520	32,730
1988	28,071	33,028	36,040	55,407	45,093	45,680	51,080	28,380
1986	25,260	31,143	33,580	50,119	41,548	42,667	45,600	26,000
1984	21,974	28,721	30,610	44,743	38,057	39,005	39,800	23,000
1982	18,945	25,673	27,424	39,649	n.a.	34,443	35,700	20,800
1980	16,100	21,299	22,904	33,034	n.a.	28,486	30,100	17,800
1978	14,207	18,115	19,590	27,738	n.a.	23,972	26,400	15,900
1976	12,591	15,428	17,122	24,205	n.a.	20,749	24,200	14,600
1974	10,778	13,285	14,659	21,082	n.a.	17,929	21,600	13,100
1972	9,705	11,879	13,117	18,392	n.a.	16,159	19,800	11,800
1970	8,635	10,686	11,665	16,884	n.a.	14,695	18,100	10,800
1968	7,423	9,367	10,260	15,283	n.a.	13,095	16,100	9,500
1966	6,485	8,328	9,252	14,052	n.a.	11,784	14,100	8,300
1964	5,995	7,908	n.a.	12,816	n.a.	11,016	12,500	7,700
1962	$5,515	$7,416	n.a.	$11,844	n.a.	$10,248	n.a.	n.a.
(1998 DOLLARS)								
1998	$39,347	$45,919	$54,625	$71,530	$63,072	$64,489	$75,154	$40,762
1997	39,030	43,613	52,150	69,076	59,982	63,262	73,384	40,825
1996	38,846	43,591	48,159	68,799	59,716	62,726	72,107	40,312
1995	39,252	44,252	48,583	69,348	60,631	63,796	72,137	40,959
1994	39,152	43,667	48,848	70,653	59,722	61,715	71,012	40,751
1992	39,182	43,485	47,809	76,099	61,564	61,684	71,555	41,270
1990	38,394	43,473	47,020	72,379	58,747	60,470	70,460	40,093
1988	38,515	44,924	49,020	75,363	61,334	62,132	69,477	38,602
1986	37,463	46,193	49,808	74,339	61,626	63,286	67,637	38,565
1984	34,199	44,704	47,645	69,643	59,236	60,711	61,949	35,800
1982	31,811	43,113	46,053	66,583	n.a.	57,840	59,951	34,930
1980	30,573	40,451	43,499	62,738	n.a.	54,100	57,166	33,806
1978	34,199	43,856	47,427	67,153	n.a.	58,036	63,914	38,494
1976	34,391	43,448	48,218	68,165	n.a.	58,432	68,151	41,116
1974	34,033	41,954	46,293	66,577	n.a.	56,620	68,213	41,370
1972	37,423	45,811	50,585	70,928	n.a.	62,317	76,358	45,506
1970	35,556	44,006	48,038	69,530	n.a.	60,515	74,537	44,475
1968	24,267	43,247	47,369	70,560	n.a.	60,458	74,332	43,861
1966	32,303	41,488	46,091	70,004	n.a.	58,705	70,243	41,349
1964	31,489	41,542	n.a.	67,325	n.a.	57,869	65,665	40,450
1962	27,469	39,983	n.a.	63,856	n.a.	55,252	n.a.	n.a.

American Federation of Teachers, AFL•CIO - 555 New Jersey Avenue, NW - Washington, DC 20001

Source: *Survey and Analysis of Teacher Salary Trends 1998*, American Federation of Teachers, Washington, DC, 1999. Used with permission.

Many observers believe that those who leave teaching do so primarily for better pay or because of dissatisfaction with teaching. Ingersoll found that, in addition to these two reasons, teachers leave because of school staffing actions (layoffs, school closings, and reorganization), personal reasons (such as caring for family members), or job change (to nonteaching jobs in education or to jobs outside the field of education).

Staffing actions cause more than twice as much attrition in private schools as in high-poverty, ur-

TABLE 8.9

Percent Teacher Turnover and Percent Teachers Reporting Various Reasons for their Turnover, by School Type

	All Schools		High-poverty, Urban Public Schools		Small Private Schools	
	Movers	Leavers	Movers	Leavers	Movers	Leavers
Rates of Turnover	7.2	6	8.7	5.7	7.8	15
Reasons for Turnover						
Retirement	—	27	—	32	—	8
School Staffing Action	41	12	34	5	22	13
Personal	33	45	40	41	42	51
To Pursue Other Job	25	24	28	28	27	31
Dissatisfaction	27	25	29	19	56	23
Reasons for Dissatisfaction						
Inadequate Administrative Support	38	30	25	18	25	34
Poor Salary	47	45	24	46	79	73
Student Discipline Problems	18	30	29	27	3	12
Lack of Faculty Influence and Autonomy	13	18	26	11	12	9
Lack of Student Motivation	10	38	27	50	3	14
Class Sizes Too Large	6	13	8	7	.5	13
Inadequate Time to Prepare	10	23	8	8	4	18
Unsafe Environment	11	2	10	26	1	0
Poor Opportunity for Professional Advancement	9	10	5	24	15	9
Lack of Community Support	12	5	11	0	2	1
Interference in Teaching	5	5	12	1	8	4
Lack of Professional Competence of Colleagues	8	4	23	10	5	4
Intrusions on Teaching Time	5	11	7	7	2	1

Source: Richard M. Ingersoll, *Teacher Turnover, Teacher Shortages, and the Organization of Schools*, 1999. Reprinted by permission from Center for the Study of Teaching and Policy, University of Washington, Seattle, WA.

ban public schools, possibly the result of lay-offs of low-performing staff — an option less available to public school administrators. Teachers in high-poverty, urban public schools were more likely than teachers in small private schools to move to other teaching jobs, possibly within the school district due to staffing actions.

Personal reasons, such as departures for family moves, for pregnancy and child rearing, or for health problems, accounted for 33 percent of migration and 45 percent of attrition. Teachers in small private schools were more likely to leave teaching because of personal reasons. Similar proportions of all movers and leavers reported departing to pursue a better job or other career opportunities. (See Table 8.9.)

Surprisingly, far more turnover in small private schools was linked to job dissatisfaction than

TABLE 8.10

Percentage distribution of public school teachers according to how well prepared they felt to perform various activities in the classroom, and the percentage of teachers who felt very well prepared, according to the number of hours spent in professional development in that content area in the last 12 months, by activity: 1998

| Activity | How well prepared teachers felt | | | | Very well prepared | | |
| | Very well prepared | Moderately well prepared | Somewhat well prepared | Not at all prepared | Hours of professional development | | |
					0 hours	1–8 hours	More than 8 hours
Maintain order and discipline in the classroom	71	24	4	1	74	68	68
Implement new methods of teaching (e.g., cooperative learning)	41	41	16	2	34	38	51
Implement state or district curriculum and performance standards	36	41	20	3	30	33	44
Use student performance assessment techniques (e.g., methods of testing, applying results to modify instruction)	28	41	26	4	20	27	45
Address the needs of students with disabilities*	21	41	30	7	17	20	41
Integrate educational technology in the grade or subject taught	20	37	34	9	11	17	33
Address the needs of students with limited English proficiency or from diverse cultural backgrounds*	20	33	30	17	14	21	41

* Percentages based on teachers who teach such students.
NOTE: Details may not add to 100 due to rounding.

SOURCE: U.S. Department of Education, National Center for Education Statistics, Fast Response Survey System, Teacher Survey on Professional Development and Training, 1998.

Source: *Condition of Education Statistics 1999*, National Center for Education Statistics, Washington, DC, 1999

in high-poverty, urban public schools. One-fourth or more of the teachers in the high-poverty, urban public schools that said they departed because of job dissatisfaction cited the following five reasons:

- Student discipline problems.

- Lack of student motivation.

- Lack of administrative support.

- Low salaries.

- Lack of influence over decision-making.

Far more private school teachers than public teachers left their jobs because of job dissatisfaction, citing two major reasons for their departure — poor salary and inadequate administrative support. About three-quarters of those departing small private schools because of job dissatisfaction cite poor salaries as the reason. (See Table 8.9.) Salaries of private school teachers are significantly lower than salaries of public school teachers, and private school teachers are far more likely to change to public school jobs than public school teachers to private school jobs.

TABLE 8.11

Students are often given the grades A, B, C, D, and FAIL to denote the quality of their work. Suppose the public schools themselves, in this community, were graded in the same way. What grade would you give the public schools here — A, B, C, D, or FAIL?

	Teachers '98 %	Public '98 %	Teachers '97 %	Public '97 %	Teachers '89 %	Public '89 %	Teachers '84 %	Public '84 %
A & B	69	46	62	46	66	43	64	42
A	17	10	12	10	11	8	12	10
B	52	36	50	36	55	35	52	32
C	24	31	30	32	29	33	27	35
D	4	9	6	11	4	11	4	11
FAIL	1	5	2	6	*	4	1	4
Don't know	2	9	*	5	1	9	4	8

*Less than one-half of 1%.

Source: "The Fifth Phi Delta Kappa Poll of Teachers' Attitudes Toward the Public Schools," *Phi Delta Kappan*, April 1999. Survey prepared by the Gallup Organization, Princeton, NJ

TEACHERS' FEELINGS OF PREPAREDNESS

According to *Teacher Quality: A Report on the Preparation and Qualifications of Public School Teachers* (National Center for Education Statistics, Washington, DC, 1999), less than half of America's teachers reported feeling "very well prepared" for their jobs.

- Only 20 percent felt very well prepared to integrate educational technology into classroom instruction.

- Twenty percent reported feeling very well prepared to meet the needs of limited English-proficient students, culturally diverse students, or students with disabilities.

- Twenty-eight percent felt very well prepared to use student performance assessment techniques.

- Forty-one percent reported feeling very well prepared to implement new teaching methods.

- Thirty-six percent said they were very well prepared to implement state or district curriculum and performance standards.

In most areas, the more professional development hours teachers received, the more likely they were to feel well prepared. (See Table 8.10.)

THE PHI DELTA KAPPA POLL OF TEACHERS' ATTITUDES

Periodically, Phi Delta Kappa International, the professional education fraternity, contracts with the Gallup Organization to survey American teachers on education issues. "The Fifth Phi Delta Kappa Poll of Teachers' Attitudes Toward the Public Schools" (Carol A. Langdon, *Phi Delta Kappan*, April 1999) reports the most recent findings. While they definitely see much room for improvement, teachers are generally optimistic about the performance of the nation's educational systems.

When asked if they thought children today get a better or worse education than the teachers did

TABLE 8.12

How important do you think each of the following is for measuring the effectiveness of the public schools in your community?

	Very Important		Somewhat Important	Not Very Important	Not at All Important
	Teachers %	Public %	Teachers %	Teachers %	Teachers %
Percentage of high school graduates who practice good citizenship	69	79 (2)	25	5	1
Percentage of students who graduate from high school	67	82 (1)	28	4	1
Percentage of graduates who get jobs after completing high school	58	63 (5)	34	6	2
Percentage of high school graduates who go on to college or junior college	47	71 (3)	45	7	1
Percentage who graduate from college or junior college	45	69 (4)	43	10	2
Scores that students receive on standardized tests	15	50 (6)	51	27	7

(Numbers in parentheses indicate where the problem ranks with the public.)

TABLE 8.13

Does the school in which you teach have difficulty in getting good teachers? If "yes," explain briefly, in a few words, why.

	1998 %	1989 %	1984 %
Yes	23	19	37
No	72	75	57
Don't know	5	5	6

(Not all columns add to 100% because of rounding.)

TABLE 8.14

Does the school in which you teach have difficulty in *keeping* good teachers? If "yes" explain briefly, in a few words, why.

	1998 %	1989 %	1984 %
Yes	32	32	48
No	65	66	47
Don't know	3	2	5

Source of above tables: "The Fifth Phi Delta Kappa Poll of Teachers' Attitudes Toward the Public Schools," *Phi Delta Kappan*, April 1999. Survey prepared by the Gallup Organization, Princeton, NJ

when they were in elementary and secondary school, 56 percent of the surveyed teachers thought today's education was better, 23 percent said it was worse, and 17 percent felt it was about the same. Most teachers (69 percent) gave their communities' schools a grade of A or B in 1998, the highest proportion since the teacher poll began in 1984. The public, however, tended to grade community schools lower than teachers did. (See Table 8.11.) The public and teachers alike rated the nation's public schools more negatively overall. In 1998, a clear majority of teachers (56 percent) and the public (64 percent) would assign a C or a D to the nation's education system.

Measures of Effectiveness

Asked to evaluate the importance of six measures of school effectiveness, the greatest percentage of teachers (69 percent) thought that the number of high school graduates that practice good citizenship was a very important measure. The greatest percentage of the public (82 percent) believed the number of students who graduate from high school was a very important indicator. Table 8.12 shows the other measures considered in the poll. Considered the least effective of the six measures of school effectiveness was standardized test scores. Though half the public considered test scores a very important measure, only 15 percent of teachers did.

Attracting and Retaining Good Teachers

The Gallup Organization asked teachers whether their school had difficulty in getting good teachers. In 1998, 23 percent said yes, compared to 37 percent in 1984 (Table 8.13). Nearly half (49 percent) of the inner-city teachers polled reported their schools had trouble getting good teachers, while fewer teachers of rural, small-town, urban, and suburban schools agreed. Teachers named low pay (28 percent) as the number-one reason for the problems their schools had in getting good teachers, followed by geographic location of the school district (18 percent), working conditions (15 percent), and teacher shortage (9 percent).

When asked if their schools had trouble keeping good teachers, 32 percent of the teachers said yes, compared to 48 percent in 1984 (Table 8.14). Again, more inner-city teachers (65 percent) responded with a positive answer than teachers in other areas. Low pay (35 percent) was the major reason given by respondents for teachers leaving. Other reasons given were working conditions, which include student discipline (17 percent); lack of support from administrators, community, and parents (15 percent); weak or poor administration (9 percent); location (7 percent); workload (6 percent); better job opportunities (5 percent); lack of respect (3 percent); and burnout (2 percent).

Salary Supplements

In 1998, fewer teachers (17 percent) favored paying higher wages to teachers in areas of shortage (science, math, technical subjects, and vocational subjects) than teachers did in 1989 and 1984 (21 percent each). Most teachers (80 percent) opposed higher salaries in certain subject areas. (See Table 8.15.)

TABLE 8.15

Today there is a shortage of teachers in science, math, technical subjects, and vocational subjects. If your local schools needed teachers in these subjects, would you favor or oppose paying them higher wages than teachers of other subjects?

	1998 %	1989 %	1984 %
Favor	17	21	21
Oppose	80	75	75
Don't know	3	4	4

TABLE 8.16

How do you, yourself, feel about the idea of merit pay for teachers? In general, do you favor or oppose it?

	1998 %	1989 %	1984 %
Favor	40	31	32
Oppose	49	61	64
Don't know	11	8	4

Source of above tables: "The Fifth Phi Delta Kappa Poll of Teachers' Attitudes Toward the Public Schools," *Phi Delta Kappan*, April 1999. Survey prepared by the Gallup Organization, Princeton, NJ

TABLE 8.17

Teachers' perceptions about serious problems in their schools, by type and control of school: 1990-91 and 1993-94

	Percent of teachers indicating item is a serious problem									
	Public school teachers					Private school teachers				
Problem area	1990–91	1993–94				1990–91	1993–94			
	Total	Total	Elementary schools	Secondary schools	Combined schools	Total	Total	Elementary schools	Secondary schools	Combined schools
1	2	3	4	5	6	7	8	9	10	11
Student tardiness	11.2	10.5	6.3	18.3	7.8	3.4	2.6	1.8	4.3	2.6
Student absenteeism	14.1	14.4	7.2	27.1	15.0	2.6	2.2	0.8	5.2	2.7
Teacher absenteeism	1.6	1.5	1.3	1.9	2.0	0.7	0.8	0.7	1.2	0.9
Students cutting class	4.6	5.1	1.3	11.9	4.6	0.7	0.7	0.2	2.4	0.7
Physical conflicts among students	6.5	8.2	7.8	8.6	8.1	1.1	1.5	0.9	2.1	2.1
Robbery or theft	3.4	4.1	3.0	5.8	3.6	0.8	0.8	0.4	1.4	1.1
Vandalism of school property	5.4	6.7	5.2	9.0	5.9	0.9	1.2	0.9	2.0	1.2
Student pregnancy	6.4	7.3	1.1	18.4	10.1	0.3	0.4	0.2	1.1	0.4
Student use of alcohol	8.2	9.3	1.6	23.1	14.2	2.4	3.1	0.3	11.0	2.7
Student drug abuse	4.2	5.7	1.0	14.2	7.1	0.5	1.3	0.2	4.0	1.4
Student possession of weapons	1.2	2.8	1.2	5.6	2.7	0.1	0.3	0.2	0.6	0.3
Verbal abuse of teachers	7.5	11.1	8.6	14.8	14.3	1.7	2.3	0.7	2.8	4.4
Student disrespect for teachers	13.0	18.5	15.3	23.6	20.3	2.9	3.4	2.2	4.2	4.7
Students dropping out	6.3	5.8	1.2	14.1	7.7	0.2	0.6	0.3	1.3	0.7
Student apathy	20.6	23.6	15.6	38.0	28.9	4.1	4.5	2.2	9.7	5.1
Lack of academic challenge	5.7	6.5	4.2	10.4	9.9	1.3	1.5	1.0	2.5	1.6
Lack of parental involvement	25.4	27.6	23.0	34.5	35.5	4.3	4.0	2.8	7.1	4.7
Parental alcoholism/drug abuse	12.0	13.1	12.9	12.3	18.7	2.2	2.6	1.6	4.2	3.4
Poverty	17.1	19.5	20.8	15.9	26.8	2.0	2.7	2.2	3.2	3.0
Racial tension	3.8	5.1	4.0	6.7	5.5	0.7	0.9	0.6	1.7	0.8
Students come unprepared to learn	—	28.8	24.3	36.0	30.9	—	4.1	2.6	7.6	4.6

—Data not available.

SOURCE: U.S. Department of Education, National Center for Education Statistics, "Schools and Staffing Survey," 1990–91 and 1993–94. (This table was prepared September 1996.)

Source: *Digest of Education Statistics 1998*, National Center for Education Statistics, Washington, DC, 1999

In 1998, more teachers (40 percent) favored merit pay than in earlier polls (Table 8.16). In 1984 and 1989 more than 60 percent opposed merit pay because of the difficulty in evaluating teacher performance and the subsequent morale problems teachers felt would result. Recently, however, merit pay systems have more often been linked to overall school performance on specific reform goals rather than individual teacher performance.

teachers (3.4 percent) as the top four problems. (See Table 8.17.)

In "The Fifth Phi Delta Kappa Poll of Teachers' Attitudes Toward the Public Schools" (see above), teachers and the public were asked about the seriousness of the following problems — alcohol, smoking, discipline, drugs, teenage pregnancy,

TEACHERS' PERCEPTIONS OF PROBLEMS IN SCHOOLS

The 1993-94 *Schools and Staffing Survey* (the latest survey published) asked teachers their opinions about serious problems in schools. Among public school teachers, the top four problems named were students who were unprepared to learn (28.8 percent), lack of parental involvement (27.6 percent), student apathy (23.6 percent), and poverty (19.5 percent). Private school teachers, who cited a much lower incidence of serious problems, named student apathy (4.5 percent), students unprepared to learn (4.1 percent), lack of parental involvement (4 percent), and student disrespect of

TABLE 8.18

How serious a problem would you say each of the following is in the public schools in your community?

| | Very and Fairly Serious Combined | | Very Serious | Fairly Serious | Not Very Serious | Not at All Serious |
	Teachers %	Public %	Teachers %	Teachers %	Teachers %	Teachers
Alcohol	69	72 (4)	19	50	28	3
Smoking	67	76 (2)	22	45	29	4
Discipline	65	76 (2)	23	42	29	6
Drugs	64	80 (1)	14	50	32	4
Teenage pregnancy	60	71 (5)	18	42	34	6
Fighting	49	64 (6)	13	36	46	5
Gangs	37	57 (7)	13	24	43	20

(Numbers in parentheses indicate where the problem ranks with the public.)

Source: "The Fifth Phi Delta Kappa Poll of Teachers' Attitudes Toward the Public Schools," *Phi Delta Kappan*, April 1999. Survey prepared by the Gallup Organization, Princeton, NJ

TABLE 8.19

**Percent of public school teachers who reported opinions on various aspects of their schools:
1987 and 1997**

Aspect of school	1987				1997			
	Excellent	Good	Fair	Poor	Excellent	Good	Fair	Poor
The qualifications and competence of teachers in your school	45	48	7	—	54	41	4	—
The relations between parents and teachers in your school	15	53	25	6	13	58	24	4
The availability and responsiveness of parents when you need to contact them	14	38	37	11	16	47	27	10
The amount of support for the school shown by the parents	17	40	30	12	19	44	28	10
The overall quality of the education that students receive at your school	26	64	9	1	37	55	7	1

—Data not available.

SOURCE: Metropolitan Life/Louis Harris Associates, Inc., *The Metropolitan Life Survey of The American Teacher, 1998*, "Building Family-School Partnerships: Views of Teachers and Students." (This table was prepared September 1998.)

Source: *Digest of Education Statistics 1998*, National Center for Education Statistics, Washington, DC, 1999

fighting, and gangs. The public considered each of the problems to be more serious than did the teachers. While the greatest percentage of teachers (69 percent) said alcohol was a very serious or fairly serious problem in school, the greatest percentage of the public (80 percent) identified drugs as very or fairly serious. About two-thirds of the teachers surveyed considered smoking, discipline, and drugs to be serious problems. Inner-city and urban teachers regarded discipline, fighting, and gangs more serious problems than did teachers in suburban, small-town, and rural areas. Over half the public (from 57 percent to 80 percent) thought all the problems were very or fairly serious. (See Table 8.18.)

TEACHERS' OPINIONS ON VARIOUS ASPECTS OF THEIR SCHOOLS

In *The Metropolitan Life Survey of The American Teacher, 1998* (Louis Harris and Associates, Inc., New York, New York, 1998), public school teachers were asked several questions about their schools. In 1997, ninety-five percent said the qualifications and competence of teachers in their schools were either excellent or good. While only 13 percent felt the relations between parents and teachers were excellent, 58 percent reported the relations were good. About one-quarter, however, felt the relations were either fair or poor. (See Table 8.19.)

When asked about the availability and responsiveness of parents when teachers needed to make

contact, nearly two-thirds (63 percent) said it was excellent or good. Ten percent of the teachers felt parent availability and responsiveness was poor. While two-thirds (63 percent) also thought parent support for the school was excellent or good, 28 only replied "fair," while 10 percent said parents showed poor support. (See Table 8.19.)

The overwhelming majority of teachers (92 percent) reported that the quality of education stu-

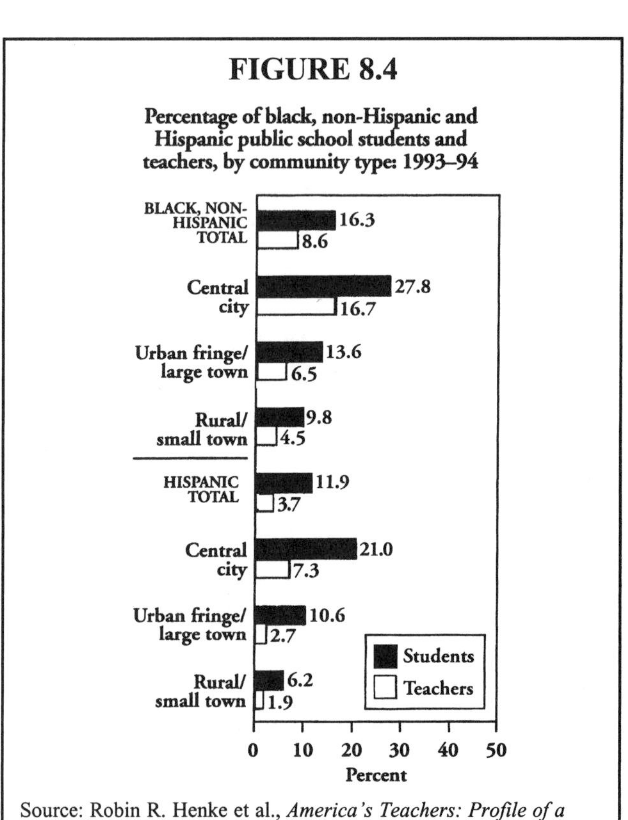

Source: Robin R. Henke et al., *America's Teachers: Profile of a Profession, 1993-94*, National Center for Education Statistics, Washington, DC, 1997

dents received at their school was excellent or good. Seven percent said the quality was fair. (See Table 8.19.) Teachers in urban schools were nearly twice as likely to say the overall quality of education students received at their school was fair or poor than teachers in rural-area schools and 3 to 4 times as likely as teachers in suburban and small-town schools.

MINORITY TEACHERS

In fall 1994, the national student population consisted of 66 percent Whites, 17 percent Blacks, 13 percent Hispanics, 4 percent Asians/Pacific Islanders, and 1 percent American Indians. However, the U.S. Department of Education reported that almost 87 percent of public school teachers were Whites. Seven percent were Black; 4 percent, Hispanic; 1 percent, Asian/Pacific Islander; and less than 1 percent, American Indian or Alaskan Native (Table 8.5). ("Hispanic" is an ethnic category; Hispanics can be of any race.) Figure 8.4 compares the proportions of Black and Hispanic teachers and students in different kinds of communities.

The difference between the proportion of minority students and the proportion of minority teachers is likely to continue to increase. The minority student population is growing rapidly, while the minority teaching force is not. Educators are concerned about the scarcity of minority teachers, who may be more aware of and sympathetic to the cultural backgrounds of minority children. Some observers note that even well-prepared, well-intentioned White teachers often fail to understand these differences. It is also becoming harder to get minority teachers, as many minority college students elect to enter other, more lucrative professions.

CHAPTER IX

COLLEGES AND UNIVERSITIES

GOING ON TO COLLEGE

The past three decades have seen a dramatic increase in the number of high school graduates going on to college. In 1960, only 45 percent of high school graduates enrolled in college; by 1994, 62 percent enrolled. The enrollment rates have fluctuated from year to year, but the trend has generally been upward, reaching a current all-time high of 67 percent of high school graduates in 1997.

Between 1970 and 1980, enrollment in higher education increased 41 percent. During the 1980s and 1990s, enrollment continued to increase, but at a slower rate. (See Figure 9.1.) In fall 1997, an estimated 14.4 million students were enrolled in American colleges and universities. Although enrollment has remained steady since 1991, the 1997 enrollment was still 18 percent more than the 12.2 million students in 1984. The National Center for Education Statistics (NCES) projects that college enrollments will reach 16.3 million by 2009. (See Table 9.1.)

Tuition at most public institutions of higher education is generally lower than tuition at private institutions. In 1997, far more students were enrolled in public institutions (11.2 million) than in private institutions (3.2 million). (See Figure 9.1 and Table 9.1.)

Part-time enrollment has accounted for much of the growth in college attendance. Between 1984 and 1997, part-time enrollment increased by 22 percent, while full-time enrollment grew by 14 percent. The increasing number of part-time students reflects the increasing availability of a college education. In 1970, about one-third (32 per-

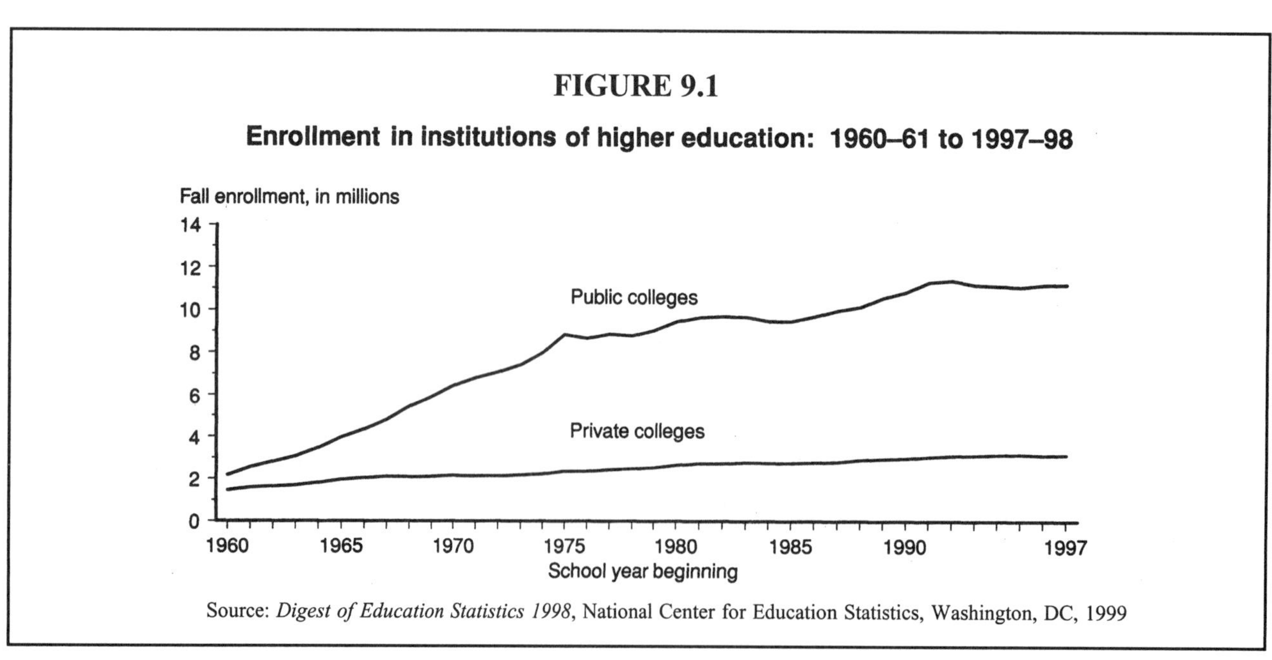

FIGURE 9.1

Enrollment in institutions of higher education: 1960–61 to 1997–98

Source: *Digest of Education Statistics 1998*, National Center for Education Statistics, Washington, DC, 1999

TABLE 9.1

Total enrollment in all institutions of higher education, by sex, attendance status, and control of institution, with alternative projections: Fall 1984 to fall 2009

(In thousands)

Year	Total	Sex		Attendance status		Control	
		Men	Women	Full-time	Part-time	Public	Private
1984	12,242	5,864	6,378	7,098	5,144	9,477	2,765
1985	12,247	5,818	6,429	7,075	5,172	9,479	2,768
1986	12,504	5,885	6,619	7,120	5,384	9,714	2,790
1987	12,767	5,932	6,835	7,231	5,536	9,973	2,793
1988	13,055	6,002	7,053	7,437	5,619	10,161	2,894
1989	13,539	6,190	7,349	7,661	5,878	10,578	2,961
1990	13,819	6,284	7,535	7,821	5,998	10,845	2,974
1991	14,359	6,502	7,857	8,115	6,244	11,310	3,049
1992	14,487	6,524	7,963	8,162	6,325	11,385	3,103
1993	14,305	6,427	7,877	8,128	6,177	11,189	3,116
1994	14,279	6,372	7,907	8,138	6,141	11,134	3,145
1995	14,262	6,343	7,919	8,129	6,133	11,092	3,169
1996	14,300	6,344	7,956	8,213	6,087	11,090	3,210
1997 *	14,390	6,313	8,077	8,114	6,276	11,214	3,175
Middle alternative projections							
1998	14,608	6,297	8,311	8,242	6,366	11,390	3,218
1999	14,881	6,370	8,511	8,449	6,432	11,602	3,279
2000	15,072	6,432	8,639	8,600	6,471	11,750	3,322
2001	15,158	6,471	8,688	8,690	6,469	11,816	3,342
2002	15,168	6,486	8,682	8,702	6,466	11,823	3,345
2003	15,262	6,525	8,736	8,787	6,475	11,894	3,368
2004	15,400	6,577	8,823	8,895	6,505	12,000	3,400
2005	15,556	6,628	8,928	9,019	6,537	12,119	3,437
2006	15,739	6,691	9,048	9,169	6,570	12,258	3,481
2007	15,929	6,763	9,166	9,325	6,604	12,403	3,526
2008	16,144	6,852	9,291	9,503	6,640	12,568	3,576
2009	16,336	6,937	9,399	9,666	6,670	12,715	3,621

*Projected

Source: *Projections of Education Statistics to 2009*, National Center for Education Statistics, Washington, DC, 1999

FIGURE 9.2

Enrollment in institutions of higher education, by age group, with middle alternative projections: Fall 1989, 1999, and 2009

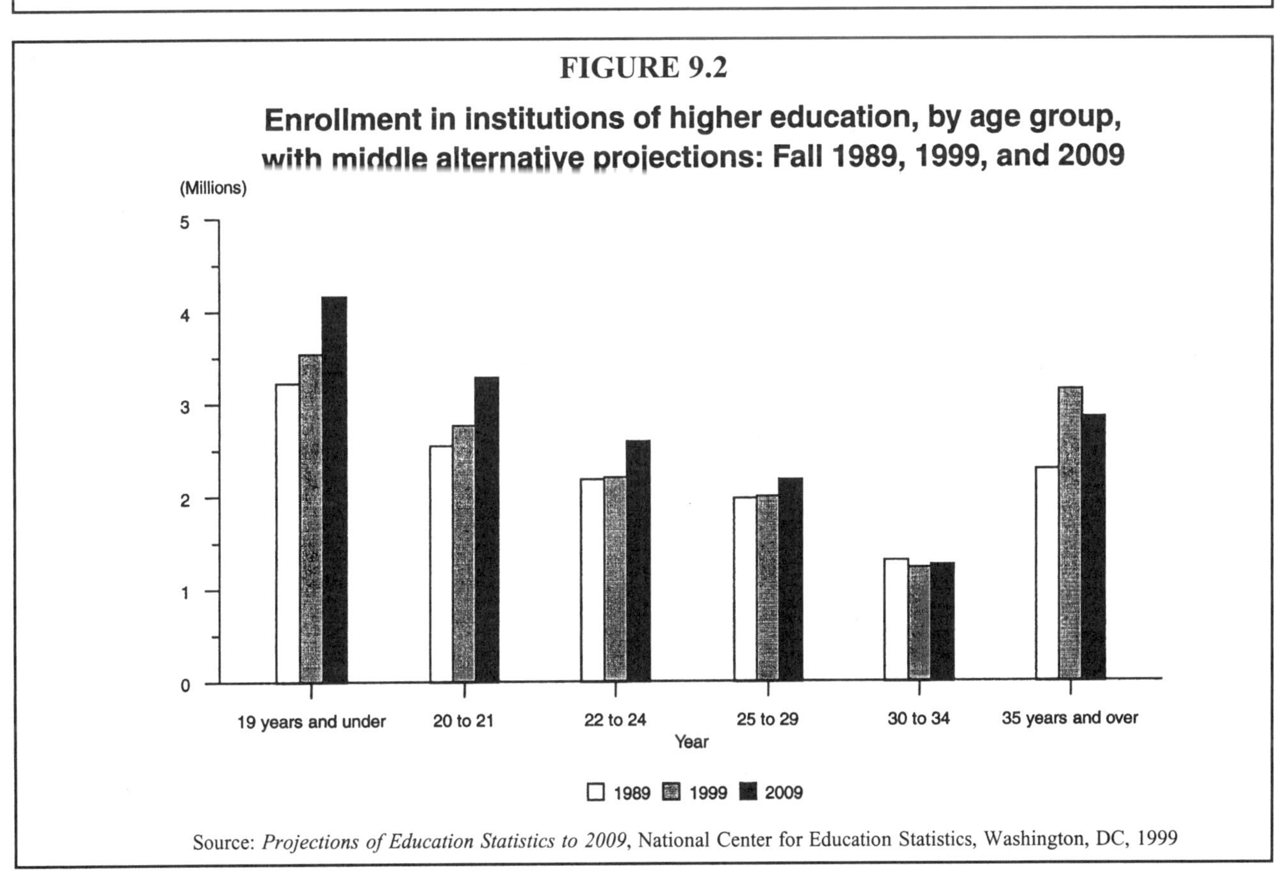

Source: *Projections of Education Statistics to 2009*, National Center for Education Statistics, Washington, DC, 1999

cent) of college students were part-time. By 1997, more than 2 of every 5 students (44 percent) attended part-time.

Increased female enrollment has also contributed to the growth in college enrollment. From 1984 to 1997, male enrollment increased by only 8 percent, while the number of females enrolled rose by 27 percent. (See Table 9.1.)

About 3 of 5 students (62 percent) in fall 1996 were attending four-year institutions, and nearly 2

TABLE 9.2

Total fall enrollment in institutions of higher education and degree-granting institutions, by level of study, sex, and race/ethnicity of student: 1976 to 1996

Level of study, sex, and race/ethnicity of student	Institutions of higher education, in thousands							Degree-granting institutions, in thousands, 1996[3]	Percentage distribution by type and control [1]						Degree-granting institutions, 1996[3]
									Institutions of higher education						
	1976	1980	1990	1993	1994	1995	1996[2]		1976	1980	1990	1994	1995	1996[2]	
1	2	3	4	5	6	7	8	9	10	11	12	13	14	15	16
All students															
Total	10,985.6	12,086.8	13,818.6	14,304.8	14,278.8	14,261.8	14,300.3	14,367.5	100.0	100.0	100.0	100.0	100.0	100.0	100.0
White, non-Hispanic	9,076.1	9,833.0	10,722.5	10,600.0	10,427.0	10,311.2	10,226.0	10,263.9	84.3	83.5	79.9	75.4	74.7	73.9	73.8
Total minority	1,690.8	1,948.8	2,704.7	3,247.7	3,395.9	3,496.2	3,609.3	3,637.4	15.7	16.5	20.1	24.6	25.3	26.1	26.2
Black, non-Hispanic	1,033.0	1,106.8	1,247.0	1,412.8	1,448.6	1,473.7	1,499.4	1,505.6	9.6	9.4	9.3	10.5	10.7	10.8	10.8
Hispanic	383.8	471.7	782.4	988.8	1,045.6	1,093.8	1,152.2	1,166.1	3.6	4.0	5.8	7.6	7.9	8.3	8.4
Asian or Pacific Islander	197.9	286.4	572.4	724.4	774.3	797.4	823.6	828.2	1.8	2.4	4.3	5.6	5.8	6.0	6.0
American Indian/Alaskan Native	76.1	83.9	102.8	121.7	127.4	131.3	134.0	137.6	0.7	0.7	0.8	0.9	1.0	1.0	1.0
Nonresident alien	218.7	305.0	391.5	457.1	455.9	454.4	464.9	466.3	—	—	—	—	—	—	—
Men	5,794.4	5,868.1	6,283.9	6,427.5	6,371.9	6,342.5	6,344.0	6,352.8	100.0	100.0	100.0	100.0	100.0	100.0	100.0
White, non-Hispanic	4,813.7	4,772.9	4,861.0	4,755.0	4,650.7	4,594.1	4,553.0	4,552.2	85.3	84.4	80.5	76.2	75.6	74.9	74.8
Total minority	826.6	884.4	1,176.6	1,399.1	1,451.7	1,484.2	1,524.3	1,533.4	14.7	15.6	19.5	23.8	24.4	25.1	25.2
Black, non-Hispanic	469.9	463.7	484.7	543.7	549.7	555.9	563.6	564.1	8.3	8.2	8.0	9.0	9.1	9.3	9.3
Hispanic	209.7	231.6	353.9	441.2	464.0	480.2	501.3	506.6	3.7	4.1	5.9	7.6	7.9	8.2	8.3
Asian or Pacific Islander	108.4	151.3	294.9	363.1	385.0	393.3	403.6	405.5	1.9	2.7	4.9	6.3	6.5	6.6	6.7
American Indian/Alaskan Native	38.5	37.8	43.1	51.2	53.0	54.8	55.7	57.2	0.7	0.7	0.7	0.9	0.9	0.9	0.9
Nonresident alien	154.1	210.8	246.3	273.4	269.5	264.3	266.7	267.2	—	—	—	—	—	—	—
Women	5,191.2	6,218.7	7,534.7	7,877.4	7,906.9	7,919.2	7,956.3	8,014.7	100.0	100.0	100.0	100.0	100.0	100.0	100.0
White, non-Hispanic	4,262.4	5,060.1	5,861.5	5,845.1	5,776.3	5,717.2	5,673.1	5,711.7	83.1	82.6	79.5	74.8	74.0	73.1	73.1
Total minority	864.2	1,064.4	1,528.1	1,848.6	1,944.2	2,012.0	2,085.0	2,104.0	16.9	17.4	20.7	25.2	26.0	26.9	26.9
Black, non-Hispanic	563.1	643.0	762.3	869.1	898.9	917.8	935.8	941.4	11.0	10.5	10.3	11.6	11.9	12.1	12.0
Hispanic	174.1	240.1	428.5	547.6	581.6	613.7	650.9	659.5	3.4	3.9	5.8	7.5	7.9	8.4	8.4
Asian or Pacific Islander	89.4	135.2	277.5	361.3	389.3	404.1	420.0	422.6	1.7	2.2	3.8	5.0	5.2	5.4	5.4
American Indian/Alaskan Native	37.6	46.1	59.7	70.5	74.4	76.5	78.2	80.4	0.7	0.8	0.8	1.0	1.0	1.0	1.0
Nonresident alien	64.6	94.2	145.2	183.7	186.4	190.1	198.2	199.0	—	—	—	—	—	—	—
Undergraduate															
Total	9,419.0	10,469.1	11,959.1	12,324.0	12,262.6	12,231.7	12,259.4	12,326.9	100.0	100.0	100.0	100.0	100.0	100.0	100.0
White, non-Hispanic	7,740.5	8,480.7	9,272.6	9,100.4	8,916.0	8,805.6	8,730.9	8,769.5	83.4	82.7	79.0	74.3	73.6	72.8	72.8
Total minority	1,535.3	1,778.5	2,467.7	2,955.4	3,077.2	3,158.5	3,254.4	3,282.1	16.6	17.3	21.0	25.7	26.4	27.2	27.2
Black, non-Hispanic	943.4	1,018.0	1,147.2	1,290.4	1,317.3	1,333.6	1,352.6	1,358.6	10.2	9.9	9.8	11.0	11.1	11.3	11.3
Hispanic	352.9	433.1	724.6	918.1	968.3	1,012.0	1,065.6	1,079.4	3.8	4.2	6.2	8.1	8.5	8.9	9.0
Asian or Pacific Islander	169.3	248.7	500.5	634.2	674.1	692.2	713.2	717.6	1.8	2.4	4.3	5.6	5.8	6.0	6.0
American Indian/Alaskan Native	69.7	77.9	95.5	112.7	117.4	120.7	122.9	126.5	0.8	0.8	0.8	1.0	1.0	1.0	1.0
Nonresident alien	143.2	209.9	218.7	268.2	269.4	267.6	274.1	275.3	—	—	—	—	—	—	—
Men	4,896.8	4,997.4	5,379.8	5,483.7	5,422.1	5,401.1	5,411.1	5,420.7	100.0	100.0	100.0	100.0	100.0	100.0	100.0
White, non-Hispanic	4,052.2	4,054.9	4,184.4	4,067.0	3,963.1	3,918.1	3,890.7	3,890.8	84.4	83.5	79.6	75.1	74.5	73.9	73.8
Total minority	748.2	802.7	1,069.3	1,270.1	1,312.4	1,339.3	1,375.0	1,384.1	15.6	16.5	20.4	24.9	25.5	26.1	26.2
Black, non-Hispanic	430.7	428.2	448.0	499.6	502.9	506.8	513.1	513.6	9.0	8.8	8.5	9.5	9.6	9.7	9.7
Hispanic	191.7	211.2	326.9	409.2	429.4	444.2	464.0	469.2	4.0	4.3	6.2	8.1	8.4	8.8	8.9
Asian or Pacific Islander	91.1	128.5	254.5	314.1	331.4	338.1	346.9	348.8	1.9	2.6	4.8	6.3	6.4	6.6	6.6
American Indian/Alaskan Native	34.8	34.8	39.9	47.2	48.6	50.2	51.0	52.4	0.7	0.7	0.8	0.9	1.0	1.0	1.0
Nonresident alien	96.4	139.8	126.1	146.6	146.6	143.8	145.3	145.8	—	—	—	—	—	—	—
Women	4,522.1	5,471.7	6,579.3	6,840.3	6,840.5	6,830.6	6,848.4	6,906.3	100.0	100.0	100.0	100.0	100.0	100.0	100.0
White, non-Hispanic	3,688.3	4,425.8	5,088.2	5,033.4	4,953.0	4,887.5	4,840.2	4,878.7	82.4	81.9	78.4	73.7	72.9	72.0	72.0
Total minority	787.0	975.8	1,398.5	1,685.2	1,764.8	1,819.2	1,879.3	1,898.1	17.6	18.1	21.6	26.3	27.1	28.0	28.0
Black, non-Hispanic	512.7	590.6	699.2	790.8	814.4	826.9	839.5	845.0	11.5	10.9	10.8	12.1	12.3	12.5	12.5
Hispanic	161.2	221.8	397.6	508.9	538.9	567.8	601.6	610.1	3.6	4.1	6.1	8.0	8.5	9.0	9.0
Asian or Pacific Islander	78.2	120.2	246.0	320.0	342.7	354.1	366.3	368.8	1.7	2.2	3.8	5.1	5.3	5.5	5.4
American Indian/Alaskan Native	34.9	43.1	55.5	65.5	68.8	70.5	71.9	74.1	0.8	0.8	0.9	1.0	1.1	1.1	1.1
Nonresident alien	46.8	70.1	92.6	121.7	122.8	123.8	128.8	129.5	—	—	—	—	—	—	—
Graduate															
Total	1,322.5	1,340.9	1,586.2	1,688.4	1,721.5	1,732.5	1,743.1	1,742.3	100.0	100.0	100.0	100.0	100.0	100.0	100.0
White, non-Hispanic	1,115.6	1,104.7	1228.4	1,273.8	1,286.8	1,282.3	1,273.9	1,272.6	89.2	88.5	86.6	83.5	82.6	81.7	81.6
Total minority	134.5	144.0	190.5	232.7	255.2	270.7	286.0	286.3	10.8	11.5	13.4	16.5	17.4	18.3	18.4
Black, non-Hispanic	78.5	75.1	83.9	102.2	110.6	118.6	125.5	125.5	6.3	6.0	5.9	7.2	7.6	8.0	8.0
Hispanic	26.4	32.1	47.2	57.9	63.9	68.0	72.7	72.8	2.1	2.6	3.3	4.1	4.4	4.7	4.7
Asian or Pacific Islander	24.5	31.6	53.2	65.2	72.6	75.6	79.0	79.1	2.0	2.5	3.8	4.7	4.9	5.1	5.1
American Indian/Alaskan Native	5.1	5.2	6.2	7.3	8.1	8.5	8.9	8.9	0.4	0.4	0.4	0.5	0.5	0.6	0.6
Nonresident alien	72.4	92.2	167.3	182.0	179.5	179.5	183.2	183.3	—	—	—	—	—	—	—
Men	707.9	672.2	737.4	771.0	775.8	767.5	760.5	759.4	100.0	100.0	100.0	100.0	100.0	100.0	100.0
White, non-Hispanic	589.1	538.5	538.8	550.9	551.4	541.6	530.2	529.0	90.2	89.2	86.8	83.8	83.1	82.3	82.3
Total minority	63.7	65.0	82.1	98.1	106.3	110.4	113.9	114.0	9.8	10.8	13.2	16.2	16.9	17.7	17.7
Black, non-Hispanic	32.0	28.2	29.3	35.3	37.7	39.8	41.2	41.2	4.9	4.7	4.7	5.7	6.1	6.4	6.4
Hispanic	14.6	15.7	20.6	24.8	27.0	28.2	29.5	29.6	2.2	2.6	3.3	4.1	4.3	4.6	4.6
Asian or Pacific Islander	14.4	18.6	29.7	35.1	38.3	39.0	39.7	39.7	2.2	3.1	4.8	5.8	6.0	6.2	6.2
American Indian/Alaskan Native	2.7	2.5	2.6	3.0	3.3	3.4	3.6	3.6	0.4	0.4	0.4	0.5	0.5	0.6	0.6
Nonresident alien	55.1	68.7	116.4	122.0	118.1	115.6	116.3	116.4	—	—	—	—	—	—	—
Women	614.6	668.7	848.8	917.4	945.6	965.0	982.6	982.8	100.0	100.0	100.0	100.0	100.0	100.0	100.0
White, non-Hispanic	526.5	566.2	689.5	722.9	735.4	740.7	743.7	743.6	88.1	87.8	86.4	83.2	82.2	81.2	81.2
Total minority	70.8	79.0	108.3	134.6	148.9	160.3	172.1	172.3	11.9	12.2	13.6	16.8	17.8	18.8	18.8
Black, non-Hispanic	46.5	46.9	54.6	66.9	72.9	78.8	84.3	84.3	7.8	7.3	6.8	8.2	8.7	9.2	9.2
Hispanic	11.8	16.4	26.6	33.1	36.9	39.9	43.1	43.2	2.0	2.5	3.3	4.2	4.4	4.7	4.7
Asian or Pacific Islander	10.1	13.0	23.6	30.2	34.3	36.6	39.3	39.4	1.7	2.0	3.0	3.9	4.1	4.3	4.3
American Indian/Alaskan Native	2.4	2.7	3.6	4.3	4.8	5.0	5.3	5.3	0.4	0.4	0.5	0.5	0.6	0.6	0.6
Nonresident alien	17.3	23.5	50.9	59.9	61.4	63.9	66.9	66.9	—	—	—	—	—	—	—

Source: *Digest of Education Statistics 1998*, National Center for Education Statistics, Washington, DC, 1999

of 5 students (38 percent) were in two-year colleges. Over 12 million were enrolled in undergraduate institutions, 1.7 million in graduate schools, and 298,000 in first-professional institutions (such as theological, dental, medical, and law schools).

Older Students

Between 1989 and 1999, the number of older students attending colleges grew faster than the number of younger students. During that period,

TABLE 9.3

Number and percent of students enrolled in postsecondary institutions, by disability status and selected student characteristics: 1995–96

Selected student characteristics	Undergraduate			Graduate and first-professional [1]		
	All students	Disabled students [2]	Nondisabled students	All students	Disabled students [2]	Nondisabled students
1	2	3	4	5	6	7
Total (in thousands)	16,678	892	15,786	2,784	89	2,695
Sex	100.0	100.0	100.0	100.0	100.0	100.0
Male	44.1	50.0	43.8	45.7	31.3	46.2
Female	55.9	50.0	56.2	54.3	68.7	53.8
Race/ethnicity of student	100.0	100.0	100.0	100.0	100.0	100.0
White, non-Hispanic	71.4	80.9	70.8	80.6	73.9	80.9
Black, non-Hispanic	11.6	7.1	11.9	6.4	10.7	6.2
Hispanic	10.3	7.7	10.5	4.9	9.8	4.7
Asian/Pacific Islander	5.3	1.8	5.5	8.1	5.6	8.2
American Indian/Alaskan Native	0.9	2.1	0.8	—	—	—
Other	0.5	0.4	0.5	—	—	—
Age	100.0	100.0	100.0	100.0	100.0	100.0
15 to 23	54.9	46.0	55.5	9.2	7.6	9.3
24 to 29	17.9	13.6	18.1	42.7	32.3	43.0
30 or older	27.2	40.4	26.4	48.1	60.0	47.7
Attendance status	100.0	100.0	100.0	100.0	100.0	100.0
Full time	40.5	38.7	40.6	32.5	34.2	32.5
Part time	59.5	61.3	59.4	67.5	65.8	67.5
Student housing status	100.0	100.0	100.0	100.0	100.0	100.0
On-campus	14.6	12.0	14.8	6.5	6.6	6.5
Off-campus	58.0	62.7	57.7	86.9	82.3	87.1
With parents or relatives	27.4	25.3	27.5	6.6	11.1	6.4
Dependency status	100.0	100.0	100.0	100.0	100.0	100.0
Dependent	49.3	40.7	49.8	50.5	48.8	50.5
Independent, unmarried	16.7	21.5	16.4	20.7	21.5	20.7
Independent, married	9.8	8.0	9.9	28.8	29.7	28.8
Independent with dependents	24.2	29.8	23.9	—	—	—
Veteran status	100.0	100.0	100.0	100.0	100.0	100.0
Veteran	5.2	9.7	5.0	5.2	10.6	5.0
Not veteran	94.8	90.3	95.0	94.8	89.4	95.0
Field of study	100.0	100.0	100.0	100.0	100.0	100.0
Business/management	15.7	13.8	15.8	17.1	14.8	17.1
Education	6.8	6.6	6.8	26.1	23.8	26.2
Engineering/computer science	9.6	10.9	9.6	8.3	3.7	8.4
Health	10.1	9.0	10.2	13.0	28.6	12.5
Humanities	11.6	13.9	11.5	9.7	6.2	9.8
Law	0.0	0.0	0.0	5.2	4.1	5.2
Life/physical sciences	5.3	3.2	5.4	6.3	2.1	6.5
Social/Behavioral sciences	7.6	7.5	7.6	7.8	5.8	7.9
Vocational/technical	2.1	3.0	2.1	0.0	0.0	0.0
Undeclared	20.3	20.9	20.3	3.5	7.1	3.4
Other	10.8	11.3	10.7	2.9	3.8	2.9

[1] Includes chiropractic medicine, medicine, dentistry, optometry, osteopathic medicine, pharmacy, podiatry, and veterinary medicine.

[2] Disabled students are those who reported that they had one or more of the following conditions: a specific learning disability, a visual handicap, hard of hearing, deafness, a speech disability, an orthopedic handicap, or a health impairment.

—Sample size too small for a reliable estimate.

NOTE.—Because of rounding and survey item nonresponse, details may not add to totals.

SOURCE: U.S. Department of Education, National Center for Education Statistics, "The 1995–96 National Postsecondary Student Aid Study." (This table was prepared October 1997).

Source: *Digest of Education Statistics 1998*, National Center for Education Statistics, Washington, DC, 1999

147

TABLE 9.4

FOREIGN STUDENT TOTAL ENROLLMENT

Year	Foreign Students	Annual % Change
1954/55	34,232	–
1959/60	48,486	2.6
1964/65	82,045	9.7
1969/70	134,959	11.2
1974/75	154,580	2.3
1979/80	286,343	8.5
1984/85	342,113	0.9
1985/86	343,777	0.5
1986/87	349,609	1.7
1987/88	356,187	1.9
1988/89	366,354	2.9
1989/90	386,851	5.6
1990/91	407,529	5.3
1991/92	419,585	3.0
1992/93	438,618	4.5
1993/94	449,749	2.5
1994/95	452,653	0.6
1995/96	453,787	0.3
1996/97	457,984	0.9
1997/98	481,280	5.1
1998/99	**490,933**	**2.0**

TABLE 9.5

LEADING PLACE OF ORIGIN, 1997/98 & 1998/99

Place of Origin	1997/98	1998/99	% Chang
WORLD TOTAL	481,280	490,933	2.0
China	46,958	51,001	8.6
Japan	47,073	46,406	-1.4
Korea	42,890	39,199	-8.6
India	33,818	37,482	10.8
Taiwan	30,855	31,043	0.6
Canada	22,051	22,746	3.2
Thailand	15,090	12,489	-17.2
Indonesia	13,282	12,142	-8.6
Malaysia	14,597	11,557	-20.8
Mexico	9,559	9,641	0.9
Germany	9,309	9,568	2.8
Turkey	9,081	9,377	3.3
Hong Kong	9,665	8,735	-9.6
Brazil	6,982	8,052	15.3
United Kingdom	7,534	7,765	3.1

Source of both tables: "Open Doors 1998-99: Report on International Educational Exchange" published by the Institute of International Education (www.iie.org) with support from the Bureau of Educational and Cultural Affairs of the U.S. Department of State. For more information: www.opendoorsweb.org.

enrollment of students under age 25 increased by 10 percent, while enrollment of persons 35 and over increased by 37 percent. However, from 1999 to 2009, the NCES projects an 18 percent increase for students less than 25 years of age and a 9 percent decrease in students age 35 and older. (See Figure 9.2.)

In 1996, almost 2.8 million students age 35 years or older and about 8.2 million students under age 25 pursued degrees. Observers attribute the increased enrollment of older students to the higher education levels required by many occupations and the growing number of students who leave school to work and return later. The main reasons older students begin or return to degree programs are career transitions and the need for new skills to obtain new jobs.

In 1996, most older students (80 percent) were part-time students, and 63 percent were women. Older students tend to study computer science, education, library science, mechanics/transportation, and public administration/social work more than any other subjects. In the past two decades, colleges have eagerly courted older students in order to maintain enrollments that otherwise would have decreased because of the decline in the number of high school graduates.

MINORITY ENROLLMENT

The enrollment of minority students (non-Hispanic Blacks, Hispanics, Asians, and American Indians) in higher education has been rising steadily. In 1976, only 15.7 percent of college students were from minority groups, compared to 26.1 percent in 1996. Much of the increase can be traced to larger numbers of Hispanic and Asian/Pacific Islander students.

While White students still comprise the large majority of college students, the trend is toward more racial and ethnic diversity on campuses. In 1976, White students made up 84.3 percent of higher education enrollment. In 1996, Whites accounted for 73.9 percent of those attending college; Blacks, 10.8 percent; Hispanics, 8.3 percent; Asian or Pacific Islanders, 6 percent; and American Indians and Alaskan Natives, 1 percent. Between 1976 and 1996, the number of White stu-dents grew by 13 percent and the number of Black students by 45 percent. Other minority groups increased by even higher proportions: American Indians by 76 percent, Hispanics by 200 percent, and Asian/Pacific Islanders by 316 percent. (See Table 9.2.)

In 1996, non-Hispanic Black and Hispanic students were underrepresented in attaining college degrees. While Black and Hispanic students made up 20 percent of the undergraduate student body, they earned only about 12.8 percent of all bachelor's degrees in 1996. Similarly, minorities were underrepresented at the master's, doctor's, and first-professional degree levels.

DISABLED STUDENTS

During the 1995-96 school year, about 5 percent of all undergraduate students and 3 percent of all graduate-level students were classified as dis-

---

TABLE 9.6

Institutions of higher education, by control and type of institution: 1949–50 to 1995–96

Year	All institutions			Public			Private		
	Total	4-year	2-year	Total	4-year	2-year	Total	4-year	2-year
1	2	3	4	5	6	7	8	9	10
Including branch campuses									
1974–75	3,004	1,866	1,138	1,433	537	896	1,571	1,329	242
1975–76	3,026	1,898	1,128	1,442	545	897	1,584	1,353	231
1976–77	3,046	1,913	1,133	1,455	550	905	1,591	1,363	228
1977–78	3,095	1,938	1,157	1,473	552	921	1,622	1,386	236
1978–79	3,134	1,941	1,193	1,474	550	924	1,660	1,391	269
1979–80	3,152	1,957	1,195	1,475	549	926	1,677	1,408	269
1980–81	3,231	1,957	1,274	1,497	552	945	1,734	1,405	[1] 329
1981–82	3,253	1,979	1,274	1,498	558	940	1,755	1,421	[1] 334
1982–83	3,280	1,984	1,296	1,493	560	933	1,787	1,424	[1] 363
1983–84	3,284	2,013	1,271	1,481	565	916	1,803	1,448	355
1984–85	3,331	2,025	1,306	1,501	566	935	1,830	1,459	371
1985–86	3,340	2,029	1,311	1,498	566	932	1,842	1,463	379
1986–87 [2]	3,406	2,070	1,336	1,533	573	960	1,873	1,497	376
1987–88 [2]	3,587	2,135	1,452	1,591	599	992	1,996	1,536	460
1988–89 [2]	3,565	2,129	1,436	1,582	598	984	1,983	1,531	452
1989–90 [2]	3,535	2,127	1,408	1,563	595	968	1,972	1,532	440
1990–91 [2]	3,559	2,141	1,418	1,567	595	972	1,992	1,546	446
1991–92 [2]	3,601	2,157	1,444	1,598	599	999	2,003	1,558	445
1992–93 [2]	3,638	2,169	1,469	1,624	600	1,024	2,014	1,569	445
1993–94 [2]	3,632	2,190	1,442	1,625	604	1,021	2,007	1,586	421
1994–95 [2]	3,688	2,215	1,473	1,641	605	1,036	2,047	1,610	437
1995–96 [2]	3,706	2,244	1,462	1,655	608	1,047	2,051	1,636	415

[1] Large increases are due to the addition of schools accredited by the Accrediting Commission of Career Schools and Colleges of Technology.

[2] Because of revised survey procedures, data are not entirely comparable with figures for earlier years. The number of branch campuses reporting separately has increased since 1986–87.

NOTE.—Includes those colleges designated as institutions of higher education by the Integrated Postsecondary Education Data System, even if they have a less than 2-year program.

SOURCE: U.S. Department of Education, National Center for Education Statistics, *Education Directory, Colleges and Universities;* Higher Education General Information Survey (HEGIS), "Fall Enrollment in Higher Education" and "Institutional Characteristics of Colleges and Universities" surveys; and Integrated Postsecondary Education Data System (IPEDS), "Institutional Characteristics" surveys. (This table was prepared September 1996.)

Source: *Digest of Education Statistics 1998*, National Center for Education Statistics, Washington, DC, 1999

TABLE 9.7

Degree-granting 2-year and 4-year institutions, by type, control, and size of enrollment: Fall 1996 [1]

Control of institution and size of total enrollment	All institutions		Universities		All other 4-year institutions		2-year institutions	
	Number [2]	Enrollment	Number [2]	Enrollment	Number [2]	Enrollment	Number [2]	Enrollment
1	2	3	4	5	6	7	8	9
Total	**3,842**	**14,367,520**	**156**	**2,984,965**	**2,044**	**5,819,228**	**1,642**	**5,563,327**
Under 200	474	54,775	0	0	249	27,519	225	27,256
200 to 499	563	188,906	0	0	247	84,757	316	104,149
500 to 999	523	384,035	0	0	346	257,487	177	126,548
1,000 to 2,499	866	1,445,889	0	0	571	929,358	295	516,531
2,500 to 4,999	563	1,946,596	5	20,988	285	973,753	273	951,855
5,000 to 9,999	459	3,228,457	28	219,382	213	1,464,502	218	1,544,573
10,000 to 19,999	272	3,751,871	55	774,630	112	1,543,842	105	1,433,399
20,000 to 29,999	94	2,273,919	45	1,098,907	20	501,744	29	673,268
30,000 or more	28	1,093,072	23	871,058	1	36,266	4	185,748
Public institutions	**1,645**	**11,120,499**	**94**	**2,226,529**	**514**	**3,579,507**	**1,037**	**5,314,463**
Under 200	28	3,519	0	0	5	281	23	3,238
200 to 499	55	19,630	0	0	9	3,200	46	16,430
500 to 999	115	88,222	0	0	31	24,246	84	63,976
1,000 to 2,499	348	618,430	0	0	87	150,946	261	467,484
2,500 to 4,999	381	1,342,602	0	0	112	402,761	269	939,841
5,000 to 9,999	368	2,613,085	6	53,094	146	1,028,912	216	1,531,079
10,000 to 19,999	235	3,263,388	27	398,838	103	1,431,151	105	1,433,399
20,000 to 29,999	89	2,146,275	40	971,263	20	501,744	29	673,268
30,000 or more	26	1,025,348	21	803,334	1	36,266	4	185,748
Private institutions	**2,197**	**3,247,021**	**62**	**758,436**	**1,530**	**2,239,721**	**605**	**248,864**
Under 200	446	51,256	0	0	244	27,238	202	24,018
200 to 499	508	169,276	0	0	238	81,557	270	87,719
500 to 999	408	295,813	0	0	315	233,241	93	62,572
1,000 to 2,499	518	827,459	0	0	484	778,412	34	49,047
2,500 to 4,999	182	603,994	5	20,988	173	570,992	4	12,014
5,000 to 9,999	91	615,372	22	166,288	67	435,590	2	13,494
10,000 to 19,999	37	488,483	28	375,792	9	112,691	0	0
20,000 to 29,999	5	127,644	5	127,644	0	0	0	0
30,000 or more	2	67,724	2	67,724	0	0	0	0
Nonprofit institutions	**1,633**	**2,942,556**	**62**	**758,436**	**1,397**	**2,108,745**	**174**	**75,375**
Under 200	292	32,125	0	0	226	25,188	66	6,937
200 to 499	257	87,446	0	0	195	66,755	62	20,691
500 to 999	315	232,625	0	0	279	207,810	36	24,815
1,000 to 2,499	470	755,555	0	0	462	743,319	8	12,236
2,500 to 4,999	168	558,903	5	20,988	162	534,974	1	2,941
5,000 to 9,999	87	592,051	22	166,288	64	418,008	1	7,755
10,000 to 19,999	37	488,483	28	375,792	9	112,691	0	0
20,000 to 29,999	5	127,644	5	127,644	0	0	0	0
30,000 or more	2	67,724	2	67,724	0	0	0	0
Proprietary institutions	**564**	**304,465**	**0**	**0**	**133**	**130,976**	**431**	**173,489**
Under 200	154	19,131	0	0	18	2,050	136	17,081
200 to 499	251	81,830	0	0	43	14,802	208	67,028
500 to 999	93	63,188	0	0	36	25,431	57	37,757
1,000 to 2,499	48	71,904	0	0	22	35,093	26	36,811
2,500 to 4,999	14	45,091	0	0	11	36,018	3	9,073
5,000 to 9,999	4	23,321	0	0	3	17,582	1	5,739
10,000 to 19,999	0	0	0	0	0	0	0	0
20,000 to 29,999	0	0	0	0	0	0	0	0
30,000 or more	0	0	0	0	0	0	0	0

[1] These preliminary data represent the branch campuses and enrollments reported in the "Fall Enrollment" survey. Includes 4-year and 2-year degree-granting institutions that were eligible to participate in Title IV federal financial aid programs.

[2] Some institutions do not report separate enrollment data for each branch campus. For this reason, counts of institutions in this table are somewhat lower than figures appearing in other tables.

U.S. Department of Education, National Center for Education Statistics, Integrated Postsecondary Education Data System (IPEDS), "Fall Enrollment, 1996" survey. (This table was prepared August 1998.)

Source: *Digest of Education Statistics 1998*, National Center for Education Statistics, Washington, DC, 1999

abled. The reported disabilities included visual and hearing impairments, health impairments, speech or specific learning disabilities, and orthopedic handicaps. Disabled students tended to be older than other undergraduate students; 54 percent of the disabled undergraduates were age 24 or older, compared to 44.5 percent of nondisabled undergraduates. (See Table 9.3.)

About three-fifths of disabled undergraduate students lived independently, and 29.8 percent not only lived independently, but also had dependents of their own. Most (62.7 percent) lived off-campus, but not with their parents. About 61 percent were part-time students, and 27.7 percent were majoring in business or the humanities. In general, disabled undergraduates chose the same fields of

TABLE 9.8

Selected statistics on historically black colleges and universities:[1] 1980, 1990, and 1996

Item	Total	Public		Private	
		4-year	2-year	4-year	2-year
1	2	3	4	5	6
Number of institutions, fall 1996	104	40	10	51	3
Total enrollment, fall 1980	233,557	155,085	13,132	62,924	2,416
Men	106,387	70,236	6,758	28,352	1,041
Men, black	81,818	53,654	2,781	24,412	971
Women	127,170	84,849	6,374	34,572	1,375
Women, black	109,171	70,582	4,644	32,589	1,356
Total enrollment, fall 1990	257,152	171,969	15,077	68,528	1,578
Men	105,157	70,220	6,321	28,054	562
Men, black	82,897	54,041	3,214	25,198	444
Women	151,995	101,749	8,756	40,474	1,016
Women, black	125,785	80,883	6,066	38,115	721
Total enrollment, fall 1996	273,931	182,063	18,506	72,383	979
Men	110,056	72,929	7,763	28,900	464
Men, black	88,257	57,845	3,657	26,348	407
Women	163,875	109,134	10,743	43,483	515
Women, black	135,241	87,659	6,381	40,696	505
Full-time enrollment, fall 1996	211,940	136,341	9,927	64,959	713
Men	87,042	56,756	4,016	25,959	311
Women	124,898	79,585	5,911	39,000	402
Part-time enrollment, fall 1996	61,991	45,722	8,579	7,424	266
Men	23,014	16,173	3,747	2,941	153
Women	38,977	29,549	4,832	4,483	113
Earned degrees conferred, 1995–96					
Associate	3,053	1,285	1,496	137	135
Men	1,111	481	535	43	52
Men, black	474	199	220	29	26
Women	1,942	804	961	94	83
Women, black	1,052	313	588	76	75
Bachelor's	29,728	20,187	—	9,541	—
Men	10,884	7,584	—	3,300	—
Men, black	9,087	6,007	—	3,080	—
Women	18,844	12,603	—	6,241	—
Women, black	16,305	10,335	—	5,970	—
Master's	5,848	4,777	—	1,071	—
Men	1,881	1,545	—	336	—
Men, black	1,088	850	—	238	—
Women	3,967	3,232	—	735	—
Women, black	2,718	2,111	—	607	—
Doctor's	236	105	—	131	—
Men	127	50	—	77	—
Men, black	83	26	—	57	—
Women	109	55	—	54	—
Women, black	83	38	—	45	—
First-professional	1,178	442	—	736	—
Men	526	212	—	314	—
Men, black	344	105	—	239	—
Women	652	230	—	422	—
Women, black	497	162	—	335	—
Financial statistics, 1995–96, in thousands of dollars					
Current-fund revenues	$3,855,794	$2,037,292	$96,108	$1,712,458	$9,936
Tuition and fees	942,423	419,116	18,198	501,837	3,272
Federal government[2]	816,612	322,323	16,992	474,154	3,142
State governments[2]	942,577	844,659	49,045	48,406	466
Local governments[2]	96,157	80,093	6,793	9,064	207
Private gifts, grants, and contracts	240,160	36,703	170	202,049	1,237
Endowment income	37,014	2,616	3	34,385	10
Sales and services	688,975	284,649	3,651	399,285	1,391
Other sources	91,876	47,134	1,255	43,276	211
Current-fund expenditures	3,744,816	2,003,637	95,818	1,634,808	10,554
Educational and general expenditures	3,112,805	1,738,574	92,034	1,271,960	10,238
Auxiliary enterprises	388,753	265,063	3,785	119,590	316
Hospitals	233,460	0	0	233,460	0
Independent operations	9,798	0	0	9,798	0

[1] Historically black colleges and universities are accredited institutions of higher education established prior to 1964 with the principal mission of educating black Americans. Federal regulations, 20 U.S. Code, Section 1061 (2), allow for certain exceptions to the founding date. Most institutions are in the southern and border states and were established prior to 1954.

[2] Includes appropriations, grants, contracts, and independent operations.

—Not applicable.

NOTE.—Because of rounding, details may not add to totals.

U.S. Department of Education, National Center for Education Statistics, Higher Education General Information Survey (HEGIS), "Fall Enrollment in Institutions of Higher Education;" and Integrated Postsecondary Education Data System (IPEDS), "Fall Enrollment," "Completions," and "Finance" surveys. (This table was prepared November 1998.)

Source: *Digest of Education Statistics 1998*, National Center for Education Statistics, Washington, DC, 1999

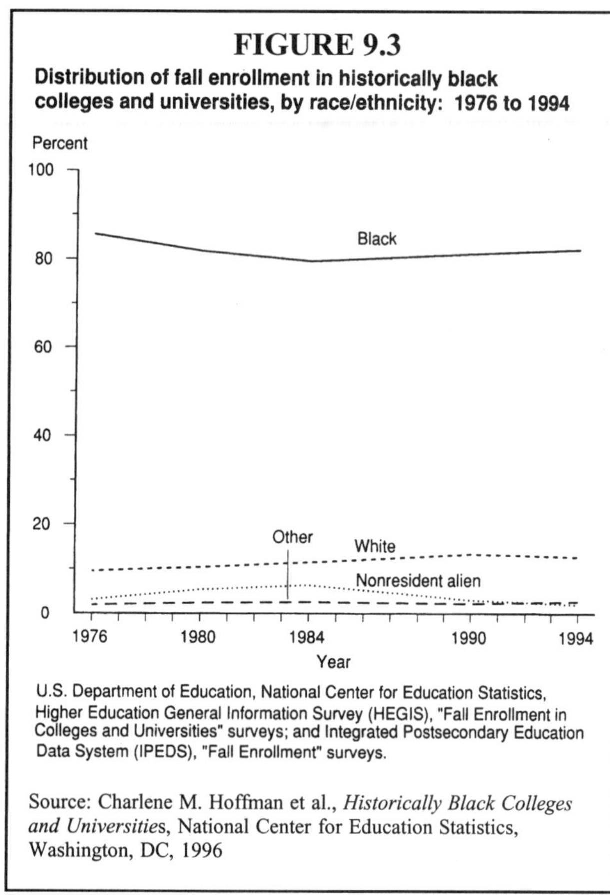

U.S. Department of Education, National Center for Education Statistics, Higher Education General Information Survey (HEGIS), "Fall Enrollment in Colleges and Universities" surveys; and Integrated Postsecondary Education Data System (IPEDS), "Fall Enrollment" surveys.

Source: Charlene M. Hoffman et al., *Historically Black Colleges and Universities*, National Center for Education Statistics, Washington, DC, 1996

study that nondisabled students did. (See Table 9.3.)

FOREIGN STUDENTS

In 1998-99, 490,933 foreign students attended institutions of higher learning in this country (Table 9.4) — 3 percent of the total U.S. college enrollment and more than 11 percent of graduate enrollments. As in the past several years, students from Asia accounted for more than one-half (56 percent) of the total foreign student population in the United States. Over 10 percent of foreign students were from China (51,001), 9 percent from Japan (46,406), 8 percent from Korea (39,199), nearly 8 percent from India (37,482), and 6 percent from Taiwan (31,043). (See Table 9.5.) European students were the second largest group of foreign students with 15 percent of U.S. foreign student enrollment. Students from Canada, Mexico, and Brazil accounted for more than 52 percent of the foreign student enrollment from the Western Hemisphere.

NUMBER OF SCHOOLS

In 1995-96, there were 3,706 schools of higher education in the United States — 1,655 public and 2,051 private. About 61 percent (2,244) were four-year institutions, and 39 percent (1,462) were two-year schools. While most four-year schools were private (1,636, compared to 608 public institutions), most two-year schools were public (1,047, compared to 415 private schools). (See Table 9.6.)

The 1990s were difficult years for many schools of higher education. From 1990-91 to 1996-97, 173 schools (including branch campuses) closed their doors. Most (68 percent) of these were two-year institutions. The 1980s had been little better; 98 schools shut down during that decade.

A LARGE SCHOOL
OR A SMALL SCHOOL?

Most students go to large colleges and universities. In fall 1996, 41 percent of institutions of higher learning had fewer than 1,000 students, accounting for just 4 percent of all college students. On the other hand, the 394 colleges (10 percent) with 10,000 or more students accounted for 50 percent of total college enrollment (Table 9.7). In 1996, the schools with the largest enrollments were the Community College of the Air Force (63,123), the University of Minnesota, Twin Cities (51,388), Miami-Dade Community College (48,795), Ohio State University, Main Campus (48,352), and the University of Texas at Austin (48,008).

HISTORICALLY BLACK
COLLEGES AND UNIVERSITIES

Historically Black colleges and universities (HBCUs) are accredited institutions of higher learning established before 1964, whose principal mission was to educate Black Americans. The first HBCU was Cheyney University in Pennsylvania, established in 1837, well before the Civil War (1860-1865). At that time, most Blacks in the nation were still slaves, and the prevailing practice was to limit or prohibit their education.

Richard Humphreys, a Philadelphia Quaker, founded Cheyney University. It began as a high school and then became a college (Cheyney State College), awarding its first baccalaureate degree almost 100 years later in the 1930s. Two HBCUs were established in the 1850s: Lincoln University in Pennsylvania (1854) and Wilberforce College in Ohio (1856). Both of these colleges were founded by Blacks to promote Black education.

Another institution whose beginnings go back to the 1850s is now known as the University of the District of Columbia. This institution was started in 1851 by Myrtilla Miner as a school to train Black women as teachers. In 1976, D.C. Teachers College, Federal City College, and Washington Technical Institute merged to form today's University of the District of Columbia.

Following the Civil War, educating the freed slaves became a top priority of the federal government, the Black community, and private philanthropic groups. Public support in the various states generally came in the form of land grants for schools buildings. Many of the HBCUs founded during this time were religious schools, such as Edward Waters College in Florida (1866), Fisk University in Tennessee (1867), and Talledega College in Alabama (1867). Howard University in Washington, DC, was also founded in 1867 by an act of the U.S. Congress. The university was established as a coeducational and multiracial private school.

In 1996, 273,931 students were enrolled in the 104 historically Black colleges and universities in the United States. (See Table 9.8.) Between 1981

TABLE 9.9

Undergraduate enrollment in all institutions, by sex and attendance status, with alternative projections: Fall 1984 to fall 2009

(In thousands)

Year	Total	Men		Women	
		Full-time	Part-time	Full-time	Part-time
1984	10,618	3,195	1,812	3,153	2,459
1985	10,597	3,156	1,806	3,163	2,471
1986	10,798	3,146	1,871	3,206	2,575
1987	11,046	3,164	1,905	3,299	2,679
1988	11,317	3,206	1,931	3,436	2,743
1989	11,743	3,279	2,032	3,562	2,869
1990	11,959	3,337	2,043	3,639	2,940
1991	12,439	3,436	2,135	3,786	3,082
1992	12,538	3,425	2,158	3,820	3,135
1993	12,324	3,382	2,102	3,797	3,043
1994	12,263	3,342	2,081	3,827	3,013
1995	12,232	3,297	2,105	3,849	2,982
1996	12,259	3,304	2,107	3,907	2,942
1997 *	12,359	3,276	2,114	3,900	3,068
Middle alternative projections					
1998	12,577	3,276	2,116	4,050	3,135
1999	12,842	3,346	2,126	4,191	3,179
2000	13,037	3,404	2,138	4,291	3,204
2001	13,137	3,450	2,137	4,342	3,207
2002	13,154	3,466	2,141	4,342	3,206
2003	13,247	3,499	2,147	4,389	3,211
2004	13,374	3,534	2,160	4,453	3,227
2005	13,515	3,569	2,173	4,530	3,244
2006	13,686	3,615	2,186	4,623	3,261
2007	13,862	3,666	2,202	4,715	3,279
2008	14,067	3,732	2,220	4,818	3,297
2009	14,253	3,797	2,237	4,907	3,312

* Projected.

NOTE: Historical numbers may differ from those in previous editions. Projections are based on data through 1996. Because of rounding, details may not add to totals.

SOURCE: U.S. Department of Education, National Center for Education Statistics, "Fall Enrollment in Colleges and Universities" surveys; Integrated Postsecondary Education Data System (IPEDS) surveys; and Higher Education Enrollment Model. (This table was prepared August 1998.)

Source: *Projections of Education Statistics to 2009*, National Center for Education Statistics, Washington, DC, 1999

TABLE 9.10

Graduate enrollment in all institutions, by sex and attendance status, with alternative projections: Fall 1984 to fall 2009

(In thousands)

Year	Total	Men		Women	
		Full-time	Part-time	Full-time	Part-time
1984	1,345	286	386	215	459
1985	1,376	289	388	220	479
1986	1,435	294	399	228	514
1987	1,452	294	400	233	525
1988	1,472	304	393	249	526
1989	1,522	309	401	263	548
1990	1,586	321	416	278	571
1991	1,639	341	419	300	578
1992	1,669	351	421	314	582
1993	1,688	355	416	334	584
1994	1,721	359	417	347	598
1995	1,732	356	412	361	604
1996	1,742	358	403	378	604
1997 *	1,744	335	422	349	638
Middle alternative projections					
1998	1,750	322	423	346	659
1999	1,760	317	424	349	669
2000	1,758	312	424	349	673
2001	1,747	309	421	347	670
2002	1,740	308	419	346	667
2003	1,740	308	418	348	666
2004	1,749	311	418	353	667
2005	1,760	313	418	360	669
2006	1,770	315	418	365	670
2007	1,780	318	419	371	671
2008	1,787	321	419	376	671
2009	1,792	324	419	379	669

* Projected.

NOTE: Historical numbers may differ from those in previous editions. Projections are based on data through 1996. Because of rounding, details may not add to totals.

SOURCE: U.S. Department of Education, National Center for Education Statistics, "Fall Enrollment in Colleges and Universities" surveys; Integrated Postsecondary Education Data System (IPEDS) surveys; and Higher Education Enrollment Model. (This table was prepared August 1998.)

Source: *Projections of Education Statistics to 2009*, National Center for Education Statistics, Washington, DC, 1999

and 1986, the number of students attending these schools dropped, but then the number steadily increased to a peak of 282,856 in 1993. Between 1993 and 1996, there was a 3 percent decline in the enrollment of students at historically Black colleges and universities. The HCBUs account for about 2 percent of all college and university enrollment.

In 1996, full-time students outnumbered part-time students by more than 3 to 1. Women made up a majority (60 percent) of all students at these institutions. Most HCBU students were Black — 83 percent of the women and 80 percent of the men. (See Table 9.8.)

Although Black students are in the majority at these colleges and universities, students with other racial and ethnic backgrounds also attend many HBCUs. In 1994, approximately 82 percent of the students were non-Hispanic Blacks, and 13 percent were non-Hispanic Whites. (See Figure 9.3.) Almost 2 percent were Hispanic, and less than 1 percent were Asian/Pacific Islanders or American Indians. Young Black students often choose to attend historically Black institutions because their parents attended there. Others seek racial companionship, an improved chance of leadership positions, and the typically lower costs of these schools.

Because of their mission and the makeup of their enrollment, historically Black colleges and universities have had to keep tuition and fees exceptionally low. The United Negro College Fund estimates that 90 percent of students in these schools receive some sort of financial aid. In 1993-

TABLE 9.11
First-professional enrollment in all institutions, by sex and attendance status, with alternative projections: Fall 1984 to fall 2009

(In thousands)

Year	Total	Men		Women	
		Full-time	Part-time	Full-time	Part-time
1984	279	166	19	83	10
1985	274	162	17	84	10
1986	270	159	15	87	9
1987	268	154	16	88	10
1988	267	151	16	90	10
1989	274	153	16	95	10
1990	273	150	17	96	11
1991	281	152	18	100	11
1992	281	151	18	101	11
1993	292	154	19	106	14
1994	295	155	19	108	12
1995	298	155	19	111	12
1996	298	154	18	113	12
1997*	286	146	19	108	13
Middle alternative projections					
1998	280	140	19	107	14
1999	279	138	19	108	14
2000	277	136	19	108	14
2001	275	134	19	107	14
2002	274	134	19	107	14
2003	275	134	19	108	14
2004	277	135	19	109	14
2005	281	136	19	111	14
2006	283	137	19	113	14
2007	286	139	19	115	14
2008	289	140	19	116	14
2009	291	141	19	117	14

*Projected.

NOTE: Historical numbers may differ from those in previous editions. Projections are based on data through 1996. Because of rounding, details may not add to totals.

SOURCE: U.S. Department of Education, National Center for Education Statistics, "Fall Enrollment in Colleges and Universities" surveys; Integrated Postsecondary Education Data System (IPEDS) surveys; and Higher Education Enrollment Model. (This table was prepared August 1998.)

Source: *Projections of Education Statistics to 2009*, National Center for Education Statistics, Washington, DC, 1999

94, HBCUs spent $231.5 million on scholarships and fellowships.

NATIVE AMERICAN COLLEGES

Although tribal and Indian colleges and universities differ widely in their stages of development, they share some similarities. The governing boards of most are made up primarily of American Indians and Alaskan Natives, as are their student bodies. Located in 12 states, most of the 31 tribal colleges are in isolated areas of the nation.

In 1996, these colleges served about 25,000 full- and part-time students, a 62 percent increase from 1990 and an almost sixfold increase from only 2,094 students in 1982. The average age of tribal college students is 32, and 64 percent are women. Most students attend on a part-time basis.

Most of the colleges are two-year and technical institutions, but four offer bachelor's degrees, and two offer master's degrees. One of their major thrusts is to reinforce traditional cultures and transmit them to the coming generation. Their curricula are primarily practical and geared to local needs. Many of them are strongly oriented toward community service.

Most funding for these schools has come from the federal government under the Tribally Controlled College or University Assistance Act (PL 95-471). In 1999, about $3000 was available for each Indian student, almost 40 percent lower than

155

Earned degrees conferred by institutions of higher education, by level of degree and sex of student: 1869–70 to 2007–08

Year	Associate degrees			Bachelor's degrees			Master's degrees			First-professional degrees			Doctor's degrees		
	Total	Men	Women	Total	Men	Women	Total	Men	Women	Total	Men	Women	Total	Men	Women
1	2	3	4	5	6	7	8	9	10	11	12	13	14	15	16
1869–70	—	—	—	[1]9,371	[1]7,993	[1]1,378	0	0	0	(2)	(2)	(2)	1	1	0
1879–80	—	—	—	[1]12,896	[1]10,411	[1]2,485	879	868	11	(2)	(2)	(2)	54	51	3
1889–90	—	—	—	[1]15,539	[1]12,857	[1]2,682	1,015	821	194	(2)	(2)	(2)	149	147	2
1899–1900	—	—	—	[1]27,410	[1]22,173	[1]5,237	1,583	1,280	303	(2)	(2)	(2)	382	359	23
1909–10	—	—	—	[1]37,199	[1]28,762	[1]8,437	2,113	1,555	558	(2)	(2)	(2)	443	399	44
1919–20	—	—	—	[1]48,622	[1]31,980	[1]16,642	4,279	2,985	1,294	(2)	(2)	(2)	615	522	93
1929–30	—	—	—	[1]122,484	[1]73,615	[1]48,869	14,969	8,925	6,044	(2)	(2)	(2)	2,299	1,946	353
1939–40	—	—	—	[1]186,500	[1]109,546	[1]76,954	26,731	16,508	10,223	(2)	(2)	(2)	3,290	2,861	429
1949–50	—	—	—	[1]432,058	[1]328,841	[1]103,217	58,183	41,220	16,963	(2)	(2)	(2)	6,420	5,804	616
1959–60	—	—	—	[1]392,440	[1]254,063	[1]138,377	74,435	50,898	23,537	(2)	(2)	(2)	9,829	8,801	1,028
1960–61	—	—	—	365,174	224,538	140,636	84,609	57,830	26,779	25,253	24,577	676	10,575	9,463	1,112
1961–62	—	—	—	383,961	230,456	153,505	94,418	62,603	28,815	25,607	24,836	771	11,622	10,377	1,245
1962–63	—	—	—	411,420	241,309	170,111	98,684	67,302	31,382	26,590	25,753	837	12,822	11,448	1,374
1963–64	—	—	—	461,266	265,349	195,917	109,183	73,850	35,333	27,209	26,357	852	14,490	12,955	1,535
1964–65	—	—	—	493,757	282,173	211,584	121,167	81,319	39,848	28,290	27,283	1,007	16,467	14,692	1,775
1965–66	111,607	63,779	47,828	520,115	299,287	220,828	140,602	93,081	47,521	30,124	28,982	1,142	18,237	16,121	2,116
1966–67	139,183	78,356	60,827	558,534	322,711	235,823	157,726	103,109	54,617	31,695	30,401	1,294	20,617	18,163	2,454
1967–68	159,441	90,317	69,124	632,289	357,682	274,607	176,749	113,552	63,197	33,939	32,402	1,537	23,089	20,183	2,906
1968–69	183,279	105,661	77,618	728,845	410,595	318,250	193,756	121,531	72,225	35,114	33,595	1,519	26,158	22,722	3,436
1969–70	206,023	117,432	88,591	792,316	451,097	341,219	208,291	125,624	82,667	34,918	33,077	1,841	29,866	25,890	3,976
1970–71	252,311	144,144	108,167	839,730	475,594	364,136	230,509	138,146	92,363	37,946	35,544	2,402	32,107	27,530	4,577
1971–72	292,014	166,227	125,787	887,273	500,590	386,683	251,633	149,550	102,083	43,411	40,723	2,688	33,363	28,090	5,273
1972–73	316,174	175,413	140,761	922,362	518,191	404,171	263,371	154,468	108,903	50,018	46,489	3,529	34,777	28,571	6,206
1973–74	343,924	188,591	155,333	945,776	527,313	418,463	277,033	157,842	119,191	53,816	48,530	5,286	33,816	27,365	6,451
1974–75	360,171	191,017	169,154	922,933	504,841	418,092	292,450	161,570	130,880	55,916	48,956	6,960	34,083	26,817	7,266
1975–76	391,454	209,996	181,458	925,746	504,925	420,821	311,771	167,248	144,523	62,649	52,892	9,757	34,064	26,267	7,797
1976–77	406,377	210,842	195,535	919,549	495,545	424,004	317,164	167,783	149,381	64,359	52,374	11,985	33,232	25,142	8,090
1977–78	412,246	204,718	207,528	921,204	487,347	433,857	311,620	161,212	150,408	66,581	52,270	14,311	32,131	23,658	8,473
1978–79	402,702	192,091	210,611	921,390	477,344	444,046	301,079	153,370	147,709	68,848	52,652	16,196	32,730	23,541	9,189
1979–80	400,910	183,737	217,173	929,417	473,611	455,806	298,081	150,749	147,332	70,131	52,716	17,415	32,615	22,943	9,672
1980–81	416,377	188,638	227,739	935,140	469,883	465,257	295,739	147,043	148,696	71,956	52,792	19,164	32,958	22,711	10,247
1981–82	434,526	196,944	237,582	952,998	473,364	479,634	295,546	145,532	150,014	72,032	52,223	19,809	32,707	22,224	10,483
1982–83	449,620	203,991	245,629	969,510	479,140	490,370	289,921	144,697	145,224	73,054	51,250	21,804	32,775	21,902	10,873
1983–84	452,240	202,704	249,536	974,309	482,319	491,990	284,263	143,595	140,668	74,468	51,378	23,090	33,209	22,064	11,145
1984–85	454,712	202,932	251,780	979,477	482,528	496,949	286,251	143,390	142,861	75,063	50,455	24,608	32,943	21,700	11,243
1985–86	446,047	196,166	249,881	987,823	485,923	501,900	288,567	143,508	145,059	73,910	49,261	24,649	33,653	21,819	11,834
1986–87	436,304	190,839	245,465	991,264	480,782	510,482	289,349	141,269	148,080	71,617	46,523	25,094	34,041	22,061	11,980
1987–88	435,085	190,047	245,038	994,829	477,203	517,626	299,317	145,163	154,154	70,735	45,484	25,251	34,870	22,615	12,255
1988–89	436,764	186,316	250,448	1,018,755	483,346	535,409	310,621	149,354	161,267	70,856	45,046	25,810	35,720	22,648	13,072
1989–90	455,102	191,195	263,907	1,051,344	491,696	559,648	324,301	153,653	170,648	70,988	43,961	27,027	38,371	24,401	13,970
1990–91	481,720	198,634	283,086	1,094,538	504,045	590,493	337,168	156,482	180,686	71,948	43,846	28,102	39,294	24,756	14,538
1991–92	504,231	207,481	296,750	1,136,553	520,811	615,742	352,838	161,842	190,996	74,146	45,071	29,075	40,659	25,557	15,102
1992–93	514,756	211,964	302,792	1,165,178	532,881	632,297	369,585	169,258	200,327	75,387	45,153	30,234	42,132	26,073	16,059
1993–94	530,632	215,261	315,371	1,169,275	532,422	636,853	387,070	176,085	210,985	75,418	44,707	30,711	43,185	26,552	16,633
1994–95	539,691	218,352	321,339	1,160,134	526,131	634,003	397,629	178,598	219,031	75,800	44,853	30,947	44,446	26,916	17,530
1995–96	555,216	219,514	335,702	1,164,792	522,454	642,338	406,301	179,081	227,220	76,734	44,748	31,986	44,652	26,841	17,811
1996–97 [3]	528,000	211,000	317,000	1,166,000	523,000	643,000	402,000	181,000	221,000	79,700	46,000	33,700	44,700	27,100	17,600
1997–98 [3]	520,000	209,000	311,000	1,172,000	523,000	649,000	406,000	183,000	223,000	78,400	46,100	32,300	45,200	27,200	18,000
1998–99 [3]	528,000	209,000	319,000	1,166,000	510,000	655,000	410,000	185,000	225,000	75,800	43,700	32,000	45,800	27,300	18,500
1999–2000 [3]	532,000	208,000	323,000	1,161,000	502,000	659,000	414,000	187,000	227,000	74,000	42,000	32,000	46,400	27,400	19,000
2000–01 [3]	543,000	210,000	333,000	1,173,000	506,000	667,000	418,000	189,000	229,000	73,100	41,100	32,000	46,800	27,300	19,500
2001–02 [3]	550,000	211,000	339,000	1,195,000	510,000	685,000	422,000	191,000	231,000	72,400	40,500	31,800	47,200	27,200	20,000
2002–03 [3]	555,000	212,000	343,000	1,214,000	515,000	699,000	426,000	193,000	233,000	71,900	40,100	31,800	47,600	27,100	20,500
2003–04 [3]	559,000	213,000	346,000	1,227,000	519,000	708,000	430,000	195,000	235,000	71,800	39,800	32,000	47,900	27,000	20,900
2004–05 [3]	560,000	213,000	347,000	1,235,000	520,000	716,000	434,000	197,000	237,000	72,300	39,900	32,400	48,300	26,900	21,400
2005–06 [3]	565,000	214,000	351,000	1,243,000	524,000	719,000	438,000	199,000	239,000	73,100	40,100	33,000	48,700	26,800	21,900
2006–07 [3]	572,000	215,000	357,000	1,256,000	527,000	729,000	442,000	201,000	241,000	74,100	40,500	33,600	49,100	26,700	22,400
2007–08 [3]	579,000	216,000	363,000	1,270,000	530,000	739,000	446,000	203,000	243,000	75,000	40,800	34,200	49,500	26,600	22,900

[1] Includes first-professional degrees.
[2] First-professional degrees are included with bachelor's degrees.
[3] Projected.
—Data not available.

NOTE.—Some data have been revised from previously published figures. Because of rounding, details may not add to totals.

SOURCE: U.S. Department of Education, National Center for Education Statistics, Earned Degrees Conferred; *Projections of Education Statistics to 2008;* Higher Education General Information Survey (HEGIS), "Degrees and Other Formal Awards Conferred" surveys; and Integrated Postsecondary Education Data System (IPEDS), "Completions" surveys. (This table was prepared May 1998.)

Source: *Digest of Education Statistics 1998*, National Center for Education Statistics, Washington, DC, 1999

what the average community college receives per student from government (federal, state, and local revenues). Tribal colleges typically do not receive state support because they have been established by sovereign nations and are usually located on federal trust land. Federal legislation in 1994 awarded 29 of the schools land-grant status, which made them eligible for more financial aid.

ALLIANCE FOR EQUITY IN HIGHER EDUCATION

The Alliance for Equity in Higher Education is made up of the Hispanic Association of Colleges and Universities, the American Indian Higher Education Consortium, and the National Association for Equal Opportunity in Higher Education and is coordinated by the Institute for Higher Education Policy, a Washington, DC-based non-profit education group. The Alliance represents 175 Hispanic-Serving Institutions (HSIs), 118 Historically Black Colleges and Universities (HBCUs) and other predominately Black institutions, and the 31 Tribal Colleges and Universities. These colleges educate 42 percent of all Hispanic students, 24 percent of Black students, and 16 percent of American Indian students.

The Alliance member colleges provide greater access to low-income and underserved populations, striving to keep tuitions affordable. In spite of underfunding, these colleges have higher student success rates than mainstream colleges. In 1996, they awarded almost 188,000 degrees.

TRENDS IN DEGREES

Trends in Enrollment by Degree Levels

Undergraduate enrollment grew from 10.6 million in 1984 to 12.3 million in 1996, a 15 percent

---

TABLE 9.13

Degrees conferred by institutions of higher education, by control of institution, level of degree, and discipline division: 1994–95

Discipline division	Public institutions				Private institutions			
	Associate degrees	Bachelor's degrees	Master's degrees	Doctor's degrees	Associate degrees	Bachelor's degrees	Master's degrees	Doctor's degrees
1	2	3	4	5	6	7	8	9
Total	451,539	776,670	224,152	28,917	88,152	383,464	173,477	15,529
Agriculture and natural resources [1]	5,418	18,471	3,778	1,246	312	1,370	474	18
Architecture and related programs	253	6,532	2,708	81	24	2,224	1,215	60
Area, ethnic, and cultural studies	52	2,980	963	87	16	2,726	676	99
Biological sciences/life sciences	1,802	36,640	3,904	3,274	77	19,344	1,489	1,371
Business [2]	75,415	142,206	37,114	970	26,511	92,117	56,695	424
Communications	1,340	33,847	2,773	266	1,820	14,257	2,369	54
Communications technologies	1,659	471	82	0	325	228	385	1
Computer and information sciences	6,716	14,793	5,661	594	2,436	9,611	4,665	290
Construction trades	1,345	38	0	0	383	75	7	0
Education	8,414	79,536	65,265	5,139	1,244	26,543	35,977	1,766
Engineering	1,908	47,026	19,314	4,277	324	15,316	9,239	1,833
Engineering-related technologies	22,521	11,550	954	18	12,211	4,083	156	0
English language and literature/letters	1,491	34,848	5,900	1,098	57	17,053	1,945	463
Foreign languages and literatures	349	8,896	2,301	563	267	4,879	835	342
Health professions and related sciences	84,962	53,101	18,049	1,468	13,512	26,754	13,194	601
Home economics and vocational home economics	7,476	13,223	1,586	248	345	2,122	1,278	140
Law and legal studies	6,208	1,242	550	10	2,932	790	1,961	78
Liberal arts and sciences, general studies, and humanities	159,722	20,906	1,096	32	11,095	12,450	1,469	58
Library science	98	45	4,176	49	3	5	881	6
Mathematics	748	8,939	3,190	867	34	4,784	991	359
Mechanics and repairers	9,880	32	0	0	1,617	34	0	0
Multi/interdisciplinary studies	8,575	20,157	1,609	171	117	5,876	848	67
Parks, recreation, leisure, and fitness studies	730	10,234	1,375	120	134	2,655	380	29
Philosophy and religion	45	2,931	496	203	36	4,345	884	304
Physical sciences and science technologies	2,397	12,505	4,251	3,052	59	6,672	1,502	1,431
Precision production trades	6,413	336	0	0	2,931	17	5	0
Protective services	19,007	19,347	1,047	26	702	4,810	659	0
Psychology	1,437	48,255	5,985	1,766	163	23,828	7,936	2,056
Public administration and services	3,499	13,349	14,206	291	383	5,237	9,295	265
R.O.T.C. and military technologies	349	6	124	0	15	21	0	0
Social sciences and history	3,251	84,021	9,596	2,303	383	44,133	5,249	1,422
Theological studies/religious vocations	35	2	2	0	572	5,576	5,238	1,591
Transportation and material moving workers	1,174	1,693	75	0	272	2,005	748	0
Visual and performing arts	6,402	28,227	5,664	679	6,142	20,463	4,613	401
Not classified by field of study	448	285	358	19	698	1,061	219	0

[1] Includes "Agricultural business and production," "Agricultural sciences," and "Conservation and renewable natural resources."

[2] Includes "Business management and administrative services," "Marketing operations/marketing and distribution" and "Consumer and personal services."

SOURCE: U.S. Department of Education, National Center for Education Statistics, Integrated Postsecondary Education Data System, "Completions" survey, 1994–95 and "Consolidated" survey 1995. (This table was prepared March 1997.)

Source: *Digest of Education Statistics 1998*, National Center for Education Statistics, Washington, DC, 1999

increase. Women outnumbered men 56 percent to 44 percent. By 2009, enrollment is projected to reach about 14.3 million. (See Table 9.9.)

Between 1984 and 1996, graduate enrollment increased 30 percent, from 1.3 million to 1.7 million. By 2009, enrollment is projected to reach nearly 1.8 million, increasing only about 50,000 from 1996. The number of women (982,000) enrolled in graduate programs in 1996 was higher than the number of men (761,000). (See Table 9.10.)

Enrollment in first-professional degree programs (medicine, law, dentistry, theology, etc.) declined between 1984 and 1988 and then rose in the early 1990s to 298,000 in 1995 and 1996. In 1996, more men (172,000) than women (125,000) were enrolled in first-professional degree programs. Proportionally, however, the enrollment of women increased from 33 percent in 1984 to 42 percent in 1996. Total enrollment is projected to drop to 291,000 by 2009, of which 45 percent will be women. (See Table 9.11.)

TABLE 9.14

First-professional degrees conferred by institutions of higher education in dentistry, medicine, and law, by sex, and number of institutions conferring degrees: 1949–50 to 1995–96

	Dentistry (D.D.S. or D.M.D.)				Medicine (M.D.)				Law (LL.B. or J.D.)			
Year	Number of institutions conferring degrees	Degrees conferred			Number of institutions conferring degrees	Degrees conferred			Number of institutions conferring degrees	Degrees conferred		
		Total	Men	Women		Total	Men	Women		Total	Men	Women
1	2	3	4	5	6	7	8	9	10	11	12	13
1949–50	40	2,579	2,561	18	72	5,612	5,028	584	(1)	(1)	(1)	(1)
1951–52	41	2,918	2,895	23	72	6,201	5,871	330	(1)	(1)	(1)	(1)
1953–54	42	3,102	3,063	39	73	6,712	6,377	335	(1)	(1)	(1)	(1)
1955–56	42	3,009	2,975	34	73	6,810	6,464	346	131	8,262	7,974	288
1957–58	43	3,065	3,031	34	75	6,816	6,469	347	131	9,394	9,122	272
1959–60	45	3,247	3,221	26	79	7,032	6,645	387	134	9,240	9,010	230
1961–62	46	3,183	3,166	17	81	7,138	6,749	389	134	9,364	9,091	273
1963–64	46	3,180	3,168	12	82	7,303	6,878	425	133	10,679	10,372	307
1965–66	47	3,178	3,146	32	84	7,673	7,170	503	136	13,246	12,776	470
1967–68	48	3,422	3,375	47	85	7,944	7,318	626	138	16,454	15,805	649
1969–70	48	3,718	3,684	34	86	8,314	7,615	699	145	14,916	14,115	801
1970–71	48	3,745	3,703	42	89	8,919	8,110	809	147	17,421	16,181	1,240
1971–72	48	3,862	3,819	43	92	9,253	8,423	830	147	21,764	20,266	1,498
1972–73	51	4,047	3,992	55	97	10,307	9,388	919	152	27,205	25,037	2,168
1973–74	52	4,440	4,355	85	99	11,356	10,093	1,263	151	29,326	25,986	3,340
1974–75	52	4,773	4,627	146	104	12,447	10,818	1,629	154	29,296	24,881	4,415
1975–76	56	5,425	5,187	238	107	13,426	11,252	2,174	166	32,293	26,085	6,208
1976–77	57	5,138	4,764	374	109	13,461	10,891	2,570	169	34,104	26,447	7,657
1977–78	57	5,189	4,623	566	109	14,279	11,210	3,069	169	34,402	25,457	8,945
1978–79	58	5,434	4,794	640	109	14,786	11,381	3,405	175	35,206	25,180	10,026
1979–80	58	5,258	4,558	700	112	14,902	11,416	3,486	179	35,647	24,893	10,754
1980–81	58	5,460	4,672	788	116	15,505	11,672	3,833	176	36,331	24,563	11,768
1981–82	59	5,282	4,467	815	119	15,814	11,867	3,947	180	35,991	23,965	12,026
1982–83	59	5,585	4,631	954	118	15,484	11,350	4,134	177	36,853	23,550	13,303
1983–84	60	5,353	4,302	1,051	119	15,813	11,359	4,454	179	37,012	23,382	13,630
1984–85	59	5,339	4,233	1,106	120	16,041	11,167	4,874	181	37,491	23,070	14,421
1985–86	59	5,046	3,907	1,139	120	15,938	11,022	4,916	181	35,844	21,874	13,970
1986–87	58	4,741	3,603	1,138	121	15,428	10,431	4,997	179	36,056	21,561	14,495
1987–88	57	4,477	3,300	1,177	122	15,358	10,278	5,080	180	35,397	21,067	14,330
1988–89	58	4,265	3,124	1,141	124	15,460	10,310	5,150	182	35,634	21,069	14,565
1989–90	57	4,100	2,834	1,266	124	15,075	9,923	5,152	182	36,485	21,079	15,406
1990–91	55	3,699	2,510	1,189	121	15,043	9,629	5,414	179	37,945	21,643	16,302
1991–92	52	3,593	2,431	1,162	120	15,243	9,796	5,447	177	38,848	22,260	16,588
1992–93	55	3,605	2,383	1,222	122	15,531	9,679	5,852	184	40,302	23,182	17,120
1993–94	53	3,787	2,330	1,457	121	15,368	9,544	5,824	185	40,044	22,826	17,218
1994–95	53	3,897	2,480	1,417	119	15,537	9,507	6,030	183	39,349	22,592	16,757
1995–96	53	3,697	2,374	1,323	119	15,341	9,061	6,280	183	39,828	22,508	17,320

(1) Data prior to 1955–56 are not shown because they lack comparability with the figures for subsequent years.

U.S. Department of Education, National Center for Education Statistics, Higher Education General Information Survey (HEGIS), "Degrees and Other Formal Awards Conferred" surveys, and Integrated Postsecondary Education Data System (IPEDS), "Completions" surveys. (This table was prepared July 1998.)

Source: *Digest of Education Statistics 1998*, National Center for Education Statistics, Washington, DC, 1999

Trends in Degrees Conferred

Between school years 1986-87 and 1996-97, the number of associate, bachelor's, master's, and doctor's degrees conferred rose — by 21 percent, 18 percent, 39 percent, and 11 percent, respectively. In 1996-97, students earned 528,000 associate degrees, 1.2 million bachelor's degrees, 402,000 master's degrees, 79,700 first-professional degrees, and 44,700 doctorates. (See Table 9.12.) Table 9.13 shows the number, level, and disciplines of degrees conferred during 1994-95.

Associate Degrees

In 1995-96, 555,216 associate degrees were earned, and an estimated 528,000 were conferred in 1996-97 (Table 9.12). Public institutions accounted for 84 percent of all associate degrees in 1994-95. At public institutions, liberal arts/general studies, health professions, and business management/administration were the most popular areas of study. At private institutions, in addition to these three areas, engineering-related technology was a popular degree program. (See Table 9.13.)

Bachelor's Degrees

In 1995-96, students earned almost 1.2 million bachelor's degrees, with the number projected to remain the same in 1996-97. Since 1981-82, more bachelor's degrees have been awarded to women than to men. Of the 1.2 million degrees awarded in 1995-96, women earned 642,338 or 55 percent. (See Table 9.12.) The largest numbers of degrees conferred were in business management/administration, social sciences and history, education, health and related sciences, psychology, and engineering (Table 9.13).

Master's Degrees

The annual number of master's degrees awarded declined during the late 1970s and the early 1980s but began to rise again in the 1984-85 school year. In 1995-96, the number reached 406,301. The proportion earned by women has steadily increased. In 1970-71, women earned 40 percent of all master's degrees; in 1995-96, the proportion rose to 56 percent and is projected to remain above 50 percent through 2007-08. (See Table 9.12.) The fields with the greatest numbers of degrees awarded were education and business management/administration (Table 9.13).

Doctor's Degrees

The number of doctorates conferred remained virtually unchanged at around 33,000 throughout most of the 1970s and 1980s. Since 1984-85, the number has increased slightly each year, reaching 44,652 in 1995-96 and an estimated 44,700 in 1996-97. Generally, men receiving doctor's degrees far outnumbered women, but the number of women earning doctorates has more than doubled since the mid-1970s. In 1995-96, women earned 40 percent of all doctor's degrees conferred. The NCES projects that by 2007-08, the gap will narrow even more, with women earning 46 percent of all doctorates. (See Table 9.12.) The majority of doctorates earned in 1994-95 were in education and technical fields such as engineering, the biological/life sciences, and physical science (Table 9.13).

First Professional Degrees

The total number of first-professional degrees (dentistry, medicine, law, etc.) awarded to women increased almost 700 percent from 1970-71 to 1980-81. (The increase for men during the same period was 49 percent.) By 1995-96, first-professional degrees earned by women had increased an additional 67 percent. Women still lagged behind men, however, earning 42 percent of all first-professional degrees in 1995-96. (See Table 9.12.) Women received 36 percent of dental degrees, 41 percent of medical degrees, and 43 percent of all law degrees in 1995-96. (See Table 9.14.) These are huge changes in just 25 years.

FACULTY

In fall 1995, 2.7 million people were involved in operating the nation's colleges and universities.

About 65.5 percent were professional staff, including executives, administrators, and instructors. Nearly 35 percent were nonprofessional, such as clerical or secretarial staff, paraprofessionals, and skilled staff, including building maintenance and groundskeepers.

Instructional and research faculty filled 931,706 positions; 215,909 research and instruction assistants were also employed. Almost 80 percent were full-time employees. Seventy percent worked in public institutions, most (74 percent) of which were in four-year institutions.

In fall 1995, men accounted for 65 percent of the 550,822 full-time instructional faculty members. Far more men (82 percent) than women (18 percent) were full professors. Three-quarters of full-time faculty members were professors, associate professors, or assistant professors. The remainder were instructors, lecturers, or other faculty. (See Table 9.15.)

Race/Ethnicity

Minorities are underrepresented in full-time faculty positions. In 1995, non-Hispanic Whites made up 85 percent of all full-time faculty members, down slightly from 88 percent in 1991. Non-Hispanic Blacks accounted for only 5 percent of full-time faculty; Hispanics, 2 percent; Asians/Pacific Islanders, 5 percent; and American Indians/Alaskan Natives, less than 1 percent. Nonresident aliens made up another 2 percent. (See Table 9.15.)

Salaries

Salaries for instructional faculty have increased slowly but steadily over the past two decades. In 1970-71, the average faculty member earned

TABLE 9.15

Full-time instructional faculty in institutions of higher education, by race/ethnicity, academic rank, and sex: Fall 1995

| Academic rank and sex | Total | White, non-Hispanic | Minority | | Black, non-Hispanic | Hispanic | Asian or Pacific Islander | American Indian/ Alaskan Native | Non-resident alien | Race/ ethnicity unknown |
			Number	Percent [1]						
1	2	3	4	5	6	7	8	9	10	11
Men and women, all ranks	**550,822**	**468,518**	**69,505**	**12.9**	**26,835**	**12,942**	**27,572**	**2,156**	**10,853**	**1,946**
Professors	159,333	142,819	15,254	9.6	4,768	2,470	7,643	373	975	285
Associate professors	125,082	108,953	14,710	11.9	5,634	2,607	6,119	350	1,179	240
Assistant professors	129,682	104,037	20,725	16.6	8,011	3,736	8,459	519	4,311	609
Instructors	66,708	55,211	10,223	15.6	4,857	2,530	2,323	513	848	426
Lecturers	12,874	10,533	1,838	14.9	798	429	557	54	426	77
Other faculty	57,143	46,965	6,755	12.6	2,767	1,170	2,471	347	3,114	309
Men, all ranks	**360,150**	**307,498**	**43,258**	**12.3**	**13,847**	**7,864**	**20,285**	**1,262**	**8,161**	**1,233**
Professors	130,940	117,844	11,987	9.2	3,085	1,912	6,691	299	879	230
Associate professors	85,313	74,160	9,985	11.9	3,214	1,723	4,826	222	989	179
Assistant professors	73,141	57,580	11,952	17.2	3,897	2,068	5,734	253	3,225	384
Instructors	33,067	27,239	5,037	15.6	2,154	1,345	1,244	294	551	240
Lecturers	5,889	4,809	812	14.4	351	193	241	27	233	35
Other faculty	31,800	25,866	3,485	11.9	1,146	623	1,549	167	2,284	165
Women, all ranks	**190,672**	**161,020**	**26,247**	**14.0**	**12,988**	**5,078**	**7,287**	**894**	**2,692**	**713**
Professors	28,393	24,975	3,267	11.6	1,683	558	952	74	96	55
Associate professors	39,769	34,793	4,725	12.0	2,420	884	1,293	128	190	61
Assistant professors	56,541	46,457	8,773	15.9	4,114	1,668	2,725	266	1,086	225
Instructors	33,641	27,972	5,186	15.6	2,703	1,185	1,079	219	297	186
Lecturers	6,985	5,724	1,026	15.2	447	236	316	27	193	42
Other faculty	25,343	21,099	3,270	13.4	1,621	547	922	180	830	144

[1] Based on the number of U.S. citizen faculty with racial/ethnic data.

NOTE.—Data exclude faculty employed by system offices. Totals may differ from figures reported in other tables because of varying survey methodologies.

SOURCE: U.S. Department of Education, National Center for Education Statistics, Integrated Postsecondary Education Data System (IPEDS), "Fall Staff" survey. (This table was prepared June 1998.)

Source: *Digest of Education Statistics 1998*, National Center for Education Statistics, Washington, DC, 1999

TABLE 9.16
Average Student Expenses, by College Board Region, 1999-00

	Tuition & Fees	Out-of-state tuition	Books & supplies	Residential			Commuter		
				Room and board	Trans.	Other costs	Board only	Trans.	Other costs
NATIONAL									
2-yr public	1,627	3,191	645	—	—	—	2,128	997	1,202
2-yr private	7,182		681	4,583	686	1,132	2,029	932	1,132
4-yr public	3,356	5,350	681	4,730	658	1,484	2,213	1,005	1,519
4-yr private	15,380		700	5,959	558	1,054	2,324	907	1,189
New England									
2-yr public	2,243	4,224	610	—	—	—	2,349	1,034	1,331
2-yr private	14,332		719	6,676	—	1,110	1,953	815	873
4-yr public	4,727	5,998	652	5,205	507	1,250	2,047	945	1,206
4-yr private	20,171		708	7,205	489	1,004	2,274	1,048	1,034
Middle States									
2-yr public	2,567	2,951	625	—	—	—	1,782	937	1,163
2-yr private	9,139		685	—	—	—	1,898	876	1,299
4-yr public	4,427	4,447	705	5,409	532	1,275	2,263	926	1,421
4-yr private	16,046		672	6,825	413	984	2,103	843	1,118
South									
2-yr public	1,290	3,067	626	—	—	—	2,105	1,142	1,060
2-yr private	8,383		628	4,143	556	1,206	1,507	976	790
4-yr public	2,748	5,676	690	4,232	789	1,479	2,145	1,189	1,532
4-yr private	13,186		713	5,214	713	1,116	2,384	939	1,167
Midwest									
2-yr public	1,850	3,400	675	—	—	—	2,464	1,024	1,213
2-yr private	7,583		690	3,964	575	1,161	1,649	1,002	1,501
4-yr public	3,813	5,057	635	4,512	533	1,543	2,270	954	1,545
4-yr private	14,558		693	5,009	532	981	2,716	807	1,196
Southwest									
2-yr public	1,106	1,678	658	2,642	830	1,078	1,946	1,128	1,184
2-yr private	5,448		655	3,759	819	1,180	2,108	1,147	1,362
4-yr public	2,536	4,880	663	4,125	939	1,432	2,180	1,333	1,464
4-yr private	11,275		667	4,634	718	1,294	2,204	1,092	1,342
West									
2-yr public	*1,076*	3,779	*651*	—	—	—	*2,137*	*761*	*1,386*
2-yr private	—		—	—	—	—	—	—	—
4-yr public	2,708	6,819	734	5,534	789	1,721	2,224	812	1,618
4-yr private	15,078		780	6,155	654	1,282	2,207	1,002	1,388

SOURCE: *Annual Survey of Colleges*, The College Board, New York, NY.
Note: Averages in *italicized type* indicate that while the number of institutions reporting data on this item was large enough to support an analysis, the sample size was marginal. Data are enrollment weighted.

$12,710; in 1996-97, the average salary was $50,829. Taking inflation into account, however, the 1996-97 average salary was about the same as in 1970-71 ($50,841 in constant 1996-97 dollars). College faculty suffered large losses in purchasing power between 1970-71 and 1980-81. While faculty salaries began to increase in the mid-1980s, they still had not recovered completely by 1996-97.

In 1996-97, the average salary of a full professor was $66,659. For associate and assistant professors, the average salaries were $49,307 and $40,687, respectively, while instructors earned an average of $31,193. Male faculty members received an estimated average salary of $54,465. The average salary for female faculty was $44,325, only 81 percent of the salaries of their male peers. The difference can be at least partly explained by the fact that fewer women are full professors.

THE RISING COST OF A COLLEGE EDUCATION

About the only thing more expensive than going to college is not going to college. — Thomas G. Mortenson, editor and publisher of *Postsecondary Education OPPORTUNITY*

The cost of a college education has been increasing dramatically. Overall costs for all institutions have quadrupled since 1976-77. Costs were

---

TABLE 9.17
Mean Earnings of Workers 18 Years or Older by Highest Level of Educational Attainment

Year	Not a High School Graduate	High School Graduate (or equiv.)	Some College or Assoc. Degree	Bachelor's Degree Only	Not a High School Graduate	High School Graduate (or equiv.)	Some College or Assoc. Degree	Bachelor's Degree Only
	MALE				FEMALE			
1997	19,574	28,307	32,641	50,056	10,725	16,906	19,856	30,119
1996	17,826	27,642	31,426	46,702	10,421	16,161	18,933	28,701
1995	16,747	26,333	29,851	46,111	9,790	15,970	17,962	26,841
1994	16,633	25,038	27,636	46,278	9,189	14,955	16,928	26,483
1993	14,946	23,973	26,614	43,499	9,462	14,446	16,555	25,232
1992	14,934	22,978	25,660	40,039	9,311	14,128	16,023	23,991
1991	15,056	22,663	25,345	38,484	8,818	13,523	15,643	22,802
1990	14,991	22,378	26,120	38,901	8,808	12,986	15,002	21,933
1989	14,727	22,508	25,555	38,692	8,268	12,468	14,688	21,089
1988	14,551	21,481	23,827	35,906	7,711	11,857	14,009	19,216
1987	14,544	20,364	22,781	33,677	7,504	11,309	13,158	18,217
1986	13,703	19,453	21,784	33,376	7,109	10,606	12,029	17,623
1985	13,124	18,575	20,698	31,433	6,874	10,115	11,504	16,114
1984	12,775	18,016	18,863	29,203	6,644	9,561	10,614	14,865
1983	12,052	16,728	18,052	27,239	6,292	9,147	9,981	13,808
1982	11,513	16,160	17,108	25,758	5,932	8,715	9,348	12,511
1981	11,668	15,900	16,870	24,353	5,673	8,063	8,811	11,384
1980	11,042	15,002	15,871	23,340	5,263	7,423	8,256	10,628
1979	10,628	14,317	14,716	21,482	4,840	6,741	7,190	9,474
1978	9,894	13,188	13,382	19,861	4,397	6,192	6,441	8,408
1977	8,939	12,092	12,393	18,187	4,032	5,624	5,856	7,923
1976	8,522	11,189	11,376	16,714	3,723	5,240	5,301	7,383
1975	7,843	10,475	10,805	15,758	3,438	4,802	5,109	6,963

Source: Created by the U.S. Congressional Research Service from U.S. Bureau of the Census data.

Note: Prior to 1991, workers with less than 1 year of college were included in the high school graduate category. Since then, they have been included in the some college or associate degree category.

Source: Linda Levine, *Education Matters: Earnings by Highest Year of Schooling Completed*, Congressional Research Service, Washington, DC, 1998

162

considerably less for students attending a state-supported school within their state of residence. In 1996-97, the estimated average annual cost for undergraduate tuition, room and board, and fees was $6,530 for a public institution and $18,039 for a private college.

In 1999-00, the average residential student paid $10,909 in total costs if he or she attended an in-state, four-year public college. At a four-year private college, total costs were $23,651. The Southwest had the lowest tuition rates at both public and private four-year institutions, while New England had the highest rates. (See Table 9.16.)

College costs, which began soaring in the early 1980s, have consistently exceeded the rate of inflation since then. Between 1980-81 and 1996-97, charges at public colleges rose by 175 percent, and those at private colleges increased by 230 percent.

Many factors have contributed to the increase in costs at public schools, including declines in government appropriations, increases in instruc-

---

TABLE 9.18

Percent of undergraduates receiving financial aid, by type and source of aid and selected student characteristics: 1995–96

Selected student characteristics	Enrollment of under-graduates,[1] in thousands	Any aid			Grants			Loans			Work study	Other		
		Total[2]	Federal	Non-federal	Total	Federal	Non-federal	Total	Federal	Non-federal	Total[3]	Total	Federal	Non-federal
1	2	3	4	5	6	7	8	9	10	11	12	13	14	15
							Percent of all undergraduates receiving aid							
All undergraduates	**16,677**	**49.7**	**36.6**	**32.0**	**39.0**	**21.9**	**27.6**	**25.6**	**25.3**	**1.1**	**5.0**	**7.4**	**2.4**	**4.8**
Sex														
Men	7,197	46.7	33.1	31.4	35.8	18.2	26.4	24.4	23.9	1.3	4.3	8.7	2.7	5.8
Women	9,481	51.9	39.2	32.5	41.4	24.8	28.5	26.5	26.2	0.9	5.6	6.5	2.2	4.2
Race/ethnicity														
White, non-Hispanic	11,681	47.1	33.2	31.1	35.4	16.6	26.9	25.6	25.2	1.0	4.6	7.5	2.5	4.8
Black, non-Hispanic	2,030	62.9	50.0	38.3	52.8	38.1	31.7	30.9	30.4	1.3	6.1	9.8	2.6	7.0
Hispanic	1,723	54.2	44.6	30.6	47.3	36.1	27.2	22.3	22.0	0.9	5.8	5.2	1.5	3.6
Asian American/ Pacific Islander	967	42.9	33.1	30.8	35.7	22.9	27.5	21.3	20.7	1.3	6.6	5.7	2.2	3.5
American Indian/ Alaskan Native	163	59.4	47.8	37.1	48.4	37.3	27.3	25.2	25.2	0.2	3.9	12.0	1.5	7.7
Age														
23 years old or younger	9,116	53.5	42.1	34.0	41.7	22.7	30.9	31.1	30.7	1.2	7.7	7.7	4.4	3.4
24 to 29 years old	3,049	49.0	37.8	29.2	38.5	25.5	23.3	25.8	25.5	1.0	2.5	7.1	0.0	6.9
30 years old or over	4,513	42.5	24.8	29.9	33.9	18.0	23.8	14.5	14.1	0.8	1.4	7.1	0.0	6.4
Marital status														
Married	3,191	16.0	27.0	20.5	25.1	19.7	24.3	16.9	16.5	0.7	1.4	7.3	0.0	6.9
Not married[4]	12,861	50.4	38.4	32.2	39.4	22.0	28.5	27.9	27.5	1.2	6.1	7.3	3.1	4.1
Separated	322	70.9	61.6	38.7	62.0	54.3	29.1	30.0	30.0	0.8	3.3	13.4	0.1	12.5
Attendance status														
Full-time, full-year	6,306	68.4	55.6	45.7	54.1	30.6	41.0	43.7	43.2	1.7	11.0	10.9	5.0	5.9
Part-time and part-year	10,372	38.3	24.8	24.0	29.9	16.6	19.7	14.4	14.1	0.7	1.4	5.4	0.8	4.3
Dependency status														
Dependent	8,201	50.9	39.2	33.4	38.8	18.9	30.7	30.5	30.1	1.3	7.8	7.7	4.9	3.0
Less than $20,000	1,543	70.2	62.9	43.0	66.3	57.0	40.4	35.4	35.2	1.1	10.9	6.5	3.0	3.6
$20,000–$39,999	1,873	60.3	49.2	40.5	51.0	31.7	38.1	38.2	37.4	2.0	10.4	7.5	4.4	3.2
$40,000–$59,999	1,865	47.4	34.6	31.8	30.4	3.7	29.2	32.4	32.2	1.1	7.8	9.0	6.3	2.9
$60,000–$79,999	1,366	42.5	28.4	28.1	25.3	0.5	25.3	27.0	26.6	1.1	5.8	8.1	5.6	2.6
$80,000–$99,999	681	37.6	24.4	24.4	50.4	0.2	20.3	23.3	23.1	0.6	4.9	9.0	6.0	3.2
$100,000 or more	873	27.5	13.9	19.7	17.3	0.3	17.1	12.6	12.2	1.0	2.7	6.0	4.1	1.9
Independent	8,476	48.5	34.1	30.7	39.2	24.8	24.6	20.9	20.5	0.9	2.3	7.1	0.0	6.7
Less than $9,999	2,470	67.4	59.0	37.5	60.5	52.3	30.8	34.0	33.7	1.1	5.7	8.4	0.0	8.2
$10,000–$19,999	1,923	50.6	38.6	29.8	38.4	24.4	23.2	23.7	23.1	1.3	1.6	7.7	0.0	7.2
$20,000–$29,999	1,382	41.9	26.0	28.3	34.0	18.3	22.9	15.7	15.4	0.9	0.9	6.3	0.0	5.9
$30,000–$49,999	1,502	36.3	16.4	27.3	24.7	6.0	21.0	12.3	12.1	0.4	0.6	6.9	0.0	6.2
$50,000 or more	1,201	29.3	7.0	25.1	20.7	0.1	20.7	5.9	5.8	0.2	0.1	4.9	0.0	4.3
Housing status														
School-owned	2,292	73.6	60.0	54.6	59.5	26.6	51.6	53.1	52.5	2.4	18.9	13.7	9.3	4.7
Off-campus, not with parents	10,188	46.1	32.5	29.0	35.5	20.6	23.8	22.2	21.8	0.9	2.8	7.0	1.1	5.5
With parents	4,197	45.3	33.7	26.9	36.4	22.6	23.8	19.0	18.7	0.7	2.9	5.1	1.6	3.3

[1] Numbers of undergraduates may not equal figures reported in other tables, since these data are based on a sample survey. Includes all postsecondary institutions.

[2] Includes students who reported they were awarded aid, but did not specify the source or type of aid.

[3] Details on federal and nonfederal work study participants are not available.

[4] Includes students who were single, divorced, or widowed.

—Data not applicable.

NOTE.—Because of rounding and/or the fact that some students receive aid from multiple sources, row details may not add to totals. Because of rounding and survey item nonresponse, enrollment data may not add to totals. Data include undergraduates in noncollegiate and collegiate institutions.

SOURCE: U.S. Department of Education, National Center for Education Statistics, *National Postsecondary Student Aid Study*, 1995–96. (This table was prepared September 1997.)

Source: *Digest of Education Statistics 1998*, National Center for Education Statistics, Washington, DC, 1999

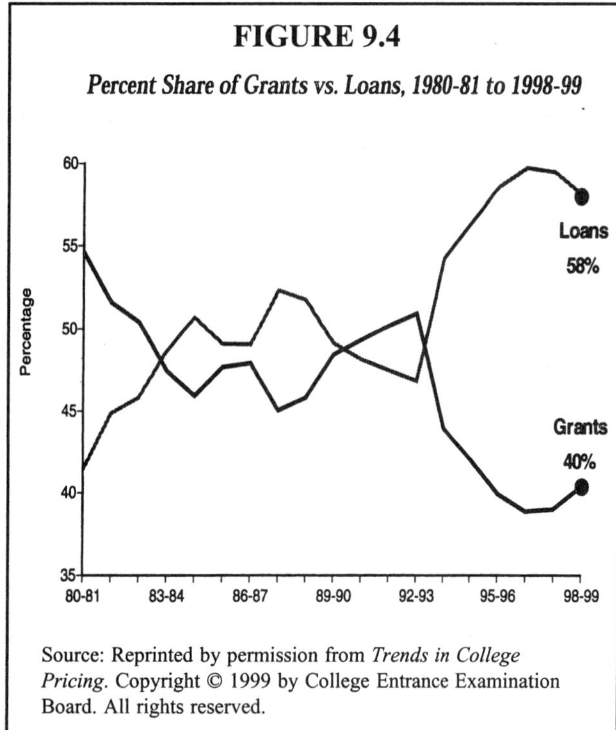

Source: Reprinted by permission from *Trends in College Pricing*. Copyright © 1999 by College Entrance Examination Board. All rights reserved.

tional and student services costs, and increases in research expenditures. Many states have raised room and board and tuition costs at once-inexpensive state schools to compensate for declining federal aid. While public schools still remain significantly less expensive than private schools, they no longer are the educational bargains that they were for many decades. Private schools blame mounting expenses on several factors, including higher student aid, increases in salaries and benefits for faculty and staff, higher energy costs, and maintenance of their superior academic programs and libraries.

Nonetheless, the investment in higher education offers impressive returns. According to Gaston Caperton, president of the College Board, "About 50 percent of people who go to college pay about $4,000 for fees and tuition, which is $16,000 over four years. If a person works for 40 years, they'll probably earn over $1 million on that $16,000."

In 1997, male workers with a bachelor's degree earned 77 percent more than males with a high school degree. Female workers with a bachelor's degree earned 78 percent more than females who graduated from high school. (See Table 9.17.)

FINANCIAL ASSISTANCE FOR STUDENTS

In 1995-96, half of all undergraduate students received some type of financial support. Almost two-fifths received federal support (36.6 percent), and almost one-third (32 percent) received nonfederal assistance, usually from the state. About 39 percent received grants (which do not have to be paid back), 25.6 percent got loans (which do have to be paid back), and about 5 percent were on work-study programs. (See Table 9.18; note that a student may receive more than one form of assistance, so the table percentages may not total 100 percent.) A full-time undergraduate student received an average of $6,832 per year.

Federal assistance that goes directly to students includes Pell Grants (the maximum was $3,000 in 1998-99), the Stafford Student Loan Program (a maximum loan of $17,250 for four years), and Supplemental Education Opportunity Grants (a maximum of $4,000). Colleges or universities receive assistance, which they in turn pay out to students, through Campus-Based Programs and Perkins Loans. In general, the federal government has shifted its spending from grants to loans (Figure 9.4). Loan aid has more than doubled between 1988-89 and 1998-99, from 17.9 billion to 37.2 billion, while grant aid has increased by about two-thirds, from 15.8 billion to 25.9 billion over the same period.

Help for the Middle Class

Middle-income families often face a dilemma in educating their children — they have too much income to qualify for many assistance programs, and too little income to meet spiraling college costs. In 1964, a family in the twentieth percentile (lowest) of income could expect to spend 29 percent of its total annual income on public college tuition, room, and board. A family at the mid-point of income levels would have spent 14.4 percent of its income, and a family at the eightieth percentile would have had to expend only 9.2 percent of its income on public college costs. In 1995, these expenditures had risen to 32.2 percent of the income of the twentieth-percentile family; the costs for families at the fiftieth and eightieth percentiles were about the same proportion as in 1964. (See Table 9.19.)

At private institutions of higher learning, the increase in tuition, room, and board escalated even more rapidly. By 1995, a family at the twentieth percentile of income would have had to spend 88.5 percent of its annual income for one year of private college, far above the 1964 level of 58.3 percent. The proportions for fiftieth- and eightieth-percentile families increased by 45 percent and 26 percent, respectively. (See Table 9.19.)

In 1992, President George Bush signed legislation increasing college assistance for middle-income families. In an attempt to help those caught in the middle — too much income to qualify for Pell Grants and too little income to meet the spiraling college costs — the new law dropped the previous practice of calculating assets by including a family's equity in a home or farm and college-savings accounts.

Students from families of four with annual incomes of up to $42,000 could now qualify for grants; the previous maximum income was $30,000. The bill also established a new unsubsidized (not guaranteed by the government) loan program for students and families who do not qualify for subsidized loans because of high incomes. Unsubsidized borrowing by students (Stafford Unsubsidized) and parents (Parent Loans to Undergraduate Students; PLUS) currently accounts for about 45 percent of federal education loans.

TABLE 9.19

Average undergraduate tuition, room, and board (in 1996 constant dollars) as a percentage of selected percentiles of income of all families, by control of institution: Selected years 1964–95

| | Public institutions | | | | Private institutions | | | |
| Year | Tuition, room, and board | Family income percentile | | | Tuition, room, and board | Family income percentile | | |
		20th	50th	80th		20th	50th	80th
1964	$4,772	29.0	14.4	9.2	$9,580	58.3	28.8	18.6
1966	4,891	25.6	13.4	8.7	10,124	53.1	27.7	17.9
1968	4,914	24.0	12.6	8.1	10,210	49.8	26.2	16.9
1970	5,083	24.7	12.7	8.1	10,814	52.5	27.1	17.2
1972	5,044	26.4	12.0	0.0	11,105	52.9	26.7	16.7
1974	4,735	22.5	11.5	7.2	10,309	48.9	25.1	15.7
1976	4,783	23.3	11.6	7.3	10,442	50.9	25.3	15.8
1978	4,567	21.8	10.8	6.6	10,339	49.3	24.4	15.0
1979	4,376	20.7	10.3	6.4	9,927	46.9	23.4	14.6
1980	4,298	21.9	10.7	6.5	9,908	50.6	24.7	15.1
1982	4,708	25.9	12.4	7.2	11,062	60.7	29.0	17.0
1984	5,056	26.8	12.7	7.4	12,167	64.5	30.5	17.8
1986	5,367	27.0	12.7	7.4	13,648	68.7	32.4	18.9
1988	5,533	27.6	13.0	7.5	14,486	72.3	33.9	19.5
1990	5,573	27.6	13.1	7.5	15,126	74.8	35.6	20.5
1991	5,829	29.8	14.1	8.0	15,788	80.6	38.1	21.8
1992	5,922	31.2	14.4	8.2	16,110	84.9	39.1	22.4
1993	6,110	33.0	15.1	8.4	16,628	89.8	41.2	22.8
1994[1]	6,223	32.7	15.1	8.4	16,907	88.7	41.1	22.8
1995[2]	6,349	32.2	15.2	8.5	17,474	88.5	41.7	23.4

[1] Revised from previously published figures.

[2] Preliminary data based on fall 1994 enrollment weights.

NOTE: Tuition data are for academic years beginning 1964–95, and family income data are for calendar years 1964–95. Both calendar and school year Consumer Price Indexes (CPIs) were used to calculate constant dollar figures. "Tuition, room, and board" are for 2-year and 4-year colleges and universities. In-state tuition and fees were used for public institutions.

Source: Thomas M. Smith et al., *The Condition of Education 1997*, National Center for Education Statistics, Washington, DC, 1997

The Higher Education Amendments of 1998 (PL 105-244) continued the authorization level for the maximum individual Pell Grant at $4,500 for the 1999-2000 academic year, increasing by $300 for each of the next three years and by $400 in 2003-04. The actual appropriation (amount funded by the federal budget), however, is likely to be less than the authorized amount. In 1998-99, the maximum Pell Grant was $3,000. The Higher Education Amendments also increased the amount of money that independent and working dependent students may earn before it is counted against their eligibility to receive federal grant aid, including Pell Grants. For those eligible, the act doubled the amount of a Pell Grant for the first two years of undergraduate study for students who graduate in the top 10 percent of their high school class.

Tax Credit Incentives

In 1997, President Bill Clinton signed legislation that established new incentives to help middle class taxpayers save for college, pay tuition bills, and repay student loans. The major provisions of the Taxpayers Relief Act of 1997 (PL 105-34) include Hope scholarships, lifetime learning credits (LLC), and education IRAs (Individual Retirement Accounts).

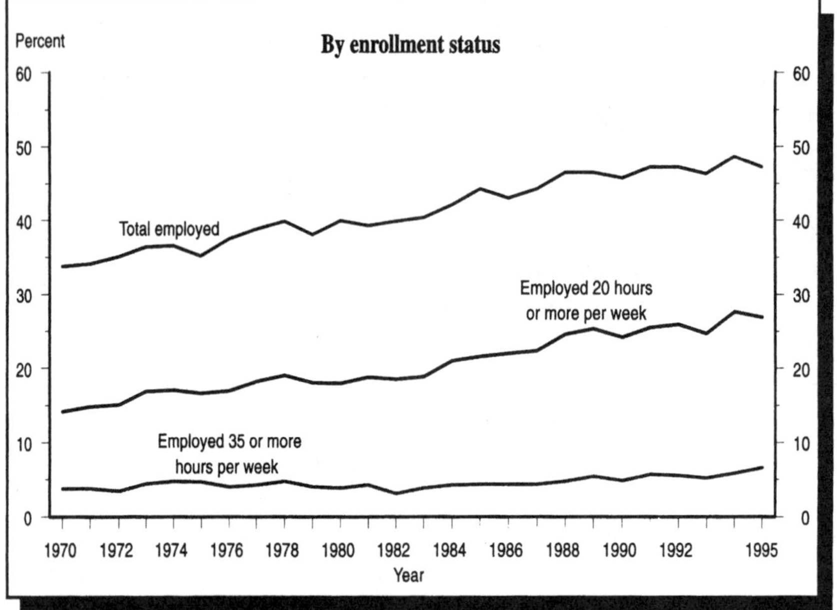

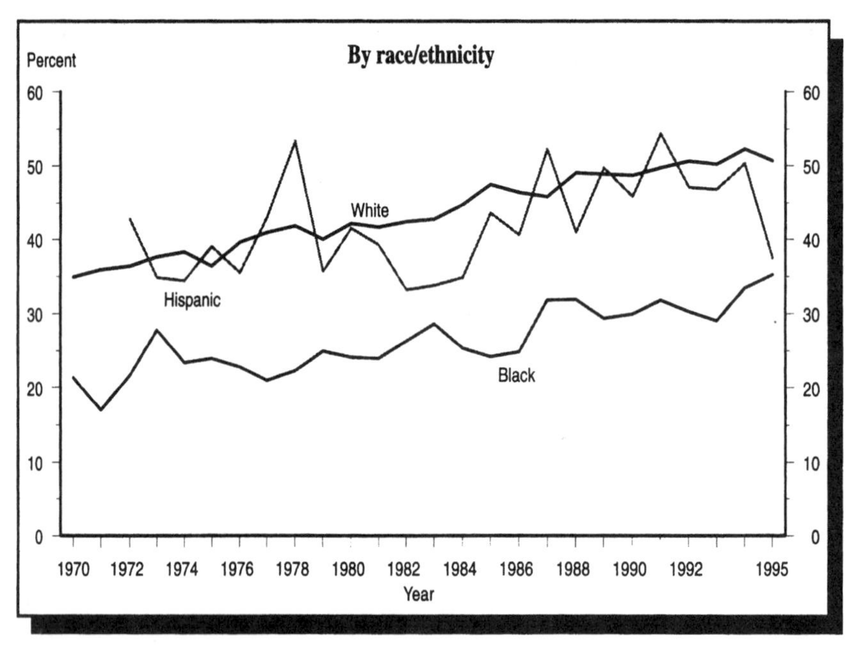

Source: Thomas M. Smith et al., *The Condition of Education 1997*, National Center for Education Statistics, Washington, DC, 1997

The Hope scholarship provides a tax credit against tuition of up to $1,500 per year per student for the first two years of postsecondary education. This benefit phases out — beginning at an $80,000 yearly income for a couple ($40,000 for single tax-

TABLE 9.20

Number and percentage distribution of 2-year and 4-year postsecondary education institutions that offered distance education courses in 1997–98, that planned to offer them in the next 3 years, and that did not offer and did not plan to offer them in the next 3 years, by institutional characteristics

Institutional characteristic	Total number of institutions	Offered distance education in 1997–98		Planned to offer distance education in the next 3 years		Did not offer in 1997–98 and did not plan to offer in the next 3 years	
		Number	Percent	Number	Percent	Number	Percent
All institutions	5,010	1,680	34	990	20	2,340	47
Institutional type							
Public 2-year.........................	1,230	760	62	250	20	230	18
Private 2-year........................	1,120	60	5	220	20	840	75
Public 4-year.........................	610	480	78	70	12	60	10
Private 4-year........................	2,050	390	19	450	22	1,210	59
Size of institution							
Less than 3,000.....................	3,800	730	19	840	22	2,230	59
3,000 to 9,999.......................	820	610	75	110	14	90	12
10,000 or more......................	400	350	87	30	8	20	5

NOTE: Percentages are based on the estimated 5,010 2-year and 4-year postsecondary education institutions in the nation. Percentages are computed across each row. Details may not sum to totals because of rounding.

Source: *Distance Education at Postsecondary Education Institutions: 1997-98,* National Center for Education Statistics, Washington, DC, 1999

payers) and ending entirely at annual incomes of $100,000 for a couple ($50,000 for single taxpayers).

The lifetime learning credit offers a tax credit of up to $1,000 per year for tuition after the first two years. It may be taken for an unlimited number of years. The income phase-outs are the same as for Hope scholarships.

Education IRAs permit tax-free withdrawals for tuition, fees, room and board, and books and supplies for undergraduate and graduate education, as well as technical training. Taxpayers may contribute up to $500 per child per year in a designated education IRA account, which grows tax-free until used. When money is needed for education, as long as the withdrawal is less than or equal to the higher education expenses, no tax is owed. This benefit also phases out, but at higher income levels.

WORKING STUDENTS

As might be expected in this time of rising education costs, college students are likely to be em-ployed to help pay their way through school. In 1970, about one-third (34 percent) of full-time students worked. In 1995, the proportion had increased to almost one-half (47 percent). White students (51 percent) were more likely to work than were Black students (35 percent). (See Figure 9.5.)

Typically, part-time students were much more likely to work while attending school. Full-time students were also more likely to work if their families' incomes were low (the bottom 20 percent of all family incomes) or mid-range (the middle 60 percent of family incomes). In 1993, the work rates were 51 percent for low-income students and 48 percent for middle-income students. Only 42 percent of students from high-income families (the top 20 percent of incomes) worked while attending school.

DISTANCE EDUCATION

Distance education is not a new concept. It started with classes taken by mail (correspondence courses) and by watching teachers' lectures on videos or cable television. Now, according to *Distance Education at Postsecondary Education Institu-*

TABLE 9.21

Trends in Annual and 30-Day Prevalence of Use of Various Drugs for Eighth, Tenth, and Twelfth Graders, College Students, and Young Adults (Ages 19-28)

| | Annual | | | | | | | | | 30-Day | | | | | | | | |
	1991	1992	1993	1994	1995	1996	1997	1998	'97–'98 change	1991	1992	1993	1994	1995	1996	1997	1998	'97–'98 change
Any Illicit Drug[a]																		
8th Grade	11.3	12.9	15.1	18.5	21.4	23.6	22.1	21.0	-1.1	5.7	6.8	8.4	10.9	12.4	14.6	12.9	12.1	-0.8
10th Grade	21.4	20.4	24.7	30.0	33.3	37.5	38.5	35.0	-3.5ss	11.6	11.0	14.0	18.5	20.2	23.2	23.0	21.5	-1.5
12th Grade	29.4	27.1	31.0	35.8	39.0	40.2	42.4	41.4	-1.0	16.4	14.4	18.3	21.9	23.8	24.6	26.2	25.6	-0.6
College Students	29.2	30.6	30.6	31.4	33.5	34.2	34.1	37.8	+3.7s	15.2	16.1	15.1	16.0	19.1	17.6	19.2	19.7	+0.5
Young Adults	27.0	28.3	28.4	28.4	29.8	29.2	29.2	29.9	+0.7	15.1	14.8	14.9	15.3	15.8	15.8	16.4	16.1	-0.3
Any Illicit Drug Other Than Marijuana[a]																		
8th Grade	8.4	9.3	10.4	11.3	12.6	13.1	11.8	11.0	-0.8	3.8	4.7	5.3	5.6	6.5	6.9	6.0	5.5	-0.5
10th Grade	12.2	12.3	13.9	15.2	17.5	18.4	18.2	16.6	-1.6	5.5	5.7	6.5	7.1	8.9	8.9	8.8	8.6	-0.2
12th Grade	16.2	14.9	17.1	18.0	19.4	19.8	20.7	20.2	-0.5	7.1	6.3	7.9	8.8	10.0	9.5	10.7	10.7	0.0
College Students	13.2	13.1	12.5	12.2	15.9	12.8	15.8	14.0	-1.8	4.3	4.6	5.4	4.6	6.3	4.5	6.8	6.1	-0.7
Young Adults	14.3	14.1	13.0	13.0	13.8	13.2	13.6	13.2	-0.4	5.4	5.5	4.9	5.3	5.7	4.7	5.5	5.5	0.0
Any Illicit Drug Including Inhalants[a,b]																		
8th Grade	16.7	18.2	21.1	24.2	27.1	28.7	27.2	26.2	-1.0	8.8	10.0	12.0	14.3	16.1	17.5	16.0	14.9	-1.1
10th Grade	23.9	23.5	27.4	32.5	35.6	39.6	40.3	37.1	-3.2ss	13.1	12.6	15.5	20.0	21.6	24.5	24.1	22.5	-1.6
12th Grade	31.2	28.8	32.5	37.6	40.2	41.9	43.3	42.4	-0.9	17.8	15.5	19.3	23.0	24.8	25.5	26.9	26.6	-0.3
College Students	29.8	31.1	31.7	31.9	33.7	35.1	35.5	39.1	+3.6	15.1	16.5	15.7	16.4	19.6	18.0	19.6	21.0	+1.4
Young Adults	27.8	29.2	28.9	29.2	30.4	30.2	30.1	30.6	+0.5	15.4	15.3	15.1	16.1	16.1	16.4	16.9	16.7	-0.2
Marijuana/Hashish																		
8th Grade	6.2	7.2	9.2	13.0	15.8	18.3	17.7	16.9	-0.8	3.2	3.7	5.1	7.8	9.1	11.3	10.2	9.7	-0.5
10th Grade	16.5	15.2	19.2	25.2	28.7	33.6	34.8	31.1	-3.7sss	8.7	8.1	10.9	15.8	17.2	20.4	20.5	18.7	-1.8s
12th Grade	23.9	21.9	26.0	30.7	34.7	35.8	38.5	37.5	-1.0	13.8	11.9	15.5	19.0	21.2	21.9	23.7	22.8	-0.9
College Students	26.5	27.7	27.9	29.3	31.2	33.1	31.6	35.9	+4.3s	14.1	14.6	14.2	15.1	18.6	17.5	17.7	18.6	+1.0
Young Adults	23.8	25.2	25.1	25.5	26.5	27.0	26.8	27.4	+0.6	13.5	13.3	13.4	14.1	14.0	15.1	15.0	14.9	-0.1
Inhalants[b,c]																		
8th Grade	9.0	9.5	11.0	11.7	12.8	12.2	11.8	11.1	-0.7	4.4	4.7	5.4	5.6	6.1	5.8	5.6	4.8	-0.8s
10th Grade	7.1	7.5	8.4	9.1	9.6	9.5	8.7	8.0	-0.7	2.7	2.7	3.3	3.6	3.5	3.3	3.0	2.9	-0.1
12th Grade	6.6	6.2	7.0	7.7	8.0	7.6	6.7	6.2	-0.5	2.4	2.3	2.5	2.7	3.2	2.5	2.5	2.3	-0.2
College Students	3.5	3.1	3.8	3.0	3.9	3.6	4.1	3.0	-1.0	0.9	1.1	1.3	0.6	1.6	0.8	0.8	0.6	-0.1
Young Adults	2.0	1.9	2.1	2.1	2.4	2.2	2.3	2.1	-0.2	0.5	0.6	0.7	0.5	0.7	0.5	0.5	0.7	+0.2
Nitrites[d]																		
8th Grade	—	—	—	—	—	—	—	—	—	—	—	—	—	—	—	—	—	—
10th Grade	—	—	—	—	—	—	—	—	—	—	—	—	—	—	—	—	—	—
12th Grade	0.9	0.5	0.9	1.1	1.1	1.6	1.2	1.4	+0.2	0.4	0.3	0.6	0.4	0.4	0.7	0.7	1.0	+0.3
College Students	—	—	—	—	—	—	—	—	—	—	—	—	—	—	—	—	—	—
Young Adults	0.2	0.1	0.4	0.3	—	—	—	—	—	*	0.1	0.2	0.1	—	—	—	—	—

(Table continued on next page)

TABLE 9.21

Trends in Annual and 30-Day Prevalence of Use of Various Drugs for Eighth, Tenth, and Twelfth Graders, College Students, and Young Adults (Ages 19-28)

	Annual									30-Day								
	1991	1992	1993	1994	1995	1996	1997	1998	'97–'98 change	1991	1992	1993	1994	1995	1996	1997	1998	'97–'98 change
Hallucinogens[c]																		
8th Grade	1.9	2.5	2.6	2.7	3.6	4.1	3.7	3.4	-0.3	0.8	1.1	1.2	1.3	1.7	1.9	1.8	1.4	-0.4
10th Grade	4.0	4.3	4.7	5.8	7.2	7.8	7.6	6.9	-0.7	1.6	1.8	1.9	2.4	3.3	2.8	3.3	3.2	-0.1
12th Grade	5.8	5.9	7.4	7.6	9.3	10.1	9.8	9.0	-0.8	2.2	2.1	2.7	3.1	4.4	3.5	3.9	3.8	-0.1
College Students	6.3	6.8	6.0	6.2	8.2	6.9	7.7	7.2	-0.5	1.2	2.3	2.5	2.1	3.3	1.9	2.1	2.1	0.0
Young Adults	4.5	5.0	4.5	4.8	5.6	5.6	5.9	5.2	-0.7	1.1	1.5	1.2	1.4	1.7	1.2	1.5	1.4	-0.1
LSD																		
8th Grade	1.7	2.1	2.3	2.4	3.2	3.5	3.2	2.8	-0.4	0.6	0.9	1.0	1.1	1.4	1.5	1.5	1.1	-0.4s
10th Grade	3.7	4.0	4.2	5.2	6.5	6.9	6.7	5.9	-0.8	1.5	1.6	1.6	2.0	3.0	2.4	2.8	2.7	-0.1
12th Grade	5.2	5.6	6.8	6.9	8.4	8.8	8.4	7.6	-0.8	1.9	2.0	2.4	2.6	4.0	2.5	3.1	3.2	+0.1
College Students	5.1	5.7	5.1	5.2	6.9	5.2	5.0	4.4	-0.6	0.8	1.8	1.6	1.8	2.5	0.9	1.1	1.5	+0.4
Young Adults	3.8	4.3	3.8	4.0	4.6	4.5	4.4	3.5	-0.9ss	0.8	1.1	0.8	1.1	1.3	0.7	0.9	1.0	0.0
Hallucinogens Other Than LSD																		
8th Grade	0.7	1.1	1.0	1.3	1.7	2.0	1.8	1.6	-0.2	0.3	0.4	0.5	0.7	0.8	0.9	0.7	0.7	0.0
10th Grade	1.3	1.4	1.9	2.4	2.8	3.3	3.3	3.4	+0.1	0.4	0.5	0.7	1.0	1.0	1.0	1.2	1.4	+0.2
12th Grade	2.0	1.7	2.2	3.1	3.8	4.4	4.6	4.6	0.0	0.7	0.5	0.8	1.2	1.3	1.6	1.7	1.6	-0.1
College Students	3.1	2.6	2.7	2.8	4.0	4.1	4.9	4.4	-0.4	0.6	0.7	1.1	0.8	1.6	1.2	1.2	0.7	-0.4
Young Adults	1.7	1.9	1.9	2.0	2.5	2.8	3.1	3.0	-0.1	0.3	0.5	0.6	0.6	0.6	0.6	0.7	0.5	-0.1
PCP[d]																		
8th Grade	—	—	—	—	—	—	—	—	—	—	—	—	—	—	—	—	—	—
10th Grade	—	—	—	—	—	—	—	—	—	—	—	—	—	—	—	—	—	—
12th Grade	1.4	1.4	1.4	1.6	1.8	2.6	2.3	2.1	-0.2	0.5	0.6	1.0	0.7	0.6	1.3	0.7	1.0	+0.3
College Students	—	—	—	—	—	—	—	—	—	—	—	—	—	—	—	—	—	—
Young Adults	0.3	0.3	0.2	0.3	0.3	0.2	0.5	0.6	+0.1	0.1	0.2	0.2	0.1	0.0	0.1	0.1	0.2	+0.1
MDMA (Ecstasy)[d]																		
8th Grade	—	—	—	—	—	2.3	2.3	1.8	-0.5	—	—	—	—	—	1.0	1.0	0.9	-0.1
10th Grade	—	—	—	—	—	4.6	3.9	3.3	-0.6	—	—	—	—	—	1.8	1.3	1.3	0.0
12th Grade	—	—	—	—	—	4.6	4.0	3.6	-0.4	—	—	—	—	—	2.0	1.6	1.5	-0.1
College Students	0.9	2.0	0.8	0.5	2.4	2.8	2.4	3.9	+1.5	0.2	0.4	0.3	0.2	0.7	0.7	0.8	0.8	0.0
Young Adults	0.8	1.0	0.8	0.7	1.6	1.7	2.1	2.9	+0.8	0.1	0.3	0.3	0.2	0.4	0.3	0.6	0.8	+0.1
Cocaine																		
8th Grade	1.1	1.5	1.7	2.1	2.6	3.0	2.8	3.1	+0.3	0.5	0.7	0.7	1.0	1.2	1.3	1.1	1.4	+0.3
10th Grade	2.2	1.9	2.1	2.8	3.5	4.2	4.7	4.7	0.0	0.7	0.7	0.9	1.2	1.7	1.7	2.0	2.1	+0.1
12th Grade	3.5	3.1	3.3	3.6	4.0	4.9	5.5	5.7	+0.2	1.4	1.3	1.3	1.5	1.8	2.0	2.3	2.4	+0.1
College Students	3.6	3.0	2.7	2.0	3.6	2.9	3.4	4.6	+1.2	1.0	1.0	0.7	0.6	0.7	0.8	1.6	1.6	-0.1
Young Adults	6.2	5.7	4.7	4.3	4.4	4.1	4.7	4.9	+0.2	2.0	1.8	1.4	1.3	1.5	1.2	1.6	1.7	+0.1

(Table continued on next page)

TABLE 9.21

Trends in Annual and 30-Day Prevalence of Use of Various Drugs for Eighth, Tenth, and Twelfth Graders, College Students, and Young Adults (Ages 19-28)

| | Annual | | | | | | | | | 30-Day | | | | | | | | |
	1991	1992	1993	1994	1995	1996	1997	1998	'97–'98 change	1991	1992	1993	1994	1995	1996	1997	1998	'97–'98 change
Crack																		
8th Grade	0.7	0.9	1.0	1.3	1.6	1.8	1.7	2.1	+0.4s	0.3	0.5	0.4	0.7	0.7	0.8	0.7	0.9	+0.2
10th Grade	0.9	0.9	1.1	1.4	1.8	2.1	2.2	2.5	+0.3	0.3	0.4	0.5	0.6	0.9	0.8	0.9	1.1	+0.2
12th Grade	1.5	1.5	1.5	1.9	2.1	2.1	2.4	2.5	+0.1	0.7	0.6	0.7	0.8	1.0	1.0	0.9	1.0	+0.1
College Students	0.5	0.4	0.6	0.5	1.1	0.6	0.4	1.0	+0.6	0.3	0.1	0.1	0.1	0.1	0.1	0.2	0.2	-0.1
Young Adults	1.2	1.4	1.3	1.1	1.1	1.1	1.0	1.1	+0.1	0.4	0.4	0.4	0.3	0.2	0.3	0.3	0.3	0.0
Other Cocaine[e]																		
8th Grade	1.0	1.2	1.3	1.7	2.1	2.5	2.2	2.4	+0.2	0.5	0.5	0.6	0.9	1.0	1.0	0.8	1.0	+0.2
10th Grade	2.1	1.7	1.8	2.4	3.0	3.5	4.1	4.0	-0.1	0.6	0.6	0.7	1.0	1.4	1.3	1.6	1.8	+0.2
12th Grade	3.2	2.6	2.9	3.0	3.4	4.2	5.0	4.9	-0.1	1.2	1.0	1.2	1.3	1.3	1.6	2.0	2.0	0.0
College Students	3.2	2.4	2.5	1.8	3.3	2.3	3.0	4.2	+1.2	1.0	0.9	0.6	0.3	0.8	0.6	1.3	1.5	+0.2
Young Adults	5.4	5.1	3.9	3.6	3.9	3.8	4.3	4.5	+0.2	1.8	1.7	1.1	1.0	1.3	1.1	1.5	1.5	0.0
Heroin[f]																		
8th Grade	0.7	0.7	0.7	1.2	1.4	1.6	1.3	1.3	0.0	0.3	0.4	0.4	0.6	0.6	0.7	0.6	0.6	0.0
10th Grade	0.5	0.6	0.7	0.9	1.1	1.2	1.4	1.4	0.0	0.2	0.2	0.3	0.4	0.6	0.5	0.6	0.7	+0.1
12th Grade	0.4	0.6	0.5	0.6	1.1	1.0	1.2	1.0	-0.2	0.2	0.3	0.2	0.3	0.6	0.5	0.5	0.5	0.0
College Students	0.1	0.1	0.1	0.1	0.3	0.4	0.3	0.6	+0.3	0.1	0.0	*	0.0	0.1	*	0.2	0.1	-0.1
Young Adults	0.1	0.2	0.2	0.1	0.4	0.4	0.3	0.4	+0.1	*	0.1	0.1	0.1	0.1	0.1	0.1	0.1	0.0
Other Narcotics[g]																		
8th Grade	—	—	—	—	—	—	—	—	—	—	—	—	—	—	—	—	—	—
10th Grade	—	—	—	—	—	—	—	—	—	—	—	—	—	—	—	—	—	—
12th Grade	3.5	3.3	3.6	3.8	4.7	5.4	6.2	6.3	+0.1	1.1	1.2	1.3	1.5	1.8	2.0	2.3	2.4	+0.1
College Students	2.7	2.7	2.5	2.4	3.8	3.1	4.2	4.2	0.0	0.6	1.0	0.7	0.4	1.2	0.7	1.3	1.1	-0.2
Young Adults	2.5	2.5	2.2	2.5	3.0	2.9	3.3	3.4	+0.1	0.6	0.7	0.7	0.6	0.9	0.7	0.9	0.9	-0.1
Amphetamines[g]																		
8th Grade	6.2	6.5	7.2	7.9	8.7	9.1	8.1	7.2	-0.9	2.6	3.3	3.6	3.6	4.2	4.6	3.8	3.3	-0.5
10th Grade	8.2	8.2	9.6	10.2	11.9	12.4	12.1	10.7	-1.4s	3.3	3.6	4.3	4.5	5.3	5.5	5.1	5.1	0.0
12th Grade	8.2	7.1	8.4	9.4	9.3	9.5	10.2	10.1	-0.1	3.2	2.8	3.7	4.0	4.0	4.1	4.8	4.6	-0.2
College Students	3.9	3.6	4.2	4.2	5.4	4.2	5.7	5.1	-0.7	1.0	1.1	1.5	1.5	2.2	0.9	2.1	1.7	-0.4
Young Adults	4.3	4.1	4.0	4.5	4.6	4.2	4.6	4.5	0.0	1.5	1.5	1.5	1.7	1.7	1.5	1.7	1.7	0.0
Ice[h]																		
8th Grade	—	—	—	—	—	—	—	—	—	—	—	—	—	—	—	—	—	—
10th Grade	—	—	—	—	—	—	—	—	—	—	—	—	—	—	—	—	—	—
12th Grade	1.4	1.3	1.7	1.8	2.4	2.8	2.3	3.0	+0.7	0.6	0.5	0.6	0.7	1.1	1.1	0.8	1.2	+0.4
College Students	0.1	0.2	0.7	0.8	1.1	0.3	0.8	1.0	+0.2	0.0	0.0	0.3	0.5	0.3	0.1	0.2	0.3	+0.1
Young Adults	0.3	0.4	0.8	0.9	1.2	0.9	0.9	1.1	+0.2	*	0.1	0.3	0.5	0.3	0.3	0.3	0.3	-0.1
Barbiturates[g]																		
8th Grade	—	—	—	—	—	—	—	—	—	—	—	—	—	—	—	—	—	—
10th Grade	—	—	—	—	—	—	—	—	—	—	—	—	—	—	—	—	—	—
12th Grade	3.4	2.8	3.4	4.1	4.7	4.9	5.1	5.5	+0.4	1.4	1.1	1.3	1.7	2.2	2.1	2.1	2.6	+0.5s
College Students	1.2	1.4	1.5	1.2	2.0	2.3	3.0	2.5	-0.5	0.3	0.7	0.4	0.4	0.5	0.8	1.2	1.1	-0.1
Young Adults	1.8	1.6	1.9	1.8	2.1	2.2	2.4	2.5	+0.2	0.5	0.5	0.6	0.6	0.8	0.8	0.9	0.9	0.0

(Table continued on next page)

TABLE 9.21

Trends in Annual and 30-Day Prevalence of Use of Various Drugs for Eighth, Tenth, and Twelfth Graders, College Students, and Young Adults (Ages 19-28)

	Annual									30-Day								
	1991	1992	1993	1994	1995	1996	1997	1998	'97–'98 change	1991	1992	1993	1994	1995	1996	1997	1998	'97–'98 change
Tranquilizers[g]																		
8th Grade	1.8	2.0	2.1	2.4	2.7	3.3	2.9	2.6	-0.3	0.8	0.8	0.9	1.1	1.2	1.5	1.2	1.2	0.0
10th Grade	3.2	3.5	3.3	3.3	4.0	4.6	4.9	5.1	+0.2	1.2	1.5	1.1	1.5	1.7	1.7	2.2	2.2	0.0
12th Grade	3.6	2.8	3.5	3.7	4.4	4.6	4.7	5.5	+0.8s	1.4	1.0	1.2	1.4	1.8	2.0	1.8	2.4	+0.6ss
College Students	2.4	2.9	2.4	1.8	2.9	2.8	3.8	3.9	+0.1	0.6	0.6	0.4	0.4	0.5	0.7	1.2	1.3	+0.1
Young Adults	3.5	3.4	3.1	2.9	3.4	3.2	3.1	3.8	+0.7s	0.9	1.0	1.0	0.8	1.1	0.7	1.1	1.2	+0.1
Alcohol[i]																		
Any use																		
8th Grade	54.0	53.7	51.6	—	—	—	—	—	—	25.1	26.1	26.2	—	—	—	—	—	—
			45.4	46.8	45.3	46.5	45.5	43.7	-1.8			24.3	25.5	24.6	26.2	24.5	23.0	-1.5
10th Grade	72.3	70.2	69.3	—	—	—	—	—	—	42.8	39.9	41.5	—	—	—	—	—	—
			63.4	63.9	63.5	65.0	65.2	62.7	-2.5s			38.2	39.2	38.8	40.4	40.1	38.8	-1.3
12th Grade	77.7	76.8	76.0	—	—	—	—	—	—	54.0	51.3	51.0	—	—	—	—	—	—
	77.7	76.8	72.7	73.0	73.7	72.5	74.8	74.3	-0.5			48.6	50.1	51.3	50.8	52.7	52.0	-0.7
College Students	88.3	86.9	85.1	82.7	83.2	82.9	82.4	84.6	+2.1	74.7	71.4	70.1	67.8	67.5	67.0	65.8	68.1	+2.3
Young Adults	86.9	86.2	85.3	83.7	84.7	84.0	84.3	84.0	-0.3	70.6	69.0	68.3	67.7	68.1	66.7	67.5	66.9	-0.6
Been Drunk[h]																		
8th Grade	17.5	18.3	18.2	18.2	18.4	19.8	18.4	17.9	-0.5	7.6	7.5	7.8	8.7	8.3	9.6	8.2	8.4	+0.2
10th Grade	40.1	37.0	37.8	38.0	38.5	40.1	40.7	38.3	-2.4s	20.5	18.1	19.8	20.3	20.8	21.3	22.4	21.1	-1.3
12th Grade	52.7	50.3	49.6	51.7	52.5	51.9	53.2	52.0	-1.2	31.6	29.9	28.9	30.8	33.2	31.3	34.2	32.9	-1.3
College Students	—	—	—	—	—	—	—	—	—	—	—	—	—	—	—	—	—	—
Young Adults	—	—	—	—	—	—	—	—	—	—	—	—	—	—	—	—	—	—
Cigarettes																		
Any use																		
8th Grade	—	—	—	—	—	—	—	—	—	14.3	15.5	16.7	18.6	19.1	21.0	19.4	19.1	-0.3
10th Grade	—	—	—	—	—	—	—	—	—	20.8	21.5	24.7	25.4	27.9	30.4	29.8	27.6	-2.2s
12th Grade	—	—	—	—	—	—	—	—	—	28.3	27.8	29.9	31.2	33.5	34.0	36.5	35.1	-1.4
College Students	35.6	37.3	38.8	37.6	39.3	41.4	43.6	44.3	+0.7	23.2	23.5	24.5	23.5	26.8	27.9	28.3	30.0	+1.7
Young Adults	37.7	37.9	37.8	38.3	38.8	40.3	41.8	41.6	-0.2	28.2	28.3	28.0	28.0	29.2	30.1	29.9	30.9	+1.1
Smokeless Tobacco[d]																		
8th Grade	—	—	—	—	—	—	—	—	—	6.9	7.0	6.6	7.7	7.1	7.1	5.5	4.8	-0.7
10th Grade	—	—	—	—	—	—	—	—	—	10.0	9.6	10.4	10.5	9.7	8.6	8.9	7.5	-1.4
12th Grade	—	—	—	—	—	—	—	—	—	—	11.4	10.7	11.1	12.2	9.8	9.7	8.8	-0.9
College Students	—	—	—	—	—	—	—	—	—	—	—	—	—	—	—	—	—	—
Young Adults	—	—	—	—	—	—	—	—	—	—	—	—	—	—	—	—	—	—
Steroids[h]																		
8th Grade	1.0	1.1	0.9	1.2	1.0	0.9	1.0	1.2	+0.2	0.4	0.5	0.5	0.5	0.6	0.4	0.5	0.5	0.0
10th Grade	1.1	1.1	1.0	1.1	1.2	1.2	1.2	1.2	0.0	0.6	0.6	0.5	0.6	0.6	0.5	0.7	0.6	-0.1
12th Grade	1.4	1.1	1.2	1.3	1.5	1.4	1.4	1.7	+0.3	0.8	0.6	0.7	0.9	0.7	0.7	1.0	1.1	+0.1
College Students	—	—	—	—	—	—	—	—	—	—	—	—	—	—	—	—	—	—
Young Adults	0.5	0.4	0.3	0.4	0.5	0.3	0.5	0.4	-0.1	0.2	0.1	0.0	0.1	0.2	0.2	0.2	0.2	-0.1

(Table continued on next page)

171

TABLE 9.21

NOTES: Level of significance of difference between the two years: s = .05, ss = .01, sss = .001.
'—' indicates data not available. '*' indicates less than .05 percent but greater than 0 percent.
Any apparent inconsistency between the change estimate and the prevalence of use estimates for the two years is due to rounding error.
SOURCE: The Monitoring the Future Study, the University of Michigan.

Approximate Weighted Ns	1991	1992	1993	1994	1995	1996	1997	1998
8th Graders	17,500	18,600	18,300	17,300	17,500	17,800	18,600	18,100
10th Graders	14,800	14,800	15,300	15,800	17,000	15,600	15,500	15,000
12th Graders	15,000	15,800	16,300	15,400	15,400	14,300	15,400	15,200
College Students	1,410	1,490	1,490	1,410	1,450	1,450	1,480	1,440
Young Adults	6,600	6,800	6,700	6,500	6,400	6,300	6,400	6,200

[a]For 12th graders, college students, and young adults only: Use of "any illicit drug" includes any use of marijuana, LSD, other hallucinogens, crack, other cocaine, or heroin, or any use of other narcotics, amphetamines, barbiturates, or tranquilizers not under a doctor's orders. For 8th and 10th graders only: The use of other narcotics and barbiturates has been excluded, because these younger respondents appear to overreport use (perhaps because they include the use of nonprescription drugs in their answers).

[b]For 12th graders, college students, and young adults only: Data based on five of six forms; N is five-sixths of N indicated for each group.

[c]Inhalants are unadjusted for underreporting of amyl and butyl nitrites; hallucinogens are unadjusted for underreporting of PCP.

[d]For 8th and 10th graders only: Smokeless tobacco data based on one of two forms for 1991–96 and on two of four forms beginning in 1997; N is one-half of N indicated. MDMA data based on one form in 1996; N is one-half of N indicated. Beginning in 1997, data based on one-third of N indicated due to changes in the questionnaire forms. For 12th graders only: Data based on one form; N is one-sixth of N indicated. For college students and young adults only: Data based on two forms; N is one-third of N indicated. Questions about nitrite use were dropped from the college student and young adult questionnaires in 1995. Questions about smokeless tobacco use were dropped from the college student and young adult analyses in 1989.

[e]For 12th graders, college students, and young adults only: Data based on four of six forms; N is four-sixths of N indicated for each group.

[f]In 1995, the heroin question was changed in three of six forms for 12th graders and in one of two forms for 8th and 10th graders. Separate questions were asked for use with injection and without injection. In 1996, the heroin question was changed in the remaining 8th and 10th grade form. Data presented here represent the combined data from all forms.

[g]Only drug use which was not under a doctor's orders is included here.

[h]For 12th graders, college students, and young adults only: Data based on two of six forms; N is two-sixths of N indicated for each group.

[i]For 8th, 10th, and 12th graders only: In 1993, the question text was changed slightly in half of the forms to indicate that a "drink" meant "more than just a few sips." The data in the upper line for alcohol came from forms using the original wording, while the data in the lower line came from forms using the revised wording. In 1993, each line of data was based on one of two forms for the 8th and 10th graders and on three of six forms for the 12th graders. N is one-half of N indicated for these groups. Data for 1994–98 were based on all forms for all grades. For college students and young adults, the revision of the question text resulted in rather little change in the reported prevalence of use. The data for all forms are used to provide the most reliable estimate of change.

[j]Daily used is defined as use on twenty or more occasions in the past thirty days except for 5+ drinks, cigarettes, and smokeless tobacco, for which actual daily use is measured.

Source: *National Survey Results on Drug Use from The Monitoring the Future Study*, Institute for Social Research, University of Michigan, Ann Arbor, MI, 1999

tions: 1997-98 (U.S. Department of Education, National Center for Education Statistics, Washington, DC, 1999), the term refers to "education or training courses delivered to remote (off-campus) locations(s) via audio, video (live or prerecorded), or computer technologies…."

About one-third (34 percent) of the nation's two-year and four-year postsecondary education institutions offered distance education courses in 1997-98, and another one-fifth (20 percent) planned to make such courses available within the next three years. Far more public institutions (78 percent of four-year and 62 percent of two-year schools) offered distance education courses than private institutions (19 percent of four-year and 5 percent of two-year schools). (See Table 9.20.) In 1997-98, about 1.4 million students, most of which were undergraduates, were enrolled in college-level credit-granting distance education courses. Tuition and fees tended to be the same as for comparable on-campus courses.

The greatest number of distance education courses offered were in the fields of English, humanities, the social and behavioral sciences, and business and management. Though most distance education courses were at the undergraduate level, more courses in education, engineering, and library and information sciences were at the graduate level. In 1997-98, about 8 percent of all postsecondary institutions offered college-level degree or certificate programs that were designed to be completed totally through distance education.

Distance education can provide access to postsecondary education where otherwise it might not be available, due to distance, work schedules, and family responsibilities. It may decrease costs by schools sharing or combining resources with other schools. Increased access to certificate and degree programs may encourage students to undertake these programs or to complete them more quickly. However, some observers question the effectiveness and fairness of online college courses. They wonder if distance learning will hinder the progress of poor and minority students who may have less exposure or access to computers. Others claim that studies have shown a higher dropout rate for Internet-based learners.

SUBSTANCE ABUSE AMONG COLLEGE STUDENTS

Illicit Drug Use

The *National Survey Results on Drug Use from The Monitoring the Future Study, 1975-1998* (Washington, DC, 1999) was prepared by Dr. Lloyd D. Johnston and his staff at the Institute for Social Research, University of Michigan, for the National Institute on Drug Abuse. The survey of drug use among college students covers all full-time students, one to four years out of high school, who were enrolled in a two- or four-year college in March 1998.

Compared to their nonstudent peers, college students showed a somewhat higher annual prevalence (37.8 percent, compared to 29.9 percent for nonstudents) and 30-day prevalence (19.7 percent versus 16.1 percent) of any illicit drug use. (Annual prevalence means using a drug at any time within the year preceding the survey, and 30-day prevalence refers to using a drug in the 30 days prior to the survey.) Drug use among college students has generally increased since 1991. (See Table 9.21.)

In 1998, more than one-third of college students (35.9 percent) reported that they had used marijuana at some time during the previous year, compared to 27.4 percent of nonstudents. Use of all forms of cocaine within the past year has slightly increased for both college students and young people not in college. While heroin use was still under 1 percent among both students and nonstudents, the annual use of heroin increased more for college students in 1998. (See Table 9.21.)

Alcohol Use

College students who responded to the 1998 survey were as likely to have used alcohol in the past year as their nonstudent peers (84.6 percent, compared to 84 percent). (See Table 9.21.) The high incidence of heavy or "binge" drinking (five or more drinks in a row in the past two weeks) among college students has been an important issue in the past several years. In 1998, nearly two in five (38.9 percent) college students reported bouts of heavy drinking in the last two weeks, compared to 34.1 percent of nonstudent young adults. (See Table 9.22.)

Overall, college students were more likely to engage in heavy weekend drinking rather than drinking on a daily basis. According to a 1997 survey by researchers at the Harvard School of Public Health, fraternity and sorority members were more likely to indulge in binge drinking than other college students — four of five were binge drinkers, compared to 42.7 percent of the general college student population.

Tobacco Use

Recent studies have shown that full-time college students were less likely than other persons of the same age group to be regular smokers, although college students showed a significant increase between 1997 and 1998. In 1998, 18 percent of college students reported daily smoking, up from 15.2 percent in 1997. Over 11 percent reported smoking half a pack or more a day, an increase of 2.3 percentage points from 1997. About 22 percent of nonstudents in the same age group reported daily smoking, while 15.6 percent said they smoked half a pack or more a day. (See Table 9.22.)

TABLE 9.22

Trends in 30-Day Prevalence of <u>Daily</u> Use of Various Drugs for Eighth, Tenth, and Twelfth Graders, College Students, and Young Adults (ages 19-28)

Daily

	1991	1992	1993	1994	1995	1996	1997	1998	'97–'98 change
Marijuana/Hashish[j]									
8th Grade	0.2	0.2	0.4	0.7	0.8	1.5	1.1	1.1	0.0
10th Grade	0.8	0.8	1.0	2.2	2.8	3.5	3.7	3.6	-0.1
12th Grade	2.0	1.9	2.4	3.6	4.6	4.9	5.8	5.6	-0.2
College Students	1.8	1.6	1.9	1.8	3.7	2.8	3.7	4.0	+0.2
Young Adults	2.3	2.3	2.4	2.8	3.3	3.3	3.8	3.7	-0.1
Alcohol[j]									
Any use									
8th Grade	0.5	0.6	0.8	—	—	—	—	—	—
			1.0	1.0	0.7	1.0	0.8	0.9	+0.1
10th Grade	1.3	1.2	1.6	—	—	—	—	—	—
			1.8	1.7	1.7	1.6	1.7	1.9	+0.2
12th Grade	3.6	3.4	2.5	—	—	—	—	—	—
			3.4	2.9	3.5	3.7	3.9	3.9	0.0
College Students	4.1	3.7	3.9	3.7	3.0	3.2	4.5	3.9	-0.6
Young Adults	4.9	4.5	4.5	3.9	3.9	4.0	4.6	4.0	-0.7
Been Drunk[h,j]									
8th Grade	0.1	0.1	0.2	0.3	0.2	0.2	0.2	0.3	+0.2ss
10th Grade	0.2	0.3	0.4	0.4	0.6	0.4	0.6	0.6	0.0
12th Grade	0.9	0.8	0.9	1.2	1.3	1.6	2.0	1.5	-0.5
College Students	—	—	—	—	—	—	—	—	—
Young Adults	—	—	—	—	—	—	—	—	—
5+ drinks in last 2 weeks									
8th Grade	12.9	13.4	13.5	14.5	14.5	15.6	14.5	13.7	-0.8
10th Grade	22.9	21.1	23.0	23.6	24.0	24.8	25.1	24.3	-0.8
12th Grade	29.8	27.9	27.5	28.2	29.8	30.2	31.3	31.5	+0.2
College Students	42.8	41.4	40.2	40.2	38.6	38.3	40.7	38.9	-1.7
Young Adults	34.7	34.2	34.4	33.7	32.6	33.6	34.4	34.1	-0.3
Cigarettes									
Any use									
8th Grade	7.2	7.0	8.3	8.8	9.3	10.4	9.0	8.8	-0.2
10th Grade	12.6	12.3	14.2	14.6	16.3	18.3	18.0	15.8	-2.2ss
12th Grade	18.5	17.2	19.0	19.4	21.6	22.2	24.6	22.4	-2.2s
College Students	13.8	14.1	15.2	13.2	15.8	15.9	15.2	18.0	+2.8s
Young Adults	21.7	20.9	20.8	20.7	21.2	21.8	20.6	21.9	+1.2
1/2 pack+/day									
8th Grade	3.1	2.9	3.5	3.6	3.4	4.3	3.5	3.6	+0.1
10th Grade	6.5	6.0	7.0	7.6	8.3	9.4	8.6	7.9	-0.7
12th Grade	10.7	10.0	10.9	11.2	12.4	13.0	14.3	12.6	-1.7s
College Students	8.0	8.9	8.9	8.0	10.2	8.4	9.1	11.3	+2.3s
Young Adults	16.0	15.7	15.5	15.3	15.7	15.3	14.6	15.6	+0.9
Smokeless Tobacco[d]									
8th Grade	1.6	1.8	1.5	1.9	1.2	1.5	1.0	1.0	+0.1
10th Grade	3.3	3.0	3.3	3.0	2.7	2.2	2.2	2.2	0.0
12th Grade	—	4.3	3.3	3.9	3.6	3.3	4.4	3.2	-1.2
College Students	—	—	—	—	—	—	—	—	—
Young Adults	—	—	—	—	—	—	—	—	—

Note: See Table 21 for relevant footnotes.

Source: *National Survey Results on Drug Use from The Monitoring the Future Study*, Institute for Social Research, University of Michigan, Ann Arbor, MI, 1999

CHAPTER X

PUBLIC OPINIONS ABOUT EDUCATION

Every year, Phi Delta Kappa, the professional education fraternity, sponsors a survey of the American public on education issues. This annual examination is considered one of the best measurements of current American attitudes towards education. Except where otherwise noted, the information in this chapter comes from "The 31st Annual Phi Delta Kappa/Gallup Poll of the Public's Attitudes Toward the Public Schools"* (*Phi Delta Kappan*, September 1999).

Keep in mind that these are surveys of peoples' opinions and feelings about public education. They may or may not coincide with facts about the nation's schools. Instead, the survey results provide trends in current American thought on educational subjects.

BIGGEST PROBLEMS FACING LOCAL PUBLIC SCHOOLS

Since Phi Delta Kappa began surveying the public's opinion of education in 1969, discipline has been at or near the top of the list of concerns. Between 1969 and 1985 (with the exception of 1971, when the top issue was finances), discipline was the most frequently mentioned problem. Drug abuse by students replaced discipline as the top concern from 1986 through 1991, and in 1992, drugs and lack of proper financial support tied, at 22 percent each. In 1993, lack of proper financial support was clearly the number-one concern, with

---

TABLE 10.1

What do you think are the biggest problems with which the public schools of your community must deal?

	National Totals		No Children In School		Public School Parents	
	'99 %	'98 %	'99 %	'98 %	'99 %	'98 %
Lack of discipline/more control	18	14	18	15	15	9
Fighting/violence/gangs	11	15	10	14	12	20
Lack of financial support/ funding/money	9	12	9	13	9	11
Use of drugs/dope	8	10	9	10	6	12
Overcrowded schools	8	8	6	5	12	11
Crime/vandalism	5	2	5	1	4	2
Difficulty getting good teachers/quality teachers	4	5	4	6	5	4
Parents' lack of support/ interest	4	2	4	2	5	1
Concern about standards/ quality	2	6	3	6	1	5
Low pay for teachers	2	2	2	2	1	1
Religious education	2	2	2	2	1	1
Poor curriculum/low standards	2	1	1	1	2	1
Busing	2	*	*	*	*	*
Pupils' lack of interest/ attitudes/truancy	2	5	2	4	2	5
Lack of respect	2	2	2	2	1	2
Peer pressure	2	1	2	*	2	1
Moral standards/dress code/sex/pregnancy	2	2	1	1	2	3

*Less than one-half of 1%.

(Figures add to more than 100% because of multiple answers.)

Source: "The 31st Annual Phi Delta Kappa/Gallup Poll of the Public's Attitudes Toward the Public Schools," *Phi Delta Kappan*, September 1999

---

* For opinions about school choice and school prayer, see Chapter VII. For teachers' opinions, see Chapter VIII.

TABLE 10.2

Thinking about the public schools in your community, how would you describe the learning environment for students in those schools — very safe and orderly, somewhat safe and orderly, not very safe and orderly, or not at all safe and orderly?

	National Totals %	No Children In School %	Public School Parents %
Very safe and orderly	24	22	30
Somewhat safe and orderly	62	62	62
Not very safe and orderly	7	8	5
Not at all safe and orderly	3	3	2
Don't know	4	5	1

Source: "The 31st Annual Phi Delta Kappa/Gallup Poll of the Public's Attitudes Toward the Public Schools," *Phi Delta Kappan*, September 1999

TABLE 10.3

Some public schools have a so-called zero tolerance drug and alcohol policy, which means that possession of any illegal drugs or alcohol by students will result in automatic suspension. Would you favor or oppose such a policy in the public schools in your community?

	National Totals		No Children In School		Public School Parents	
	'99 %	'97 %	'99 %	'97 %	'99 %	'97 %
Favor	90	86	89	84	92	89
Oppose	10	13	11	15	8	10
Don't know	*	1	*	1	*	1

*Less than one-half of 1%.

Source: "The 31st Annual Phi Delta Kappa/Gallup Poll of the Public's Attitudes Toward the Public Schools," *Phi Delta Kappan*, September 1999

21 percent mentioning it as the biggest concern for public schools in their communities. In 1994 and 1995, lack of discipline was back on top. Drug abuse edged out discipline as the top concern of 1996 (16 percent).

In 1999, the three top problems identified by the public — lack of discipline (18 percent), fighting/violence/gangs (11 percent), and lack of financial support (9 percent) — were the same top three identified in 1998. Use of drugs and overcrowded schools (8 percent each) tied for fourth place. (See Table 10.1.) Twenty-eight percent of those age 50 and older were most concerned about lack of discipline, while younger ages (18- to 29-year-olds) thought fighting/violence/gangs (16 percent) the top problem.

How Safe Are Schools?

When respondents were asked how safe and orderly they thought the schools in their community were, 24 percent felt they were "very safe and orderly," while 62 percent felt they were "somewhat safe and orderly." Only 10 percent believed their community schools were not safe and orderly. (See Table 10.2.) When parents were asked the same question about the school their oldest child attended, the percentages increased — 42 percent responded "very safe and orderly," and 50 percent

TABLE 10.4

Students are often given the grades A, B, C, D, and FAIL to denote the quality of their work. Suppose the public schools themselves, in this community, were graded in the same way. What grade would you give the public schools here — A, B, C, D, or FAIL?

	National Totals		No Children In School		Public School Parents	
	'99 %	'98 %	'99 %	'98 %	'99 %	'98 %
A & B	49	46	47	43	56	52
A	11	10	10	8	15	15
B	38	36	37	35	41	37
C	31	31	31	31	31	33
D	9	9	10	9	8	9
FAIL	5	5	4	5	4	4
Don't know	6	9	8	12	1	2

Source: "The 31st Annual Phi Delta Kappa/Gallup Poll of the Public's Attitudes Toward the Public Schools," *Phi Delta Kappan*, September 1999

TABLE 10.5

How about the public schools in the nation as a whole? What grade would you give the public schools nationally — A, B, C, D, or FAIL?

	National Totals		No Children In School		Public School Parents	
	'99 %	'98 %	'99 %	'98 %	'99 %	'98 %
A & B	24	18	26	19	21	16
A	2	1	1	*	3	2
B	22	17	25	19	18	14
C	46	49	43	48	50	52
D	16	15	16	15	17	13
FAIL	4	5	4	6	5	4
Don't know	10	13	11	12	7	15

*Less than one-half of 1%.

Source: "The 31st Annual Phi Delta Kappa/Gallup Poll of the Public's Attitudes Toward the Public Schools," *Phi Delta Kappan*, September 1999

TABLE 10.6	TABLE 10.7

TABLE 10.6

Suppose you could send your oldest child to any public, private, or church-related school of your choice, with tuition paid by the government. Would you send your oldest child to the school he or she now attends, or to a different school?

	Public School Parents		
	'99 %	'98 %	'96 %
School now attends	51	51	55
Different school	46	46	44
Don't know	3	3	1

TABLE 10.7

Would you send your child to a private school, a church-related school, or to another public school?

	Public School Parents		
	'99 %	'98 %	'96 %
Private school	22	22	19
Church-related school	17	17	17
Another public school	5	6	8
Don't know	1	1	–

Regarding the factors respondents would use in choosing a school, 98% select the quality of the teaching staff; 89%, the

Source of both tables: "The 31st Annual Phi Delta Kappa/Gallup Poll of the Public's Attitudes Toward the Public Schools," *Phi Delta Kappan*, September 1999

said "somewhat safe and orderly."

Following the Littleton, Colorado, shooting in April 1999, an ABC News/*Washington Post* poll asked high school students and parents of high school students about personal feelings of safety from violence. Eighty-nine percent of the students felt very or somewhat safe from violence at their high school, while 83 percent of the parents believed their children were very or somewhat safe from violence in their high school.

Drugs and Alcohol at School

Although zero-tolerance policies toward alcohol and drug violations have been debated in the past two years, the public, especially parents, still strongly supports the automatic suspension of any student in possession of any illegal drug or alcohol. Ninety percent of respondents supported a zero-tolerance drug and alcohol policy, up from 86 percent in 1997. (See Table 10.3.)

TABLE 10.8

Here are different factors that might be considered in choosing a public school for a child, assuming free choice of public and private schools were allowed in this community. As I read off each of these factors, would you tell me whether you consider it very important, fairly important, not too important, or not at all important in choosing a local school?

	Very Important %	Fairly Important %	Not Too Important %	Not at All Important %	Don't Know %
Quality of the teaching staff	98	2	*	*	*
Maintenance of student discipline	89	10	1	*	*
Curriculum (i.e., the courses offered)	89	10	1	*	*
Size of classes	75	19	4	2	*
Extracurricular activities, such as band/orchestra, theater, clubs	51	40	7	2	*
Proximity to home	47	40	10	2	1
Size of the school (number of students)	46	33	15	6	*
Reputation or prestige of school	45	35	12	7	1
Having your child exposed to a more diverse student body	41	38	12	4	5
Athletic program	34	46	13	7	*
Proximity to the parent's workplace	22	38	26	12	2
Having your child exposed to a less diverse student body	17	28	28	21	6

*Less than one-half of 1%.

Source: "The 31st Annual Phi Delta Kappa/Gallup Poll of the Public's Attitudes Toward the Public Schools," *Phi Delta Kappan*, September 1999

<table>
<tr><td colspan="4">

TABLE 10.9

If there was one thing you could change to improve the public schools in your community, what would that be?

</td></tr>
<tr><th></th><th>National Totals %</th><th>No Children In School %</th><th>Public School Parents %</th></tr>
<tr><td>Discipline/more control/stricter rules</td><td>12</td><td>13</td><td>9</td></tr>
<tr><td>More teachers/smaller class size</td><td>10</td><td>8</td><td>14</td></tr>
<tr><td>Better/more qualified teachers</td><td>7</td><td>8</td><td>5</td></tr>
<tr><td>Funding</td><td>5</td><td>5</td><td>3</td></tr>
<tr><td>Security</td><td>4</td><td>4</td><td>5</td></tr>
<tr><td>Prayer/God back in the schools</td><td>4</td><td>4</td><td>3</td></tr>
<tr><td>Dress code/uniforms</td><td>3</td><td>4</td><td>3</td></tr>
<tr><td>Higher pay for teachers</td><td>3</td><td>3</td><td>4</td></tr>
<tr><td>More parent involvement</td><td>3</td><td>3</td><td>4</td></tr>
<tr><td>Academic standards/better education</td><td>3</td><td>3</td><td>4</td></tr>
<tr><td>Curriculum/more offered</td><td>2</td><td>2</td><td>3</td></tr>
<tr><td>More/updated equipment/books/computers</td><td>2</td><td>2</td><td>1</td></tr>
</table>

| | | | |

TABLE 10.10

In your opinion who or what is the main obstacle to improving the public schools in your community?

	National Totals %	No Children In School %	Public School Parents %
Finances/funding	13	14	13
Parents/lack of parent involvement	12	12	12
Government	10	11	10
Board of education/superintendent	8	6	11
Better teachers	5	6	3
Politics/politicians	4	3	6
Taxpayers/general public	4	4	3
Unions/teacher unions/NEA	3	3	2
Lack of discipline/teachers can't discipline	3	3	2
Students/kids	2	2	*
Administration/administrators	2	1	2

Source of both tables: "The 31st Annual Phi Delta Kappa/Gallup Poll of the Public's Attitudes Toward the Public Schools," *Phi Delta Kappan*, September 1999

GRADING THE SCHOOLS

Every year, the Phi Delta Kappa survey asks respondents to grade the public schools, just as students are graded. In general, the survey has found for many years that the closer ties a respondent has to a school system, the more highly he or she grades the school. A school attended by a respondent's oldest child, for example, is graded more highly than the schools in the community as a whole, and community schools are given a higher grade than are the nation's whole school system.

Overall, the 1999 survey found that half (49 percent) of those surveyed felt the schools in their communities deserved an A or a B. Most (56 percent) public school parents awarded an A or B grade to their community schools. (See Table 10.4.) When asked to grade the school attended by their own oldest children, two-thirds (66 percent) of public school parents awarded an A or a B.

Respondents graded the American public school system overall much more harshly. Only 24 percent felt the nation's public schools, overall, deserved an A or B grade, while 62 percent assigned a grade of C or D. (See Table 10.5.)

TABLE 10.11

Here are some ways that have been suggested for attracting and retaining good public school teachers. As I read off each suggestion, would you tell me whether you favor it or oppose it as a way to attract and retain good teachers?

	Favor %	Oppose %	Don't Know %
Increased pay for teachers who demonstrate high performance	90	9	1
Loans and scholarships for prospective teachers	86	12	2
School-financed professional development opportunities	85	12	3
Tax credits for teachers who demonstrate high performance	63	37	*
Increased pay for all teachers	62	37	1

*Less than one-half of 1%.

Source: "The 31st Annual Phi Delta Kappa/Gallup Poll of the Public's Attitudes Toward the Public Schools," *Phi Delta Kappan*, September 1999

CHOOSING A SCHOOL

Public school parents were asked where they would send their oldest child if tuition were paid by the government. In 1999, 51 percent said they would send their child to the same school the child now attended, while 46 percent would choose a different school (Table 10.6). Among those who responded a "different school," 22 percent would send their child to a private school, 17 percent to a church-related school, and 5 percent to another public school (Table 10.7).

Nearly all of the respondents (98 percent) considered the quality of teaching staff as a very important factor in choosing a local school. Parents also considered student discipline and curriculum (89 percent each) very important considerations. Three out of four public school parents felt class size was very important, while about half (51 percent) believed a school's extracurricular activities would be a very important consideration when choosing a school. (See Table 10.8.)

In a November 1999 Public Agenda poll, parents of school-age children were asked if they would rather send their child to a good school near their home or a better school that is rather difficult to get to. Fifty-four percent chose the better school, while 40 percent chose the closest school. According to the interviewers, parents gave three main reasons for settling for the closest, rather than the better, school.

- The child's safety.

- The child's feelings.

- The family's convenience.

It appeared that many parents wanted a school close enough to allow them to get to their child quickly in case of an emergency.

TABLE 10.12

How important do you think each of the following factors should be in determining a public school teacher's salary? Very important, somewhat important, not very important, or not at all important?

	Very Important %	Somewhat Important %	Not Very Important %	Not at All Important %	Don't Know %
Level of academic degree earned	60	33	5	1	1
Years of teaching experience	52	35	9	4	*
Scores the teacher's students receive on standardized tests	47	38	10	4	1

*Less than one-half of 1%.

TABLE 10.13

In your opinion, are student achievement standards in the public schools in your community too high, about right, or too low?

	National Totals %	No Children In School %	Public School Parents %
Too high	6	5	9
About right	57	56	60
Too low	33	34	30
Don't know	4	5	1

Source of above tables: "The 31st Annual Phi Delta Kappa/Gallup Poll of the Public's Attitudes Toward the Public Schools," *Phi Delta Kappan*, September 1999

IMPROVING SCHOOLS

The 1999 Phi Delta Kappa survey asked respondents to name the one thing they would change to improve the public schools in their community. Not surprisingly, since the public considered discipline the top problem faced by public schools, discipline (12 percent) also topped the list of desired changes. Ten percent of respondents thought more teachers/smaller class size would be a desirable change, and 7 percent wanted better/more qualified teachers. (See Table 10.9.)

Respondents were then asked who or what was the main obstacle to improving the public schools in their community. Finances/funding was noted by 13 percent of the respondents, followed by parents/lack of parent involvement (12 percent) and

government (10 percent) (Table 10.10).
Nonwhites (17 percent) and those from
the South (18 percent) put parents/lack
of parent involvement at the top of the
list. Republicans (15 percent) believed
government was the greatest obstacle.

A Public Willingness to Pay for Improving Schools?

A National Public Radio (NPR)/
Kaiser Family Foundation/Kennedy
School of Government survey on education found strong public support for
specific school improvements. In this
1999 survey, 3 out of 4 Americans
claimed they would be willing to have
their taxes raised by at least $200 a year
to pay for measures designed to improve
community public schools. More than
half (55 percent) said they would be
willing to have their taxes raised by $500.

When asked whether states should
equalize school funding even if it means
taking funds from wealthy school districts to give to poor districts, 83 percent of respondents said yes. Nearly 70 percent
thought the spending in wealthy districts should
be "capped so that poor districts are not left behind."

ATTRACTING AND RETAINING TEACHERS

In light of concerns over possible teacher shortages, the Phi Delta Kappa survey asked respondents to consider several suggestions for attracting and retaining good public school teachers.
Ninety percent favored increased pay for teachers
who demonstrate higher standards. High percentages also favored loans and scholarships for pro-
spective teachers (86 percent) and school-financed
professional development opportunities (85 percent). Most respondents also supported tax credits
for teachers who demonstrate high performance (63
percent) and increased pay for all teachers (62 percent). (See Table 10.11.)

TABLE 10.14

Social promotion means moving children from grade to grade in order to keep them with others in their own age group. Would you favor stricter standards for social promotion in school even if it meant that significantly more students would be held back?

	National Totals %	No Children In School %	Public School Parents %
Favor	72	70	75
Oppose	26	27	24
Don't know	2	3	1

TABLE 10.15

As you know, many high school students are allowed to choose many of their academic courses. Would you favor or oppose requiring high school students to take a standardized core curriculum of certain courses?

	National Totals %	No Children In School %	Public School Parents %
Favor	78	78	76
Oppose	21	21	23
Don't know	1	1	1

Source of both tables: "The 31st Annual Phi Delta Kappa/Gallup Poll of the Public's Attitudes Toward the Public Schools," *Phi Delta Kappan*, September 1999

When asked what factors should be considered
in determining a public school teacher's salary, 60
percent felt the level of academic degree earned
was very important, 52 percent believed years of
teaching experience to be a very important consideration, and 47 percent thought the scores the
teacher's students received on standardized tests
were very important. (See Table 10.12.)

STANDARDS

Raising standards, accountability in meeting
those standards, and requiring high school students
to take a common core of courses are major issues
in education reform. Survey participants were
asked about the student achievement standards in
the public schools in their community. Most (57
percent) believed that standards were about right,
although one-third felt standards were too low
(Table 10.13). A specific question about social pro-

motion standards was asked. Three-quarters of public school parents favored stricter standards for social promotion even if it meant that significantly more students would be held back a grade (Table 10.14).

When asked if they would favor or oppose requiring high school students to take a standardized core curriculum, 78 percent of respondents supported the standardized curriculum (Table 10.15). Those feeling the strongest about a core curriculum requirement included college graduates, those with annual incomes of $50,000 and over, and those age 50 and older (84 percent each).

TO TEACH OR
NOT TO TEACH VALUES

The Phi Delta Kappa polls have been asking questions about the role of values or ethics/morals in public education since 1975, when 79 percent of the public favored public-school instruction about morals and moral behavior. The following year, respondents rated "high moral standards" among the top four qualities that should be developed in children. A 1984 poll listed "develop standards of right and wrong" as second only to "develop the ability to speak and write correctly" among the most important goals of public schools.

The 1999 survey presented a list of 12 values and asked respondents to indicate whether or not each one should be taught in public school. At least 9 of every 10 respondents favored teaching honesty, democracy, acceptance of people of different races and ethnic backgrounds, caring for friends and family members, moral courage, and patriotism. Eighty-six percent supported the teaching of the Golden Rule. Most respondents also wanted acceptance of people who hold unpopular or controversial viewpoints (71 percent), sexual abstinence outside of marriage (68 percent), and acceptance of people with different sexual orientations (55 percent) to be taught. Fewer (48 percent) supported teaching acceptance of the right of a woman to choose an abortion. (See Table 10.16.)

TABLE 10.16

I am going to read off a list of different values that might be taught in the public schools. For each one, please tell me whether you think it should be taught, or should not be taught, to all students in the public schools of your community?

Should Be Taught	National Totals '99 %	National Totals '93 %	No Children In School '99 %	No Children In School '93 %	Public School Parents '99 %	Public School Parents '93 %
Honesty	97	97	97	97	97	97
Democracy	93	93	94	92	91	93
Acceptance of people of different races and ethnic backgrounds	93	93	93	92	93	96
Caring for friends and family members	90	91	90	90	90	93
Moral courage	90	91	90	91	89	94
Patriotism/love of country	90	91	89	91	92	93
The Golden Rule	86	90	87	90	84	89
Acceptance of people who hold different religious beliefs	–	87	–	87	–	87
Acceptance of people who hold unpopular or controversial political or social views	71	73	71	73	70	75
Sexual abstinence outside of marriage	68	66	68	66	66	67
Acceptance of people with different sexual orientations; that is, homosexuals or bisexuals	55	51	57	52	51	50
Acceptance of the right of a woman to choose abortion	48	56	52	56	45	57

Source: "The 31st Annual Phi Delta Kappa/Gallup Poll of the Public's Attitudes Toward the Public Schools," *Phi Delta Kappan*, September 1999

IMPORTANT NAMES AND ADDRESSES

American Association for
Employment in Education, Inc.
820 Davis St., Suite 222
Evanston, IL 60201-4445
(847) 864-1999
FAX (847) 864-8303
www.aaee.org
aaee@nwu.edu

American College Testing (ACT)
2201 N. Dodge St.
P.O. Box 168
Iowa City, IA 52243-0168
(319) 337-1000
www.act.org

American Federation of Teachers
AFL-CIO
555 New Jersey Ave. NW
Washington, DC 20001
(202) 879-4400
FAX (202) 879-4545
www.aft.org
online@aft.org

Centers for Disease Control and
Prevention (CDC)
1600 Clifton Road
Atlanta, GA 30333
(404) 639-3311
(800) 311-3435
www.cdc.gov

Child Trends
4301 Connecticut Ave. NW
Suite 100
Washington, DC 20008
(202) 362-5580
FAX (202) 362-5533
www.childtrends.org
swilliams@childtrends.org

Children's Defense Fund
25 E St. NW
Washington, DC 20001
(202) 628-8787
FAX (202) 628-3510
www.childrensdefense.org
cdfinfo@childrensdefense.org

The College Board (SAT)
45 Columbus Ave.
New York, NY 10023-6992
(212) 713-8000
FAX (212) 713-8184
www.collegeboard.org

Council of the Great City Schools
1301 Pennsylvania Ave. NW
Suite 702
Washington, DC 20004
(202) 393-2427
FAX (202) 393-2400
www.cgcs.org

Educational Testing Service
Corporate Headquarters
Rosedale Road
Princeton, NJ 08541
(609) 921-9000
FAX (609) 734-5410
www.ets.org
etsinfo@ets.org

Higher Education Research Institute
UCLA Graduate School of Education
and Information Studies
3005 Moore Hall
Mail Box 951521
Los Angeles, CA 90095-1521
(310) 825-1925
FAX (310) 206-2228
www.gseis.ucla.edu/heri/heri
heri@ucla.edu

Home School Legal Defense Association
P.O. Box 3000
Purcellville, VA 20134
(540) 338-5600
FAX (540) 338-2733
www.hslda.org

Institute of International Education
809 United Nations Plaza
New York, NY 10017-3580
(212) 984-5400
FAX (212) 984-5358
www.iie.org
info@iie.org

National Catholic Educational
Association
1077 30th St. NW, Suite 100
Washington, DC 20007-3852
(202) 337-6232
FAX (202) 333-6706
www.catholic.org/ncea
nceaadmin@ncea.org

National Center for Children in Poverty
The Joseph L. Mailman School of
Public Health, Columbia University
154 Haven Ave.
New York, NY 10032
(212) 304-7100
FAX (212) 544-4200
http://cpmcnet.columbia.edu/dept/nccp

National Education Association
1201 16th St. NW
Washington, DC 20036
(202) 833-4000
www.nea.org
neaadmin2@aol.com

National Law Center on Homelessness
and Poverty
1411 K St. NW
Suite 1400
Washington, DC 20005
(202) 638-2535
FAX (202) 628-2737
www.nlchp.org
nlchp@nlchp.org

Phi Delta Kappa International
P.O. Box 789
Bloomington, IN 47402-0789
800-766-1156
FAX (812) 339-0018
www.pdkintl.org

U.S. Department of Education
National Center for Education
Statistics
555 New Jersey Ave. NW
Washington, DC 20208-5574
(202) 219-1828
FAX (202) 219-1736
http://nces.ed.gov

U.S. Department of Education
Office of Educational Research and
Improvement (OERI)
555 New Jersey Ave. NW
Washington, DC 20208-5500
(202) 219-1385
FAX (202) 219-1466
www.ed.gov/offices/OERI

U.S. Department of the Interior
Bureau of Indian Affairs
Indian Education Programs
1849 C St. NW
Washington, DC 20240-0001
(202) 208-6123
FAX (202) 208-3312
www.doi.gov/bureau-indian-affairs

RESOURCES

The National Center for Education Statistics (NCES) of the U.S. Department of Education (Washington, DC) is a valuable source of information about the state of education in America. Its two annual publications, *Digest of Education Statistics* and *The Condition of Education*, provide a detailed compilation of education statistics from prekindergarten through graduate school. Five other NCES publications were of major assistance in the preparation of this book: *Projections of Education Statistics to 2009* (1999), *Schools and Staffing in the United States: A Statistical Profile, 1993-94* (1996), *NAEP 1998 Reading Report Card* (1999), *NAEP Writing Assessment Results for the Nation* (1999), and *NAEP 1996 Trends in Academic Progress* (1997).

The Office of Educational Research and Improvement (OERI) of the Department of Education routinely issues reports on specific areas of education. *The State of Charter Schools 2000* is the fourth report of a four-year research program to document and analyze the charter school movement, and *National Excellence: A Case for Developing America's Talent* (1993) describes the need for increased support of the education of gifted and talented students. In *The National Education Goals Report: Building a Nation of Learners, 1999*, the National Education Goals Panel supplied the most recent data on the nation's progress toward meeting the National Education Goals.

The U.S. General Accounting Office (GAO: Washington, DC) has published numerous studies on American education. Reports concerning disadvantaged and disabled children included, among others, *Migrant Children: Education and HHS Need to Improve the Exchange of Participant Information* (1999) and *Special Education Reform: Districts Grapple with Inclusion Programs* (1994). On topics relating to financing reform, the GAO has published *School Finance: State Efforts to Reduce Funding Gaps Between Poor and Wealthy Districts* (1997) and *School Finance: State Efforts to Equalize Funding Between Wealthy and Poor School Districts* (1997). *School Facilities: America's Schools Report Differing Conditions* (1996) reflected on the poor physical condition of many American schools.

The Congressional Research Service (CRS) is a government research agency that works exclusively for members and committees of the U.S. Congress. Two of its reports used in this publication are *Head Start: Background and Funding* (1999) and *The Federal Migrant Education Program: An Overview* (1998).

The U.S. Department of Justice (Washington, DC) monitors the problem of crime and violence among the school-age population. Two 1999 publications, *Juvenile Offenders and Victims: 1999 National Report* and *Criminal Victimization 1998* provided detailed insight into the problem of violence and victimization among juveniles.

America's Children: Key National Indicators of Well-Being (1999), the third report in an annual series prepared by the Interagency Forum on Child and Family Statistics, provided statistics on early childhood education and "detached youth." Child Trends, in its December 1999 *Facts at a Glance*, gave permission to use its data on teen pregnancy and births.

The Centers for Disease Control and Prevention (CDC; Atlanta, Georgia), in its "Youth Risk Behavior Surveillance — United States, 1997" (*Morbidity and Mortality Weekly Report*, vol. 47, no. SS-3, August 14, 1998), reported on behaviors such as alcohol and drug use and violence and weapons at school. The CDC presented the results of the "National Youth Tobacco Survey — United States, 1999" in its January 2000 *Morbidity and Mortality Weekly Report* (vol. 49, no. 3). Another CDC publication, *HIV/AIDS Surveillance Report* (vol. 9, no. 1), provided a look at the spread of AIDS.

Phi Delta Kappa, a national teachers' fraternity, publishes numerous reports on the condition of education in the United States. Information Plus thanks Phi Delta Kappa for permission to use much of its "31st Annual Phi Delta Kappa/Gallup Poll on the Public Attitudes Toward the Public Schools," as well as "The Fifth Phi Delta Kappa Poll of Teachers' Attitudes Toward the Public Schools." These polls are a primary source for the nation's opinions about the educational system.

The College Board kindly granted permission to use charts from the *1999 Profile of College-Bound Seniors National Report* (New York, 1999). We also thank American College Testing for the use of materials from its *1999 ACT National and State Scores* (Iowa City, Iowa, 1999).

We especially appreciate Dr. Lloyd Johnston of the University of Michigan's Institute for Social Research. With support from the National Institute on Drug Abuse (NIDA), the Institute for Social Research annually performs the *Monitoring the Future* study, an in-depth survey of drug use among high school and college students. Our thanks also extend to the Council of Great City Schools in Washington, DC, who provided the National Urban Education Goals for the year 2000 and compiled demographic details in *Key Facts: 1997-98 Data about Council Member Districts* (1999).

Several private sources also provide valuable information about education in America. Information Plus thanks the American Federation of Teachers (*Survey and Analysis of Teacher Salary Trends: 1998*, Washington, DC, 1999) for permission to use its materials. The Institute of International Education also graciously granted permission to use information provided in *Open Doors 1998/99: Report on International Educational Exchange* (New York, 1999).

Lawrence M. Rudner allowed Information Plus to use information from his *Scholastic Achievement and Demographic Characteristics of Home School Students in 1998* (Education Policy Analysis Archives, Arizona State University, Tempe, Arizona, 1999), and Stephen Krashen shared information on bilingual education that was presented at the Georgetown Round Table on Languages and Linguistics in May 1999. Richard M. Ingersoll, in *Teacher Turnover, Teacher Shortages, and the Organization of Schools* (Center for the Study of Teaching and Policy, University of Washington, Seattle, Washington, 1999), reported on his study of teacher attrition and migration.

INDEX